1, 10, 100 YEARS OF
FORM, TYPOGRAPHY, AND INTERACT
AT PARSONS

ORO Editions
Publishers of Architecture, Art, and Design
Publisher: Gordon Goff

www.oroeditions.com
info@oroeditions.com

Published by ORO Editions
Copyright © 2021

Managing Editor: Jake Anderson

10 9 8 7 6 5 4 3 2 1 First Edition
ISBN: 978-1-954081-51-2

ORO Editions makes a continuous effort to minimize the overall carbon footprint of its publications. As part of this goal, ORO Editions, in association with Global ReLeaf, arranges to plant trees to replace those used in the manufacturing of the paper produced for its books. Global ReLeaf is an international campaign run by American Forests, one of the world's oldest nonprofit conservation organizations. Global ReLeaf is American Forests' education and action program that helps individuals, organizations, agencies, and corporations improve the local and global environment by planting and caring for trees.

CONTENTS

ABOUT THIS BOOK
Jarrett Fuller, editor

This book is a celebration. It's not lost on me that it's being released after a year of profound change and uncertainty between a global pandemic and a racial reckoning, a near-overthrow of the United States government and unrest around the world. So this is a celebration of work from this year's graduating seniors, whose last year at Parsons was not what they expected as they sat in their homes scattered around the planet working odd hours. It's a celebration of their resilience; a sign of their dedication to the future. But it's also a celebration of the Communication Design community at Parsons: this past year but also the last decade. And the last century.

The current Communication Design program was conceived in 2011 and built upon a rich history of visual design at Parsons, which launched the first program of its kind over 100 years ago. In the last century, the program cycled through names, classes, teachers, and students and we've collected just some of this history here. It's a book about both the past and the future. Indeed, to describe the Communication Design program at Parsons is to describe a series of paradoxes: equally excited about the tradition of print and the potential of digital, in pursuit of both formal excellence and critical thinking, both rooted in history and looking towards the future, it is conceptually rigorous and commercially minded. This book interrogates these intersections and attempts to outline how the faculty thinks about the education of a contemporary designer.

This past year proved that change is inevitable, the only certainty is uncertainty. Design, too, is always changing. This work is different from ten years ago and will be different a decade from now. To teach design is always to teach a moving target. This book shows how they've tried to do that.

Jarrett Fuller is a designer, writer, editor, and Assistant Professor of Graphic Design at North Carolina State University.

100 Years

INTRODUCTION

A teacher from my university days once mentioned that becoming a designer would be to elect a life in visual hell. As macabre as the warning was, it did little to dissuade my classmates and me from continuing our graphic design studies. Today, I can attest that there is truth to this statement, but its sentiment of designers in pursuit of perfect craft is an elision of something far greater and much less grim: a pursuit for an understanding of visual form. In fact, this is a delightful pursuit. Form is an interface between two individuals vacillating between its dual roles as both a record of past thought and a living carrier of meaning. It is this quality that allows it to captivate our imaginations. As social beings, we cannot help but express ourselves through language made visible and ideas made material. This is at the heart of communication design.

Despite these innate needs, the discipline itself is relatively new and is the result of the successive forces of industrialization, modernization, computeri-zation, and globalization that reoriented and reordered activities related to the mass transmission of word and idea. At Parsons, this dynamic has played out within Communication Design—the oldest program of its kind in the United States—since the first courses were offered in 1905 under the moniker of Poster Design and Advertising. At that time, the school was called the New York School of Art and was the successor to the Chase School of Art which itself was founded less than a decade earlier by a group from the Art Students League.

The beginnings of Communication Design at Parsons reflects a distinctly American (or perhaps New York) attitude where its value was solely measured by its usefulness to trade and commerce. Early program leaders could not make up their minds as to what to call this course of study and performed titular acrobatics every few years with words like advertising, art, commercial, design, graphic, and illustration. It was not until 1972 that the department finally settled on the name Communication Design under the chairmanship of John Russo. The name was remarkably prescient for it was not until the turn of the millennium that the International Council of Design officially declared the discipline be called visual communication design[1] and eleven years later, simply communication design.[2]

One of the first outlines of the course of study is from the 1912-1913 bulletin of The New York School of Fine and Applied Art. Defining the discipline as Commercial Advertising, it states:

> The rapidly growing importance of advertising, the desire on the part of the public for artistic expression in this field, and the inability of the art student to do practical things, has led to the establishing of this course. It aims to make the connection between art and the trade easier and more effective.

It includes:

Drawing from life, nude and costume model.

Free hand drawing of objects accessory to all illustration work.

A course in pen and ink, wash and color technique for purpose of reproduction.

A course in lettering.

Lessons in placing, spacing and arrangement of type, illustrations, decorative materials and color in car-cards, posters, magazine covers, catalogues and related fields.

Weekly criticisms of this work of the entire class with suggestions for placing work.[3]

From this pithy description, the contours of what we now call Communication Design can be seen including the development of attitudes towards the organization of disparate elements like image, type, and form. Current graduates might even recognize the weekly critique format and the anxiousness in finding a job. More importantly, the attention paid to the reproduction of images is the first of many nods towards the importance of interrogating methods that allow for the mass produced dissemination of ideas. That the early days of Communication Design should have this complicated relationship with advertising should come as no surprise. Walter Benjamin observed as much when he wrote that the beginning of the 20th century marked the first time all known works of art could be reproduced.[4] Such changes had begun to make inroads into artistic practice and was changing the way society regarded the value and role of art. For the school's early instructors, recognizing these invisible forces through the new lens of advertising would have been reasonable, even if we regard it as myopic today.

Perhaps the school faintly grasped these implications. When the program appointed its first department head, Zerelda Rains, in 1913, she took a slight pedagogical turn and modified the course's goal from making connections between art and commerce "easier and more effective" to include the reassurance that such connections would be done "without losing either the artistic or the practical viewpoint."[5] For good or ill, the program's, and indeed the larger school's, affinity for industry had been baked into its core and into the aspirations of its students. However, the tension held by this phrase represents what I observe to be the unique position that today's Parsons Communication Design finds itself in: a community that is neither strictly industry-minded nor oriented towards the white cube, taught by faculty who maintain active professional practices without shunning the more esoteric dialogue of wider design discourse.

By 1915, the first true definition of Communication Design at Parsons emerges—albeit still under the guise of advertising: "Advertising is taught as the means by which ideas are conveyed from one person to others."[6] This was recast nearly half a century later when the program was renamed Graphic Design: "The essential skill of a graphic designer is his ability to communicate ideas forcefully and effectively in a wide variety of media. In the highly complex culture we live in, the problem of effective communication among the diverse business, social, and individual interests of a mass society has become a major concern."[7] Variations of this definition have remained until the present day.

However, this definition did not resolve a compulsion to enumerate the tools, media, and formats designers engaged. Traditionally, an artist meant that a person was a specialist in a particular craft, and through habit or convention, types of artists were often defined by their medium and tool. In contrast, the emerging communication designer was a generalist wielding multiple tools and directing activity on a metaorder like a chef working with ingredients harvested by farmers and fishermen. The 1947 catalogue stresses the wide scope of the field that includes "illustration, painting, industrial design, display design, package design, advertising layout design and publication formats."[8] The 1990 catalogue mentions that instruction in "computer graphics and design is offered in Mac and PC computer labs"[9] which five years later is revised to "industry-standard computer programs as Adobe Illustrator, Adobe Photoshop, QuarkXPress and Director."[10] By 2000, a veritable buffet of "information, publication, advertising, packaging, broadcast, network, and corporate design, as well as web and multimedia environments"[11] is proudly touted as a way to "take the lead in the fast-changing fields of the visual world."[12]

How much of this is marketing-speak remains unclear, and this tools-based notion of the discipline continues to be difficult to disabuse. Sensing a moment where the forest was lost for the trees, Charles Nix offered a more reflective assessment during his chairmanship in 2004:

Communication designers associate with all disciplines. It is their job to understand the specifics and peculiarities of a body of knowledge—to associate with experts, and to become "momentary experts" themselves. Through their facility with visual language, they communicate essence and intention to a wider audience. This process repeats itself throughout the designer's career, each time leaving a residue of the experience in the designer's mind and creating pathways and patterns for greater understanding.[13]

There is a focus here on the whole designer, as an individual, whose worth is not predicated on servicing industry but offering a way of making and thinking that is as valuable to others as to one's own understanding of form and ultimately of the visual world. The curricular reforms of the past decade of Communication Design at Parsons has been focused on strengthening this idea.

Throughout its evolution, communication design has negotiated between material form and the changing methods of production that have enabled word and image to be transmitted broadly across different cultural contexts. Thus, a constant of the discipline has been typography—the study of the visual shape of language—and adjacent investigations of sign, symbol, and image as a way of conveying meaning. But unique to Communication Design at Parsons has been the emphasis on interaction: the study of the cause and effect relation-ships between people and the digital networks and systems that mediate our daily experiences. While type is the systematic reproduction of a script and ultimately, of ideas, interaction is the means by which those ideas are given responsiveness and life.

Indeed, communication design has evolved from a one-way distribution of fixed mediums to a two-way conversation that is media agnostic. Hardly anything in our day-to-day is not negotiated through the interface of language and image or more literally through a piece of paper or screen. As both method and material, type and interaction offer manifold ways for us to create this membrane stretched over the activities of contemporary life. It is through communication design that we have the means to understand this interface, to articulate its intentions, and to make it visible.

Caspar Lam, Assistant Professor of Communication Design, joined Parsons in 2011 and is the Director of the BFA Communication Design Program.

1. *Icograda Design Education Manifesto.* Icograda Millennium Congress, 2000.

2. Bennett, Audrey and Omar Vulpinari, eds. *Icograda Design Education Manifesto 2011.* International Council of Design Associations, 2011.

3. *1912-13 bulletin of The New York School of Fine and Applied Art.* The New York School of Fine and Applied Art, 1912.

4. Benjamin, Walter. "The Work of Art in the Age of Its Technological Reproducibility." 1936-39.

5. *1913-14 bulletin of The New York School of Fine and Applied Art.* The New York School of Fine and Applied Art, 1913.

6. *1915-16 bulletin of the Winter Session of the New York School of Fine and Applied Art.* The New York School of Fine and Applied Art, 1915.

7. *1963-1964 catalog of Parsons School of Design.* Parsons School of Design, 1963.

8. *1947-1948 catalog of Parsons School of Design.* Parsons School of Design, 1947.

9. *Parsons Under-graduate Portfolio & Catalog.* Parsons School of Design, 1990.

10. *Parsons: 1 Century of American Design.* Parsons School of Design, 1995.

11. *Parsons: 2000-2001 Undergraduate Programs.* Parsons School of Design, 2000.

12. Ibid.

13. *Parsons: 2004-2005 Undergraduate Programs.* Parsons School of Design, 2004.

00 Years

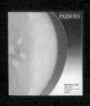

ON DESIGN EDUCATION

TEACHING DESIGN IS TEACHING A MOVING TARGET

A Conversation with Lucille Tenazas

Jarrett Fuller

Lucille Tenazas joined Parsons in 2006 where she is the Henry Wolf Professor in the School of Art, Media and Technology. Before this, she taught at California College of Arts in San Francisco since 1985 and was the Founding Chair of their MFA program in Design. From 1996 to 1998, she was national president of AIGA. In this conversation, Lucille reflects on her experience in design education and the ever-changing nature of graphic design.

Jarrett Fuller
The reason that I love the word design so much is that it is both a noun and a verb. Something I've found is that when students just start out in design, they think about it as the noun. They want to make something: the poster, the book, the app. But you've talked often about how teaching design is sort of like teaching a moving target; about how the field is changing so fast—the nouns are changing so fast. This makes me think it doesn't always make sense to teach the noun, as in "here's how you make apps or here's how you bind a book". What actually makes more sense is to teach the verb. I'm curious how you think about teaching design as a process over teaching a result?

Lucille Tenazas
When a student tells me "Lucille, I have a thesis idea. I want to make a website." I say, "No, that's not a thesis idea." A website is a platform, not an idea. A thesis idea is a subject that you would like to investigate further—it can be the weather, geography, traffic patterns—any topic that you're interested in that you can explore in various ways. After exhaustive research, you can then decide what form best expresses that idea. Give me the essence of that idea then we can talk about whether you want to do a book or a map or a

website. Our smart phones are the most pervasive portals of communication we have, but how do we know what the next medium will be? Maybe there will be chips embedded in our wrists. But your brain will continue to operate as a designer. So as an educator, I ask myself, "What can I do to prepare students to think like that and ensure that they learn to be adaptable, to be observant, and to use the faculties that they have to engage with the process, and at the same time, be generous and hospitable to new forms?"

When I was a student—way ahead of you—there were no computers in the studios but when I graduated from Cranbrook in 1982, I considered myself a designer. It's now 2021. That's 39 years! I have been away from school for 39 years and I am still a designer. The tools have evolved but my approach has stayed the same. The artifacts, the tools, the conditions will change based on the time but what's important is that one have the headspace, the tactics, the approach. I tell this to my students: it's 2021 and if we add 40 years to that, we get to 2061. What will you be doing? I will be dead, but you'll still be a designer! I'm proof that you can continually evolve as a designer and still be relevant, years after you have left school.

JF
When I first started teaching, somebody older than me said that when they think about their job as an educator, they see it not necessarily to train students for that first job immediately after college but for the one after that. That job is harder to get in some ways, because everything's changing and when I hear you talk about being a designer in 2061,

it's the same idea. How do you think about that long term thinking with students who are often coming to New York, taking out loans, knowing that this is costing them money, and thinking "I better get a job after this"?

LT
Yes, I believe in that approach and understand that attitude from the students. I think of parents who pay a lot of money for their children to be educated and the first thing they want to know is the employability data. This is why college websites always list the companies their alumni work for and it's not easy to say "don't worry, your child has a degree in Design!" But when you look at design with a capital D, it is as you say, both the verb and the noun, it is both process and artifact. I want to tell these parents "your child is actually getting an education in understanding how the world works. They may end up making an artifact. That's easiest because they're educated in a discipline where that is a byproduct of the profession, but the bigger lesson is that they are eminently qualified to think through problems in a bigger context that maybe somebody with a business degree or a law degree will never have."

JF
But often it seems like the design education system is just following what the professional world is looking for. We'll hear companies say, "We want app designers" or "we need people who can do X" and then we're like "OK! Let's add this into our classes so students can do this!" In thinking about design more holistically, thinking about the process and the thinking and the approach, there's actually some switch that could happen where the next generations of

students could actually influence the industry instead of vice versa.

LT

This reminds me of the time when I was developing the graduate design program at CCA [California College of Arts] in 1999. I was in the process of preparing the prospectus for the program and had, at that point in my career, been through a leadership experience as the national president of the AIGA from 1996–98, had taught for several years since 1985, and had been practicing as a designer for almost 15 years. I believed that through this new program, I could create the pedagogical pathways for these three experiences to come together. I wanted to incorporate writing, leadership, and design into one curriculum. So I included a mandatory writing class because as designers, we are often the recipients of existing text written by someone else, but if designers are trained to write, we could be the authors of our own text. A designer could both write and design it.

The second pillar was leadership. I often ask myself, "Will it ever come to pass in my lifetime, that the CEO of a major fortune 500 company was someone who has an MFA in Design?" That became my goal. Most CEOs and top-level managers have either a law degree or an MBA, and I wanted design to pave the way for those C-suite positions! Teaching design can give people a holistic understanding of complex problems. My thinking is that if you have enough of these people in high-powered decision-making positions and you find out they have a design background, we begin to change how design is perceived and understood.

So to answer your question, educators who are developing design curriculums should anticipate the cultural, political and social landscape that they are preparing their students to enter. We shouldn't wait for the industry to tell us what they are looking for. When people ask me what it is that designers can do, I say it's the development of synthetic thinking. It is the mindset that takes the best of all the things one knows and finds out how they can adapt it to the situation at hand. I want students who can engage with the world, who are literate in different areas, and not just in design. "See more, think more" espouses the art critic and author, Jed Perl.

JF

One thing I appreciate about the Parsons curriculum is that in addition to this synthetic thinking, it also retains an emphasis on craft. I think often those two get disconnected. Between the thinking and the craft, one of them always takes priority where it's either "let's just make stuff that looks good so you have a good portfolio seeking a job" but then there's no thought behind it. Or it's "let's be really thoughtful, lets you do all this research" and then by the time it gets to the actual artifact it's a letdown. How do you make sure that those two are always in sync?

LT

I often show my students examples of design practitioners and their body of work, and ask them what qualities make their work stand out. The best designers are the ones who balance quality of thought with the quality of craft. You can be a smart thinker but then you also have to pay attention to the quality of the work because in the end, the work needs to stand on its own.

I say to them: there are hundreds of thousands of you who will graduate from this discipline every year. How will you stand out? Will your work just be like everybody else's? Or are you telling a visual story that will trigger something so that when somebody sees it, they would have to pause and try to decipher something, not out of confusion, but out of interest? It might not make everyone stop, but when someone does, it means you've found your match. They will see the potential in what you have done and will want to know more about you. Those are the people you want to give time to.

JF
The field of design has just gotten bigger and bigger. There's all sorts of things that students are designing now that didn't exist when I was in school and certainly didn't exist when you were. What do you see as next? Looking back over your history and looking forward to the next 40 years, what stands out as the next big changes in the field?

LT
We've come full circle because when you asked me about design as the moving target, this is it. Books were around in the 17th century but the way we read and the way we address reading systems will change. Why is

there still an attempt to mimic the physically of "turning the page"? The forms may change but we still think about the actions of the body that allow for this to happen. In short, our humanity will transcend any techno-logical advances made.

Over the years, many words have been affixed to design—we have design thinking or service design or experiential design or whatever is trendy at the time. We add these adjectives to legitimize our profession but the word "design" stays, it is the common denominator. Design has become the locus that ties all these other areas of study. Here at The New School, of which Parsons is a part of, we have a program on Design and the Future of Publishing and a newly-developed area of study in Anthro-pology and Design. Whatever is next, Design will be there. It's evergreen, regardless of how it'll be defined. So my sense is that there are the things that change and the things that remain the same, and the important thing is for the things that remain the same to continually evolve. That's the core, I think, of how we practice design.

Jarrett Fuller is a designer, writer, editor, and Assistant Professor of Graphic Design at North Carolina State University.

Juliette Cezzar

When I joined the full-time faculty at Parsons in 2011, I came in as director of the BFA Communication Design program, a program that was and still is one of extraordinary scale closely connected to commercial practice. Rather than finding this concerning, I found it liberating. I had gone to graduate school in graphic design in the early 2000s and had struggled to make sense of the art-inspired conceptual focus of the learning there because I found meaning in graphic design work as a practitioner. I took on the directorship role at Parsons because I saw an opportunity to connect theory and practice in one place.

A lot of things were aligned at that moment in 2011. The scale of the program—with over 100 classes offered each academic year—provided greater flexibility in designing and communicating the curriculum, as well as the ability to bring in new faculty. The panic following the 2008 recession meant that there was institutional support for fully integrating digital and interaction design into what was a patchwork of courses designed and unevenly maintained since 1970. The most promising condition was that interaction courses were already required in the sophomore year, left over from an unsuccessful merger with the BFA Design & Technology program a few years earlier. When I joined, my primary goal was to break the persistent belief that "digital" was an alternative to "print" (and therefore something that a student could opt out of) because my experience within the field and the hundreds of conversations I had with practitioners—mostly in recruiting for this large program—pointed directly at our already hybrid world.

It would seem that an alignment with practice would naturally lead to a more vocationally-focused program. But in the years that followed, it's become more and more evident that the value and purpose of a four-year design program has never been the production of competent individual designers for an imagined future American job market. I'm not the first to declare this: certainly there have been calls towards design as a liberal art[1] or to follow the educational and cultural model of architecture.[2] Elite schools have also long proposed and borrowed progressive art education structures and formats.[3] But none of these models were or are possible to implement in a program with over 400 students and 100 part-time faculty embedded in the commercial design world of New York City. Moreover, both the liberal arts and architecture models presume a substantial amount of prior canonical cultural knowledge: something we cannot assume with our diverse and large international student population.

The value and purpose of a graphic and communication design education is its ability to take in students with a wide range of visual, linguistic, and computational abilities and deliver them into an even wider array of outcomes without tracking students into separate paths. This is true of all of the design disciplines and even the arts, but it is particularly true in graphic and communication design which, in part because of its close relationship with technology, is well-positioned to deliver a sound education amid the forces shaping education, practice, and private life. It's also important to recognize that the American school is still very much a social experience—whether that social experience is online, offline, or a mix of both[4]—all of which is both bound up in and beyond the content of the classroom.

The three forces that have been reshaping academia for years—globalization, digital technology, and an increasingly market-driven education economy[5]—have driven every aspect of who comes to design school at Parsons and what those students do while they are here. During my time here, the number of students as a whole almost doubled while the proportion of international students rose until it was just over half. Most students came and many more continue to come because of institutional messaging about individual success within creative careers. This language exists not because it is what faculty aspire to but because consistent user testing of university marketing campaigns has shown that it increases applications. Meanwhile, across schools and professional organizations, the drumbeat to match design education to job statistics has been increasing, culminating most recently in the AIGA Designer of 2025 report[6] which later rebranded itself as Design Futures.[7]

The Communication Design programs at Parsons did not grow and develop by creating checklists that match the wishes of future employers with the desires of students and their families. Schools are like rivers: they look like fixtures in the landscape, but they are ever-changing. They are also made of people. On the faculty side, with the help of Pascal Glissmann, we brought interaction courses under the umbrella of the program (when they were previously served from another program) and made active practice a requirement for all faculty teaching Communication Design courses. This changed the nature of the part-time faculty who still teach the vast majority of courses in the program. What really shifted the character of the program, however, is the introduction of new full-time faculty who served as directors after my term—YuJune Park from 2014–2017, E Roon Kang from 2017–2020, and Caspar Lam starting in 2020—as well as the addition of Brendan Griffiths, Kelly Walters, and Lynn Kiang, all of whom have served or continue to serve in leadership across multiple Communication Design degree programs. All, like me, are rooted in practices that straddle the real and the virtual, and all are deeply committed to education. Most importantly, we have worked so closely together as a team that it's difficult to see where one person's work ends and another begins. Like contemporary design, design education is not a solo sport.

So if we are not serving industry-ready content to fill the minds of our students, what are we doing? Students are not empty vessels or computers waiting to be programmed. All students already arrive with areas of strength that can be either excised or exercised during their time in school. The group of students that make it through the enrollment algorithms comes with above-the-median skills in *translation*, *creation*, and *articulation*—strengths that are often found in successful designers. By design, each classroom in our program contains that range of individuals with vast differences in prior experience and skills. It is imperative to develop each student towards increasing levels of mastery and confidence in each of these three areas while acknowledging that they will not all be the same upon graduation and that they will continue learning and strengthening these competencies throughout their lives.

CREATION

During the late 2010s when I was conducting interviews for a book, I asked over forty interviewees what they looked for in new hires. Many of the responses were what I would have expected, but some were not. In less visually-oriented and team-oriented environments like consultancies and tech companies, people told me that they had great difficulty knowing if a candidate was a good fit until *three months after* the candidate began. This was the case despite long interview processes, challenge assignments, group meetings, and reviews of portfolio work and prior experience. Most surprisingly, when I pressed people in interdisciplinary agency environments to explain what graphic designers or communication designers do, they would start talking about prototyping. Designers may collaborate with their teams to design products, but the one thing that they did regularly that other team members didn't do was *make stuff*.

Creation is a skill that each design student possesses at some level, but it is not an inborn talent. It's not a given that they really understand how to make something in the first place. In a networked world, they see representations of creations or creativity, but processes are almost entirely hidden. Students have the impression that the most important works are made by individuals who are geniuses who come up with genius ideas. They even often mistake thinking the artifact is the idea ("My idea is an app. My idea is to make a magazine"). It shouldn't be surprising, then, for students to try to replicate this process and then become crestfallen when the thing they bring to class draws either a lukewarm reaction or worse, criticism. Ideally, by the senior year, students see the critique as part of a design process rather than a performance, feedback more of a gift than a burden.

TRANSLATION

If there is a skill that is already well into development by the time students arrive at design school, it's the skill of translation. Fifteen years ago, the majority of my design students already came aligned to mainstream culture and could move with it or against it with little friction. Only those who were outsiders needed to develop translation skills, but even those skills were contingent on the people and materials in their proximity. Today, our students are constantly moving between contexts and cultures, often occupying two or more at the same time.

This no less true for designers as translation is also required as projects of all scales now call either for universality or for intimate knowledge of specific conditions or specific audiences. But translation for designers is not just a movement between cultures and languages. The designer also translates ideas into form, ideas from one form into another, or ideas across multiple physical and digital forms. The last category is especially important. There are very few modes of communication that aren't already mediated by templated or automated design processes. Moreover, a "single" digital instance fragments into dozens of forms in response to different devices, user accessibility preferences, and language. Translation has become a requirement and a norm.

ARTICULATION

If you ask designers what they took away from their undergraduate education, those new to the field will point to "making" as their main takeaway. Everyone else will tell you that they had learned how to think, how to speak, how to write, or some combination of the three. Articulation is an extension of these skills of thinking, writing, and speaking clearly to an audience. It's a necessary competency for designers because without onboarding project commissioners and collaborators, no work of design will be realized. And most of those people—whether they are supporting that work or executing it—know very little about design and do not understand any of its specialized language.

However, articulation is not just about speaking to people outside of the discipline. Without a shared design language, there is no discipline. More recently, we have required that students in our core design courses attend curated lectures and that all sections of core classes share common readings. While this may seem obvious, it's rare for a program of this size to coordinate such shared experiences because it is often extra, unacknowledged work. The result, however, has been greater fluency in the more specialized language of design and a deeper understanding between designers both in and out of school.

Within the Communication Design programs at Parsons, the shift in our teaching towards new, structured methods built around translation, creation, and articulation has required more effort than teaching through individual intuition. It has even presented some conflicts since every structural addition reduces student agency. But in order to eventually have that agency, a student must first develop the skills that they have already brought to design school. If we want to value students as people and not just future workers, we should focus on the designer they are now and on making that designer better. In our current global, market-driven, and digitally-focused world, these are the skills they need at home, at work, and in their communities.

Juliette Cezzar, Associate Professor of Communication Design, joined Parsons in 2011 and was the Director of the BFA Communication Design Program (2011-2014).

1. Gunner Swanson has written eloquently in defense of graphic design as a liberal art since the 1990s. See Swanson, Gunnar. "Graphic Design Education as a Liberal Art: Design and Knowledge in the University and the 'Real World.'" *Design Issues* 10, no. 1 (1994): 53–63. https://doi.org/10.2307/1511656.

2. David Cabianca, "A Case for the Sublime Uselessness of Graphic Design," Design and Culture, 8:1 (Routledge: 2016), 103–122. https://doi.org/10.1080/17547075.2016.1142347.

3. See, for example, Judy Chicago, "Feminist Art Education: Made in California," in *Politics of Study*, Sidsel Meineche Hansen & Tom Vandeputte, eds. (London: Open Editions, 2015), 90.

4. This is largely why American students rarely go to school abroad, even though the quality of education for its cost is almost always greater outside of the U.S.

5. Joan Ockman, *Architecture School: Three Centuries of Educating Architects in North America* (Cambridge, MA: MIT Press, 2012), 10.

6. aigaeducators. "AIGA Designer 2025." August 22, 2017, accessed September 8, 2021. https://educators.aiga.org/aiga-designer-2025/. In August of 2017, AIGA, the American professional association for for design, published and distributed two PDFs under this header. One document outlined the current undergraduate competencies (what every undergraduate is supposed to learn) excerpted from the handbook of NASAD, which, until recently, was the accreditor for most name-brand art and design schools. (Accreditation has its own interesting history: until the GI Bill was passed, art schools didn't offer accredited degrees, because they didn't need to. Parsons was started in 1896, but didn't offer degrees until 1948, in partnership with NYU.) The other provided an executive summary of what it identified as seven "trends." Beneath each of these trends are lists of competencies to be expected of undergraduate, graduate, and professional continuing education students in communication design.

7. Davis, Meredith. "Introduction to Design Futures." 2019. Accessed March 31, 2020. https://www.aiga.org/aiga-design-futures/introduction-to-design-futures/ Both of these missives cite U.S. Bureau of Labor statistics job forecasts that show "traditional" graphic design work as stagnant or declining, and web design and software design climbing. Design Futures also kicks off with a nod to the "designers' anxiety and self-described challenges regarding their place in the future" in the 2017 Design Census. Both data sets are flawed: the Bureau of Labor Statistics separates any digital work that designers do into a separate "Computer and Information Technology" header, uncomfortably stating that "web developers design and create websites." The Design Census was sponsored by Google and written by the designers there, which is why issues such as "Advertising supported content model" and "Algorithm bias" turn up throughout the survey.

TIMELINE

Communication Design at Parsons has its origins in the first classes offered at the school's founding. Leadership transitions are highlighted. The AAS program begins as a separate division in 1975 before becoming fully integrated with the establishment of AAS Communication Design in 2019.

Year	Program Name	Leadership & Developments
1896		(Chase School of Art is formed by a group from the Art Students League) *Art Nouveau's popularity in the United States is exemplified by publications like Harper's magazine.*
1898		(Chase School of Art is renamed the New York School of Art)
1905	Poster Design and Advertising	(Classes first formed under the direction of Frank Alvah Parsons)
1909	Poster Design and Advertising	(New York School of Art is re-incorporated as New York School of Fine and Applied Art) *Futurist manifesto published*
1912	Commercial Advertising	(First courses in lettering and placing, spacing, and arrangement of type)
1913	Illustrative Advertising	Zerelda Rains, Head of Department, Illustrative Advertising and Costume Design
1914	Illustrative Advertising	Zerelda Rains, Head of Department, Illustrative Advertising and Costume Design *American Institute of Graphic Arts is founded*
1915	Illustrative Advertising	Zerelda Rains, Head of Department, Illustrative Advertising and Costume Design
1916	Illustrative Advertising	Zerelda Rains, Director, Illustrative Advertising Department
1917	Illustrative Advertising	Zerelda Rains, Director, Illustrative Advertising Everett Henry, Assistant Director, Illustrative Advertising
1918	Advertising or "Commercial Art"	Zerelda Rains, Director, Illustrative Advertising
1919	Poster Advertising and Commercial Art	Zerelda Rains, Director, Poster Advertising, Costume and Stage Design
1920	Poster Advertising and Commercial Art	Zerelda Rains, Director, Department of Advertising *The Art Directors Club of New York is founded*
1921	Poster Advertising and Commercial Art	Zerelda Rains, Director, Department of Advertising Elizabeth Cole Tucker, Assistant to the Director
1922	Graphic Advertising	Zerelda Rains, Director Department of Advertising *Constructivist manifesto is published*
1923	Graphic Advertising and Commercial Design	Zerelda Rains, Director of the Departments of Life Drawing and Graphic Advertising
1924	Graphic Advertising and Commercial Design	Zerelda Rains, Director of the Department of Graphic Advertising Frank Fiore, Assistant Head of Department of Graphic Advertising
1925	Advertising Illustration and Commercial Design	Zerelda Rains, Head of Department, Advertising Illustration Frank Fiore, Associate Department Head, Advertising Illustration and Process of Reproduction
1926	Graphic Advertising and Illustration	Zerelda Rains, Head of Department, Graphic Advertising and Illustration Frank Fiore, Associate Department Head, Graphic Advertising Illustration, Lettering and Process of Reproduction
1927	Graphic Advertising and Illustration	Zerelda Rains, Head of Department, Graphic Advertising and Illustration Frank Fiore, Associate Department Head, Graphic Advertising Illustration; Lettering and Process of Reproduction
1928	Graphic Advertising and Illustration	Zerelda Rains, Head of Department, Department of Graphic Advertising and Illustration Elsie Brown Barnes, Associate Department Head, Department of Graphic Advertising and Illustration *Jan Tschichold publishes The New Typography*
1929	Graphic Advertising and Illustration	Zerelda Rains, Head of Department, Department of Graphic Advertising and Illustration Elsie Brown Barnes, Associate Department Head, Department of Graphic Advertising and Illustration
1930	Graphic Advertising and Illustration	Zerelda Rains, Head of Department of Graphic Advertising and Illustration Elsie Brown Barnes, Associate Department Head of Advertising Illustration and Costume Design (First mention of the Modern Art Movement in course catalogues)

1931	Graphic Advertising and Illustration	Zerelda Rains, Head of Department of Graphic Advertising and Illustration Elsie Brown Barnes, Associate Department Head of Advertising Illustration and Costume Design
1932	Graphic Advertising and Illustration	Zerelda Rains, Head of Department of Graphic Advertising and Illustration Elsie Brown Barnes, Associate Department Head of Advertising Illustration and Costume Design
1933	Graphic Advertising and Illustration	Zerelda Rains, Head of Department of Graphic Advertising and Illustration Elsie Brown Barnes, Associate Department Head of Advertising Illustration and Costume Design *Staatliches Bauhaus closes*
1934	Graphic Advertising and Illustration	Elsie Brown Barnes, Department Head of Advertising Illustration and Costume Design Betty M. Carter, Associate Department Head of Advertising Illustration
1935	Graphic Advertising & Illustration	Elsie Brown Barnes, Department Head of Advertising Illustration and Costume Design Betty M. Carter, Associate Department Head of Advertising Illustration
1936	Graphic Advertising & Illustration	Elsie Brown Barnes, Department Head of Graphic Advertising and Illustration and Costume Design and Illustration Betty M. Carter, Associate Department Head of Graphic Advertising and Illustration
1937	Advertising Design	Elsie Brown Barnes, Head of Departments of Advertising Design, Costume Design and Illustration Betty M. Carter, Associate Head of Department of Advertising Design
1938	Advertising Design	Elsie Brown Barnes, Head of Departments of Advertising Design, Costume Design and Illustration Betty M. Carter, Associate Head of Department of Advertising Design
1939	Advertising Design	Elsie Brown Barnes, Head of Departments of Advertising Design, Costume Design and Illustration Betty M. Carter, Associate Head of Department of Advertising Design (First mention of the study of typography in course catalogues)
1940	Advertising Design	Elsie Brown Barnes, Head of Departments of Advertising Design, Costume Design and Illustration Betty M. Carter, Associate Head of Department of Advertising Design
1941	Advertising Design	Elsie Brown Barnes, Head of Departments of Advertising Design, Costume Design and Illustration Betty M. Carter, Associate Head of Department of Advertising Design
1942	Advertising & Industrial Design	Elsie Brown Barnes, Head of Departments of Advertising and Industrial Design; Costume Design and Illustration Betty M. Carter, Associate Head of Department of Advertising and Industrial Design; Flat Design (New York School of Fine and Applied Art is renamed Parsons School of Design)
1943	Advertising & Industrial Design	Elsie Brown Barnes, Head of Departments of Advertising and Industrial Design; Costume Design and Illustration Betty M. Carter, Associate Head of Department of Advertising and Industrial Design; Flat Design
1944	BS Advertising and Industrial Design	Elsie Brown Barnes, Head of Departments of Advertising Design; Costume Design and Illustration; Flat Design Betty M. Carter, Associate Head of Departments of Advertising Design; Flat Design (Bachelor of Science is offered through an affiliation with New York University)
1945	BS Advertising	Elsie Brown Barnes, Head of Departments of Advertising Design; Costume Design and Illustration; Flat Design Betty M. Carter, Associate Head of Departments of Advertising Design; Flat Design
1946	BS Advertising	Betty M. Carter, Head of Department of Advertising Design *Type Directors Club is founded in New York*
1947	BS Advertising	Betty M. Carter, Head of Department of Advertising Design *Paul Rand publishes Thoughts on Design*
1948	BS Advertising	Betty M. Carter, Head of Department of Advertising Design
1949	BS Advertising	Elsie Brown Barnes, Director, Departments of Costume Illustration and Design, Flat Design, Advertising Design, and Illustration Betty M. Carter, Assistant Director, Department of Advertising Design

1950	BS Advertising	Elsie Brown Barnes, Director, Departments of Costume Illustration and Design, Flat Design, Advertising Design, and Illustration Betty M. Carter, Assistant Director, Department of Advertising Design *Yale's graduate graphic design program, the first of its kind in the United States, begins*
1951	BS Advertising	Elsie Brown Barnes, Director, Departments of Costume Illustration and Design, Flat Design, Advertising Design, and Illustration Betty M. Carter, Assistant Director, Department of Advertising Design
1952	BS Advertising	Betty M. Carter, Head of Advertising Design and Illustration James Frangides, Assistant Head of Advertising Design and Illustration
1953	BS Advertising	Betty M. Carter, Head of Advertising Design and Illustration James Frangides, Assistant Head of Advertising Design and Illustration
1954	BFA Graphic Design and Advertising	Leo Lionni, Head of Department (Bachelor of Fine Arts is offered through an affiliation with New York University)
1955	BFA Graphic Design and Advertising	Leo Lionni, Chairman of the Department
1956	BFA Graphic Design and Advertising	Leo Lionni, Chairman of the Department
1957	BFA Graphic Design and Advertising	Leo Lionni, Chairman of the Department *Black Mountain College closes*
1958	BFA Graphic Design and Advertising	James Frangides, Chairman of the Department
1959	BFA Graphic Design and Advertising	James Frangides, Chairman of the Department
1960	BFA Graphic Design and Advertising	James Frangides, Chairman of the Department
1961	BFA Graphic Design	James Frangides, Chairman of the Department
1962	BFA Graphic Design	James Frangides, Chairman of the Department
1963	BFA Graphic Design	James Frangides, Chairman of the Department
1964	BFA Graphic Design	James Frangides, Chairman of the Department
1965	BFA Graphic Design	James Frangides, Chairman of the Department
1966	BFA Graphic Design	James Frangides, Chairman of the Department
1967	BFA Graphic Design	James Frangides, Chairman of the Department
1968	BFA Graphic Design	James Frangides, Chairman of the Department
1969	BFA Graphic Design	James Frangides, Chairman of the Department
1970	BFA Graphic Design	John Russo, Acting Chairman, Graphic Design Department (Parsons and the New School for Social Research merge)
1971	BFA Graphic Design	John Russo, Chairman of the Department
1972	BFA Communication Design	John Russo, Chairman of the Department Patrick Norado, Associate Chairman
1973	BFA Communication Design	John Russo, Chairman of the Department Patrick Norado, Associate Chairman
1974	BFA Communication Design	John Russo, Chairman of the Department Patrick Norado, Associate Chairman
1975	BFA Communication Design (AAS Graphic & Advertising Design)	John Russo, Chairman of the Department Patrick Norado, Associate Chairman
1976	BFA Communication Design (AAS Graphic & Advertising Design)	John Russo, Chairman of the Department Patrick Bairado, Associate Chairman
1977	BFA Communication Design (AAS Graphic & Advertising Design)	John Russo, Chairman of the Department Patrick Bairado, Associate Chairman *First mass-produced personal computers are introduced*
1978	BFA Communication Design (AAS Graphic & Advertising Design)	John Russo, Chairman of the Department Patrick Bairado, Associate Chairman *The New York Times transitions from Linotype to photocomposition*
1979	BFA Communication Design (AAS Graphic & Advertising Design)	John Russo, Chairman of the Department (Parsons is affiliated with Otis until 1991)
1980	BFA Communication Design (AAS Graphic & Advertising Design)	John Russo, Chairman of the Department Richard tum Suden, Assistant to the Chairman
1981	BFA Communication Design (AAS Graphic & Advertising Design)	John Russo, Chairman of the Department Richard tum Suden, Assistant to the Chairman
1982	BFA Communication Design (AAS Graphic & Advertising Design)	John Russo, Chairman of the Department Richard tum Suden, Assistant to the Chairman

1983	BFA Communication Design (AAS Graphic & Advertising Design)	(Leadership transition in progress)
1984	BFA Communication Design (AAS Graphic & Advertising Design)	Albert Greenberg, Chairman Richard tum Suden, Assistant Chairman (First time "Computer Design" course appears) *HP introduces the first low-cost laser printer; Adobe releases PostScript*
1985	BFA Communication Design (AAS Graphic & Advertising Design)	Albert Greenberg, Chairman Richard tum Suden, Assistant Chairman
1986	BFA Communication Design (AAS Graphic & Advertising Design)	Albert Greenberg, Chairman Richard tum Suden, Assistant Chairman
1987	BFA Communication Design (AAS Graphic & Advertising Design)	Albert Greenberg, Chairman Richard tum Suden, Assistant Chairman
1988	BFA Communication Design (AAS Graphic & Advertising Design)	Albert Greenberg, Chairman Richard tum Suden, Assistant Chairman (First mention of "Computer Graphics" in course descriptions)
1989	BFA Communication Design (AAS Graphic & Advertising Design)	Albert Greenberg, Chairman Richard tum Suden, Assistant Chairman (Communication Design Advisory Committee established and runs to the 1994-1995 academic year)
1990	BFA Communication Design (AAS Graphic & Advertising Design)	Albert Greenberg, Chairman Richard tum Suden, Assistant Chairman
1991	BFA Communication Design (AAS Graphic & Advertising Design)	Albert Greenberg, Chairman Richard tum Suden, Assistant Chairman *First web page is launched at CERN*
1992	BFA Communication Design (AAS Graphic & Advertising Design)	Albert Greenberg, Chairman
1993	BFA Communication Design (AAS Graphic & Advertising Design)	Albert Greenberg, Chairman
1994	BFA Communication Design (AAS Graphic & Advertising Design)	(Leadership transition in progress) Krista Bergert, Assistant to the Chair *Muriel Cooper presents "Information Landscapes" at TED 5*
1995	BFA Communication Design (AAS Graphic & Advertising Design)	William Bevington, Chair (First appearance of Computing Procedures and Advanced Computing Techniques courses)
1996	BFA Communication Design (AAS Graphic Design)	William Bevington, Chair *Palm introduces the first commercially succesful handheld, the Pilot*
1997	BFA Communication Design (AAS Graphic Design)	William Bevington, Chair
1998	BFA Communication Design (AAS Graphic Design)	William Bevington, Chair *CSS2 is published by the W3C*
1999	BFA Communication Design (AAS Graphic Design)	William Bevington, Chair *CSS3 drafts published by the W3C*
2000	BFA Communication Design (AAS Graphic Design)	William Bevington, Chair *International Council of Design calls for the discipline to be renamed visual communication design*
2001	BFA Communication Design (AAS Graphic Design)	William Bevington, Chair
2002	BFA Communication Design (AAS Graphic Design)	William Bevington, Chair
2003	BFA Communication Design (AAS Graphic Design)	Charles Nix, Chair
2004	BFA Communication Design (AAS Graphic Design)	Charles Nix, Chair
2005	BFA Communication Design (AAS Graphic Design)	Charles Nix, Chair (Communication Design and Design & Technology, a program started four years earlier, briefly merge into one department)
2006	BFA Communication Design (AAS Graphic Design)	(Leadership transition in progress) Ted Byfield, Associate Chair
2007	BFA Communication Design (AAS Graphic Design)	Jane Pirone, Director
2008	BFA Communication Design (AAS Graphic Design)	Jane Pirone, Director *Apple launches App Store for iOS; Google launches Android Market (Google Play) for Android*

2009	BFA Communication Design (AAS Graphic Design)	Jane Pirone, Director *Yahoo! GeoCities is shut down in the United States*
2010	BFA Communication Design (AAS Graphic Design)	Jane Pirone, Co-Director Juliette Cezzar, Co-Director (Spring 2011) (Communication Design and Design & Technology departments begin the process of separation) *Web Open Font Format (WOFF) is published by the W3C as a working draft*
2011	BFA Communication Design (AAS Graphic Design)	Juliette Cezzar, Director, BFA *International Council of Design calls for the discipline to be renamed communication design; Coding bootcamps and later, design bootcamps, appear in the United States.*
2012	BFA Communication Design (AAS Graphic Design)	Juliette Cezzar, Director, BFA Pascal Glissmann, Associate Director, BFA
2013	BFA Communication Design (AAS Graphic Design)	Juliette Cezzar, Director, BFA Pascal Glissmann, Associate Director, BFA (Communication Design minor is offered)
2014	BFA Communication Design (AAS Graphic Design)	YuJune Park, Director, BFA Juliette Cezzar, Associate Director, BFA (Communication Design and Design & Technology programs are fully independent)
2015	BFA Communication Design (AAS Graphic Design)	YuJune Park, Director, BFA Juliette Cezzar, Associate Director, BFA
2016	BFA Communication Design (AAS Graphic Design)	YuJune Park, Director, BFA E Roon Kang, Associate Director, BFA *Variable fonts introduced*
2017	BFA Communication Design MPS Communication Design (AAS Graphic Design)	E Roon Kang, Director, BFA YuJune Park, Associate Director, BFA Brendan Griffiths, Director, MPS *Adobe Flash is deprecated*
2018	BFA Communication Design MPS Communication Design (AAS Graphic Design)	E Roon Kang, Director, BFA YuJune Park, Associate Director, BFA Brendan Griffiths, Director, MPS
2019	BFA Communication Design MPS Communication Design AAS Communication Design	E Roon Kang, Director, BFA Caspar Lam, Associate Director, BFA Brendan Griffiths, Director, MPS Pascal Glissmann, Director, AAS
2020	BFA Communication Design MPS Communication Design AAS Communication Design	Caspar Lam, Director, BFA Kelly Walters, Associate Director, BFA Brendan Griffiths, Director, MPS Pascal Glissmann, Director, AAS

10 Years

TRANSLATION, CREATION, ARTICULATION

A Conversation with Juliette Cezzar and Pascal Glissmann

Andrew LeClair

This remote conversation between Juliette Cezzar, Pascal Glissmann, and Andrew LeClair took place in April 2021, and charts the development of the new core curriculum across Communication Design programs (BFA, AAS, and MPS). Juliette Cezzar, Associate Professor of Communication Design, joined Parsons in 2011 and was the Director of the BFA Communication Design Program (2011-2014). Pascal Glissmann, Associate Professor of Communication Design, joined Parsons in 2012, served as the BFA Communication Design Program Associate Director (2012-2014), was chair of the School Curriculum Committee (2013-2016), and is the Director of the AAS Communication Design Program.

Andrew LeClair
I'm interested in hearing more about the conditions that were in place when you were thinking about what these two programs—BFA Communication Design and BFA Design and Technology—could be. What was the context institutionally? How did you see designers operating in the world and how you saw that potentially changing in the future? How did you understand the history that you were building on?

Juliette Cezzar
I may as well start with the published history. The Communication Design program is the oldest graphic and communication design program in the United States, if not the world. It started off as an advertising and commercial illustration program in 1910. By 1970, Parsons had about 1,000 students and was both a commercial type of school but also a freestanding art school. If you go back and look at all the catalogues, it's right around that time, in 1972, that the name changes to Communication Design. I've always been curious

about why. Josef Müller-Brockmann's *The History of Visual Communication* came out in 1971, which might have precipitated that. What is weird is that if you look at the course listings from the late 1960s, you have all these wild-sounding, abstract courses, especially in the Graphic Design program. When the name changed to Communication Design, it got commercial. That's when you started seeing a lot of classes like "corporate design" and "book design," where everything starts getting laid out by medium. At that time, there were already well-known faculty working in the department like Cipe Pineles, who was art directing magazines like *Glamour* and *Mademoiselle*. Lance Wyman joined the faculty in 1973, and taught for another 40 years.

In the financial distress of the early 1990s, there was another push to hire more faculty and increase the number of students. During this time in the late 1980s, early 1990s, the computer was starting to become a thing, and everybody was asking, "Well, are we going to use this thing or are we not going to use this thing? What is it for?" A lot of the 90s was trying to figure out what to do with computers. Near the height of the dot-com boom, in 1999, both the BFA and MFA Design and Technology programs were launched. What's interesting to me—and this is not specific to Parsons—is that in a lot of these schools, instead of integrating the computer into existing programs, like Illustration or Fine Arts, the choice was to build new, separate programs.

For a while, as a person working in New York, I knew the Design and Technology program because it would graduate all these kids who could use a lot of different software.

When I worked at VH1 in the mid-2000s, we would have a whole bullpen of interns from Parsons who all knew how to use Flash and Photoshop. Communication Design wasn't even in my periphery. A lot of the 2000s were about kicking off Design and Technology, and then trying to define Communication Design against it, with it, for it, or whatever. There were periods where the programs were combined into "CDT."

I joined as director in 2011 and took over the program directorship from Jane Pirone, who was much more attuned to technology and business. There was this despair about how communication design was this mothballed thing that needed to wake up and develop a better relationship with technology. It's funny, because there was a certain moment right after I started where I was worried that I had made a mistake because I was much more interested in the web and what we now refer to as UI/UX and product design. I was like, "Did I sign up to teach in the wrong program?" I wasn't interested in teaching in a program that was only going to teach how to make logos or letterhead or whatever. Pascal came a few months later, with some of the same questions. It was a program that was confused about what its relationship to technology was going to be.

The thing that never seemed to factor in for everybody who was thinking on a more thematic level was that the Design and Technology BFA was small. It was about a fifth of the size of Communication Design, which was always about a hundred people per level. The scale of Communication Design never computed in anyone's decision making because people were always thinking about other questions like, "Should designers have to use computers?" Add into this a ton of pressure from The New School and from Parsons to either blur or destroy the boundaries between programs. Parsons did away with departments in 2009 in favor of programs that could operate as buckets of classes. The idea was that there would be people who would steer subject areas, but all the courses would be open to everybody and students could float around. This push to "break down all the silos"—again, not specific to Parsons—made it very challenging to direct an undefined program in an already confused discipline. "What is a program? What does it mean to direct a program? How do you do all this?" There were all these questions.

But the thing I immediately wanted to change when I arrived in terms of curriculum was that, as a Communication Design student, you had required courses that were coded as Design and Technology courses. You had to take Creative Computing and Core Interaction, and both of them were Design and Technology courses. There was also the confusion of having required courses where you had a selection, like Topics, and you had electives that were "required electives." Everything curricular was all over the place. And then thematically there was still this belief among both students and faculty that we were there to teach students how to use software, since that's what would get them jobs. When the director of BFA Design and Technology left about a year after I started, I volunteered to direct that program as well, and lobbied for Pascal to be named Associate Director so that we could do this work together.

Taking classes in Design and Technology as a Communication Design major was a big deal for students. They were like, "I didn't sign up for this. You can't make me take it. I'm not going to do this in my job." In 2013, all of Parsons was engaged in curricular restructuring in response to a newly redesigned first year, the introduction of minors, and a mandate to reduce the number of credits from 133 to 120. When Pascal led the work for the 120-credit curriculum, those courses that were previously required but outside the major were brought into Communication Design, which made a big difference in terms of how the students saw themselves and how the faculty felt either included or not included into the program.

Pascal Glissmann
It was a good moment to officially redesign the whole curriculum, and since we were in charge of the BFA Design and Technology curriculum at the same time, it was helpful to distinguish the two. We had to explain to the world how these two programs were different. It became clear that all the programs need to have core classes, everything that whoever directs the program believes you need to learn. These are the skills, the methodologies you need to have when you leave school, that need to happen in the core classes. The electives at that point, we decided, these can be wild cards. These can be whatever you want it to be. We even pushed students to take a class in psychology, anthropology, whatever. But this commitment to the core classes, at least in my impression, was new or was seen as outspoken in that moment. That made it easier to focus on.

AL

What do you remember about the state of the design world and the broader forces that were affecting education?

JC

2006 and 2007 was a bonanza. There was money on the streets: you could go walk around and pick it up. There was work everywhere. Then the 2008 recession came and people who had established practices for many years all of a sudden had a hard time. In New York City, in particular, that was pronounced. Work in publishing and advertising shrank by almost half, and what came up in place of all that was the rise of branding and UI/UX. There was a lot of digital work, but everything else went down.

But Pascal, what was it like in Europe? You were in Hong Kong at the time? You were in Beirut. What was it like worldwide?

PG

I don't have the New York perspective since I had been teaching for many years in Germany then Hong Kong and Beirut. What happened, at least in my perception, is that I was able to study four years of visual form. If I think back to my undergrad program, what we did is just form, right? That is an amazing opportunity because you can study it in detail, but I wasn't forced to make an interview or to be super reflective. I observed that, in all these different places, it became more and more obvious that using Photoshop was not a skill. People weren't interested. This was nothing you would develop a future around. I think I had a full semester learning QuarkXpress, because if you could publish a magazine using this weird software, you had a life, we thought.

But when the iPhone came out in 2007, technology in general became more democratized and people could do cool things on a tiny device. I think we all noticed that this was not our future: being able to use technology won't help you. Other questions, that looked at social science or social practice through the lens of design, seemed important. So this is why I was excited to come to Parsons in 2012 because, in my perception, you were light years ahead. It was clear that this is what design needs to be. The way we talk about design today, to me, started ten years ago in the Communication Design program. That was the biggest shift that I noticed.

JC

There was a nice, long period for about ten years where a lot of the people who were in charge didn't know how to use computers or use software, and they would hire hands to do all this work. As soon as we had that recession, that ended. If you weren't thinking *and* designing, instead of just entering things in the computer, you weren't useful to anybody, because anybody who couldn't do the work as well as think about it was already out of a job or a practice by then, or on thin ice. It was a big shift in terms of who was practicing design and how broad their skills were. This also has contributed in the last ten years to who is here on our faculty. Most of us are generalists. Almost all of us can design a book, design a website, or design a typeface. We do not have the specialization that in good times is a benefit. And yet, the urge toward specialization in the university context is always there. We've been incredibly resistant to it in the last decade, in part because of the history right before this period began.

PG

This goes back to the curriculum changes that happened at the time. Not all classes had course templates or even syllabi available to look at, and even if they did, then the learning outcomes would be something like "choose a paper" or "understand how a pencil works." Having proper learning outcomes for the classes was something we changed immediately. The learning outcomes we created for classes still had students making things but we added more holistic thinking processes. There's an accountability for faculty and for students to not only choose paper but to critically reflect on what those choices would mean.

JC

It was a shift away from thinking of each class as its own independent universe. I would say the big innovation, in a way, was to have a curriculum at all. We did it in concert with the rest of the programs in the school, but it was still met with a considerable amount of resistance from both faculty and students, who were used to an environment where they could take each class and try to teach everything within each class, as their own independent project.

AL

How did you approach that process? A lot of the things you mentioned sound like solving practical problems or addressing practical expectations.

JC

It doesn't sound like innovation, does it?

AL

But they're necessary things! I'm curious what were the high-level objectives that you were after?

PG

That's a good question. One thing that changed in the shift from looking at skills to looking at a holistic person that would graduate as a critical thinker, is this whole idea that we try to make them unlearn and learn, see things new. We aim to educate people who are not robots or soldiers in industry but visionaries of the community. If we want our graduates to rethink the processes within the community, have fresh ideas and visions, then we need to teach that.

One of the key moments to implement this philosophy was Thesis. We completely redesigned Thesis, this year-long experience of looking at a topic or a theme and developing a critical response. Again, redesigning the BFA curriculum came near the end of a complete redesign of the first year curriculum, where students learn specific methodologies and research. We took this into the second, third, and fourth year. We needed to make sure there's not a research-focused first year, then two years of typesetting and coding, then all of a sudden, there's the research thesis, but they forgot over two years what research means: the idea of criticality and initiating your own projects; not always waiting for the faculty to say, "Hey, here's your little assignment and do this in two weeks;" the accountability of, what's your voice as a designer, what do you want to do, that this happens throughout the program so that they would be able to come up with a solid thesis project. Saying that out loud, "solid thesis project," it's a lot to expect, but I would say that creating that thesis space was key to building the identity of Communication Design.

JC

We had to define Thesis first because when I came in, it was wholly framed as an independent study. Whatever the student wants to do for a year, we're going to assign them to a faculty and they're going to do it. Then we'll have an exhibition and we'll be done with it. All of which is fine and kind of works in a less commercial setting, but our students from their first year lean towards the commercial, and they rarely let go.

Even before Thesis, there is this confusion about whether students are going to be specializing or not, and there is a mixed bag of ideas about how to prepare for what they see as separate tracks or trajectories. I would have all these conversations with students where they would say, "you should waive this interaction class for me because that's not what I'm going to do. You don't understand. This is not relevant to my career. I'm going to be in branding." Other students had similar arguments about what they did not need to know how to do when designing for web and mobile.

So we changed Thesis from "I'm thinking about making this specific thing that's going to help me go do a career I'm interested in doing," to "this is the design process. Let's go and think about it again, now that we know ourselves and the field a little better." How are you going to be able to create your own brief in a way that takes into account what your capabil-ities are, what your interests are? How do you do all that? It's psycho-logical work,being in charge of your own trajectory.

Then we started to move backwards from there. What is it they need to know in order to be able to be prepared for this experience? Then slowly, everything started picking up and as we structured, especially the second year, it really helped. That work was very visible in the fourth year, two years later. Education in general is a long game.

PG

You shouldn't forget that people come into the program and look at what people do when they leave the program. If you join this program, you look at the thesis work, and in your mind, this is where you're going to, but of course, it's not, and it shouldn't be. This is why it takes like almost two generations to make that shift in philosophy and perspective.

JC

I came from architecture, which has a specific theme to each year, and I started to borrow a little bit of that here where I could. In architecture, the first year is incredibly abstract. You do everything with squares and circles, and there's nothing to do with buildings at all. The second year, you start to think about materials as form and function to some degree. In the third year, you get a site. The fourth year is exploration, and the fifth is synthesis.

In thinking about what we're doing here, in my mind, the second year is building both abstractly and a little bit concretely, though it's still not as abstract as I would hope, is building the foundational skills in typography and interaction during that whole year. Then the third year is about being able to situate that learning, meaning, being able to use typography and interaction in various contexts. Typography and interaction in branding, typography and inter-action in digital product design, in editorial design. Then, in the thesis year, being able to synthesize all of that and map it back to the design process, understanding how to frame a project and how to communicate a project in a much more conscious way.

This is still a work in progress, in part because of the primacy of interaction. Interaction is still hard to understand as something that is integrated into everything, it's still incomplete in a way. But for me, the ideal is that you understand those foundational skill sets as driving everything. If you're making and crafting one-off things, for the type of work that people are professionally engaged in, there's no part of that you're not using in every single project, in my view, especially for identity work. You need to know all of it.

PG

There was a shift in the early years when I organized the Thesis course. We shifted away from the artifact that came out in the end and focused more on the research documentation, which I'm sure we're still doing. The idea that you end the year not only with this one thing or a series of small things, but you also have a well-designed documentation of all your research that is even printed in a book form. That became as important as the work itself, and I think students could read into that what it means to be a designer and to reflect on your own work.

JC

Yes, totally. And then when YuJune Park became director, the structure of Thesis changed completely. We started to meet all together as a cohort twice a semester, with common deliverables posted where everyone could see them. As a student, you were doing your thesis not just by yourself, with your faculty, or with your class, but with everyone

in your year. She really understood how to create a student experience that made students feel like they were part of something bigger than themselves, and to be proud of that.

AL

I was thinking about how the structure is there for the students but it's also there for the faculty. Teaching is one of the things that they do, but they also practice. When I started teaching, I was like a student in that I had an image of Parsons and an idea of the curriculum coming in. There was enough structure, but there was also openness to how to approach it, and that made it an interesting process. It was enjoyable.

JC

Right. We have about 115 part-time faculty now teaching across the programs. How much should they be the same and how much should they be different is another question. If everybody is too different from each other, they have nothing in common and they don't feel the sense of camaraderie that will make them come back next year. If they're all too much the same, the student is getting too much of the same experience, which we worry about all the time.

Obviously, I want us to have much more full-time faculty, but at the same time, we are super lucky to have these 115 or so part-time faculty. Students are super lucky to have them. They live and breathe. They work. They're designers. Most of them are not people trying to make a career in education. They know what's going on in the world. They know what time it is, and that's huge. But keeping that in a way that can have social glue, this is where I would say E Roon Kang, in particular, is really good at looking at that as an opportunity to try to get people to feel cohesive, feeling like a team at that scale. That's a skill in itself, and it's a lasting gift from his time as director of the BFA.

But Andrew, can you tell the story of what that first semester was like? You've been with us now for almost 10 years. What did you see during that time—culturally, curricular, otherwise?

AL

When I was in grad school, the work I was interested in was work that combined programming and typography because those were the two primary influences that had led me into graphic design. I had this Swiss influence from the books that we had at home which were my initial exposure to graphic design. And at the same time, I had learned how to program early. When I graduated, I started teaching at Parsons the year after. What appealed to me at that time was that there were other people who had similar interests, and it felt like a program where those two threads were intermingled in an interesting way.

My experience learning design was different from many of the students, because I had made a decision to study graphic design after I had already studied other things. When I started teaching at Parsons, I didn't have a lot of experience teaching, but having learned the subject matter so recently, it helped me think about how to teach it. My feeling as I arrived in New York and was looking around is that all these great designers teach at Parsons, and it seemed appealing to be part of that.

PG

That whole philosophy, that type and interaction are the two things that you need to learn and then apply across various sub-disciplines has been the guiding principles to develop the MPS program, and then later to redesign the AAS. AAS is a completely new program since we relaunched it, but I think it's important that the three programs are connected through that way of thinking. And, thankfully, all full-time faculty totally subscribe to that, because otherwise, it would be impossible, right? Having that same thought in all three programs makes it easy for faculty to move around and teach in MPS, and then in BFA, then maybe direct AAS. That creates a community of faculty that can work across all programs and courses.

JC

All of us can teach typography, interaction, topics, thesis, without feeling at a loss in any of these categories.

PG

Both of you can answer this better for the US, but from the European perspective, or other places I've been, this concept is different, because in many schools I know, if somebody who teaches typography would teach interaction the next year, students wouldn't trust that system.

They would say, "I want to study with an expert, and I want somebody who does only type for their whole life. And it needs to be that dude who's like sixty years old. He can teach me type." And then there's this young person who's doing it. The whole idea that you can teach across sub-disciplines, to me, it's Parsons specific, but maybe it's different in the US.

JC

What I think is interesting is how this maps back to the history of Parsons as an industry-focused school. What we've done, in a way—at least I hope—is we haven't lost that part entirely. We're not like, "Oh, no, we're just going to be totally abstract. We don't care if nobody gets a job." We have not done that. And yet, what we've done is we've said, "here are the things that we see as necessary for all of the things that you might possibly do out there."

If you want to work in industry, these are the things you need to know. The things that we've pulled out, in this case typography and interaction, are, in fact, more general and more abstract than, let's say, magazine design or logo design or whatever. We decided that it would be easier if we made it clear to everyone how foundational it was to design practice in general, and that it wasn't an anti-practice move to do this.

You came in, Andrew, in 2013 or 2014; pretty soon after. You probably got one of my spiels about what we were doing, what was going on, how this curriculum was changing, what we were thinking. The alignment was easier to have once we had a few general principles that were hard to ignore.

AL
Yes, I remember, you and I, Juliette, had coffee. I started teaching Core Interaction in 2013. At that point, there were standardized learning objectives. There was a course template. I didn't know at the time that there was a time not too long before where those things weren't in place, because they felt like structures that made a lot of sense at the time and seemed to be working.

You also have written about abstract skills layered on top of typography and interaction that a Communication Design student could strengthen through their education and are broadly useful post graduation, right?

JC
The question becomes, "Okay, well, what if you did this whole degree program and you never went into the field?" Would it be useful if you were a community organizer, if you were a teacher, if you were doing something completely different? What would you bring with you in this?

There were three things that Caspar Lam and YuJune Park landed on. One was translation, understanding content and bringing it into a place where it could then be re-communicated to somebody else. The second was creation, meaning not just solving problems, but imagining new futures, new things, things that don't exist yet, that are related to that translation. And the third was articulation.

What we ended up with, as a layer on top of typography and interaction, was this translation, creation, articulation, as a way of understanding: What are we teaching that continues? And, not just continues, but what do students come with? Students—especially our students, and they're more than 50% international—they come with incredibly strong skills in all three of these areas. These are the things that they arrive with.

A lot of what we do, in my mind, is see that and then strengthen that, as they go through all of these classes so that they know that their ability to interpret, their ability to make things, their ability to talk about the things that they've made just keeps getting better and better. But it's not something that's new to them when they show up.

AL

Now that you know how this all transpired, were there decisions that felt more tentative at the time that have been proven out over the past ten years?

JC

All of the answers I had about what we were doing. Pascal would back me up on this! The conversations that we had, I was always like, "I don't know if this is going to work, I might not be here next year. I don't think this is working." None of it felt possible. It wasn't that there was a united opposition, but it didn't seem possible that people could cohere enough from my perspective. It felt like you could pull the sandpile together and it would all scatter away again.

I still feel like that, to be honest with you. I still feel like we've done all this awesome stuff and I think it's great. I'm so proud of what the faculty have done, and this includes part-time faculty, not just the full-time faculty trying to wrangle things. But it's always tentative, and I know too from other work situations and other academic situations, that when the wind is blowing, it's blowing, and it's going. People will go with that. But when it changes, it changes, and you have to appreciate it when things are moving in a good direction and try to keep hanging on to it as much as possible.

I think we—both students and faculty—feel a sense of a whole group coming together to make something rather than being served as a unit by this entity who's supposed to serve them in some imagined way. That has changed enormously, and I would say this is where I have to give huge credit to Caspar. Some of that was unspoken before, but as soon as Caspar took over as director, a lot of this is explicit. "No, look, this is what we do, what we are, how we're doing it. These are the protocols by which we operate as a group, and as a group of people learning and teaching together in New York." As much as the previous ten years was a group project in coming up with those things, it's not until Caspar came along that we had these ideas written down and articulated.

One last thing to say is I've been reading a lot about education and educational histories, art history, and other schools' histories. In the end, I think my conclusion is that when education suffers, it's not from lack of innovation. It's not because people don't come up with enough good ideas. It's because people don't put in the work to maintain what's there and care for it. When the care work doesn't happen, and when people let the house fall, it falls. When a few people start neglecting pieces of it, it becomes easy for other people to be like, all right then, I'm out.

So we all should be grateful and somewhat protective of what we have, but realize none of these things are ever forever, you know? Every story, every educational institution you've ever heard of, it's usually six or seven years that it had a real synergy, and then it's hard to hold. You should never relax into thinking, it's going to be cool now, we're good.

PG

I do want to reiterate, though, that the biggest difference and what makes me happy looking back on those almost ten years is that we understood and accepted our responsibility. These young human beings, they trust us. Their parents trust us as educators. And then if you're sitting in a thesis class, you're looking at the work and you feel like, "I don't know. I really don't know what happened over the last four years, but I'm not feeling very confident sending these people out into the world." If you think that, you just did not live up to that trust. In my first moments, I had that impression and I wasn't sure if all this was the right thing to do. That completely changed.

If I look at the thesis course now, I'm super happy, super proud, and that is because we created a working curriculum. It always needs to change, of course. It is because we had these amazing people who joined us, full-time and part-time faculty. It is a completely new setup and what I'm happy about is that the responsibility that I feel welcoming these students or saying, "hey, goodbye, have a nice life," totally works. It's never 100 percent—but I feel confident about what we're doing.

JC

I would fully agree with Pascal on that. In those early years, it was like, "Is this right that I'm doing this?" It was a big question. More recently, I feel so much like spending my time doing this is worth it, feels like a more true statement than it did in those early moments. The students, they're not just happy, they're equipped to go out there and do what they want to do, and that's all that we want for them.

Andrew LeClair is a designer in New York and Part-Time Assistant Professor at Parsons.

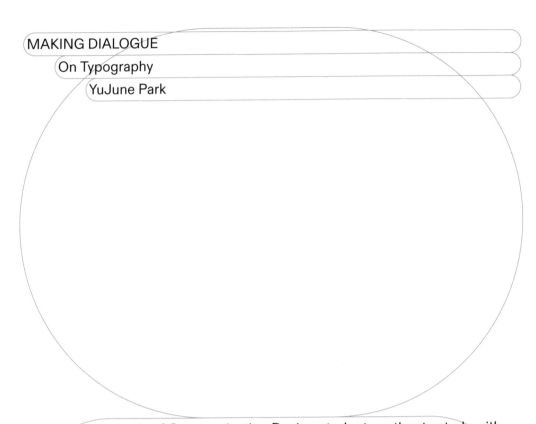

Each year, hundreds of Communication Design students gather to study with us in New York City, a global crossroads where over 800 languages are spoken daily.[1] We face the unique gift and challenge of educating students of diverse cultural backgrounds. Nearly half of the students in our program are international, each carrying within them a unique visual and typographic landscape forged by place and memory. Our graduates will continue their journey as designers in cities around the world. Their work will live simultaneously *somewhere*—a physical place rooted in history with a living culture—and *everywhere* through the screens at our fingertips. How can we teach typography in a way that equips our students to practice across radically different contexts and mediums?

Typography is language made visible. It is an act of visual articulation, giving clarity to thought and feeling. Our typographic curriculum embraces an expansive vision of typography, one that holds a multitude of viewpoints and expressions and supports the open exchange of knowledge across cultural contexts. To study typography is to study the visual shape of language and, in the process, discover a history of ideas made manifest through forms.

We begin with the letter or character, the smallest unit of information, manifoldly expressed around us. We ask each student to stop and examine the visual and textual world around them: the text on a receipt, bitmapped and smudged, or the gold-leafed lettering above the door of an old bookstore. Indeed, as Stuart Chase and Marian Tyler write in the *Power of Words*, an exploration of the facets of communication, "We live in an ocean of words, but like a fish in water we are often not aware of it."[2] Each letter is a window into a place, culture, time, and perspective. This context matters. Form carries meaning.

Observation begets curiosity. Where do typographic forms come from? The narratives from the past illuminate the connection between form, meaning, and tool. This, in turn, inspires how type can shape meaning in the here and now. From Futura in the New Frankfurt project as an expression of modernism and industrialization to the Hong Kong font in Bibles as a reflection of the tension between technology and script, letterforms are born from a confluence of history, culture, ideals, and the maker(s) expression. Yet language and type are living entities, dynamically evolving. As letterforms travel through time and across cultures, they gather the residue of different meanings.

While we begin with the letter, our projects quickly scale in complexity from word to phrase to sentence to typographic system. Communication designers interface with all other disciplines and work across mediums. We are expert generalists, examining how the form of language translates across contexts. Our projects shift from page to screen to space, so students can study the relationship between typography and the medium in which it is rendered. Type is form, but it is also software. By examining the underlying systems that shape communication, our students can begin to see the invisible structures that mediate our experience.

Typography is manifest through form, but it is brought to life through dialogue. Our job is to create an environment that facilitates an open and lively exchange. We embrace varying critique styles weekly, shifting from peer-to-peer, group, and individual critiques. We incorporate a reflective critique process in the classroom through independent writing and written peer review feedback. Through Instagram, Dropbox Paper, and Slack, we create open channels of communication between faculty and students that empower all voices to be heard equally. We endeavor to create a community within each class and build trust, so our students can move with confidence from creating work that speaks in monologue to dialogue. Who is the audience? The reader? The user? By creating and sharing work together, they traverse the distance between a work's intent, meaning, and its perception. Everyone is a maker and an audience, a student and a teacher.

While language is universal to all human beings, no one faculty can prepare all students to work with all scripts. However, we aim to connect students to a global network of organizations and initiatives rooted in local communities like the Khatt Foundation Center for Arabic Typography and the Typojanchi International Typography Biennale in South Korea. This empowers us to examine typography within a contemporary context—highlighting its impact on community and culture today—while also examining its history and potential future evolution. We strive to create a program that reflects the plurality of our city, where students can encounter new scripts and ways of making meaning. By creating a distributed network of typographic expertise, we become a conduit for the exchange of knowledge. In that process, our students shift from being consumers to participants. They discover that engagement and responsibility go hand-in-hand.

Lastly, we acknowledge and embrace diverse typographic viewpoints, even (and perhaps especially) when they are challenging. Typography is a deeply human story. The desire to codify experience through language is foundational, and the ideas that drive each maker's journey range far and wide. The best typography not only reflects culture, but also shapes it; the beauty of the form is that it somehow reflects the lives behind it.

To teach typography is to wrestle with form and dialogue. Our students shape words with pixels and ink and journey to new visual territories. They move between cultures and connect to the material world, each other, and a global community of makers. We ask them to pause and look at each letter closely so they might see. And, in this process, discover their voice, its form and meaning.

YuJune Park, Assistant Professor of Communication Design, joined Parsons in 2012 and was the Director of the BFA Communication Design Program (2014-2017).

1. https://www.nytimes.com/ 2010/04/29/nyregion/ 29lost.html

2. Chase, S., & Chase, M. T. (n.d.). *Power of words, by Stuart Chase, in collaboration with Marian Tyler Chase.* New York: Harcourt and Brace.

STRANGE LOOPS

On Interaction

Brendan Griffiths

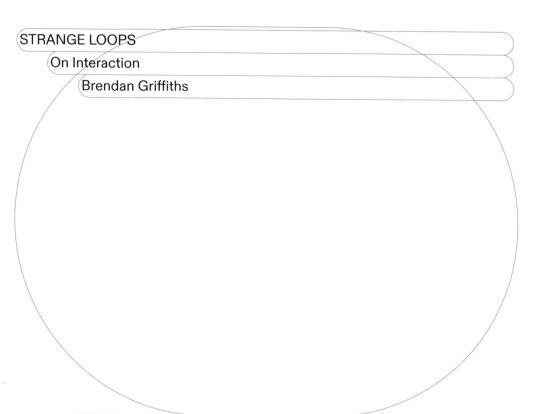

Though these words are intended for a printed publication, it's more likely than not that you're reading them on a screen—perhaps on a laptop, a tablet, or phone—and your journey to them was mediated by an interface. It was little more than a decade ago that we lived in a world without smartphones, mobile apps, and social media, and yet today these platforms have become the primary way in which we tell stories and share information. The interfaces which give form to these surfaces all have designers behind them—designers steeped in the language of interaction design.

But what is interaction design? It could be argued that all design is now interaction design—the way in which books, posters, and exhibitions now employ the language and methods of interaction to define the experience of reading or viewing. Working within this expanded context, interaction design could be seen as any design which considers an audience's relationship to content through visual form—the connective tissue that engages us as readers, viewers, or users.

While the term "interaction design" traces its origins to interface design in the 1980s, communication designers have been defining how we engage with content and the vessels that carry it since the beginnings of the discipline. Communication design has historically always evolved in lock-step with technology—from early block printing, the printing press, and movable type, to offset lithography, xerography and desktop publishing, designers have always been there, evolving and often inventing both new means and forms for communication.

Interaction design, then, inherently performs a sort of strange loop—in which we use the tool to make the tool. This reflexivity has always been present in the medium; for example, the first web browsers also served as web page editors. Likewise, we find the pedagogy of interaction design no different, wherein the teaching materials can be found in the discipline itself. As faculty, we extend the principles of interaction design to the classroom wherein we enable our students to build their own journey towards learning—not only in the field of interaction design but any number of new technologies or methods they may encounter.

When we teach interaction design, we ask students to consider and engage with the principles of interface design as well as the logic patterns embedded in the systems which run them. We see code as material, one which can be shaped by a designer much like clay and paint, as well as a tool that gives us the agency to create and ability to circulate. We see the classroom as a laboratory—for us as faculty, to experiment with different assignments and exercises, and for our students, a safe testing ground to engage what is for most of them a totally new medium, to articulate our voice within this space of interaction design. The projects deployed in our core interaction sequence are scaffolded in a way that each builds upon the prior, both from a conceptual and technological standpoint.

Students in the Parsons Communication Design program go on to pursue rich and varied design careers spanning across the discipline—from branding, editorial and exhibition design to motion, user experience, digital product design and beyond. But the underpinnings of interaction design and the principles students explored in their time here are applied back to projects in any medium and in a multitude of contexts. Our aim and hope is that the students' biggest takeaways are not students leave Parsons not simply with technical expertise and software acuity, but also with the ability to create their own tools in defining their work and, as the tides of technology shift, the power to give meaning and form to worlds yet to be discovered.

Brendan Griffiths, Assistant Professor of Interaction Design, joined Parsons in 2011 and is the Director of the MPS Communication Design Program.

A core component to the structure of the Communication Design department is that all of the faculty, both full-time and part-time, are engaged in the practice of design outside of the classroom. For some, this is professional, client-driven work and for others it's speculative, research-driven projects. In this conversation hosted by Pascal Glissmann, Assistant Professors of Communication Design Lynn Kiang and Kelly Walters discuss the various ways design manifests itself in different contexts. Lynn joined Parsons in 2016. Kelly joined Parsons in 2018 and is also the Associate Director of the BFA Communication Design Program.

Pascal Glissmann
How do you define creative practice and research in the context of communication design and how does your work relate to this?

Lynn Kiang
The research we do as communication designers is extremely broad. Typically there is a message that needs to be conveyed to an audience. In my creative practice, I am not limited to any device or specific media channel and I think since I started my career I am understanding this with even more flexibility.

Kelly Walters
Communication design is a way of thinking across disciplines. I learned design in the context of fine arts. Today, I am really interested in thinking beyond printed artifacts: there are so many different ways that design can be captured digitally, in the environment, or in the world and I think that Communication Design allows for an expansiveness of making. We are studying global systems, the ways we interact with them, and new directions to shape them in the future.

PG
You both work with clients but also self-initiate research investigations. Kelly, you just published the book *Black, Brown + Latinx Design Educators: Conversations on Design* and, Lynn, you worked with a variety of museums including the Cleveland Museum of Art and the Women's Health Leadership Institute. How would you describe that these two different ways of working and thinking inspire each other?

LK
Almost all of our clients at Dome, the studio I co-founded with my partner Katie Lee are women. As a consequence, a lot of our work represents women's voices in our culture and in diverse communities. This has never been our intention but I am really excited that it came together this way. Since we already explored this topic in depth, we decided to start a self-initiated project for the Women's March. We made protest posters which became a huge sprawling campaign with unexpected awareness. We are less intentional with these kinds of projects. We are usually driven by the urge to respond to the moment—to things that happen in society and that we are passionate about. I think it is also important to point out that running a studio is an intense work experience that does not always leave a lot of space for your own research. Working in academia offers a form of intellectual release and a space to explore new research inquiries.

KW
I agree that the academic environment nurtures my inquiries into various directions and I really appreciate this as a balance to my client based work. My recent book project stemmed out of wanting to have conversations with design educators of color. In that project I was able to co-design a publication, with BFA CD alum Iyana Martin Diaz, that captured the interviews I had with designers about topics around race, representation and design. In February 2020, I chaired a panel at the College Art Association where I was able to share a first draft of the book. In the past I have always thought my primary skills as a designer were to only create design artifacts like books, posters and small editorial publications. However, as I've evolved as a designer I have been really excited to expand on that skillset, as a way to facilitate discussions, curate events and really think about how one designs for an environment.

PG
I am interested in the graphic design skills you just mentioned and how they are part of your research process. How would you describe the skills or qualities that Communication Designers bring to the table that might distinguish us from other disciplines?

KW
I think communication design is really about creating spaces, rethinking larger systems, and shaping ways of existing. I think we have the capacity to design for experiences, from artifacts like an editorial publication to a motion-based work viewed on a digital screen. I think our ability to work across mediums is an asset and it enables us to conceptualize design for a multitude of scales, languages and audiences.

LK
At the same time, the skills to actually make things will always remain important and actually help our understanding of the larger context.

For instance, we learn about type hierarchy in a studio class which really is the first step of understanding the hierarchy of content—including multilayered information databases and processes of entire businesses. Our abilities as designers to simplify complex systems and address larger problems makes us so valued in the industry—way beyond the traditional disciplines of design.

PG

I am excited to hear that you both talk about connections to other people, to other disciplines, and to the world. When you reflect on communication design skills, collaboration seems a core value in your creative practices—perhaps distinguishing you from the artist who creates artifacts in solitude in their workshops. Can you talk more about your perspective on collaborating and ways to make it successful?

KW

My graduate experience in design was a formative time that taught me how to understand and shape resilient collaboration. One memorable design project I created as a design student, provided an opportunity for me to learn how to reach out to people, conduct interviews and create an exhibition. This activated a lot of new skills and it was also an amazing opportunity for me to understand what collaboration meant for me and its importance in my design practice. Collaboration is not only an exchange of tools; you are taking care of someone's ideas, narrative or someone's experience and that requires thoughtful and respectful balance in the context of a design process.

LK

I have been co-directing my studio with my business partner for the past seven years and just this collaboration between the two of us is essential and shapes the ethos and the mission for the studio. In extensions, we are collaborating with a variety of people from very diverse disciplines to be able to realize the huge projects we are commissioned to develop—ranging from technologists to writers to furniture designers. Sometimes, our clients don't really have a brief that would initiate our work. In those cases, we have to launch our process with interviews to get all the insights from the companies or the institutions. And if you imagine this conversation with eight stakeholders from the institution you will find yourself in the middle of at least five different perspectives on the topic. We do understand this work with our clients—especially those lasting over years—as a collaboration that is fruitful in both directions.

PG

Talking about the research process and studio practices: in academia we try to educate our students to look at the things around them anew and apply critical thinking when redesigning a societal process, for example. Yet the reality of a junior design position might be a very different one. Do you have any advice for graduates to navigate the transition from design school to industry?

LK

The senior year, specifically the thesis class, can be a springboard into your career. I highly encourage students to use this time to develop something they are really passionate about. This is an opportunity to set your own creative practice and research, prototype something that is completely new and differentiates yourself from all other graduates. It could be your first step on a future career path and connect your academic career, where you are allowed to take advantage of a protected exploratory playground, with your practice outside of school.

KW
Thesis gives you the opportunity to test your own limits and design capacities—what are you really passionate about and how much are you willing to give to that work? In our Parsons Communication Design program, Thesis is a time when you can explore a line of inquiry for a year on a topic or subject matter that you have great interest in. It may plant a

seed for the type of design work you might continue doing for the rest of your career or a time for immense growth in learning about yourself.

PG
This is so important to remember and also reflects my personal experience: if you just graduated and you are holding this book in your hands thinking that thesis or capstone was not one of the best things you created so far, you will appreciate all you learned from it in a couple of years.

Pascal Glissmann, Associate Professor of Communication Design, joined Parsons in 2012, served as the BFA Communication Design Program Associate Director (2012-2014), was chair of the School Curriculum Committee (2013-2016), and is the Director of the AAS Communication Design Program.

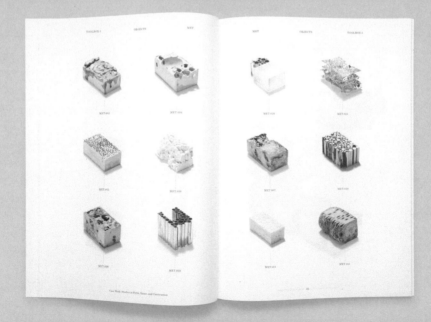

JULIETTE CEZZAR
Associate Professor of Communication Design

My studio work explores the ways that graphic and communication design shape contemporary culture. The work spans print and digital media to create systems and forms for food, art, and architecture.

Juliette Cezzar is a designer, author, and educator based in New York City. Her award-winning design practice spans a variety of media for cultural clients. She is an Associate Professor of Communication Design at Parsons School of Design, where she directed the BFA Communication Design and BFA Design & Technology programs from 2011–14. She served as President of AIGA NY from 2014–16 and has been a board member of The Brooklyn Rail since 2019. She holds a Bachelor of Architecture from Virginia Tech and an MFA in Graphic Design from Yale University.

→ juliettecezzar.com

1. Design for *Tartine Book No. 3* by Chad Robertson. Published by Chronicle Books in 2013.

2. *Case Work: Studies in Form, Space, and Construction* by Brad Cloepfil / Allied Works. Published by Hatje Cantz in 2016.

PASCAL GLISSMANN
Associate Professor of Communication Design

My journey through diverse urban habitats with eclectic everyday artifacts activated research interests that span across cultures and beyond disciplinary boundaries. I am specifically interested in the merging of the natural, the artificial, and the speculative.

Pascal Glissmann is a designer, media artist, and educator based in New York & Berlin. Since 2001, he has held academic positions alongside his creative practice in Cologne, Hong Kong, Beirut, and New York. He is currently full-time faculty at Parsons School of Design, director of the AAS Communication Design program, and co-director of the Observational Practices Lab.
→ subcologne.de

1. *Electronic Life Forms*, Installation View, Collaboration with Martina Hoefflin, electronic-life-forms.com

2. The Phaistos Project — Forty-five Symbols, Publication, Collaboration with Olivier Arcioli & Andreas Henrich, 45symbols.com

nonfood

BRENDAN GRIFFITHS
Assistant Professor of Interaction Design

My work explores the materiality of digital artifacts and the ways in which networks and systems inform visual culture.

Brendan Griffiths is an interaction designer and educator based in New York City. He is a partner in the design practice Zut Alors!, and currently serves as Director of the Master of Professional Studies program in Communication Design at Parsons School of Design. He holds an MFA in Graphic Design from Yale University.
→ zutalorsinc.com

1. Nonfood algae-based food company website.

2. Core77 Design Awards Call for Entries poster.

E ROON KANG
Assistant Professor of Interaction Design

I investigate the relationship between design and technology for an increasingly computational society, to rediscover the essence of communication design as a practice of giving visual structures to knowledge.

E Roon Kang runs a design studio, Math Practice, in New York City. He is also a co-founder of 908A, a research-driven consultancy focused on constructing new computational design tools, with project support from the Knight Foundation. He has worked in partnership with a range of cultural institutions and events, including Seoul Biennale of Architecture and Urbanism; the Korean Pavilion of the Venice Architecture Biennale; and educational institutions and their research labs. He is a TED Senior Fellow, was previously a research fellow at SENSEable City Laboratory of MIT. He holds an MFA in Graphic Design from Yale.
→ eroonkang.com

1. *Personal Timekeepers* on view at the Los Angeles County Museum of Art, collaboration with Taeyoon Choi.

2. Poster for MIT Architecture's Spring 2016 Lecture Series.

4.7%

OF SENIOR-LEVEL OFFICIALS
AND MANAGERS IN
S&P 500* COMPANIES
ARE WOMEN OF COLOR
AS OF 2017

21.8%

OF SENIOR-LEVEL OFFICIALS
AND MANAGERS IN
S&P 500* COMPANIES
ARE WHITE WOMEN
AS OF 2017

WOMEN
OF COLOR
IN THE
WORKPLACE

MEN
85¢

AWAIIAN
C ISLANDER
N INDIAN
A NATIVE
RE PAID 62¢
RE PAID 58¢

LYNN KIANG
Assistant Professor of Communication Design

I am an experience designer working at the inter-section of media and the built environment for cultural and social impact institutions. My practice is technology-agnostic and explores how stories can be delivered in more seamless, meaningful, and responsible ways.

Lynn is the co-founder and partner of Dome, an experience design studio in New York City. She is a multi-disciplinary designer and creative director in experience design, graphic design and built environments. She is Director of the MPS Communication Design and Assistant Professor at Parsons School of Design. Previously she was a design lead at SYPartners, Local Projects, and Fathom Information Design. She received her MFA in Graphic Design from the Rhode Island School of Design, a Certificate of Collegiate Teaching from Brown University, and a BS in Psychology from the University of California at Los Angeles.
→ domecollective.com

1. *Seat at the Table* exhibition at the Kimmel Center, Philadelphia, PA.

2. Immersive film for *Revealing Krishna: Journey to Cambodia's Sacred Mountain* at the Cleveland Museum of Art, Cleveland, OH.

CASPAR LAM & YUJUNE PARK
Assistant Professors of Communication Design

Our collaborative practice unlocks human stories and reveals connections through design, language, and information.

Caspar Lam is a partner at Synoptic Office. He holds an MFA from Yale and degrees in biology and design from the University of Texas at Austin. He formerly led design and digital strategy at Artstor, a Mellon-funded non-profit developing digital products related to metadata and publishing for institutions like Harvard, Cornell, and the Philadelphia Museum of Art. Adobe, AIGA, and the ID Annual Design Review have recognized his work. He has been a visiting critic at the Hong Kong Design Institute and served as an Adjunct Associate Research Scholar at Columbia University's GSAPP. He sits on the board of directors of AIGA NY.

1. Installation view of *Faraway Places* at Palazzo Mora at Time Space Existence in Venice 2021.

2. View of *Point, Line, and Shape* exhibit on Chinese typography.

YuJune Park is a partner at Synoptic Office. She holds an MFA from Yale and a BFA from RISD. YuJune has partnered with studios including Base Design, Graphic Thought Facility, Rockwell Lab, and Pentagram for a variety of clients, and her work has been recognized by AIGA, ID Annual Design Review, and the ADC. She serves on the board of directors of the TDC and was the Program Director of the BFA Communication Design program from 2014–2017 and Associate Director from 2017–2019. In addition to teaching, she speaks internationally on design education and typography, most recently at Typographics, Northside Festival, and AIGA NY.

→ synopticoffice.com

1. View of Carnegie Hall's online Timeline of African American Music

2. View of How the World Sees, an experimental news viewer for Hong Kong's 2021 deTour Design Festival.

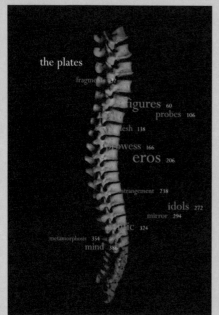

the plates

fragments 32

figures 60
probes 106
flesh 138
prowess 166
eros 206
estrangement 238
idols 272
mirror 294
logic 324
metamorphosis 354
mind 386

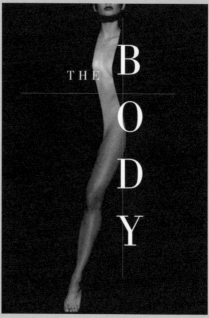

THE B O D Y

LUCILLE TENAZAS
Henry Wolf Professor of Communication Design

My work is at the intersection of typography and linguistics, with design that reflects complex and poetic means of visual expression. I focus on typography as the armature of my work because it serves as a mediator of meaning that can be heightened and manipulated. As a multi-lingual designer, I question the authority of any one language and the relativity of meaning—in the process freeing myself of its colonial nature, to subdue it and make it my own.

Lucille Tenazas is a graphic designer and educator based in New York and San Francisco. She is the Henry Wolf Professor of Communication Design and previously Associate Dean in the School of Art, Media and Technology from 2013-2020. An authority in the evolving state of design education, she has conducted workshops in institutions throughout the United States, Asia and Europe. Lucille was the national president of the AIGA from 1996-98 and was awarded the AIGA Medal in 2013, for her lifetime contribution to design practice and outstanding leadership in design education. She was the recipient of the National Design Award for Communication Design from the Cooper-Hewitt National Design Museum in 2002. Originally from Manila, the Philippines, Lucille received her MFA in Design from Cranbrook Academy of Art.
→ tenazasdesign.com

1. *The Body: Photographs of the Human Form*, book cover and contents page.

2. CCA Graduate Show poster.

KELLY WALTERS
Assistant Professor of Communication Design

My ongoing design research interrogates the complexities of identity, systems of value, and shared vernacular in and around Black visual culture.

Kelly Walters is an Assistant Professor and the Associate Director of the BFA Communication Design program in Parsons School of Design at The New School. In her independent design studio Bright Polka Dot, she works across platforms to create publications, exhibitions, and digital experiences for educational and cultural institutions.
→ brightpolkadot.com

1. *Black, Brown + Latinx Design Educators; Conversations on Design and Race*, Princeton Architectural Press, 2021.

2. Exhibition design for *The Black Woman is God: Assembly of Gods*, SOMArts Cultural Center, 2018.

ON FORMATS

Rachel Berger

CD Lecture Series

The Auditorium, Room A106
Alvin Johnson/J.M. Kaplan Hall
66 West 12th Street

2019-10-11

First of all, thanks, E Roon, for welcoming me to Parsons. Thank all of you for coming to this super nice place. This is a really nice building to be in on a Friday afternoon. I know some of you are doing it for school credit, which I think is great. I love education, obviously, from my bio.

Today, what I want to talk with you guys about is a very, very simple topic, and that topic is format. Don't worry, there's not some kind of trick here. There's no hidden meaning. Format is exactly what you think. Format is the way in which something is arranged or presented. You can format a document by changing its font and margins, you can format a website by changing its CSS styling, you can decide to switch formats between a website and a document. Like most English words, format comes from a Latin root *forma*, meaning to mold or to give shape to something.

This talk has three parts. The first part is my own thoughts. The second part is a little bit about my work. And in the third part, I hope you will talk and I can not talk as much, but instead answer questions or hear your thoughts on what I've talked about. The thoughts I'm going to offer are about design's changing and increasingly ambivalent relationship with format. The work I'm going to show describes some ways that I've tried to approach format and ways I've thought about format in my own work.

PART ONE, AMBIVALENCE.

(By the way, this display typeface is by one of our students at CCA, his name is Kevin Lee. It's called Dwelling and for me, is just the right amount of hard to read, and is kind of funky looking. So thanks, Kevin.) What does ambivalence mean? It's a really great word to know. It means to have simultaneous and contradictory feelings about something, to love and hate it at the same time. And designers, as I see it, have an increasingly ambivalent relationship with format. Historically, format has been quite important to designers because, well obviously, designers are interested in form. We are trained to make ideas into stuff. So, it is no surprise that we care about how stuff looks and how it feels, maybe even how it smells or tastes or sounds. To go back about 10 years in time, in 2009, Michael Rock published an essay called "Fuck Content." (As a content warning, this is the first but not the only time I'm going to say fuck in this presentation.) So "Fuck Content" (I said it again, sorry) is a critique of the idea that content is more important than form. Rock superhates this subservient mindset, and he mostly blames Beatrice Ward and her crystal goblet for indoctrinating generations of designers with that idea. Rock is the founder of a design studio called 2×4, which is mostly based here in New York, and is best known for its bold branding work for the Italian luxury fashion house Prada. Ward was the typography scholar best known for writing the iconic modernist essay, "The Crystal Goblet or Printing Should Be Invisible". In it, she compares fine typesetting to a perfect, crystal-clear wine glass. As she sees it, good type and minimalist stemware are both transparent showcases for their content. Everything about them is calculated to reveal rather than hide the beautiful thing they are meant to contain. Despite Rock's dismissal of Ward, I actually see the two of them as natural allies in the larger debate around form that I'm going to be talking about today. Both of them believe in the vital importance of form, casting the designer's every

move as a high stakes matter. Ward decries the "thousand mannerisms in typography that are as impudent and arbitrary as putting port in tumblers made of red or green glass." Rock argues that the graphic forms and advertisements for everyday things like ink and cigarettes and spark plugs have the power to change the world. To me, the form versus content debate has become kind of quaint, like a half-hearted argument on the ride home from an AIGA studio tour. There is a larger existential threat to formal designers—which is to say pretty much all designers—and that threat doesn't give a fuck about form.

So a lot of this has to do with the changing definition of design. I studied graphic design at Yale. Then, my first job after school was interning on Michael Bierut's team at Pentagram. So, I had a very privileged and very, very particular design education. I was trained to think of designers as creative people who make books and posters and websites and lots of other but mostly flat stuff, and that designers make a living by making those things for clients. After I finished my internship, I moved to the Bay Area and started working at a company called SYPartners. SYPartners, which also has an office here in New York, is a strategy and design consultancy that helps leaders and teams and organizations become better versions of themselves. At SYPartners, I learned a much more expansive definition of design. I learned that you can design an experience. I learned that you can design a conversation. I learned that you can design a whole darn company. I learned great design wasn't reserved for designers— writers were designers, CEOs were designers. As a designer at SYPartners, I was expected to apply my design training to inspire change within companies, and in turn, I did not expect to make much of anything that would ever see the light of day. At SYPartners, I learned that "strategist" could be a job and not just a personality type. I met people who went to business school yet called themselves designers, and I thought, isn't this a funny California thing, this way of thinking and talking about design.

Then in late 2011, a small but notable thing happened back in old New York. This is what 2×4's website looked like in late September of 2011. Besides noting the use of ASCII art, which I think is pretty awesome, I'd like to call your attention to the descriptive statement that's at the top of the page. It says "2×4 is a multidisciplinary studio, focusing on design for art, architecture, fashion, and cultural clients worldwide." Very clear and very straightforward. By early October, the website looked like this. If you go on the Wayback Machine, which is what I did to get these, literally 10 days later, the screengrab now looks like this. And more importantly, it sounds like this: "2×4 develops brand strategy and design systems for diverse clients worldwide. We identify and articulate core values and develop innovative ways to express them, drawing on both modernist traditions and the exuberance of contemporary life." I remember feeling a chill when I first read this. I couldn't believe that the mighty form gods at 2×4 felt the need to invoke horrible business-oriented vapor phrases like "brand strategy," "design systems," and worst of all, "core values." To me, it signaled a sea change in design practice. Where it used to be that focusing on design was good enough, it was no longer. To stay relevant, it seemed that designers had to develop strategies and systems, to identify and articulate values, and that expression was pushed down to the end. Frankly, it seemed like format was fucked. Form and content have both been relegated to a lower spot on the food chain to make way for systems thinking and strategy.

Since then, it seems like things have only gotten more polarized and confusing. For example, Jessica Helfand and Michael Bierut spend more time teaching at Yale's business school than at its art school. And my first grader is learning design thinking at his school. Meanwhile, the art book fair industrial complex continues, and you get 67 million hits when you search for hand lettering on Pinterest. So by day, designers make big money doing invisible work for giant technology companies, and by night they pour themselves into hyper crafted anti-digital side projects like Riso-printed zines, silkscreened totes, and hand lettered signs. Today this chaos is exemplified by the AIGA, in particular the tension between its Eye on Design project and its Design Futures project. So, let's take a look at Eye on Design's popular Instagram feed, featuring the best new work by the world's most exciting designers.

Do you love it? Do you think it's a soft bag of millennial pink frosting squeezed through default Cinema 4D filters and puked onto a poster no one will ever see or buy in real life? Either way, it is most certainly a celebration of good old fashioned making, and a fairly convincing Fuck Off to content. Meanwhile, at the grown ups table, we've been subjected to the "AIGA Designer 2025 Report" now known as "AIGA Design Futures." There is no better come down from the irrational exuberance of AIGA Eye on Design.

Its authors, design education elders like Meredith Davis and Hugh Dubberly, have seen the future and determined that it is decidedly not zines, totes, and posters. The report starts by citing scary US Bureau of Labor Statistics projections about a steep decline in traditional print design jobs. Then, it warns of a market oversaturated with people *like you*, design students unprepared for a new digital economy. The report is not concerned with petty debates over form and content. It chalks all that up to an "industrial-age perspective," obsessed with "improving the appearance and function of messages, products, and environments." The report doesn't use familiar terms like form-making, referring instead to something called an "object-driven process." This suggests a rigidity and narrowness of thinking that seems largely unaware of the boisterous joy we're seeing next door at AIGA Eye on Design. Next, the report introduces the notion of the knowledge economy (as compared to the industrial-age economy we were talking about a moment ago) where in the knowledge economy, the things people learn in business school like user-centered research strategies have supplanted the things that people learn in traditional design schools like maker-centered, informed intuition. The report mocks designers for their interest in making perfect objects, while celebrating companies like Zipcar for making nothing. No wonder it feels like our brains are being ripped apart. Michael Rock's Crystal Goblet Hangover seems downright chaste compared to the bender of format-loving uppers and strategy-loving downers we've been on ever since. Fuck that.

PART TWO, FUCK THAT!

Unless I want to feel bad about myself and what I do, I try to avoid spending too much time wallowing on either side of this debate. On the one hand, the infinitely scrolling visual feast of Eye on Design is kind of gross. And on the other hand, the self-hating fealty to capitalism in the Design Futures report is also kind of gross. So I like to think about format in other ways, and I'm going to offer some of those to you guys now.

So today, I'm going to talk about three ways that I try to think about format in my own work. These are totally made up terms. They're not real terms, it's just a handy way to have two words on a slide. So don't worry about it. But let's just, for the sake of this talk, talk about *default format, open format,* and *total format.*

So first, *default format.* I'm going to, hopefully, as many professors do, give you two contradictory pieces of advice, the first being to avoid defaults, and the second being to embrace defaults. And hopefully this will make more sense in a little bit, I promise. Just to explain what I mean by default, a default is something that is standardized, automatic, and prescribed. For example, when you create a new Google Doc, several defaults are activated, a page size, an orientation, a font (in this case Arial 11 is Google Docs's default font, which is, wow, I mean, Google has invested a lot in fonts so it's interesting that Arial 11 is where we start). Anyways, a font, margins. The default text color is black. The default page color is white. And for most people, these default settings are basically invisible. They are part of the atmosphere of the application. For designers, these settings are opportunities, opportunities to make a design decision, to make a choice about format.

For designers, to choose to use a system font like Arial or Courier or Comic Sans or Times, as in this T-shirt series by Dynamo, has had a sort of clever reverse reverse snobbery to it. That said, my wife, who is a lawyer, is required to use Times New Roman in the briefs she files for the courts, and she is totally confused as to why sophisticated designers, who have every font in the world at their disposal, continue to choose to use Times. She's into type though, which is cool.

The defaults we see when we open a tool are embedded in its technology. And this type of default is what we could think of as a technical artifact, to be embraced or undone depending on the designer's intent.

There is another type of default, which is default thinking, or to put it more simply, trend. In the same way non-designers do not question or even notice default settings in a Google Doc, designers are susceptible to unthinkingly adopting the trends and styles of the day.

Suddenly, it just feels right to use IK blue, or a lot of em dashes or slashes, or to center everything, or to take a picture of yourself holding up your poster. Clients will ask for it and your friends will think it looks cool. This kind of trend-driven groupthink happens in the book fairs and in the boardrooms. It deserves just as much caution and deliberation as using technical defaults, because when defaults are used unthinkingly, they are uncreative, but when they are used deliberately, they can make your design sharper and smarter.

So, my personal current favorite default format is printing in black ink on 8.5×11 inch letter size paper. Many designers see it as a dumpy, inelegant format compared to the rational, graceful proportions of the ISO A series used pretty much everywhere else in the world. Michael Bierut once said he's avoided this format his entire life. But for me, its defaultness offers both practical advantages and creative opportunities. Practically speaking, it is cheap, available, and portable. So, it's great, especially if you're a student and you're on a budget. Every printer can handle black ink on 8.5 by 11 inch letter size paper. Certainly, my little home printer and my crappy office printer can. I don't have to waste time or money sourcing or producing it, it fits easily in a folder, in an envelope, on a screen, on a wall. It makes *super* tiny PDFs. It is very basic. And its basicness is for me what makes for its creative opportunities.

This first project deals with 8.5×11 and *interpretation*. I work at a school, as we've said, so there are ugly flyers posted everywhere. This creates a good environment for using the flyer format in new ways. For this series, I reinterpreted Ekene Ijeoma's Ethnic Filter project as a series of flyers promoting his upcoming visit to CCA. So I don't know if you guys are familiar with this project, but it's a webcam project that is based on data from the design census from a couple years ago and is about the racial breakdown of people working in design in the United States. Design is mostly white, and so, white people, when they look into their webcam, get a super crisp image of themselves, and the word white overlaid on it. Black people are very underrepresented in design practice in the United States, so they're super blurred out and hard to see.

As for the flyers, black ink is a default. I think something that's sad is that dark colored paper is avoided by people who are printing using black and white printers, because you can't read the goddamn ink. Why is black ink the default? Why isn't white ink the default, because if it was, then this beautiful dark brown paper would have this beautiful white image on it and it would look terrific. Instead it looks like shit! I think something that students can think about is, if you were to redo one of your favorite projects as a series of flyers, what would you do? What would it look like?

This is another flyer project, in this case, exploring the idea of 8.5×11, and *defamiliarization*. I was asked to design a poster for a lecture series at my school and the speakers had nothing in common with each other at all. There was no theme that could help give me ideas for what to do. So I decided to make a mini poster, also known as a flyer, for each lecture. Then, we used 100% scale photographs of the flyers as a poster and posted it back onto the hallways around school. We printed maybe a couple thousand copies of it and sent it to other schools where they probably also have hallways that look like this. I had this image of people trying to line it up with their industrial yellow bricks. Through this tactic, with a familiar presence in this case, flyers on the wall became exaggerated and strange. So, a question for you based on this is how can you play with context in your work to alter its meaning in some way?

This project takes advantage of 8.5×11 and *modularity*. A few years ago, I traveled to Korea to participate in an event called the International Design Congress. I was asked to create an exhibition about my school for the conference, and was sent an extremely complex instruction manual that gave me all sorts of opportunities to rent various lighting conditions and build sort of really elaborate structures, which seemed both daunting and exciting.

Unfortunately, I had no printing or shipping budget, I would be traveling to the conference by myself, and I only had one hour to install my show. So, obviously, I couldn't take advantage of any of this.

I decided to create the show out of 8.5×11 inch misprints of design student work, since that would not require any budget, and there's thousands of misprints produced every day all over the school, I decided to use the simplest possible construction and display method, which was in this case, 1 inch metal binder rings. It was created using a couple hundred prints and binder rings. I ended up needing some zip ties, which I was able to scavenge from the conference crew, and I think it's a nice way to deal with a lot of constraints and still feel like you're making something respectable. So, a question for you is how can you simplify your design without sacrificing its impact?

The final 8.5×11 project I want to show is about *distribution*. When I came back from Korea, I wanted to share my experience with the CCA design community. I created a simple tabletop exhibition of the books and photos I had collected on my trip. I wanted the exhibition to be extremely easy to share and distribute, so I used a copy machine to create 8.5 by 11 inch tiles that would serve as a blueprint for the show, as well as providing information about the works. I could easily disassemble the tiles, collect them in a folder, store them, and send them along to anyone who would like to host the show next. So, a question for you is what are some distribution methods for your work that you haven't tried yet?

To go back to that confusing contradiction earlier in the presentation, what did I mean when I told you to both avoid defaults and embrace defaults? I guess I meant to try to be deliberate about which tool defaults you accept and which ones you change. For example, in InDesign, I think 8 point type defaults to 9.6 leading. So, for any of you who are sophomores and just starting, if any of your faculty ever look at your file, and they see that you have 8 point type with 9.6 letting, they're gonna scream at you because that is such a dumb weird random leading and they know that's the default. So just change it to 10, or 9, 8, even 7, 7 is better than 9.6, I swear to God. Anyway, it's real. Just be deliberate about which tool defaults you accept and which ones you change, and beware of thoughtlessly applying trendy default design moves to your work. And at the same time take advantage of the practical advantages of default formats (for example, they're often cheap) and of the creative and critical opportunities presented by the culture's associations with various defaults.

So that was *default format*. Now we're going to talk about *open format*, and an even more confusing piece of advice: stop worrying about format (which of course, like, what the hell? All I've been talking about is format.) I'm not sure if this is the same at Parsons, but at CCA, a lot of our most popular classes are named for formats. Classes like packaging design, motion design, exhibition design, identity design. It makes sense. Students want to know what they can expect to learn and make in a class. This is probably the right model for people who want to skill up. But a crucial aspect of the design process is sacrificed when the format is a foregone conclusion.

So what does that mean? That means if you already know what you're going to make, you never get a chance to *decide* what you're going to make. And that means you miss out on getting to make a really, really important decision about a project. That's the tricky part of classes that are all about a particular format.

Every discipline has its favorite formats: industrial designers love plastic, furniture designers love joinery, interaction designers love post it notes, graphic designers love printed matter. And we all run the risk of falling victim to the law of the instrument, a cognitive bias that involves over-reliance on a familiar tool, or as Abraham Maslow put it, "I suppose it is tempting, if the only tool you have is a hammer to treat everything as if it were a nail." All of which is to say, don't worry about the format until you've understood the question. Try to keep the format open.

In my practice, I do three basic things—freelance work, writing, and self initiated projects—and they are all sort of bundled up in this larger project, which is trying to understand things about design and culture. I tend to start projects with a question, not a format. Then I try to stay open to all the possible formats I could use to address that question. For example, I'm currently in the midst of a body of research that started with a question about virtual reality and violence. So far, the formats this research has assumed are a series of experimental

VR applications exploring haptics and social interaction in VR; an exhibition of rare video game peripherals, including some of the first consumer grade, haptic, gesture, audio, and motion technology; a critical survey of visions of VR in science fiction literature, and film; a prototype for an empathy box, which is inspired by Philip K. Dick's writing, and finally a set of speculative VR goggles inspired by Ernest Cline's writing.

I think that the open format method should feel intuitively relevant to the students in the room, but it might seem impractical or even irresponsible for actual professional practice, so I want to address that. Your client might hire you to make a logo and they're not going to be happy if you come back to them with logo goggles, right? However, I do think that in any decent project, there's an opportunity for a designer to push the client on format. Clients often think they know what they want, until you show them what they need. Say it's a book project that really wants to be a film project or a podcast or an exhibition. What if you put together a storyboard or a trailer, a little teaser to show your client at the end of the next meeting just to see what they say about it? I think communication designers often choose formats they feel comfortable with, projects they know they can do. That leads to a particular type of learning, one of continuous refinement of a narrow set of skills. Deep skills, of course, are important, but truly exciting opportunities arise when designers put down their favorite tools and try new ones, or find collaborators with other deep skills that are complementary to but very different from theirs. I would encourage you to challenge yourself to try a new tool.

The last format method I'm going to talk about today is something I'm calling *total format*. The advice here is probably the most straightforward so far, which is: don't settle for swag. So what is swag? Swag is the cheaply made, heavily branded totes and lanyards and notebooks and water bottles and pens and flashlights and stress balls and USB sticks. In California, we get granola bars—I don't know if that happens in New York. Stuff you get at conferences, parties, and events. I know that clients, collaborators, and family members alike will always expect me to get so excited about designing it. When the topic of swag comes up at a meeting, it's like time slows down. Everyone in the room turns to the designer and expects them to light up like a cell phone at a Coldplay concert. So, I always—and this is a good thing to keep in mind—I always get a little wary if it seems like the thing I'm expected to care most about in a meeting is the thing everyone else clearly cares least about.

So, in a sense, Beatrice Ward's Crystal Goblet, is just another piece of swag, right? It's a much nicer version of this water bottle I got at the Oculus Developer Conference last month. Then as now, if the wine had been shitty, no one would care about this beautiful crystal goblet. It's just swag. So when I say *total format*, I mean designing everything, thinking of every aspect of an event as within your purview, not just the swag. So with *total format*, we designers are not just thinking about making a cute sticker to put on a beer bottle. We're thinking about which beer and how many beers and how to make sure they're cold, what to give the folks who don't drink beer, what time the beer will happen, what snacks to serve with the beer, what to talk about during the beer, what comes right before and right after the beer, and why. With *total format,* we designers are no longer off the hook if the beer is warm and flat. But at least we get credit if it's delicious. (In full disclosure, I did design the cute stickers that are on these beers.) But I also helped design everything else that's going on in the picture.

Over the summer, some colleagues and I planned a retreat, where a group of 15 female artists, writers, designers, architects, and musicians gathered in Point Arena, California to explore the topic of beauty. I didn't have a name for it then, but this gathering was an example of *total format* design. Over two nights and two days, we staged conversations, working sessions, readings, service projects, pop up installations, meals, field trips, workshops, and performances. Every part of the agenda was a piece of design. And there was swag, of course, and I designed it, of course, but it was always part of a larger context that I also had the opportunity to design.

Those were some quick thoughts about format, and now we're at this part, which is your thoughts.

Rachel Berger is Chair and Associate Professor of Graphic Design at California College of the Arts.

10 Years

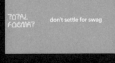

Andrew Shurtz

Authenticity, CD Symposium

Wolff Conference Room, Room D1103
Albert and Vera List Academic Center
6 East 16th Street

2019-05-15

A few weeks ago I was in an extreme state of hereness, and I was collecting a bunch of Tibor Kalman related material for my Advanced Type course here at Parsons. When I got E Roon's email I was super excited, because what would be more relevant to the topic of authenticity than Tibor Kalman? I was especially excited about a reading that I tracked down: Tibor and Karrie Jacobs' "We're here to be bad" from 1990. I've finally been able to get the actual back issue of Print Magazine from when it was originally printed, and it's amazing. I was so excited I actually even considered stealing their title for this talk. But I wasn't quite sure if Tibor's idea of "badness" was really appropriate for this—specifically Design Badness, or "being bad" in his case, in opposition to Design Good, like "good design". I didn't think it was really relevant now. So I wanted to go with something that was a little bit more specific, or what I want to talk

about, specifically, "We're here to wrong, wrong, shiny, shiny, choochoo." And this is my official title for the talk.

I want to talk about a few things: good versus bad, authentic versus inauthentic, success versus failure in design. I've noticed, especially on social media these days, there's a tendency to view work in really extreme terms. It's either extremely good or extremely bad, totally authentic or totally inauthentic. It could even be iconic or completely canceled. But I'm interested in work that sort of blurs those boundaries, or manages to be both at the same time. So, I want to talk about two pieces of design that I've been really inspired by, things that I think about a lot, things that bring up a lot of questions about what it means to design and what is good design, specifically.

The first is a record cover for the group The Four Seasons: their album

Genuine Imitation Life Gazette from 1969, designed by Don Snyder with Desmond Strobel. This is the cover. So as you can see, the cover is done like a newspaper. I don't know if it was the first record cover that was ever made like a newspaper, but it was one of the first and then it set off a trend. John Lennon and Yoko Ono did one a few years later, Jethro Tull did one too. But the year was 1969. The Four Seasons were at their peak cultural level but starting to fade off and feeling the pressure of the rise of psychedelia. Everybody was into Sgt. Pepper, everybody was into turning on, tuning in, dropping out and all that stereotypical stuff. They wanted to ride that wave. The main songwriter of the group teamed up with another songwriter that he saw play at a coffee shop in Greenwich Village, and they decided to create a concept album about the issues America was facing at the time. So instead of the normal Four Seasons stuff, Sherry, Rag Doll, all the classic Jersey Boys hits, they did this psychedelic concept album that was a musical suite. The album cover is extremely lavish for the period, it has a double gatefold and the whole thing is completely full of incredible details. The type is also incredibly well done too. Here's a close up: a comic making fun of The Beatles, a few general hippie jokes, a nice Uncle Sam thing. And then inside the second gatefold is a little mini newspaper. This is an actual photo of the group at the time. The Four Seasons were popular, but not counterculture. The whole thing is interesting because it's incredibly well done, it's incredibly detailed, basically everything you look for in a design project. If this was done in one of my classes as a thesis project, you would say, "Okay, this is an incredible success." Another thing about it that makes it really authentic is that it's a recreation of an already existing thing. They did a newspaper, a fake newspaper, but it's authentic to the means of production. Everything is done exactly how it would have been done if you were producing your own newspaper. These are some tiny little ads, there's a real crossword puzzle, everything, the details are just so completely incredible. You can't get over it, you keep finding new things. And they even went far enough to have legit underground comics artists do a comics page. It's clear that the record label, Phillips, had a ton of money they were throwing at this, it's clear that the guys that were working on this realized this was an opportunity. So again, Don Snyder was, although the credits aren't super clear, the art director for the project. Desmond Strobel was the guy that was in charge of all the graphics; he had a long career as a record cover designer, and among other things was the designer for Fleetwood Mac's *Rumours*. They basically saw this as an opportunity to do something really cool, and put everything they could into it, making an amazing thing. I would not be shocked if there isn't anyone in the room who has ever heard of this, partly because the record was almost a total flop. The band, The Four Seasons, which still exists, doesn't mention the album at all. The guy that wrote the songs will talk about it in interviews, but everybody's just pushed it aside. To a certain degree it's a total failure because of that. The cover is really, really busy, but most importantly, it doesn't really fit what we think of as the group, so in a sense it's inauthentic. The production is authentic, but the cultural aspect of it is inauthentic.

The other record that I wanted to talk about, that's almost the opposite, is by a dub reggae group, The Congos, their album *Heart of the Congos*, designed by Gillian A. Gordon in 1977. This is the cover. The handwriting at the top is not original, but still pretty cool. This was a production of the great Lee Perry, one of the most influential dub reggae producers of all time. It's considered to be one of the best dub reggae albums, and it is just a really amazing album. The cover I find fascinating, A, because it's great, but B, because it's also not great. At the same time, it basically does all of the things that I try to teach my students in Core Type and it does the things that I tell them not to do. There are a number of things that could either be mistakes or could be intentional, and it's hard to tell, which is where it gets fuzzy. This is the front cover, it's got this interesting and appropriate picture of the main members of the group playing congas. But it's also kind of strange, it feels almost randomly chosen. The back cover, if we look at it in detail, you can see some of the weirdness in the type with the song titles. If you notice carefully, the spacing is totally off, side two is a little bit shifted. There's an arbitrary space between side one and side two. There's a weird mixture of Times Roman and Univers that seems to exist for no specific reason. Then, to top it all off, the display typeface is a really weird semi-obscure Letraset typeface originally released in 1973: Beans by Dieter Zembsch of West Germany. It was a winning typeface from Letraset, who had a competition in 1973, people could just submit typefaces and they picked all the winning ones and released those. Part of the weirdness of this cover comes from the fact that it was made in paste up. There would have been an actual person sitting down with reproduced images of Letraset type that they were rubbing down manually, doing it on a board at actual size and getting it to work. Normally in a paste up you want to make sure that everything lines up, everything is really nice. But in this case, they're doing something just to get it out. One of the most fascinating things to me is how clear you can see that the label of the record is not cut in a perfect circle. There's actually a series of notches around it, which raises the question: were there issues in cutting perfect circles in Jamaica at that point, or did they just not care, or were they trying to be rough on purpose? Then, my favorite detail of the whole thing is that the stripes on the front cover, famously, were originally printed in the wrong color. They were supposed to be green stripes with red underneath, obviously, to represent the colors of Jamaica, but they came back blue stripes with red. Lee Perry was completely freaked out, he did not want the colors of Babylon, i.e. USA on the cover. And so Jah Wise, who was one of the members of the whole shebang, was instructed to hand paint over a batch of the color stripes with yellow paint to make it green again. So all of these original pressings are totally unique, the stripes are all different. Again, I'm fascinated by this because it's totally amazing. It feels like this holy object. Even if it does things that you're not technically supposed to do as a designer, it's still good. What's bad and good?

So let's look at both of them again. Looking at the Four Seasons, it's the one that's definitely more professional, all the production is totally perfect. Everything lines up, everything is exactly in the place it should be. The Congos is the exact opposite. Nothing is where it should be. Everything is kind of weird and strange. I'm interested in the sort of intersection between these two, so what does that mean? To go back to the original pirated title that I was thinking about using, this is a spread from Tibor and Karrie Jacobs' *We're here to be bad*. This is the original one scanned from a bound copy of Print Magazine that I was able to get from the library here at The New School. I had heard about this essay for a while, I'd actually used it in classes, but hadn't seen the original thing. It originally struck me as a really neat manifesto of Tibor's practice. He basically argues against good design, or at least the concept of good design that existed in the 80s of corporate perfection, and argues that basically, we need to inject badness, we need to inject art into commerce. The details of the design are really fasci-nating and completely relevant to the sort of work that I find interesting right now. This also has a lot of arbitrary decisions, a lot of wrong choices, a lot of awkward moments. They mix lots and lots of different typefaces. If you look around, you'll see that anything they're highlighting, they basically switch it to a different font. One of my favorite things is that the words "selling out" are overprinted—they're basically enlarged and printed over a paragraph. My other favorite thing is there's an actual mistake in the layout. If you look up at the top image over there, you'll notice a whole line of type is printed under the image. I honestly don't know if this was inten-tional or not, you can't read what it says underneath, and it could be a mess up, it would be a ridiculous mess up, but it's still still fascinating. I also love the bold move of having the

generic, free Art Deco font right in the middle of the text. There's so much that you can learn about, so much you can tell about the meaning of this text just by looking at it. The version that I was most familiar with is something that was on somebody's website, I don't even remember where because the link doesn't even work anymore, but just a plain text version. A lot of the readings that I use in my classes are things that I encounter either like this, or republished in some form, basically re-typeset, and I think that there's a certain authenticity to the real object and inauthenticity to the re-typeset version. It brings to mind an idea: that design texts are never really just texts. If you're reading an article, an essay, a piece of criticism that's designed by a designer, the image of it, the visual language is as important or sometimes more important than the text itself. And so in my Advanced Type course here at Parsons, I assign a really obnoxious number of readings for my students to look at, and I've been going out of my way to find the original versions. I found that no matter what the original version is, no matter how bad it is, you can get more context by looking at the original version and under-standing how the thing was made. One of the wildest examples that I've found so far is the transcribed version of Katherine McCoy and David Frazier's "Typography is Discourse" from 1989. This is a text that I had assigned because it fits in with the whole 80's, 90's postmodernism shift, and again, I always liked it, it felt like a nice little manifesto, but I always wondered what it looked like. When I actually looked it up, this is the actual printing from Communication Arts back in 1989. So this is two spreads, this is the first spread that we're seeing right now, and the design is completely crazy. And sideways! There are images that illustrate the topic, you can basically glance at it and immediately tell what's going on here in the middle of a magazine that's filled with two column text and black and white ads. And something like this jumps out, it screams at you what the message is.

A subtler distinction, but again, really interesting, is "The Crystal Goblet", originally titled "Printing Should Be Invisible", by Beatrice Warde. Anyone that's ever taken a design course or graduated has read this at some point, you've probably seen it in a pure text format, people will retype it, you'll design a little book for it. It's great. It's a really important text. I actually haven't been able to find the absolute first printed version because it was done in a British printing newspaper that I think I have to go to the British Library to find. But the earliest I could find is this 1937 edition, printed here in New York at the Marchbanks Press. This is in the NYU library, if anybody wants to see the actual book. Seeing the original, I believe, gives more context and a greater understanding of what the article is about than when you see it as a typed text and it just feels like language. But here you get a sense of the whole idea of fine printing that she was talking about, the whole idea of this purist, Eurocentric typography that she was advocating. Possibly even better is the version from the library here at The New School. This is from the 1955 collection of her essays, and is completely densely layered with decades of annotations by New School students. You get this sense of institutional memory of how the school has processed this article, so it's visually beautiful, but also at the same time, clarifies her idea of a

text being a sort of neutral space that allows room for a reader.

So, continuing on the reading idea and going back to Tibor, again, this is Tibor, J. Abbot Miller, and Karrie Jacobs' article from 1991, "Good History/Bad History". I like it because it also is much much better in the actual design version than the typeset version. But it also talks about one of the things that I wanted to bring up. Here, there's a big quote up at the top, about the whole idea of good history and bad history. "Good history, in general, presents ideas in context in a way that teaches us more than how things once looked. It's not just a roster of names, dates and battles, but the history of how we've come to believe what we believe about the world. Likewise, good design history is not just a roster of names, dates and objects, it is the history of how we have come to believe what we believe about design." So, this gets back to my main point that design is never really just about form, but instead about every-thing that happens in and around the work itself. Design is always a means to an end and a connector to other worlds and other possibilities.

Now I want to talk about three diagrams for evaluating and discussing design. So the essays and articles are really good ways to unpack the ideas behind how things are made behind certain movements. But I'm also interested in tools that can allow us to talk about work, and to place it in a certain context and unpack and understand it. These three diagrams that I'm about to show are ones that I find all work together to kind of expand how we think about something beyond the simple "iconic or canceled" binary that everybody's into. The first is Lorraine Wild's *Great*

Wheel of Style. I first encountered this in *Eye* Magazine, sometime around like 2000. And this, like any good diagram, illustrates a simple point well. Here, she's talking about how style can be re-circulated and come back to itself. So something can go from mass market to being an embarrassment, then back to being a fetish, and then back to being interesting, eventually circling back to good style. It's useful because you can see how these things connect, but also how everything can cycle back. When you realize that this is the way that style works, you can hop on the train at a certain point. If you see something that's out of style, you'll know that eventually it's going to swing back again.

The second that I find really interesting is Harsh Patel's *Association Map*. He uses this in his classes to pinpoint what the purpose of a certain piece of design is. The idea is that any piece of design can fall on a set of two axes: personal or shared, actual or abstract. The personal is something that you made for yourself. The shared is something that's done for a public. Then there's actual and abstract. Actual is something that's really straightforward and figurative. Abstract is something that's vague, fuzzier, and weirder. Once you understand that design can fall on any of those poles, there's not one way of doing design, there's not one audience for design, it opens things up to a greater sense of possibility.

And then the last, and possibly my favorite, is Desmond Wong's *Re-Designed Expanding Brain Meme Template*, which was a toss-off Twitter joke from a couple of years ago, back when everybody was doing the expanding galaxy brain thing. Instead of taking the galaxy brain to

extending levels, the joke is that you have a clever idea that gets more and more and more intense as you go along. This shows how a good idea, as it expands, get more and more insanely good, but then cycles back to being something really, really dumb and stupid so easily.

Which brings me to Comic Sans. I wanted to talk about Comic Sans partly to justify using it at the beginning. But also because I find that it's something that exists at all of these points that I talked about earlier. So we're all familiar with Comic Sans. It, of course, came out as a byproduct of the development of Microsoft Bob, which was an amazing failure of Microsoft in 1995. For those of you that aren't familiar, Microsoft Bob was created to be an overlay of Windows that would simplify computers to non computer people. So instead of going to a computer, and finding an icon and typing a bunch of stuff, you would do everything in a cartoon house that you would decorate with certain things. So there's a nice chair that you can sit in, there's a day planner, there's a bag of money, there's a calendar over the fireplace, these are all things that you can do on your nice, exciting computer. You'll notice in the bottom right corner, there's a little cartoon dog that will give you hints on how to use things. When they were making this program, the type designer Vincent Connare, who was employed by Microsoft at the time, was really horrified that the programmers had set the cartoon speech bubble in Times New Roman. He said, "It's a speech bubble, it needs to be in a comic book font." Basically, in a couple of evenings, he dashed out Comic Sans, and everyone got excited, but the programmers came back and said that it didn't fit their spacing and they still wound up with Times New Roman anyway. The fascinating thing is that because he worked for Microsoft, Microsoft owned it, and so they just bundled it with Windows, and here we are in 2019, and Comic Sans is everywhere. Interestingly enough,it was made for an authentic purpose: Times New Roman is not authentic for speech bubbles, but comic book text would be.

I'm gonna do a little detour here and talk about Philip K. Dick, who is a science fiction writer. He is famous for a number of things. He did *Do Androids Dream of Electric Sheep*, which was the basis of *Blade Runner*, *The Man in the High Castle*, that was the inspiration for the Amazon program of the same name, and a crazy book called *Valis*. He did tons of stuff, he had a career as a pulp sci fi writer, he did lots of amphetamines, wrote prolifically, basically was this frantic freelance writer who got crazier and crazier as he got older. He had this epic event happen in his life where after recovering from some kind of terrible illness/surgery, he was on a tremendous amount of pain medication, and got a delivery to his home when a woman brought some pain medication to his house. When she showed up she had this Christian fish necklace that hit the light and blinded his eyes, and he saw this as a message. It basically changed his life. He started obsessing with the idea that the Roman Empire had never ended, and that we were basically living in Roman times, and he saw this as a parallel to the sort of societies of control that he was writing about in his own books. In his book *Valis*, which is probably one of the craziest ones based off of this event, he has a quote: "Once, in a cheap science fiction novel, Fat had come across a perfect description of the Black Iron Prison, but set in the far future. So if you superimposed the past (ancient Rome) over the present (California in the 20th century) and superimposed the far future world of *The Android Cried Me a River* over that, you got the Empire, as the supra- or trans-temporal constant. Everyone who had ever lived was literally surrounded by the iron walls of the prison; they were all inside it and none of them knew it." He's talking about societal control, and he's implying this Roman connection has always existed. But looking at this, it immediately struck me that he's actually talking in a certain sense about typography. He was a writer, he made his living doing writing, he basically was an obsessive writer who's hammering stuff out all the time. Think about a black iron prison. If you think about metal, you think about metal type. But then if you also think about the Roman Empire, you realize the fact that our alphabet is essentially, especially the capitals, completely unbroken from the Roman influence. If you imagine that visual communication is something that connects us all, the Roman Empire is basically in control of our visual and linguistic communication. That brings the question, how can we resist the Empire with its own visual language? How do you break out of it if you want to do something new? What's left to do?

So then there's Comic Sans. These are a bunch of random pictures on the internet of Spain; one of my colleagues from Spain was going on about the fact that there's always Comic Sans everywhere. Spain, of course, has a really strong Roman history. When you think about this whole Philip K. Dick Roman idea of the Black Iron Prison, Comic Sans is something that basically rejects that

Roman impulse, but at the same time works within the means of production to be a perfectly functional, perfectly legible typeface, operating in a certain sense as almost a protest. It's a resistance. At the same time, Comic Sans is able to be everything at once, existing on every axis of each of these diagrams. It's both mass market and revival at the same time. It can be personal and shared. It's also brilliant, completely brilliant, and the worst possible idea, the best possible idea and the worst possible idea. So thinking about this requires us to imagine all of these diagrams in a single advanced multi dimensional hyperspace, we have to conceive this as an N dimensional zone. But to possibly put this in a way that could be a little bit simpler, it's basically Howard the Duck.

Let's wrap this up. I want to go back to these diagrams, these record covers again. Both of these have issues that might make them failures. The Four Seasons is so over the top, it's almost obscure. It feels, at times, like it's completely inauthentic, a put on by the band, it has nothing to do at all with how they were perceived or understood in culture at the time. It basically feels like somebody's trying to be hip. It's Steve Buscemi, howareyoudoingkids.jpg. The Congos is a total formal mess. Its roughness teeters on the verge of feeling tossed off, and almost obscures the brilliance of the work that went into it from all directions. But at the same time, they're both truly, truly great. The Four Seasons is so over the top that its reception doesn't matter, even if it wasn't a commercial or cultural success. As an example of something weird and slippery, it's unimpeachable. The Congos is a near perfect artifact of a group of people working to overcome extreme technological and cultural limitations. Its failures, what we'd normally consider bad design, are total and complete triumphs. Both of these fall into complicated, mushy places like Comic Sans: simultaneously in and out of style, good and bad, authentic and inauthentic. Taking all this in, maybe the way something becomes good isn't really about the way it looks at all, but instead how it's made and why it's made, who it's made for and who it's made with. If we can expand our definitions of design to allow for more oddness and complexity, we can create design that's truly about openness and possibility. Okay, and that, my friends, is the end. Don't forget to finish high school.

Andrew Shurtz is a Part-Time Assistant Professor at Parsons and co-founder of We Have Photoshop.

We're here

We're here to be bad
Tibor Kalman & Karrie Jacobs
1990

Let's talk about
good vs bad
authentic vs inauthentic
success vs failure
in design

The 4 Seasons
Genuine Imitation Life Gazette
Designed by Don Snyder with
Desmond Strobel
1969

The 4 Seasons
Genuine Imita
Designed by D
Desmond Str
1969
Album Cover

The 4 Seasons
Genu
Desi
Des
1969
Gate

The 4 Seasons
Genuine In
Designed
Desmond
1969
Detail of ty

The
Ger
Des
Des
196
Gat

The 4 Seasons
Genuine Imitation Lif
Desi
Desn
1969
Gatef

The 4 Seasons
G   azette
Design   ith
Des
1

The
C   Gazette
D   with
1

The 4 S
C   e
D
E
1
C

The 4 Seasons
Genuine Imitation Life Gazette
Designed by Don Snyder with
Desmond Strobel
1969

The 4 S
C   e
D
E
1
C

The 4 S
Genuin   azette
Design   r with
Desmo
1969
Back C

The Congos
Heart of the
Designed by
1977
Album Cove

The Cor
Heart of
Designe   rdon
1977
Back co

The Congos
Heart of the Congos
Designe
1977
Back co

The Congos
Heart of the Congos
Designe
1977
Bac

The Congo
Heart of the
Designed   lon
1977
Record lab

The Congos
Heart of the Congos
illian A. Gordon
etail

Hey let's look at

We're here to be bad
Tibor
1990

We're here to be bad.

We're h
Tibor Ka
1990
Detail

We're her
Tibor Kalm
1990
Transcrib

Design "texts"
are never really just "texts"

Typography as Discourse
Katherine McCoy &
David Frej
1989
Transcribed version

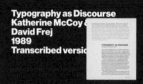

Typogr
Katheri
David F
1989
Authen

Printing Should Be Invisible
Beatric
1933
Transc

Printing Should Be Invisible
Beatrice War
1933
Authentic ver
Printed 1937

Printing Should Be Invisible
Beatrice Wa
1933
Authentic v
Printed 195

Good History/Bad History
Tibor Kalman &
J. Abbott Miller &
Karrie Jacobs
1991
Authentic version

Three diagrams
for evaluating
and discussing
design

Lorraine Wild
The Great Wheel of Style

Harsh Patel
Association map

Desmond Wong
Redesigned expanding brain
meme template

On the importance
of Comic Sans

Microsoft Bob
1995

Philip K. Dick

Philip K. Dick
Valis "Once, in a cheap science fiction novel, Fat had come across a perfect description of the Black Iron Prison, but set in the far future. So if you superimposed the past (ancient Rome) over the present (California in the twentieth century) and superimposed the far future world of *The Android Cried Me a River* over that, you got the Empire, as the supra- or trans-temporal constant. Everyone who had ever lived was literally surrounded by the iron walls of the prison; they were all inside it and none of them knew it."

Philip K. Dick
Valis "Once, in a cheap science fiction novel, Fat had come across a perfect description of the Black Iron Prison, but set in the far future. So if you superimposed the

Spain

Everything
at once

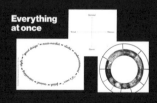

Evaluate in advanced
multi-dimensional
hyperspace

Evaluate in advanced
mu
hyp

Hey let's look at

AUTHENTICITY: A CONVERSATION

Featuring Andrew Schurtz, Elaine Lopez, and Lukas Eigler-Harding

Moderated by Kelly Walters

CD Symposium Panel, Authenticity

Wolff Conference Room, Room D1103
Albert and Vera List Academic Center
6 East 16th Street

2019-05-15

How is a designer's work "authentic"? Whether for a brand, a publication or a self-initiated work, our level of craft and the set of principles we use, influence how one perceives something to be "real" or "genuine." While building on pre-existing elements from open source platforms are widely accepted methods in a digital context, design also has the capacity to initiate dialogue and act as a provocation for unrestrained individual expression. The performative spaces we inhabit as designers, educators, family members or friends allow for multiple authentic selves that are all contextually driven.

In this symposium, we ask designers to consider the ways in which authenticity takes shape (or not) in design practice. What tools are we using? What values do we hold? How does our design engage with audiences outside of ourselves or the networks we use? Does emphasis on personal identity make design more authentic? At what point does design overstep and become so heavily edited that authenticity is lost?

Kelly Walters
Thank you all for your presentations. I think the diversity in terms of the way that you're thinking about design—from looking at historical references, to thinking about digital interfaces, to even really thinking about participatory engagement and how design can act as a provocation and allow for individuals to respond in various ways. I think that it's really, really—for me—interesting to see where we position ourselves as designers, based on whether we're working for agency, or working independently or dependently, as you have mentioned, or we're thinking about making a self initiated work that doesn't necessarily have a function particular to a particular client, but

might be just the way that you want to engage with others. And so I think part of what I wanted to do in terms of this discussion, is ask a few of you each specific questions, and then we'll allow for the larger group conversation. But to start, I think we'll work backwards and start with Andrew, just as we've just seen your presentation. I think something that I'm curious is, why did you select these particular examples as references for this discussion?

Andrew Schurtz
The short answer is that their records that I have and I've always been obsessed with. They are things that I've found in the world. One of the things that I find fascinating is that you get a stronger connection when you encounter something unexpectedly. When you just stumbled across something that you don't know about. The two covers I found to be at first, almost opposites, when I originally was thinking about the talk, I was considering that the Four Seasons was inauthentic, but good design, and the Kongos with bad design, and totally authentic but the more I thought about it, the more I realized that it's actually like this total mushy thing. Good and bad in different ways, and different respects. It's really all about the story about how things got made. It makes it really fascinating. So I think that's what I kept coming back to. Each of those, it's like this dense tax, it's this history that you can unpack each of them, that I find so exciting.

KW
I think it's interesting. I'm not sure the particular one that was hand crafted or hand painted.

AS
Yeah. The Kongos.

KW
I think that, for me, seemed like it was signaling into another space of the handicraft of making, and how we put value on something that is made by hand versus something that perhaps is a digital rendering, or something that was made with a computer. So I think another question that I have in alignment with that is just thinking: is there a prioritization of things that are made by hand versus things that are happening on the computer?

AS
The Kongos is an extreme example because it has those hand painted stripes. But one of the other things that I find interesting about it is that it was totally made in Jamaica. Printed in Jamaica, the record was pressed in Jamaica, signed, or did all of that in Jamaica. And it is a mass produced object. It was pressed at a record pressing plant. But there's a certain quality to a lot of the Jamaican pressings that you see from that period, that are old-fashioned way of looking at it. The bad way of thinking about it is that it's bad, it's not good. There's a roughness to it, there's an awkwardness to it, there's an imprecision to it. But anytime I see something like that, it's completely exciting. You get this jolt of amazement when you see texts that don't line up. Because we're so used to seeing everything so perfect all the time. And so then the question is, why is that exciting? And I think the excitement comes from the fact that you can tell a human did it. You can tell that there's a human connection. And once you know that, you know there's a story behind it. So I guess it's not so much that it has to be handmade, but I think that there has to be a sense that there was a hand behind it.

KW
I think about the examples that you were showing and think about your work, Elaine, specifically looking at an example of something that came out of Jamaican culture, but thinking about Cuban culture too, and some of the references that you were pulling into the particular work that you have generated. I was interested in and thinking about what you were finding also and how that's driving some of your thinking around authenticity and the making process?

Elaine Lopez
What I found in researching human design at all is that it actually just comes back to American design. It's people trying to imitate, or trying to look like us, or trying to look like a certain thing. The history of colonialism just is rampant. A lot of the work that I showed and when I tried to make work about Cuba, I wanted it not to look like that. Because I want people to really pay attention to the content and not just follow the trope. Cigars and the car... we all know what that is, and that's so expected. And I think there's so much nuance and a deeper history through a lot of this stuff. I think by subverting how we present that information, then people can change their minds. Our brains put things in patterns, and we're always just trying to find similarities. But I think design needs to break out of that. And I think that's why things that do break out of that are so exciting.

KW
What's interesting about that too is just thinking about the idea of control. You had also spoken in the way that when you're teaching typography, there's certain fundamentals and structures that you are imparting, so that your students are learning in a particular way. And I think what's interesting about thinking about design as control, is the moments when we are letting it go, and the moments when we're just making things off the cuff, or they're messy, or they're confusing. Again, in one particular work that you showed Elaine, I think it was using a templated system to input and then get signs back. There was somewhat of a lack of control in what types of object options you would have at your disposal. And so, I guess I was also interested to hear a little bit more about what it meant to relinquish some of the control to a system that's essentially creating for you and you're feeding in content in that way.

EL
It was awesome. It was so much fun to not have to use the Adobe software. It was just this wonky interface and I was just typing words. I don't have to worry. It was really liberating, actually, not to have to worry about rules and these standards that we've set, and just let something communicate. And ultimately, I think those things communicate better than the things that are typically type that. They just communicate different things depending on what you're going for and who you're trying to reach. I actually think templates communicate more and can communicate at that level of. It signals more importance to the thing that's being made, not to the design. Sometimes I think what we do is inauthentic. We're trying to make something feel like elsewhere, a template is just like, "That's what it is. I have to get this big shop out the door, here's this cookie." And it's like, "I'm going to buy back." Someone wrote that by hand versus label that I think signal realism and corporate

interests, and maybe something that's not.

KW

Again, pulling in Lucas here as well, I think about systems that you use, or that we use as designers, but also the creation of a system, or a network, or an interface I would also be interested to hear how in the construction of some of the work that you showed from some of your students, or even the construction of the project as a brief, to allow them to think about making a portal that in which they're putting into content, but also modifying on top of that, and still allowing for a sense of authenticity in that space too.

Lukas Eigler-Harding

My impulse there is to draw us towards almost the amount of time that it takes. So with the templates you were talking about, even printing the record, is perhaps a dense timeline, a deadline that needs to be reached.

KW

In thinking about this construction of this simultaneous function between content and making, but also the systems that we're using, another question that I was also just interested in is what are imitations in design, what is an imitation? Do you think that we are creating imitations in what we make or how we're reproducing ideas? Do you think that that contributes to a lack of authenticity of ideas?

AS

I feel like there's a tendency that I see with students when they're starting out to want to imitate something. You start designing something and you want to make something that looks like something else. So you make something that looks like something

you're familiar with, recreate something on Instagram. But you could also get to a point where you try to recreate a newspaper on a record cover. I think the imitation is like a part of what you create.

KW

Because what's interesting about it is, it's a reference. From a reference we make a new thing and I think sometimes there's that blurred space of, is that reference copy? Is it authentic? Is it borrowing the elements that we need to say a certain thing? But is there a problem with that? How do we rationalize within our making and the way that we think about that?

EL

I feel like I think about this question once a day. I think about this so much and I never get an answer because I actually think the imitation part as a designer is your thinking about functionality. You want someone to purchase something, or to believe that something does something, then you need to borrow from that language that that person recognizes. And I think it speaks to your words too. You need to lean into the things that we, as humans, have become familiar, that we identify as patterns. So I think imitation is part of it. It has to be, because we are simple creatures and we respond to things that we recognize. And is that good or bad? I don't know. I just think it's part of what we do and in every project, depending on what we're trying to achieve, we either lean into that or we don't.

KW

I think you had mentioned too about coffee shops, wood textures, and Airbnb. It's interesting to think about it in relation to that. And especially for those of us that end up working at agencies or large corporations, we're feeding into these systems that almost require us to make it that way.

LEH

My impulses to say cite your sources. I think there's an honoring, or an opportunity, to let people follow the trail and I think that, that's where perhaps imitation shifts into something that's a little bit more about building. Maybe the hamburger menu is something that we can all identify at this point. That's like a classic example on phones. But every hamburger menu I see has like a little bit of a shift, and it's a constant modification that happens. If you're going to be blunt about it, looking at something on Instagram and trying to redo it in your own, in Sketch, or InDesign, or whatever, there's shifts that are going to happen in that imitation. And so in that sense, there's an opportunity.

KW

Thinking about the digital context, I think something that I've been fasci-nated by, or trying to rationalize around, is thinking about how our inputs are our responses to certain systems that we either design for or use to put in content, thinking about the authenticity around what we put in as a bio, or what we put in as a description of ourselves, or our work on our portfolios, or the work snapshots on Instagram. Thinking about what these layers that we're using to guide our methods around what we say or how we operate. I'm interested for everyone, in your view and the way that you're presenting yourself as a designer in industry, and the classroom, and just space, how do you feel like you are either modeling different versions of self, or having to respond accordingly depending on the audience, and if

that feels like you're being less authentic in one space versus another?

EL

I can just say, for me, that's a really loaded question at this moment in time where I've just finished a two year program that has scrambled my brain. I had a 10 year career as a designer where I did the things I was supposed to do. And then I go to grad school, and it's like, "What?" It was really a moment of panic in the fall, where I had this body of work that is super weird. It's not like I'm going to go get a job at a regular design studio after a lot of this stuff. I've also been advised like, "You have your art school portfolio, and then you have your moneymaker portfolio that shows that you know how to make a logo and that you know how to do a layout?"

I think it's a fascinating thing about our industry currently. And something I've noticed just in general, sometimes portfolios or work that I see online, Instagram, whatever, that's the stuff that's gorgeous and stunning. And I'm like, "Yeah, that's awesome." When you hear it spoken about, it's just like, "Oh! That just looks like..." There's not much depth to it, but the work that's very strange. You look at someone's website and you're like, "I don't know what this person does." And then you watch that person speak, and you're completely blown away. So I think maybe our practice is moving in a direction beyond first appearance. There's a depth happening, and I think that's what we require. Inter-esting maybe, I don't know.

AS

Personally, I'm really obsessed and have almost a tremendous amount of anxiety every time I have a class situation and I have to discuss the use of a certain typeface that a student is using because I'm always trying to unpack, "Do I not like this choice because it's an incorrect choice, or do I just like have my own certain personal preferences?" And I get sick and I apologize. I'm like, "Maybe you could use Helvetica, but maybe it would be more appropriate." I'm really obsessed with the difference there. There are certain things that I really like. I think Janson is a fantastic typeface, possibly the best italic ever but then I look at somebody's choice that they've made and I'm like, "Why did you pick that?" And they say like, "It was in Adobe fonts." And I'm like, "Maybe that's not a good thing." But I'm always obsessed like, "Is it just me? Am I imposing my own will on that?"

KW
I'm always interested about where our bias is. But we're bringing all of this baggage of what we see or what we've seen before. And I similarly struggle with that too. At what point do we say it's here or it's here. I think it's definitely a challenge. I don't know if this has ever come up too for you?

LEH
Definitely, without a doubt. But I wonder if it's more a matter of positioning recommendations as opposed to absolutes. Quite frankly, the fonts at your disposal is in some cases, a perfectly valid option. There are implications or reasons as to why those fonts are chosen. I think it's in that context, there's the excitement of making it work despite that.

AS
Absolutely.

KW
I think there was one other question too, that I was just thinking about. Someone had mentioned hiding the

construction of design. Does something feel more authentic because it's been revealed to us, that we know what happened, or is it more that it's about this polishness and the shininess of something in the way that it's been created? Does that hold more weight perhaps in terms of just the way that it stands in space, whether it's online, or in print, or something like that?

LEH
I feel like with any piece of design there's... Other panelists have said, a story that involves around. And part of the technique is in delivering that story and revealing parts of that—maybe bolstered that idea or the excitement that you have. I don't know if process could always be shown, but I think in a lot of this, is a method of opening up.

EL
I think we're lacking transparency in design in general. I love opening up an InDesign document in a classroom and be like, "This is how it's made." Or like, "Show me your InDesign. Let's get in there." Because there is this mystery, and I think these are the types of things that keep design unwelcoming for a lot of people. There's this mystery that maybe we hang onto, because that's how we make our money although I think there's much more to design than that. I'm interested in just radical generosity and openness and trans-parency about how I do everything.

KW
There is a mystique. I think about how something should be presented and where and in which form and I think to your point, thinking about the closed nature of how some people may feel connected to or excluded from design and what are the systems that we are either reinforcing that are

connected to authenticity, or connected to the appearance of authenticity, are a way to create boundaries for people. That's something that I'm always constantly thinking about too: how do we become more open and how do we engage in a way that we're making?

I think something that I really loved about your presentation was highlighting that matrix set: there was one that had the access point. There was abstraction, and personal, and shared. And so I'm curious how that also surfaces for you in your research?

AS

It's an essay by Harsh Patel, and he wrote an essay that I always give on the first week of my advanced type class. He talks about his own experience as a designer of color, and as a designer that teaches in a public college and feels a lot of responsibility to open up design to students and not necessarily students from America. He talks about how design tends to be totally secluded in this Western European idea and he uses the chart, which he talks about as a way for students to think of design, not as just one thing. There's just one way of doing it, but there are lots of different possibilities and lots of different ways of being appropriate. So that's what I was excited about.

EL

To build on that, in your talk, it was interesting to compare these two albums, and to say that theoretically one is bad. What does bad mean? What does good mean anymore? I think we need to look at the language that we're using for design and story. That's why I like to look at definitions of words and their origins. Maybe we need to reflect back and analyze why things were made and question

whether or not this is the right language anymore? Can design even be good or bad? What is the goal of design? is it just to get someone to know something? There's just a lot of unpacking to do and a lot of revisiting of language behaviors of processes. It's going to be hard.

KW

I definitely think it is. What I thought was really poignant also from your presentation was thinking about, finding the original source of the texts that you might be sharing in your classroom, and thinking about what that means. I was thinking about "The Crystal Goblet", when I think it was just like a text version that I had also gotten. To be able to source it and track it back to one of the earlier forms, I think that, that also changes the read in the context. And I think everything is so contextual and so really allowing yourself, or students, or anyone who's engaging with the text, to really feel where it came from. Because I feel like the distillation, over, and over, and over again, these reproductions, replications, all things start to get lost. I'm fascinated by your process and tracking it back to aluminate what it looked like originally.

AS

To be perfectly honest—to be perfectly authentic—it started from just this collector's impulse, to just see if I could find the original and touch it or whatever. I get really excited getting books from the library. It's really, really fun. And in the process of seeing these, it just hit me. You see it and you realize that there's so much more information. It's so much more rich to look at something like that. You can tell something about it. Even if you don't know design history, there are certain cultural things that you get from it that make a lot more sense and are way, way, way, way, way more rich for a student that's coming into it. I think that's just totally thrilling. I also just love collecting PDFs. That's really satisfying.

KW
And Lucas, I think in your practice, how do you see looking at footnotes? When we had spoken earlier, we were talking about looking at the sources and finding the references. What does that mean from a digital context? What does it mean from building a website and constructing the traces of something that was its original source, even as much as code that might be used and then manipulated to become something else?

LEH
I think what excites me about it, maybe is that there isn't an original. Even with the collection of a PDF library, there's always a physical copy, or the first printed, or something that you can go back to that. That immediately puts you in a situation where just a little bit of research has opened up other avenues and opened up the opportunity for others. We have often relied on this idea of hyperlinks, of jumping up in a web surfing. And I think that that's always an exciting thing to bring into this. It means that there's a sense in that you don't necessarily know where you're going to end up, even if you have a goal in mind and it's a walk on the way.

KW
One other question and I think we can open up to the audience after that. What should we resist and what should we amplify to be more authentic designers?

EL
What I'm trying to do with my work is allow people to respond or to participate in the work as well. Posters can be nice and it can just tell you something and you can walk by but when someone can engage with that or respond to that, or actually participate in that conversation, I think that's more exciting. That brings people into design. I just think we need to be more transparent, bring more people into this, and allow more opportunities for engagement with design breaking, playing, understanding what we do.

AS
I can say on the resist angle, teaching here at the New School with such a diverse and international student body, resisting my own cultural biases is so important. Especially when thinking about a design, because I think it's really important to understand that there are different reasons for doing different things at different times.

LEH
I think amplifying, in a sense, is an opportunity to focus and resist. What does this community look like? What values are shared?

KW
Are there any questions in the audience?

Audience
It feels like there's perhaps something about authenticity—and I don't know if I want to use the word obscurity, or peripheral, or something that is marginal—but it feels like all three of you in your presentations were talking about things that we don't necessarily think about, or we don't have access to. They somehow are behind something and we have to excavate it. We have to somehow find it in a

record store somewhere, in order for it to feel authentic. And maybe sometimes that borders on fetish. I also think there's something interesting in that language, it's also about personal experience. Is there a connection there?

AS

I'm actually glad to hear you mention the fetish thing. That's totally right. There's a certain friction to these objects, there's a certain quality to them. I guess it's tricky. The whole idea of authenticity was so heavy. When I heard that was the topic, I was like, "Okay, great." And then I'm like, "Oh wow! What does that even mean?" And so I tried to purposely resist actually defining what it is. But I think something feels authentic when you can tell that it's real and it feels real. When you sense that there's some human connection to it, when it's evidence that it was actually made for and by people and then it wasn't something that was tossed off. When something is fake or inauthentic, it feels like people didn't care. I think when something does feel authentic, it's really, really authentic, it reaches that level of fetish, where you're just so into it.

LEH

In my mind, maybe the difference becomes what you use that object for. You might have it put up, but there's also an opportunity to use it in a presentation, to refer to that point. And I think that it being as the end object, perhaps defines it as a fetish, but enables you to jump to another step.

EL

I think personal narrative is maybe the only thing that's authentic in the world. What we've lived through and what each of us individually has experienced. There's nothing more

real than what you have experienced. And if we can use design to share those experiences in a way that might be fine art. But we can move design towards expressing the narrative of things that have happened to us.

Audience

Just going back to the touch on the hand behind the design. In interaction class we, at one point, talked about designs done by AI in the future—there are some logo designs that AI can generate that already exist on the internet now. I was just wondering if in the future, could AI take over designers? Would that be losing authenticity? AI, they can think of the most ideal outcome and…

KW

But is it ideal?

Audience

Yeah. I don't know, Maybe in the future? I don't know, I'm just throwing a lot of—

AS

I think it's totally possible, because the AI comes from somewhere. Somebody makes it, and so there's some personality to it. The musician, Holly Herndon, just released an album called *Spawn*. There's one song where she trains some AI to sing it. And it's it's really, really weird. It's really wild. But there's a total personality to it, because she programmed it. She coached it. She did it. So it has an essence of her in it. I think there's a total dystopian *Matrix* version of that, where everything is controlled and we're all in little bubbles or whatever. That probably wouldn't be so good. And then, maybe there's a middle ground where all design is made by AI, and it just feels lame. And I think that would be the worst possible outcome. Everything is just like, "Okay."

KW

It's flat.

AS

It's just flat.

LEH

And you design your own AI. There's a skill set that I think design school tries to give, which is that of problem solving. I think that, to me, is a huge amount of optimism in it. It's like, "Okay. If AI is producing all the design, but then..." Like you said, who gets to jump up to the next level. Not everyone programs websites, but a lot of people design websites. Not everyone has to know how to program an AI to understand the systems to perhaps design for shift.

EL

I think it's inevitable, honestly. It goes back to what design is? What is design really? That's what's exciting to me about design and I'm like, "I think we need to embrace AI and robots." They're here already and they're coming. I love my Roomba! I don't know. But we do need to think about it, before we go forward.

KW

Great. Thank you so much for your presentations and your discussions.

Andrew Shurtz is Part-Time Assistant Professor at Parsons and co-founder of We Have Photoshop. Elaine Lopez is a designer and Assistant Professor of Communication Design at Pratt Institute. Lukas Eigler-Harding is a designer based in Berlin. Kelly Walters is an Assistant Professor of Communication Design at Parsons.

ON THE EARLY INTERNET

Anil Dash

CD Symposium, Digital Materiality in the Age of Design Systems

Wolff Conference Room, Room D1103
Albert and Vera List Academic Center
6 East 16th Street

2018-05-15

Hi, I'm Anil, and I'm not a designer.

I've been an entrepreneur. I've been a writer. I've been a lot of other things. My experience is much more in designing systems and in creating design systems. I get introduced, understandably, as CEO of a software company, which is actually my job, but a lot of my work has been in interrogating the tech industry, being a bit of a critic (as much as one can be from the inside trying to be), an activist and a writer. And so trying to bridge those things together, I think, really connects into a lot of the things we'll hit today.

I wanted to give a little bit of background about what it is to be somewhat "non standard" within the tech industry because I say I run a software company and in our culture, that sort of means certain things about design and how it functions, but the company I run is small and independent, and yet, has impact.

How many of you have ever—if you are coders—looked at Stack Overflow and got an answer? A couple of you. Or if you've done project management, do you use Trello? And then I understand that a lot of you have used Glitch?

All those were created or co-created at our company, Fog Creek, and then spun out over time. Glitch is still at home because it's young and little. Yet, we as a company never had venture capital investments. We are small and privately held. Our team has three dozen people and most of them are downtown. It's a very, very different thing. That informs everything about design and everything about our ability to consistently make things that millions of people use. When we talk about design systems, that's your dream; to make something that has an impact on a lot of people's lives.

114

What I want to do is share a perspective about having been creating experiences, particularly on the web. Now, this is not to dismiss desktop and mobile software and all the other sorts of ways of creating digital experiences. But I'm going talk about the web because this is something that we've lost the history of. I'm going to talk a little bit about where that history went, why it went away, and how we sort of reconstructed an imagined version of it. I'll sort of zip through a lot of the concepts that are around that along the way.

So the first interesting aspect about the web is that it was a folk medium, which is to say: we invented our practices for creating and designing it, ad hoc, amongst each other, in the early days on the web. I got on the web in 1992, when it was mostly text and it was less than a year old. By 1994, I'd seen a graphical web browser and decided this is what I was going to do the rest of my life. I just knew this was something overwhelmingly compelling. That was a quarter century ago, so I'm obviously incredibly old. One of the things that comes out of that is that epiphanic moment of "This is how I'm going to express myself. I may not be a great singer or a great dancer, but this is the way that I can put myself out in the world." And I don't think that is most people's experience of the web today. It's not a folk medium. It's a box that companies run that you put your stuff into, and if you're lucky, they give your stuff back to you sometimes. That's a very, very different concept of how many of us in the early days of the web encountered the web. The reason why is, very quickly, companies recognized there was a lot of opportunity here. Tech companies in particular, are

radically anti-historical, and this is particularly true of the investors that make most of the large technology companies run these days. They are, and I don't say this lightly, not merely inattentive to history, I mean all of our cultures are inattentive to history. They are aggressively, stridently anti-historical. They try to erase history.

So I'll ask you something: think about your favorite album that you listen to your favorite music. Think about your favorite film. Do you know who performs on the songs? Do you know who directed the film? You probably do. And then think about the apps that you've used. And then ask yourself, do you know who made them? I don't mean, who's the CEO of the company? I mean, who made them? Can you name one person? And now granted, this is New York, and you're all educated designers, so maybe you know that one person, and you're connected through LinkedIn or they got a job at one of these companies. But for the most part, billions of people use technologies and have no idea who created them. Go back to "who made these things more deeply?" "Who invented this category of app?" And that's where we start to see why there is not a shared culture on the web anymore.

We have obliterated the ability to even see who makes apps. There is no IMDb for apps. There is no "what we used to have back in the end of the web view" source. Now, you can still View Source in your browser, technically, sometimes you have to enable the tools to do it. Most mobile devices are abysmal at this. But being able to see how a web page was made used to also give you hints as to who had done so, and give you a connection into those creatives. It's wild that we've seen so much progress in remix culture, music, and film and all these other disciplines where you can see that history. Sometimes, if you're extremely tech savvy, you can go to GitHub, and you can find where some of the pieces and parts were made. But those are the raw materials. That's not the experience. That's not the thing you're using. This manifests itself all the way into the tools of expressiveness.

The tools we use for shared culture these days are generally closed, proprietary networks, like Instagram, you see the filters. Who made the filters? Their cases were inherited originally from the iPhone, from iOS. The phone said, these are the filters you're gonna get Instagram just made them accessible and easy. But where did those transformations, the math to make those images look that way and to do those effects, where do those come from? A lot of that's public research. If you dig deep enough, you can see the academics and the researchers that created those Instagram filters. But you can't trace the line from scholarly research saying "these are ways to add effects to images" all the way through into the app in your pocket, and see how these things are connected, and there's huge loss to that, a huge loss of expressiveness, and shared culture.
What if you think, "Well, look, I want to make a filter, what would I do? How would I even petition Facebook, which owns Instagram, to say I have a way of manipulating images that the world should see? It's not designed for that?" You're not meant to do that.

Why do we erect these barriers to creating technology that's participatory, to creating design systems where we can imagine ourselves being part of the design? It's interesting, because the rhetoric of the tech industry is "we want to teach everybody to code," "We want to teach the kids in classrooms, teach everybody in grade schools, if it means they're going to come in and be coders and lower the cost of wages for working at the tech companies." But in terms of actually empowering creativity, outside of the walls of the few giant tech companies that have been funded by a couple giant venture capital firms, they're not really interested in that. And I can say that, because I've been there. I've done that. I've built companies funded by those people, and I know what they fund.

You see this sense of "user generated content." This is such a great, very telling phrase, because nobody calls themselves a user. No artists calls their work content unless they're being ironic. And certainly the creative act is not generation. I'm not a user generated content. I'm a person expressing myself. So what you do through language is that you separate people from the idea that the digital medium is one that you express yourself in, just as you would with words, poetry, art, film, with all the other media that we have in front of us. This is especially galling, because the people who created the first generation technologies are still alive and still creating vital, interesting technologies. Tim Berners Lee, who invented the web, is very active, creative, and still has lots of ideas about how the web should evolve.

How many of you have ever used a spreadsheet, like Google Spreadsheets? Microsoft Excel? Like most of you, I love spreadsheets. I'm a nerd. I think they're a really creative, expressive tool if used correctly. Who invented the spreadsheet? Charles Simonyi was influential in creating multiplayer in Excel, one of the most popular spreadsheets. The inventor of spreadsheets is a man named Dan Bricklin. He's pretty young. He's in his early 60s. He's in good shape. He's still making apps. He went on to create some of the first pen computers that influenced everything all the way through to the iPhone. The very last keynote that Steve Jobs did when he was showing off the iPad, Dan built an app for the iPad, and went up afterwards, saying, "Just like I made the first spreadsheet called Visicalc on your Apple computer in the late 70s, I made another touch app that people can take notes on on the iPad 35 years later." And there's still a connection.

So, these are people that are creative, vital. Dan's been a mentor of mine since I just emailed him out of the blue and he replied back. The folks that invented presentation software like PowerPoint are still alive out there and accessible. They want to share their knowledge. Yet we've erected all these barriers. Can you imagine talking to the people that invented the first tools for creating film, or creating television, to have access to them, have them alive, and not knowing about it, not being taught it when we're teaching what technology is? We're getting scammed, right? I bring this up, because I come from the old way. I don't have some great reverence for it, it's not like the good old days were better, they were crappy! A lot of the tools were primitive, what you could do was primitive because nobody was there. None of your friends were online. It was like a ghost town. But still, there were some parts, because they hadn't been locked down, that

were really interesting, expressive, and open.

There are some interesting vestigial memories. Are people familiar with one or more of these names of old communities like MySpace, LiveJournal, Neopets, GeoCities? There was this website called AngelFire where anybody can put up a webpage. Nowadays, people love content that follows your cursor on the screen. On an AngelFire, that was hot 20 years ago. So everything old is new again. And that's not to say that's not an original idea. But why are there echoes and we don't know the antecedents to it? Why have we been scammed into believing that there isn't a full tradition of trying these same experiments and carrying them forward?

That's the thing. Think of how much creativity is lost because you can't go back and refer to it. It's not like you have to have a museum store in the old artwork to be able to refer back to it like, "Oh, I wish I could fly to that city and see that work in person." It's the web, right? It used to fit on floppy disks. You could bring it with you.

And so where did it go? Is it somewhere in the web archive? Probably. But how do you get to it? How do you make it accessible? Why has it been erased? Why have we been separated from it? These are really important questions about how to express ourselves.

A lot of the work our team is doing now with Glitch is about explicitly trying to bring back these kinds of communities where people are helping each other create, and it might be a little rough around the edges, but you can try out new things, learn different ways of expressing yourself. I think about this a lot as the web we lost. Again, I am cautious about saying this because there's this sentimental or nostalgic view of "the good old days are better." I don't believe that. I think the best days of the web, and digital expressiveness are ahead of us. But there are still elements of this that we have to be informed about, that we have to know to feel the loss of cultural wealth before we can bring them back. While I was thinking about this, about those sites that some of you may have not heard of, some of you may vaguely heard of one and never tried. Millions of people did though. It wasn't billions, but most sites don't have billions of users. But millions of people liked a band enough to make a fan page on MySpace. Millions of people had to get out their email thoughts by making a LiveJournal blog. Millions of people wanted to just put up some art project on GeoCities, or these other sites. These weren't obscure things that only geeks did. And back then, the people were creating much more inclusive communities, by gender, by race, by class, by all the other indicators that have been squeezed out of who gets to make technology in the industry today.

What we've done has also erased the fact that we were always here—all the rest of us—we're always here creating things on the web and using it to express ourselves. And that's something that I think we can reclaim. I mean, I look at this crowd and it looks a little bit more like New York City, which is good. But we look at who's actually building the apps that dominate our digital experiences today and it doesn't look like this room. It doesn't look like this city. That's a big gap to be filled.

The other part is that there are billions more people on the web now and using apps every day but don't know about this history. I don't care if they know about any of these websites, I'm not trying to say people need to know the website that people used to put their NSYNC fanfic on. I think what's more interesting is to say is "this is a medium that used to be expressive and to claim that for yourself. You all have something to say, to share this idea that these are expressive tools." These are expressive systems, I think that's one of the things that I am beseeching you all to be voices for me, to think about design systems, not merely, "Can people understand this message," but, "Can they see it as participatory?" Is it something you create a negotiation with the community you serve, with the people you serve, with the audience you serve, as opposed to something delivered to them? Think about business models.

Now, this is something where in an art school and a design context, you're not supposed to talk about this stuff too much. We are supposed to "free your mind." Let me tell you something though, the thing that is going to constrain your artists is the business models of digital platforms, period. Your ability to express yourself is going to be locked down by this unless you understand it. Typically, what happens is you come out of here, you have great ideas, and you get a job because you have to pay off your school loans. You end up finding yourself five years down the road saying "I can't really express myself the way I want. These ideas can't get out there." It's about fluency and understanding the business context in which you're able to work. I'm not saying this as some unapologetic capitalist, I'm very conflicted about being a CEO in tech. But it's the thing I wish I had known earlier in my career to understand why I couldn't build some of the things I wanted to build. It's not saying they're all evil, there's great things like the fact that I can send a WhatsApp message to my cousins on the other side of the world and know what's happening in their lives. That is a triumph of good design. That is a triumph of accessibility, a triumph of technology doing what it's supposed to do. But we have a world where the predominant business model of large scale internet platforms is surveillance capitalism. They monitor what you're doing and then sell either your data or abstractions of your data to other companies, allowing those networks to be manipulated by actors, as we've seen in media and press, in ways that are bad for society.

That tension is going to have to be resolved, there are going to have to be other models. That's necessary for society to serve, for politics to serve as healing in the public sphere, but it's also necessary for expressiveness. We have a generation of people that think the primary way you get a message out is to go to Facebook and the page is going to be whatever shade of blue light you want it to be. I think a web, the web, the internet, can be whatever you want it to be. And we have our default templates of how we think, how communicating with each other online works, and those are very recent assumptions. Those are very fragile assumptions. Those are things that you can blow up really easily. Maybe you should think about this, because I think what we have in the digital realm is not emotionally sustainable right now. Whether it's like FOMO on Instagram, or the nonstop noise on Twitter, or all kinds of drama in different Facebook groups, the ways we interact with each other online are not sustainable. They are emotionally draining, they don't nurture our souls in the way that good art and good expressiveness does. It's very easy to put in your headphones and listen to a great album, or a great song, and lose yourself in it. It's very easy to be swept away in the world of a film for a few hours. It's a great joy to lose yourself in a book.

Then think about your digital experiences. I don't mean when Netflix gives you a film that's a great film. Think about an actual experience of the web or of an app. How often has it been immersive? How often has it been expressive? How often have you felt like you understood somebody else better? How rare is that? That is not imaginary, impossible. There's nothing intrinsic about the internet that precludes it from being that thing. We've already seen really interesting things, evocative visuals, design elements, and ways of expressing ourselves in code. That could be, if we nurture each other, every bit as expressive, and every bit as meaningful as the greatest art and the greatest expression we see in other media. There's no reason it can't be the same.

There's an interesting intersection here where we have this need for emotional sustainability or wellness, as individuals need to be connected with each other artistically and expressively, as well as this idea of critiquing the business models. There's nothing that says that large internet companies couldn't be thoughtful. It's not as if it limits their ability to succeed, and not intrinsic to whatever their metrics of success are.

We just haven't pushed them, we've forgotten how to. We can point to these prior examples, people empowering millions and millions of people to create, and having that be the sustenance of how they make something meaningful online. They made design systems that were not top, down, bottom, up, right. They made design systems that were participatory. There's no reason we can't do that again.

I want to close with a reflection I've been having on what so much of the framing of what technology should be, of criticizing technology mindfully, is based on. All histories are fiction, right? We construct our histories. So, I don't want to pretend that there is some one truth that you can go back to and can carry forward, a truth that is going to solve all these problems. But what I look to is the idea that all of you, collectively in a community like this, can create a new history, a new version of that past to reflect on and to use as a basis for making something in the future. A new version that delivers that promise, which is why we all got interested in designing things together in the first place. And with that charge, I leave you to the work and I can't wait to see what you create.

Thank you.

Anil Dash is the CEO of Glitch.

ON NETWORKS

Mindy Seu

CD Symposium, The Pedagogy of Design in the Age of Computation

Starr Foundation Hall, Room UL102
University Center
63 Fifth Avenue

2018-01-07

First, thank you so much to E Roon, Geo, and Brendan for organizing and inviting me to this Symposium. The conference itself is called the Pedagogy of Design and the Age of Computation, but what exactly is the Age of Computation? Are there clear boundaries for this era and if so how can we expand what this phrase actually means, not only in terms of the timeframe, such as when the age of computation begins, but also to the materiality? Can we learn from earlier analog forms? And finally, how can we expand our reference points for who we actually associate with computing and design?

Since I'm the first of the four speakers, I wanted to provide historical context. We're going to go backwards about 60 years. When we think about the origins of the internet, it's rooted in the military industrial complex with organizations such as ARPANET and Bell Labs. But now

when we think of the internet, we probably think of the platform oligopolies of Twitter, Facebook, Instagram, etc, one that is surveilled and in many ways restricts our online behaviors.

This talk is not going to be a nostalgic plea but rather a prompt to reconsider the importance of counter narratives and revisionist histories.

Today, in the next 30 minutes, I'll quickly address historical resonance between grassroots publishing and alternative networked cultures. I'm especially interested in publications, so when you hear this word, especially in a communication design program, you may consider the printed and bound book, but we can rethink publication to mean the site at which the public is formed. This is especially meaningful when you're considering audience and the distribution methods for online and offline publishing. When we think of networks, we probably think of social networks and platforms, or networking which probably connotes schmoozing. While social media activism is highly relevant in today's day and age, I'll be focusing on earlier, much more utopian ideas of networks.

The World Wide Web, and code in general, is not merely software protocols, texts, and data files, but it's also the sum of how this protocol is used, whether it''s for marketing, scholarship, or personal expression. Agnes Cameron stated that cookbooks are protocols and protocols are performances, so I'd wanted to start by showing a proto internet publication that spawned a network of guides, cookbooks, and manuals for living. Some of the excerpts or snapshots you can see behind me. This is the first issue of the *Whole Earth Catalog* that emerged in Fall 1968 and the founder, Stewart Brand, was motivated by a very utopian vision. This was a push away from that military industrial complex, and it was one of hippie modernism, LSD, back-to-the-land movement and frontierism. In the early 60s, NASA had not yet released a photo of the entire earth, so Brand believed if we were able to see an image of the planets, we may gain a better understanding of how we connect to those around us, as well as have an urge to work towards sustainable living. On the back cover, you'll see their famous tagline, "Stay Hungry, Stay Foolish." The *Whole Earth Catalog* was considered a proto-internet publication for several reasons. It was an early example of user generated content. Kevin Kelley, who was an editor of the Whole Earth Catalog, and later, the founder of *Wired Magazine*, called it a precursor to the blogosphere. It was even heralded for creating a network of

publications, as well as connecting counter-cultural resources in its pages. Steve Jobs, in his Stanford commencement speech, also called it "Google before Google." It was a catalog but nothing was actually for sale. Rather, it collected books and diagrams and organizations, and Brand was really motivated by providing access to tools and ideas.

In *Writing Machines*, Katherine Hayles describes encyclopedias, catalogs, and indexes as early forms of hypertext, because they have multiple reading paths and a system of extensive cross references that serve as pseudo-linking mechanisms. These text entities are separated typographically and visually from one another. These types of connections have always existed. But what digital hypertext structure adds to this is not necessarily a new model, but just an exponential increase in scope and speed of what can actually be connected.

Decades after the first issue, the *Millennium Whole Earth Catalog* came out in 1994. And in it, they had analog hyperlinks that refer you to different parts of the catalog. If you look kind of towards your left, my right, or my right left, you'll see this cat jumping into a hole. Here it says, "See restoration, forestry page 90." This was from page 70. It pushes you to different parts of the catalog. This occurs all throughout the Millennium issue. This one says "Preserving plant knowledge. See also traffic biomes plant communities plant knowledge."

One of the catalogs in the *Whole Earth Catalog* network was the very overlooked *New Women's Survival Catalog* from 1973. It was built by the authors Susan Rennie and Kristen Grimstad as the feminist Whole Earth Catalog. However, you can't even find it on Wikipedia, because there aren't many secondary sources about this. It was also excluded from the MoMA exhibition about the *Whole Earth Catalog* network. So while in many ways, the *Whole Earth Catalog* was outside the mainstream for some, it still excluded many marginalized communities and tools that might be useful for them. A quick analysis of the titles reveals this: the *Whole Earth Catalog* contains a Universalist and Environmentalist ethos for people who actually have the luxury of going "back to the land". What about those who were on those lands before who were actually involved in this whole Earth? And meanwhile, the self help ethos of the *Survival Catalog* is apparent in its title. Here, they provided references that you can see on the back cover for support after rape, how to get an affordable divorce, for an organization of self defense and healthcare. Their slogan was "A Nationwide Network of Alternative Feminist Culture," and "A Woman Made Book. There were only two spin offs of this, the *New Woman's Survival Catalog* and the *Survival Sourcebook*. And the tagline for that was "Another Woman Made Book." (And just as a side note, you can actually read an interview with Meg Miller, Susan Rennie and Kirsten Grimstad on AIGA Eye on Design.)

The *New Woman's Survival Catalog* started off as a bibliography during Kirsten Grimstad's graduate studies at Columbia. Her advisor told her that a revolution could never occur within an institution, so in order to make this movement happen, they needed to work with grassroots organizations. There have been a lot of conversations about the politics of bibliographies and archives, but it might be reframed as "bibliographies show the politics of the author or

creators." In Alessandra Ludovico's *Post Digital Print*, he speaks of the value of bibliographies because they're a result of a thoughtful and time consuming effort of searching and making connections. It's oftentimes much more sophisticated than even the most ingenious Advanced Search. This process typically links through search queries or keywords, but bibliographies, associations, or links that we build are often based on abstraction of experience or sometimes sheer interest. In *Rethinking the Public Sphere*, Nancy Frazier's principal example is the late 20th century *US Feminist Subaltern Counterpublic*. A clear artifact of that is the *Survival Catalog*. This is a collection of resources like journals, bookstores and distribution networks, and the constitution of this public is a "multicontextual space of circulation, organized not by a place or an institution, but rather self organized around a circulation of discourse."

So in many ways, the *Survival Catalog* is still very similar to the *Whole Earth Catalog*, especially due to its DIY cut up aesthetic and alternative connections. The visual language, while it points to DIY, is really a result of the material means of production at that time, having to use cut ups and the software needed to quickly and affordably create a book. The car culture of that time is also reflected in both these publications. Stewart Brand created the Whole Earth Truck store, whereas Rennie and Grimstad actually collected all of this content during a three month cross country road trip across the US. Grimstad and Rennie had a utopian vision, removed from patriarchal suppression, and they proudly called themselves second wave feminists.

I realize there might be people in the audience that aren't familiar with the various waves of feminism in the US context, so I just wanted to give a quick overview. First wave feminism deals with basic rights like suffrage or the right to vote. The second wave dealt with the consciousness raising movement, the politics of domesticity and the private sphere, such as sexual abuse, divorce and child care. Third wave feminism is largely defined by intersectionality. And you might call what we have now, fourth wave feminism, largely marked by its use of social media activism. There is value in demarcating these different waves because nothing occurs in a silo; it gives credit to the work that those have done before us, or it actually gives us a point of retaliation and conflict. Whether you agree with the history you've been taught or not, we must reckon with them by revisiting them or affirming them.

In the 1992 essay, "Audiencing," John Fiske states that culture circulates within a social order. While culture may secure the social order, or destabilize it, nothing is ever neutral. Around the same time, in the late 60s, there was a growing network of mail artists, and the mail art movement, in many ways, was also utopian. Here, these artists tried to disregard and circumvent the commercial art market and the elitism of the gallery worlds.

So behind me, you'll see a postcard by Ray Johnson, who was considered to be the founder of correspondence or mail art. On the lips, it says, "end slips to Lucy Lippard," another member in the New York correspondence school. This wasn't a school in an institutional sense, but rather a collection of artists who believed in the dance or correspon-*dance* between various actors in this network. Mail artist's use the Postal Service and existing distribution network and claim that anyone could be an artist. They believe that in principle, every mail art is unfinished. From their manifesto they write, "It is an aesthetic text asking for a reply. Mail artists always communicate again and again, and the keystone of mail art is reciprocity." Behind me, you'll see a postcard by Ben Vautier called *The Postman's Choice*. It's identical on both sides, the author would write a different address on either side of the postcard and the postman would actually have to make the choice of where it would end up.

Guy Bleus said, "A mail artist is often a disappointed artist, not disappointed in art, in the art industry at the leading galleries and museums. Being a member of a planetary art movement helps [them] to transcend this isolation and alienation in art." This is an excerpt from another leading mail artist at the time, Anna Banana, and for her, mail art represented an extension of the burgeoning 1970's counterculture. She created *Vile Magazine* and dedicated its sixth issue to fe-mail art in 1978. (Also, a side note, *Vile* was a parody of *File Magazine*, which was a parody of *Life Magazine*.) This included contributions by women mail artists like Yoko Ono, Beth Anderson and Alison Knowles. This mail art movement led to the arts strike of the late 80s and asked artists to examine their own reasons for contributing or participating in cultural discourse. The art strike mantra reads, "We want to show you a strategy for attaining art strike Nirvana. We want to show you how you can fight art as status, art as commodity, and art as hierarchy. Our strategy will help you lose your egotism, self importance, self indulgence and self esteem."

This past summer, I was a fellow at the Internet Archive, as mentioned, where I co-organized the centralized web summit with Sam Hart. The goal of the summit was to bring together technologists, policymakers, humanitarians, and artists, to consider what a redecentralization of the web might be. We're very aware of the blurry lines between these tracks, as oftentimes artists and designers actively use technology for social justice or education. For the arts track, we wanted to consider how *peer-to-peer* comes from a longer line of distribution technologies and networks like the Postal Service, and how experimental art forms arise when artists use these existing structures.

So how can artists be networked in an ideological sense?

The phrase "artist as networker" was used by Chuck Welch when he was writing *Eternal Network: a Mail Art Anthology*. This was before networking was pushed into its current connotation as schmoozing or that of platforms. It was trying to indicate an active engagement with others. After this art strike, H.R. Fricker proposed that we channel that energy into preparing for the first Worldwide Decentralized Network Congress of 1992. After that, several mini congresses sprung up to continue this conversation.

The theme of issue two of Open Net Mag was this 1992 Worldwide Decentralized Network Congress, and the goal was to conceive communication and organization systems, as well as the willingness to participate in the projects of others. Beyond correspondence or dance or the performative element, it attempted to bring networkers together in an ideological sense, so people could meet in the same space and work together.

Here's Tim Mancusi's collage cover design for *Net Shaker*. The special issue of 1995 was devoted to the *Networker Telenetlink*. Netlink refers to interconnected networks. The graphic language is also quite powerful. Pioneering telecommunication artists like Judy Malloy and Anna Couey were all active mail artists during the early 1970s, before they moved towards telecommunications arts which would then include email art. Networkers use both telecommunications and mail art as tools rather than boundaries. EMMA, the Electronic Museum of Mail Art, describes, "The hallmark of both mail and telecommunications art resides in attitudes of creative freedom, collaboration and the abolition of copyrights, and independence outside of mainstream art systems." Also, a side note: the *Whole Earth Review* introduced this issue and their readers to the *Networker Telenetlink* and the article is called "Art that Networks."

This mail art movement was then pushed into larger performances, and mail artists not only sent artifacts like paper, envelopes, and stamps, but they also considered how to bridge this analog and digital divide by sending floppy disks and other electronic media. In 1993, Losif Kiraly wrote, "Mail art, it was for me, and for many artists from communist countries, the only possibility to have contact outside of our borders. Even in this way, I had a lot of problems with censorship. And the message of this performance from 1982 was that you can travel out of the country only by post and only if you are lucky."

So what is the Eternal Network? This was actually stated when the mail art movement was happening in the early 1960s by Robert Falu, along with George Brecht, and they describe this as the ethereal, open ephemeral nature of process aesthetics that acts in networking. They have four primary goals. The first was to make artists realize they're part of a network. The second was to refrain from competition. The third was to advertise other artist's performances alongside your own. And the fourth was to acknowledge that networks exist within networks like netlinks, and to understand that this eternal network going on around them was happening at all parts of the top at all times and all parts of the world.

At the same time of this worldwide Decentralized Networker Congress and the early internet of the 1990s, a group of cyberfeminists began to emerge. This term was coined by the cultural theorist Sadie Plant and the Australian art collective VNS Matrix. (The VNS is actually a faux acronym of DNS, and you can guess what the V stands for.) One of their members Dahl Yoko stated, "Cyberfeminism is one of many feminisms and feminism has not gone away." In 1991, they created the *Cyberfeminist Manifesto for the 21st Century*.

This manifesto was remixed a number of times; this particular one is a billboard. Because of the way texts circulate, this becomes the basis for further interpretations. This convinces us that publics have activity and duration. It was also remixed as this video. If you note the folder structure is on the side, it actually is a source of citations.

[Plays the Video]

Like Stuart Brand, Kirsten Grimstad, Susan Rennie and mail artists, cyberfeminists are also utopian thinkers. Utopia is contingent on the people making them or imagining them, and they saw technology as a way towards liberation. In an essay for *Motherboard*, the musician and writer, Claire L. Evans writes, "VNS Matrix was on a mission to hijack the toys from techno cowboys and remap cyberculture with a feminist bent."

For them, the web was a space for creative experimentation, a place to transform and create in collaboration with the global community of like minded artists. They were able to tell their mission through interactive code and games, like the one behind me, All New Gen. So in this game, you became a node in the matrix and your goal was to sabotage a villain called Big Daddy Mainframe in order to achieve Data Liberation. All battles would take place in the Contested Zone, which was a terrain of propaganda, subversion and transgression. As the protagonists, you were fueled by G Slime and which helps you question your gendered construction while fighting against an antagonist like Circuit Boy, which they describe as a dangerous Techno Bimbo. In 1997, the Old Boys Network was formed in Berlin (this was a group of women who satirically picked the name Old Boys Network.) During the first cyberfeminist alliance, they created a manifesto of *100 Anti-Theses* that described what cyberfeminism was not. For example, "Cyberfeminism is not a fragrance or a fashion statement. It's not a separation." Note the multiple languages. They also produced a number of catalogs from these meetings. On the left, you can see the cover of the first Cyber Feminist International from '97. And on the right is a mapping of the 100 antitheses based on what was positive or negative by Cornelia Solfrank.

This brings me to a more modern website. This past summer in Toronto, I led a workshop with Jürg Lehni and Jon Gacnik, called LAN or Local Area Network. This was for A-B-Z TXT, a computational typography summer school. LAN typically refers to a computer network that interconnects computers within a limited area, such as this college campus, but we want to question the intimacy that could be involved in a local area network beyond the technicalities. What is something that you can make that was intended for a small group of people, the local community of this school? It resulted in this online publication. Each participant made a page in the publication and defined it with a phrase that collectively might read as a manifesto or a guide. A few of them were *A website that keeps you warm, A manual to close down the streets, A tutorial for creating a dark aesthetic, A text that shows the value of collective unified thoughts, A reading experience for slow life*, and *A page that reconsiders local area network through neighborhood civic infrastructures*. This might look like any typical browser, but it's actually using Beaker, which was released in 2017 and allows people to surf the peer-to-peer web. You'll notice in your address bar, instead of HTTP, it reads dat, since it's using the dat protocol. With Beaker, you can build and host static websites from your computer without the need to upload your files to a server. So in this sense, your computer is your server. You and your other peers then can become your data center. It also distributes the cost of bandwidth across multiple users and rehosts your content.

An example here was *A text that strengthens from collective readership* by a participant Brian Huddleston. In the top right of the address bar, you can see a 1. This shows you the number of peers visiting or seeding the site. As more peers see the site, the number increases, so keep your eye on that corner. His concept was having this guide for a local area network, so the more peers that are seeding the site, the more legible the text becomes.

This was *A set of directions that takes you on a blind date* by Steph Schapowal. When you come to the page, it gives you a set of instructions that are quite nondescript, but encourages you to browse the area around Interaccess, the gallery in which A-B-Z TXT took place. And if you were to print this website as a map, it would then reveal the images that these directions led to.

Another example is *A map that connects connected peers* by another participant Sam Panter. He describes this as, "A map as a kind of dream, a connection from our minds to the physical that distorts, skews and exaggerates. The mind travels, but the body doesn't. It's an interface, an abstraction with utility. Where will this one take you?" It also maps the different peers that are currently seeding the site.

And finally, I wanted to share another participant example by Mubashir Baweja, *An acknowledgment of the context in which the internet operates and this space exists*. It was largely informed by land acknowledgement statements, which notes the labor and unceded land of the indigenous populations who came before us.In this case, he wanted to make that acknowledgement for internet infrastructures, and I'll let you read it.

I wanted to close by reading the Open Proposal from the Networker Telenetlink from 1995, about the Eternal Network and the Mail Art Congress:

The Mail Art Congress body left in 1992. A spirit

networks now, that spirit lives in everyone. We met a network infant. A media child was born. Telenetlink is its name, it lives in Netlands now. The future of the networker is telenetlinked. Mail art is email art, fax mail art. Embrace the child Telenet link in 1995 and beyond.

Mindy Seu is a designer and Assistant Professor at Rutgers University.

MINDY SEU
Fellow, Berkman Klein Center
for the Internet and Society

WHOLE EARTH CATALOG

The New Woman's Survival Catalog

art
abortion
child care
health care
books
films
theatre
work
products
marriage
&
divorce
self-defense

A Woman-made Book

A mail artist is often a disappointed artist. Not disappointed in art, but in the art-industry of the leading galleries and museums. Being a member of a planetary art movement helps [them] to transcend this isolation and alienation in art.

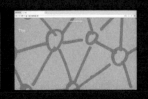

DIGITAL MATERIALITY: A CONVERSATION

Anil Dash, Jacob Heftmann, Tiff Hockin, Laurel Schwulst, and Allan Yu

Moderated by Carly Ayres

CD Symposium Panel, Digital Materiality in the Age of Design Systems

Wolff Conference Room, Room D1103
Albert and Vera List Academic Center
6 East 16th Street

2018-05-15

Over the last twenty years, design education has had an evolving but uneasy relationship with code. Graphic and communication design programs in the late 1990s were already struggling with the idea that designers would use computers to design, so the idea that students could be taught to code—or should be taught to code—was deferred indefinitely. In the meantime, dozens of adjacent programs in new media and creative technologies sprung up to fill the gap, with many designers and artists finding their first experiences with code in those programs, while other designers elected to learn on their own, or not at all.

Twenty years later, it's still an open question how, or whether, the surging number of students studying graphic and communication design should learn to code. Despite the increasing "program or be programmed" urgency in contemporary culture, there are new challenges. Computer interfaces are increasingly opaque, dampening both understanding and curiosity. Students pressured into narrow definitions of "career" struggle to find relevance in learning methods, techniques, and theory that don't fit neatly into specific job titles, and even the embrace of "digital design" has taken a turn towards prototyping rather than designing digital experiences. As a result, there have been many innovations in teaching code in K-12 environments, or to artists, but learning to code is still seen as alien to the design context, even if it is nothing new.

In this symposium, we brought together designers, programmers, and educators to unpack their approaches and philosophies towards code and pedagogy in design.

Carly Ayres

When I was asked to moderate this panel, I definitely had a moment of, "What the fuck is this about?" What is digital materiality And what is the value of it today? I really loved, Anil, what you had to say around the fact that we don't know who makes the tools that we use or who designs the tools that we use. I have no idea who designs most of the things I interact with on a daily basis and I think aside from the sad little bit of lost history there, there's an interesting dialogue to be had around accountability. When you don't know who makes the things that you use, who do you hold accountable when shit really goes wrong?

Anil Dash

I think there's a lot of negative externalities from the lack of accountability, from not having names. I think the first part is you can dodge being held responsible for...you make Uber and you're like, "We're going to mistreat our people and we're going to destroy communities and we're going to upend entire labor markets. And then we're going to sneak out the back door and get rich." That happens because there's no name on it.

We see this with agencies so much. If you do really great creative work and the client can claim credit or no one can claim credit, you don't have this thing to trade on. And so, they've not just extracted value out of you in the moment, but over the rest of your career. So there's just a huge power imbalance. This week was the first time we had Google workers walking out because they're enabling surveillance technologies for the government to do things they don't agree with, and it's like, why did it take 20 years for somebody to be like, "I think Google's gone too far"? It's

because they can't take credit for what they do, so they can't go to their next employer and be like, "I made this thing at Google."

CA

How complicit do you see designers being in those systems? What's your responsibility in operating within these systems and executing within them?

Allan Yu

That is a complicated question. Yeah, there's a responsibility there, but there's also livelihood. You want a job but you do the thing and it seems like you're not damaging anything, but you are. I don't know. I don't have an answer to this. We're responsible, but I guess there's no real support group to create that backlash. What am I going to do? I'm now going to make this button.

Tiff Hockin

Well, advertising in particular is just the worst. Everyone in the building knows that it's really bad. We still have to see ads for stuff on the web that you may or may be interested in or that you shouldn't be seeing that on a website. It's easy to forget who's actually on the other end of these products. We think that people want to know what we're doing or Bloomberg's thinking about what we're reading, but they are.

CA

What questions should designers be asking themselves in those situations? You had a few great ones up on screen. What questions should designers be asking themselves?

Jacob Heftmann

I hope that I can answer this, albeit indirectly. But I guess the funny thing about growing up is it's easy to be like, "Yeah, but those guys..." You're young and then you end up under-

132

standing why these systems exist. I don't get to think about design in a super intellectual way because I run a business. So I don't expect designers to...I hope they ask these questions, but I also understand that they're limited in what they can actually do. So I would hope that they're asking them, but sometimes they just aren't possible.

AD

I think one of the questions I think about asking our designers a lot, or when I'm making decisions about design: is what if this works? I think we're so obsessed with what if this fails and we don't anticipate what if this works. I go to the news example, because that's the world I've spent a lot of time in, and the Taboola and Outbrain, these are the related links at the bottom of the site and they will put them under a story and they will say things that are false. Sometimes they'll say, "This celebrity is dead," and then you read it and it's like, "Well, we don't mean dead. We just mean their career is in bad shape." You've all seen that, right? Everybody knows what I'm talking about. So which people in a news organization are allowed to put false things on a news page? That's an interesting question. And what we've decided is the ad team is. That comes down to it's probably an individual director level person that's like, "I got to make my quarterly numbers for ads." And the CEO doesn't know what Taboola is. So somewhere in between is a decision maker. It's probably like a VP and they're probably making a lot of money and they're probably not being called out. And this is not just you, we're all in that position. We've all been in that position. So how do you get the power to call out that VP and say, "This person can't do their job well enough to make their numbers

without putting lies on the newspaper. On the page." And that's by organizing. That's it collectively. How do you empower your designers and your team to be able to push back on the client if they can't go get the button somewhere else?

TH

I agree. One of the things I've been thinking about a lot is asking questions but also in the spirit of rallying and complaining. Because you can raise the issue but at the end of the day the designer's job is to solve the problem and I think it's really hard to stand and complain when the recipients of those complaints are going to turn around and be like, "Okay, cool. Well that's your job." So how do we fix it? And also, that's like a $50 million revenue gap that we now have to fill. So can you design a $300 million button? But I think for me, the way I think about it is how do we change the vision internally so that Taboola doesn't feel like a viable option? That makes sense in a world where it's all about click-through rates and impressions.

CA

Totally. I think that also speaks to what we were talking about, or two of you hit upon earlier, around creating experiences that are sustainable and emotional. How do you approach designing something that is sustainable and emotional? What does that conversation look like? I'm looking at Laurel. Something I love about your work in particular is I feel like you're being as a person, and having met you outside of this context, you are just so incredibly thoughtful in so many of the things you do. And the way you approach even answering this question, you're thinking about it in a way where the people who know me know that I just talk continuously. And I think it's almost, perhaps, your internal ethics or how you live your life. That becomes part of that process.

Laurel Schwulst
Yeah, totally. I mean, maybe I could talk from a very personal point of view. I got rid of social media a year ago and I recently got back on. But I don't really know what I'm doing exactly, but I recently read this poem called *Diving Into The Wreck* by Adrienne Rich. It was written in 1973. It's all about how to understand the wreck, we have to become one with it. So I guess I've just been thinking about that a lot. And then one other thing, the cool thing about the Creative Independent is that I've been able to interview a lot of artists. I interviewed this video artist, Sara Magenheimer, and she has this manifesto PDF that's instructions for artists when they wake up in the morning and they feel crazy and one of them was, "Allow contradiction and permit multiples," because that's confusing to corporations and stuff like that. I don't know, I feel like those are principles I've been trying to think through but I don't know how that's exactly applying to my design yet, but I think it's all permeating.

CA
Speaking of process, which is kind of a dirty word in some circles but in general is a good set of guiding principles for making things in some context. Allan, you spoke about how not having a process kept you from being able to work collaboratively on a team. But then being able to create a process allowed you to give other people on your team agency.

AY
Yeah.

CA
How did you figure that out? How did you create that process that enables that?

AY
We set up experiments. We were doing things that weren't business oriented so we set out days to work on our version of a thing, regardless of whether those met any metrics. Just to exercise that muscle. And I think that's what designers are excited about. Just so that when we talk about it, we were able to glean out what units that were relevant or that we can incorporate and those units come from a better place. They don't come from a place of solving a problem, but rather like, "Ah, that's a dope thing to do because I haven't seen done." And taking those applications that didn't have a meaning, and applying that meaning later on. We're just having an ice box of those little moments.

CA
How do you enable a member of your team to have that agency that they bring to the table; to bring their own voice, bring their own perspectives? How do you enable someone to bring problems to you in a way that you can then work together to find a solution?

AY
Be a better communicator? I just talk. There's very little power dynamic between me and anyone. It's very much like, "What do you want to do? Oh, we should do this." Or like, "They told me to do this and we have to get these things done. So we gotta get that done, but what else do you want to do?" Just having an open dialogue or just having room for that, I think. There's no, "I report to this dude." There's none of that stuff. It's very casual to me.

CA

Yeah. I'd say you and Laurel, perhaps, the most out of these panelists, work very independently, and oftentimes you are being injected into an existing system. I suppose, Jacob, with the studio, is probably somewhat similar to that but you're coming in and you're trying to operate within the context of a system that existed before you got there, for the most part, or you're establishing it for the first time. Do you have any tools or processes you use in those experiences?

AY

I have some there. For going into a process that already exists. Don't change anything. Just figure out what they're doing and then just go with the flow. And then you can start seeing why there's friction points with this, but they may not be about you. That's fine. And then you're there for a bit and then maybe you're gone later. You don't have to make any changes.

If they don't have a process, you should figure out how the team wants to work and what the goals are, and then try to prioritize. Then through prioritization of the goals and what the team members want reveal a process organically.

LS

I feel like one of my favorite parts of the design process is the research or absorbing phase where you're just fitting in and being a sponge. Because so much of design—design is such a huge word—is invisible. Every formal thing you see on online is just a ripple of the underneath structure. I guess I've mentored just a few people, but I feel like the best thing is, as long as you trust them and not micromanage.

CA

What does that look like as a studio, Jacob?

JH

I kind of started off with this anti-establishment approach. We work for these big tech companies, which is a bit weird, and I get that. I worked in agencies and worked with really big companies. I'm terrible at managing and I didn't like it. It wasn't a good fit for me, so that's part of why I wanted to work on my own. And so, even as a studio working with those companies, we work very, very independently. We like working at our own scale. We're a lot better matched to work with small teams.

CA

Big is bad feels, perhaps, like a large sweeping statement. I think I came in here today thinking that we would spend a lot of time talking about how we can retain our own agency. I was pleasantly surprised to see you in particular speak about how you operate within these systems and how systems do give you guidelines. And I think Allan touched upon this as well, and Tiff, around systems enable you to scale in a very real way. I think scalability is something that perhaps not everyone is seeking, but in some contexts there's a lot of value there. In terms of the work you did for Dropbox or Google, did you have to choose between the interests of a company, or the interests of a user, as well as your own agency at all?

JH

Yeah. I mean, I'm sure that we didn't do everything we could've, or didn't do everything right. In a perfect world we'd do things better. I mean, I don't know. I guess I have mixed feelings about working with big corporations. Whatever I did to reconcile that, maybe there is a real difference, maybe that was just me feeling like that.

CA

In starting our own studio, I have to say, I remember the feeling of, "Oh my gosh, we're going to do something. It's going to be so different. We're not going to do anything like any of those places we worked before." I had previously worked in Google's Creative Lab and I was like, "Ah yeah, we're going to start a studio where everything is different." And then bit by bit you start to realize why people do the things the way they do things and then your hopes and dreams get utterly shattered. How do you hold on to your hopes and dreams?

AD

We've been building this product, Glitch, and we start every one of our planning meetings by asking about the team's hopes and dreams. That's actually literally true. So that's sort of an interesting thing. Part of it is we're in tech, so it's heavily straight, white male dominated. And by having a lengthy conversation about everybody's feelings at the beginning of the meeting, it just sort of resets everything. I think everything we do in terms of design is really starting from getting everybody to a place of feeling comfortable being vulnerable.

I've worked with big companies and everybody goes through that. Where are we drawing the line between we got to pay the bills and we're selling out? That's this never ending question. Breaking out of that for me, not that I have, but the attempt to break out of that, has been recognizing that they're terrified of us. Google, more than they even want to be good, they don't want to be getting caught not being good. That's the thing they're terrified of. If somebody's going to say to them,

"You did the bad thing," that's the end of the world for them. They can't conceive of not having money, but they can conceive of not being seen as good. And those things are linked. So that thing of how much power the people in this room have to say, "That giant company, you screwed up..." There are starting to be a few that just don't care, like Uber for its first six or seven years. Now even they're trying to get back into like, "You don't hate us, right?" It's like, "Too late." Just delete Uber. My gosh, I can't even believe people still use it. But Google is complicated. They're a good example. I used their stuff. It's great. It's handy. And then there's stuff you're like, "Whoa, what are you doing?" And so, how do you get them to see their angels when they stop saying, "Don't be evil anymore?" The thing is, there are good people there. So how do you encourage them and support them and promote their stuff? That's where, I think, design has this important role. Be the amplifier and shout from the rooftops.

I have a lot of agency. I'm lucky, because I'm the CEO at a company that's got owners who are indulgent. But that's not normal. It could be. There's no reason products can't come from companies that are still run by people.

Anyway. I'm off topic. But the point is, you can make spaces where you can have a little bit of agency, but the trade-off is to stay small. It's like, "I don't want to be the biggest agency in the history of the world, or I don't want to run a multi-billion dollar giant company. I want to have control over a space and then I can have agency." That's actually a doable thing. And so, if you're merely optimizing for being wealthy enough to live in one of the most expensive cities in the history of the world yet not be a billionaire, okay good. We're all here. We're not hurting. We're good. And then if you can just temper your ambition by like 2%, which I think we're all inclined to do, and then encourage the people at those companies to do the same where somebody at Google's like, "Look, you're going to be fine. Just don't build the system that's enabling killer drones," and then they're like, "Oh okay," then it's not the end of the world. It's not this binary thing.

I think that's the thing about recognizing the decision makers who are like, "We need to get that other 2% and put false news onto the..." I've been this guy. I'm working through my own therapy here. I've been the person who's like, "You have to put garbage on the site with the news and undermine trust in the story in order to make the revenue numbers." Well, how about we don't make the revenue numbers? Let's not do it. That's the moment. And then you can put that fear of God into them. Because they're like, "Well, I'll get fired as VP of sales." I'm like, "Good. You're bad at your job. You can't make your job without putting lies on the news site? Then you're bad at your job." And if you can't make your search and email company work without making killer drones, you're bad at your job. And then they're like, "Oh shit." That's fun. That to me is the pinnacle of design.

TH
I think I've had to shift what my hopes and dreams are a little bit, and it's okay. I can always go back and work for myself and I can always work at a small place. I know I'm going to be fine without putting on the suit and speaking the other people's language. How can you fix design in a way of

seeing the people who are on the line to put the ads.

I think that one of the things I've come to realize is when you're operating by yourself or you're at a small place, you define your goal and you define your process and what it means to go from point A to point B and what the research phase looks like and what you do in the research phase. When you work on a bigger company, my role is in some ways defined by the context that I'm in and the way other people see what I do.

CA
What do you hope for in design?

LS
I went to a two hour silent film about plants over the weekend. There was an amazing Q&A with the film director at the end, and I guess the reason I'm bringing this up is because I've been thinking about it a lot. He started making experimental films in the '60s and he said, "Oh, when I was doing that in the '60s and I was reacting by having an unstable shot and things like that. But now what I am reacting against is thay actually the whole world is avant garde. Banks are avant garde. I'm literally just putting some humanity into images." And I feel like that's what I want for design. I asked a question at the end and I was like, "Do you see your film being used for therapeutic purposes?" The designer in me wants to install it in my house or in a hospital. He said something funny about needing a silent film at the right speed or something. I feel like I just want to see the humanity in things, and yeah, be able to *view source* to see authorship. I want to be able to trace back.

AY
Oh geez. I don't know. I don't know what I want to see. Oh God. Maybe

ask more questions? I don't know what I want to see from people, from kids, because I think the situations are different. What do I want to see from products? I want to see more...I don't know. I guess I want more individualized products. I don't have an answer to this question. I'm so sorry. I'm so stumped. I don't know. How do I even answer that question?

AD

I'm hoping for more fearlessness and advocacy and stronger points of view. It's a moment where the urgency couldn't be higher. All the excuses are valid. I don't diminish... All of us have been there when you have to compromise. Excuses will all just be valid. So what? And I think there's this sense of how we support each other being braver and being more vulnerable. That is a really tall order, but that's it.

I just keep coming back to pretending I'm not afraid all the time. Courage is contagious. If you say this thing and everybody else that agrees with you stands up and you're not alone anymore, but somebody's always waiting for somebody else to be first. And I think that's true for everything we design, every product we create. The products are just the artifact of the process. The process is: did you make a space where everybody can talk about the elephant in the room whatever that is.

I'm at a different stage in my career. I think about people at the beginning of their career. You can't do that, I understand that. But it's not always the person with the most positional authority or the place in the org chart. It's almost never them. They have the most to lose, so they're not going to be the one that's brave. They're like, "I'm good." And so, I think more than anything else, those

moments where everybody in the room is real quiet because they all see what you should be doing and nobody's doing it, that's an opportunity. And it doesn't take much. It just takes the slightest nudge. People want to do the right thing. They want to be pushed into doing the right thing. They want to be led, they want to be guided, or they want us to go to...not even led, by all of us doing it together. They want that. I see that all the time. And it's just, do they clear their throats and be like, "Did we think about this?" And you don't have to be confident in it and you don't have to be like, "I know the answer." That's my temperament and that's a rhetorical thing I find useful to do. But you could be tentative. And don't apologize, but you can be whatever voice you have and say that idea. I think that's the thing I'm most hopeful for.

AY

I want to see more beef. I want to see companies calling each other out, like rappers call each other out and just say it and stop being so cordial to each other. It'll be sick if Google Drive goes, "Dropbox sucks," and say it publicly. People say that all the time anyways, right?

TH

I'm going to stick with questions, asking good questions. And I think what you said of being an agitator in the room, that really resonates with me, because I feel like I am always saying the thing that I regret five seconds later. But the point is to change the conversation. People can recognize a good idea or an interesting thought and if you speak to someone in the right way, then hopefully it inspires them to continue to radiate and grow.

JH

I came to teaching through not design per se, but more coding actually. Because I thought it was so amazing that you could self publish. That's so powerful and you can put something online yourself. I thought that was such an amazing idea.

CA

Well, that's all I have for you all today. Thank you so much, Brendan and E Roon, for inviting us, all our wonderful panelists. Please give them a round of applause. Oh my gosh. You're beautiful. As well as our student presenters who I believe we still have a few of those. They are the future.

Anil Dash is CEO of Glitch. Jacob Heftmann is principal of XXIX. Tiff Hockin is design director at McKinsey & Company. Laurel Schwulst is an independent artist, educator, and writer. Allan Yu is a product designer at Shopify. Carly Ayres is a UX Content Strategist at Google.

ON DESIGN AND POWER

Chris Lee

CD Lecture Series

The Bob and Sheila Hoerle Lecture Hall, UL105
University Center
63 Fifth Avenue

2019-11-22

Thanks for the introduction and the invitation. I'm very happy to be here and feel privileged to be able to share my work because being able to talk about my work and show my work to people also helps me think about it. I also have this problem where my name is not good for Google, you can't find me, so I've given up on the internet.

What I'd like to do today is show you some projects, because lately, in the past few years, when I've given talks, they're more about research projects, and tend to be kind of lofty and theoretical, because I'm trying to figure things out, as I talk to people, and they get rambly. I might also ramble today. But I want to ground what I'm going to talk to you about through some projects that I've done in the past few years. I'm going to talk about the projects that fall under three broad categories. And I'll just list them here, you can see them in my very sophisticated presentation format. One of these categories is "Currency." Another category is work that thinks through what I sometimes refer to as the Asian diaspora or Asian diasporic politics or race politics. And then another theme relates to this talk because I was led to understand that this series of talks is about different kinds of modes of practice and introducing students to a variety of ways in which graphic design is practiced beyond the conventional, commercial client oriented types of practices. So this category is titled, "Designing as Reading." It's one way that I think about what I do as a designer. And just to say something briefly about that, a lot of the client-oriented work that I've done in the past has been in the cultural sector and for academia. As a design student, when I was an undergraduate student, we didn't do a lot of reading. It was almost like a trade school, with a very modernist corporate client-oriented pedagogy.

But when I got out of school, I guess I had some editorial design chops, so the people that tended to call me up for work were people who write things and write very interesting things. And through doing work for art spaces and academia, I started reading a lot and I was like, holy shit, there's this whole world of ideas out there that I didn't know existed.

There's some people who are here who look like they're professional practitioners, and maybe you've done editorial work. But at a certain point, you realize, Oh, you can't read everything, because it takes too long to read *and* design. But in my earlier, more naive moments, I did read and I handed in projects late. So those are going to be the three main categories of projects I'm going to talk to you about. Also, the way that I tend to do these talks is I invite questions. I know they're supposed to be questions at the end. But if something jumps out at you, or is burning your mind, please throw your hands up and we can have a conversation.

So this theme of currency is something that I started working on as a graduate student when I studied at the Sandberg Institute, which is a small design master's program in Amsterdam that's associated with the Rietveld Academie. The Sandberg Institute was a graphic design program that I was in and can be characterized as more politically oriented. The concerns of the faculty and the students were questions about how to articulate or manifest the relationship between design and politics. It was a two year program, and I, to be frank, struggled there for a really long time to figure out what I was doing. I knew that was something I was interested in, but I didn't really know what that meant.

Then about a year and a half into a two year program, I was like, oh, there's this thing called money, that's very interesting, and it's interesting because I don't have any of it. But I'm a graphic designer, and money is designed, so why can't I design money? This, on the surface, is a very basic question, but one that I've continued to find being very generative, "why can't I design money." So some of the projects that I have been able to do for my cultural sector clients and collaborators inject this interest in currency and money into some of the work.

This was a tote bag that I designed for a typography summer school in Toronto called ABZ-TXT. We printed these in an edition of 50, and then one of the 50 we put it up for sale on eBay. And over the course of the workshop, which was a week, people were allowed to bid on this one tote bag. When the bidding closed, it closed at like $10.50, we took that value, that dollar value and inscribed it onto the tote bags. So each tote bag would from that point on represent, or be convertible to US dollars, at a rate of one tote bag to $10.50. That was the conversion rate. The conceit of this project is that this tote bag functions as both a tote bag but also as a currency, right? The face value of it is established by how much it was sold for on eBay. It's this way to think about these dubious premises, I mean, it's not really $10.50 and you can't really spend it anywhere for that value. But that inability to do so is the provocation that I wanted to make with this, like why can't we say that this is money when it has a lot of things that money has?

This is another publication project that I did for a space called Art Metropole. You guys know Printed

Matter, right? The founders of Printed Matter actually started this place called Art Metropole a few years before that. It's still around and it's in Toronto. In 2012, the director of the space, Corinn Gerber, invited me to design their catalog. And my proposed response to that was to suggest, "why don't we make the catalog a prospectus or an advertisement for creating a new kind of currency?" She had approached me because she knew I had this interest in currency, and they had a curatorial thematic going on that year about alternative economies. So we had this dialogue about how we can make the catalog, a very banal object, be a vehicle for thinking about the curatorial theme throughout the year.

My response, again, was to design the catalog as a prospectus for an alternative currency. So the idea here is that one would order books or whatever that the shop carried and instead of having it shipped, or delivered to them, you could have the books banked at the shop. So let's say I ordered $10 worth of books. Instead of having them delivered to me, I could have them kept in the shop, and then the shop would issue me a serial number. I would then write on the back of this part here, which you could cut out, "$10." So it has a serial number, and a face value. And then the conceit, again, is that I could take this book money that's backed by books, to a local shop, one of their neighbors, or some cafe and say, "Hey, I have $10 worth of books at the shop down the street, can I buy lunch with this?" And if they say, yes, they take my money. Then if they want to cash that in for $10, or for the books, they could go down the street and do that. So the idea was to try to set up a system, to make this thing work, again, going

back to the question of why can't I make money? Of course, nobody actually did this. So it lives mostly as a thought experiment. I think it's too risky and that these questions of money, maybe are too burdensome or not compelling enough. But it's a way for me to think about these things.

Here's one more similar project. There was an exhibition curated by Denise Ryner called *Interim Measures* and she asked me to design the exhibition flyer for the exhibition. My counter proposal was to turn the exhibition flyer into a currency. I designed three different faces for a flyer, but it was actually like a large tabloid sized newsprint thing, because I wanted to print thousands of each of these designs. I just wanted to have volume, but like a lot of volume. We did this on a web press in newsprint, so it was very affordable. So these posters, or flyers, function both as publicity for the exhibition but again, could exist as currency. Money is printed, flyers are printed, there's a material production correlation there. In this case, I projected onto it a fictional scenario where there's this political entity called the greater Midwestern Co-rosperity Sphere that issues this currency. The Greater Midwestern Co-rosperity Sphere is a political entity that spans both Canada and the United States, so the conversion rate to be able to obtain one of these currencies is one US dollar and one Canadian dollar. It exists, again, more as a conceptual exercise. The gallery would then convert this newspaper money back to one USD, one CAD. Here's an installation shot of that, the blue and yellow ones people could just take but the red ones were special, because it was the one that you could convert, so that had to be kept securely. It was kept in the back of the gallery and it wasn't visible. So in spite of the fact that nobody actually really did this, again, it's was the fact that we had to *not* distribute something in order to make it valuable, that was an interesting component of it for me.

Since these ways to think about money through actually making money, or trying to make money, I've also done some more scholarly (or quasi-scholarly) work around this. This is a program booklet for a conference that I co-organized in Buffalo, New York called Money Lab. Money Lab is actually a conference that's organized by the Institute of Network Cultures in Amsterdam. We organized the first North American iteration of it last year. There's nothing conceptually profound about this design, but the design came from something that I had researched while I was doing a research fellowship in the Netherlands. In 2017, I heard a story about how the first Dutch paper money used typography that was created for musical notation to create more secure security patterns and decorative elements. The reason they did this was because this typeface for music, which was only the second, if I understand correctly, typeface designed or ever cut for musical notation at that point in history. It was a commercial failure at that time, because composers in the mid 1700s thought that it was not amenable to the way that they created music. Typography implies this hard standardization—there's a certain limited set of glyphs and characters. So composers at that time were frustrated because there were marks that they wanted to make in their musical notation, but were not available in the typography. Long story short, again, this typeface was a commercial failure, it was sitting on

the shelves of this printer in Haarlem, in the original Haarlem in the Netherlands, for 100 years, and so this printer, when they were approached by the Dutch National Bank to design and print the money, they were like, "Oh, we have just the thing. There's this typeface that nobody has. And so if you use it, you can be very sure that your bills will be secure, because nobody can copy it, they don't have this typeface."

Anyways, this conference was a franchise of a Dutch conference, in Buffalo, which actually, when it was first founded, was the private property of a company called the Holland Land Company and was called New Amsterdam. These graphic typographic references narrates the relationship between Dutch capital and American colonialism, so this was one of the themes in the conference.

That is all to say that another way that I think about my work is as a way to narrate my research. Like these forms. You wouldn't know that without me telling you, but well, luckily, I'm here. I think about design or graphic design as a way to make signals in history, as a way to remember things.

Briefly, this is a giant board game that I co-designed with one of my classmates from graduate school, Femke Herregraven. This is one moment where I think both of us were starting to think more about how designed artifacts have a systemic dimension, right? It's not just the design artifact, but you also have to look at the system within which these design artifacts circulate. Making a game gave us a way to make sense of how that relationship works between the discrete design artifact and the system within which it circulates. A lot of games rely on point based systems. This was actually an adaptation of *Settlers of Catan*, so there's a point based system, there's things that function as currency. Again, it was a way to think about that through making something.

These are just some images from a landscape architecture journal that I used to design and co-edit. This is one issue that I co-edited on the theme of currency, obviously. One of the formal conceptual moves for the front and back cover was to list the cover price in as many currencies as would fit here. It was 20 Canadian dollars, so it had all these national currencies and also local currencies. Then if you look down here at that time, it was only 400 Bitcoin, which means that I'm a sucker for not jumping on Bitcoin.

But yeah, there's all these. It was a way to not only do this practical thing of listing the cover price, but also it's speak to this idea that there are multiple forms of currency in circulation. I won't go into the details of that. I think it's sufficiently surprising, or at least to me, when I started researching, to learn that there are forms of money beyond national currencies. For example, this image comes from a Spanish artist named Emilio Moreno, who was doing research about the Spanish Civil War. During the Spanish Civil War, there was the fascist side and the Republican side. Republican means something different in this context—the more democratic, socialist, anarchist, communist side. Within the Republican side, there were nearly 7,000 currencies in circulation. So this is a historical precedent for how a demos, a democratic social body would create their own money to be able to facilitate and lubricate their economy.

I put this one in because I wanted to point out that this is a book review for a book called *The Art of Not Being Governed: An Anarchist History of Upland Southeast Asia* by James C. Scott, which I read in grad school. I just wanted to point this out because this is something that's been very influential to me in my own work.

So another thread of work that I've done follows questions and tensions and controversies around race, particularly around the status or the position in what can be called the racial hierarchy in the West of East Asian presenting people. So these are just some graphics that I did for an East Asian North American Art Gallery called Gendai. This is a flyer/envelope. A lot of this work is being done in extremely low budget contexts, so this gallery didn't have money to print flyers for their exhibitions. The solution to that was to just have rubber stamps designed every time they did an exhibition. It's not super cheap, but it's way cheaper than printing flyers and posters. Every time they did an exhibition, we designed the stamp and stamped these envelopes, the envelopes became a flyer, and there would be some 8.5 by 11 thing printed inside it. The gallery was in a "rough" neighborhood, and it got tagged all the time. The first tag that it got was this one here, I think it says "wild core" or something. But we said, "We can't afford to clean it up. Let's just make that the logo of the gallery." So we made a stamp out of that tag, and stamped all of the materials with that.

The identity uses the Roman character set of a Japanese typeface, and so the way that I used it, was a way for me to think through, what I think of as ethnic typography. When you're scrolling through your font menu in Adobe, or InDesign or whatever, you can go through the glyphs set. There's a lot of Chinese, Japanese, and Korean typefaces that have all these extra characters that are not commonly used in Latin orthography. So I made it a point to overuse these things in ways that are unusual, to inflect the typography and the type setting with an accent in some sense. That became what characterized the identity.

These are two flyers that were done for artists commissioned projects that I curated for a project called *Model Minority*. And I'll come back to that in a second. So I've been involved with this space, first as a designer, then in programming and curating. But this year, we're all retiring from the project, so this is a flyer requesting people to take over an art institution. What I'm starting to do, as part of that, is to create an archive of what Gendai has done for the past 20 years. I'm designing these long scrolls that will carry the archival memory of this institution and it can be used as a presentation. It doesn't have the same kind of linearity that a PowerPoint slide has, you can maybe tell that I'm adverse to linear slide presentations by how I'm presenting my work today.

This is a project that I spent two and a half years on, that I co-curated, and then eventually designed a publication for, it's a project called *Model Minority*. I don't know if you know anything about arts funding in Canada, but it's very good. It's a quasi-socialist country, so there's a lot of public funding for art. But our institution was very poorly funded and we were in an existential crisis. And we were like, maybe we should just stop.

Part of the reasoning or thinking behind that was like, maybe we shouldn't be helping the Canadian state because we're also coming from a position where we're critical of the Canadian state as a settler state, as a colonial state. So why should we make Canada look good by making it diverse, reinforcing this narrative of multiculturalism? We are quite critical of multiculturalism, at least in the way that it's been used in Canada, because in Canada, it's used as a way to say, "Hey, we're doing good here. We're inclusive or diverse, multicultural." But what's never part of that narrative is that this multiculturalism is premised on the erasure and colonization of Indigenous lands, cultures, and people. For example, this space, right? I mean, how many of us know or are very familiar with the fact that this is Lenape land? Or Canarsie land? We have these histories, these knowledges that have been brutally erased. So we were thinking, "why should we continue supporting a cultural policy that plays a role in colonization."

So we took on, ironically, this notion of the model minority, the "good" minority, and tried to subvert that by including, in this publication, examples of East Asian identifying people in North America that were involved in radical political activism. This image, for example, is of an activist who was based in Harlem for a long time, named Yuri Kochiyama. She was involved very closely with the Puerto Rican independence struggle, but also with the Black Power struggle. If you've seen photos of Malcom X's assassination, she's the person cradling his head as he's bleeding to death. This is a very undertold, underrepresented story, and that there are still people out there like her. Part of this project was also a screening series, so we did interviews with filmmakers, and had articles from a lot of people from New York City, who are involved historically with Asian American political activism, particularly activism that intersects with Latinx and Black struggles. Because what we're really trying to do here is to conduct a critical self examination of the East Asian diaspora in North America. The model minority is a racist concept that says "there's a good minority, and all these other minorities, their grievances are invalid, because look, the Japanese Americans, in spite of the fact that we put them in prison and expropriated all their property, they bounced back, they got education, they make more money than white people." This is very problematic because it again invalidates the legitimate grievances of Native American struggles, and Black and Brown struggles, as well as Asian people themselves. So we really wanted to look at where this idea came from, and it actually has a very precise origin. The term "model minority" comes from the *New York Times* and from *Newsweek* magazine, who were writing these articles in the mid 80s about how well Asians were doing.

So this book has art projects that we commissioned, historical documents and interviews. Like I mentioned before, again, this was under the rubric of Gendai Gallery We didn't have a space, we didn't have anywhere to exhibit work. So the publication became our exhibition space, and not just our exhibition space, but a space that allows us to propel this work beyond the finite limits of an exhibition that might run for two months. Hopefully, we'll be around for much longer than that, and can continue to challenge the notion of the model minority continuously.

This is a poster that I did for a space here called Interference Archive, which is in Park Slope. It's a repository of political graphics from all over the world and around history. One of the protagonists of that space, Josh MacPhee, has a poster series called Celebrate People's History, and he asked me to design a poster about something. What I chose to do was to make a poster that tells a brief story about this group called Futeisha. Futeisha was a Japanese and Korean anti-imperialist anarchist group that was operational in the early 1920s during the period of Japanese imperialism and occupation of Korea. What I really love about this story is that there was solidarity between Japanese citizens and Korean subjects in Japan. This is a story that I know my parents never told me and I didn't get in school. For me, it's very inspiring to be able to do this kind of research and be able to share this story.

This is a publication that I designed for an artist named Jacqueline Hoàng Nguyễn. This project began when we commissioned her to do a research project for the *Model Minority* publication and developed into this. What she was looking at were alternative archives of immigration, so this book collects essays that have to do with her work and our research. This is one that I got to read actually. But I want to say something about the graphical approach here. This could be a very straightforward task to design a book. But I tried to do it in a way that allows me to think through and articulate some of my research concerns or my political questions and interests. So here, I'm trying to think through form and in a very, well, formal sense. Since her work is premised on researching state archives, when I'm thinking about archives, I think about databases, I think about spread-sheets, very rational, pragmatic grids. So what I wanted to do in this book was to counterpose the image of the state archive with another formal language that's more irregular, less rational, less accountable, maybe "ugly," maybe "illegible." Again, this could have been a very straight-forward book, but I actually made it a point to be really deliberate about not setting things super straight, having irrational patterning on the page. This may be pretentious (to say), but I think of it as poetic, there's an ineffable quality to it that I can't verbalize. But I was thinking in terms of typographic convention, like what is justification? What is left justification? Why do we tend to have only three options? How can this manifest a different way of thinking about the three standard options, the options that are very much premised on the existence of a grid?

This is a part of the book that I really like. It's called "The Host Laws" and they read, "Everybody eats. Every woman is entitled to a house. Everyone has access to the wealth of the land. Only take what you need." These were spoken by an Indigenous, Sto:lo West Coast grandmother, named Lee Maracle who's also a playwright and intellectual. She shared these host laws as an alter-native option to colonial immigration laws, because this book is all about immigration and immigrant commu-nities. We thought it'd be really good to have another possibility of how we think about immigration to this land, how if this were a space that were commanded along the lines of Indigenous principles and values, right, this might be a way that we could welcome—or, well, I'm a settler,

right?—that we could be welcome in this land.

So, I think about designing a lot as reading, or it's afforded me the ability to do a lot of reading.

Being a designer, I think a lot of that reading gets filtered through that disciplinary lens. I do a little bit of writing, but I wasn't trained in a tradi-tional scholarly discipline. I had the opportunity to co-edit an issue of this magazine called *C Magazine* early last year, and I co-edited it with a fellow named Ali S. Qadeer. This is the cover for it. The theme of this issue is graphic design. We didn't want it to be like a portfolio issue, we didn't want it to be the thing that I'm doing with you now, just showing work, we wanted it to introduce writers, thinkers, and practitioners that were practicing design in ways that aren't typically recognized, either in the market or in the academy. Originally the theme of the issue was going to be "graphic design and power." But we decided to just call it "graphic design," because for us, graphic design is always a matter of power, graphic design is always entangled with power, it's just a matter of how that relationship is articulated. That's the tricky part.

The contributors that we assembled, I think, do that in a variety of ways. We had, for example, one interview that I did with an artist and designer named Joi Arcand, who works with the Cree syllabary. This is an image of her work. We did an interview about that with an oral history scholar (Dr. Winona Wheeler). We had a piece that intersects with disability studies. We have a short genealogy of an Indian design school in Ahmedabad and this interesting, intense relationship between that school and the Bauhaus tradition. So there are all these ways in which we were able to think about or have design conversations that we typically hadn't had.

These are some images from a research project that I've undertaken for two and a half years now, it's a sprawling one. Sometimes I feel like I don't know what I'm doing. Sometimes, I think I'm fucking genius (but it's probably not true!). But this project is just really big, so I don't know how this is going to end up, but I want to keep doing it. I had the opportunity to exhibit some of my research about this research last year, and basically, this project is a historical project. What I'm trying to do here is rethink the history of graphic design, in a way that centers what some refer to as the genre of the document. The thing that I'm looking at is, why don't we look at things like passports, tax forms, driver's licenses, contracts, menus, receipts, all these really, really boring things that are graphic design artifacts but we don't teach them in school because we think of them as already designed or that we don't have access to the decision making powers to implement them? These things, like passports or driver's licenses, the ID documents for example, are highly consequential. These are probably the most consequential design thing that you'll ever touch, yet, we don't teach them, we don't really talk about them. So this history that I'm trying to figure out and articulate, looks at that, and I do it through a variety of ways. In one way, I look at this historically, chronologically, so there's the 6000-year narrative that begins with the earliest clay documents in ancient Mesopotamia, which I should note that while it is recognized as the first forms of systematized writing, we should also recognize that writing wasn't invented for the purposes of literary expression. Writing was invented as an accounting practice. Writing was invented for management, for politics. Writing was political writing in the beginning—it was who gets their memories inscribed, and who doesn't? It starts from there and then it goes all the way to contemporary forms of documentation through technologies like blockchain, which became popularized through things like Bitcoin.

So, the narrative centers the document, but more specifically, I'm looking at the relationship between money and typography. Again, ancient clay tablets were invented for the purposes of accounting, and this narrative ends or maybe continues with blockchain, which was popularized by Bitcoin, this very contemporary form of money. So I'm looking at a chronological span, but I'm also looking at it materially. These three clay tablets each have inscribed in them a hash value. So I don't know if you know what a hash value is, but it's a string of, let's say, 40 random characters that can function as a signature for a digital artifact. Something that is a unique identifier. So I made this cipher where you can generate a hash value in your terminal (if you're on a Mac). It gives you a string of 40 characters, so I made this 40 level cylinder, that's a cipher between this hash and the alphanu-meric characters, which it turns into a disk. I made a 3D printing of this cylinder and then pressed it into clay, playing with this idea that we don't know that hard drives or digital storage will last more than 50 years. We haven't had hard drives for more than 30–40 years. But we know clay lasts 6,000 years, so what if we embed that onto clay? It's very impractical, but it's, again, a speculative thought experiment.

The conceit of this exhibition was an idea that I kind of stole from Julia Born, a Swiss designer, where as you go through the exhibition, you can take pictures of the walls, and these become pages for a history book about graphic design. So I also include images and pieces from collaborators and people that I've been talking to that share similar research interests.

This is an image of coins that I had minted. There's this gaming token company in Ohio, I forgot what it's called, but the minimum order is 5,000 pieces. These are the coins that you use in arcade machines and stuff. You can send them custom designs. So I ordered these. I want to end with this idea, that how I think about design is like a narrative or an index, and that coins are a thing that helps people remember things. If you have money, what it's supposed to mean is that you've contributed something to the world, right? That this is your token that represents that you've contributed something. But it doesn't really work that way, right? Because there's people who have billions of dollars that didn't do shit for it. But that's what money is supposed to remember. So I'm talking about memory through the design of money, and all of the surfaces on these coins are surfaces that helped me to narrate my research. The three surfaces of this coin refer to three different techniques of document making that I've discerned from my research. It sounds weird to say that, but one of them is that documents secure themselves through the threat of violence. This inscription here reads "To counterfeit is death" which is copied from early American colonial era money, the kind of money that people like Benjamin Franklin are printing around the time of the American Revolution. When you think about paper money, it's highly insecure, because if you have a printing press, you can just print shitloads of money, or copy it very easily, so one of the ways that paper money was securitized in the American context was by threatening people with a death penalty. On the other side, it's a similar kind of documentary function. The image that appears at the top is of Hammurabi. If you've taken art history or design history, you might have heard of Hammurabi's Code of Laws. It's a black stone monument that has inscribed on its surface one of the earliest systematized code of laws. The inscription reads, "these laws were not written by the human King Hammurabi, they are passed down," (I'm paraphrasing, of course), "by the God of the sun, the God of justice, Shamash, therefore, don't fuck with this, it comes from heaven and you can't argue with the gods, therefore, these laws are legitimate." So it's this other way that form, images, and graphics are used ideologically to impose power. The third surface of this coin is the edge of the coin. This coin has a reeded edge, which was an invention from an era when coins were made out of precious metals like gold and silver and there was a criminal practice called clipping where people would shave the outer edge of a coin. So if you had a gold coin, and its face value was, let's say, one pound, well, that's just a typographic inscription, and the actual material content of that coin might not actually be one pound. So the visible appearance of this reeded edge functioned as a guarantee that the typographic face value inscription matched the actual content of that coin.

I'll just end by saying that that's the space that I'm really interested in thinking about, graphics, communications, all of this stuff. These are all kinds of fictions, right? They're not real, they're signs, they float, they change, they morph, they mutate. But how does a sign remain stable? By thinking about documents, I hope I can figure out a way to articulate and get some insight into how that works and how that is political. Thank you.

Chris Lee is a graphic designer and Assistant Professor at the Pratt Institute.

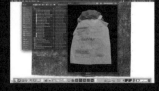

Chris Lee

Parsons School of Design
Communication Design
November 22, 2019

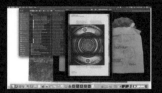

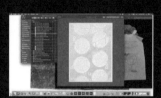
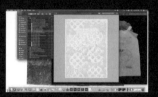

10 Years

My name is Renda Morton, and I'm currently a design director at Dropbox. I'm going to use the time today to walk you through how I got here. I'll do a deeper overview of what I've done before Dropbox and I'm going to give you a bunch of unsolicited advice about how to negotiate, because when I was a student, that's something I wish I'd known.

When E Roon asked me about this talk and I asked him what to talk about, he thought sharing my experience of being a designer in different industries would be valuable. I've had experience running my own design studio, working in journalism at *The New York Times*, and now working in a tech company, which few people do.

So to start at the beginning. I'm just personally really envious of people who have career goals. I graduated from MCAD in Minneapolis and I had a career goal then when I graduated: I really wanted to end up in my own design studio and I thought that would be my entire design career, just having that studio. I left with a degree in interactive media in 2003. I had absolutely no savings for college so I had to take out about $45,000 in student loans, which took me a long time to pay off. And in this project pictured, there's a wall, and on the other side there's a switch. It can be pressed by gallery visitors and it would trigger that computer that you see to dial a payphone at the Minneapolis airport. Then whoever picked up that payphone could speak with the visitors in the gallery. I was really excited about this. This is obviously well before Chatroulette or video roulette. So, I put this in a portfolio with some other graphic design projects, and I tried to get a job. And it didn't work out very well.

So after I graduated and with no concrete plans to figure out how to get a job, I took out another $3,000 loan to do a three week summer program in the Netherlands, called DeProgramme. It's run through the College of Creative Studies in Detroit. I think they still run it. I knew I needed to get a job but I didn't know how to do that. So I just did this program instead, trying to stall and figure out how to actually get a job. And so through this program, the students do workshops with different design studios and you visit designers. One of the studios that they worked with was called Lust. They were a small design studio in The Hague. Through getting to know them in this program, I was able to get an internship with them. It was just a three month internship, and they only paid me 300 euros a month. I was able to rent a place for 200 euros, living off 100 euros a month. The place I was renting was a really small one bedroom apartment. I had a roommate, and we only had one sink. So I was often brushing my teeth in the kitchen while they were in the bathroom. It was a very lean situation.

Then after my internship there ended, they hired me full time. At that studio, they did a lot of really interesting work for cultural clients, like artists in museums, a lot of the stuff that I was excited about when I was studying design in school. None of their clients paid them very well. Most of these projects were backed by government support, subsidies, and grants. But they were all really interesting opportunities to do visually interesting design work. So what you see here on the left, this is a digital interface for a museum's permanent collection, the Women's Museum at Rotterdam. This is a gallery that you can browse through all the stuff that

they can't put on display. In the top right, this was a website for an art and technology festival that we had in the Hague. In the bottom right, this was a self portrait of myself and my boss at the time working at our desks. Working there for two years helped me figure out a lot about what type of design I was interested in. Leaving art school, the type of design that they did was what I thought I was interested in doing, but after practicing it with them for two years, I kind of learned that that just wasn't for me.

So here's that same image of that art and technology website, or the art technology festival website I worked on in this image. This is an interactive map showing the different venues from the events and had some motion and audio. So you have to imagine that this is an image of a website from 2004. Visually, this map, this website is really interesting. It's really striking, we've created an interesting form. But functionally, it's not very helpful or useful. If someone actually wanted to use this to figure out where that venue was or what was at that venue, it's really difficult. So that latter aspect of design is something I realized I was more interested in working on than the formal part of making something visual and making forms that are more interesting. So when I left, I ended up leaving the studio really wanting to focus on usability and user experience.

So after working in Holland, I moved to New York. I'm not from New York, but I had family living there I could stay with until I found a job, which is a privilege. I started freelancing at a number of small design studios who would pay me by the hour or by the day, but with no benefits. I was able to get an offer for a full time job at a studio that I truly loved and admired, but I had to turn it down because the pay was so low that I wouldn't be able to pay for my rent and my student loans in New York. So I had to keep freelancing. I didn't really have a lot of choices economically, or I didn't think I did. So even though I really wanted to work at a studio, and I thought that was the best path into starting my own studio, I couldn't afford to so I kept freelancing. Because I kept freelancing, I ended up amassing clients, projects, and work that I ended up growing that studio from. I started a studio called Rumors with two partners, Holly Gresley and Andy Pressman. Our first studio space was in this building that we rented on the left in Brooklyn. It had fantastic views but no heat. It's now a luxury condo if you want to live there. I think it probably has heat now. We were doing lots of fun projects. We were able to hire our own interns and an employee. We were able to move to a different kind of dumpy building in a different part of Brooklyn, but this one had heat, which is nice. And we were doing lots of fun work like websites for type foundries, doing magazines, book covers. illustrations for *The New York Times*, identities for art galleries, exhibition design. This is just like a whole collage of different things that we worked on. It's exactly what I thought my goal was as a designer. But what's not included in this collage was all of this other unglamorous design work that we also were doing in order to make enough money to do the fun projects. We would do a website for a lawyer three or four times a year. Like most small businesses, I think we felt like we're always on the edge financially.

As we got bigger we started hiring an accountant to do our taxes. And this accountant, he was recom-

mended by other designers in their studios in New York. I'm pretty sure he had worked with all the design studios in New York. And I'd heard that he did Tibor Kalman's taxes. Y'all know who Tibor Kalman is? He was a very well known designer in the '80's and '90's. He passed away from cancer in 1999. He had this iconic design studio M & Co and he was the editor-in-chief of *Colors* magazine. He was interested in social issues and he was known (and this is really cringy reading it now when I looked it up) as "the bad boy of graphic design." I don't think we would call someone that in 2021, but here's a quote from his obituary in *The New York Times*: "He was the self-styled bad-boy of the graphic design profession and a harsh critic of formulaic or what he pejoratively termed 'professional' design. He wanted designers to take greater responsibility for how their work influenced the surrounding culture." So, working with this accountant and knowing he worked with this design icon, he would tell us all the secrets. *Watches*. He said Tibor only made money from watches. And he went on to lecture us about how we need to develop some copyrightable intellectual property so we can actually make money off of our work because our design studio was never going to be successful unless we were doing what Tibor was doing, which is selling watches. These images show different watch designs that Tibor did with Swatch Watch. So to hear this was kind of a downer because I have no interest in designing watches or selling Swatch Watches or copyrightable actual property, I didn't even know what he was talking about.

So, we seemed to have negative prospects of just continuing to do design work for our clients. Our accountant was up in White Plains, so we had a long train ride back to our office. On that train ride, I thought about an essay I'd read back when I was a student in 2002. This is an essay by Dimitri Siegal, called "Fuck Tibor." He wrote this when he was an MFA student at Yale. He was critiquing this idea of being a bad boy in graphic design and that underlying privilege in his work. "Tibor was a New York designer. He had great parties, yelled at people, and lived in a loft. Downtown New York in the '80s can be pretty well summed up by a list of his clients: The Ramones, The Talking Heads, Laurie Anderson, Restaurant Florent. Fuck Tibor. My friends are mostly a) uncool, b) broke, but *the tenets of Tiborism state that doing work for them is more important than cultivating paying clients, or even generating self-initiated projects.* Students of design need to develop their own means of producing work that is interesting and generative. In my experience, going to New York and trying to meet bands is not a process."

So it's a little harsh, and the emphasis here is mine. But it's so hard for me now to think about that and reconcile the watches and selling the watches to subsidize a design practice and an image that was criti-cizing other people for being profes-sional designers. It enabled him to do so much, and he railed against professional design but participated in it at the same time. That all was a little disillusioning for me. After that experience, I thought about money a lot.

Here's an image of how we used our studio meeting room to play poker and gambling. Our studio was finan-cially stable, and I didn't end up leaving the studio because of money.

In fact, my partner, Andy, after I left the studio after four years, he kept it going for a much longer time and he was doing well with that. I left because the work no longer felt challenging. I wasn't learning or growing as I thought I would, and I wondered if this was the dream that I had when I was in college. On top of thinking about the money aspect, it didn't seem worth it either. In the last year of running the studio, I was just spending so much time redesigning projects, and we weren't involved after we launched them. So I wasn't learning from those design decisions or iterating on that work. Running a small business means you have to wear a lot of different hats, and it was very hard to focus on the design process. And it wasn't what I thought it would be.

So I found a new goal. I got an opportunity to work at *The New York Times*, and I took it. I didn't really have a goal with that. It just sounded like a good idea. It's an iconic place. I've been reading *The Times* for years, it felt exciting to be a part of something so much bigger. But I was terrified. I've been working as an independent designer for over 10 years, and I've worked a lot. There were nights and weekends. Having a studio took over my life and became part of my identity. So leaving that behind was scary because it meant that I was changing who I was. I had no separation between my work and who I was as a person.

And this is what it felt like the first year at the *Times*. I've been working in design for 10 years, but I'd never worked at a company that had more than five or six people, literally *The Times* is part of a corporation called the New York Times Company. A lot of culture shock there. I felt really feral, and I made a lot of mistakes. Then to top it off, the first project I had to do there was redesign NYTimes.com, which was huge, like a major undertaking that took over a year and involved many designers and many, many people like 60+ engineers. And through that project, I learned what it meant to work as a team rather than working with clients or running your own business. I thought that the whole experience I had with clients had prepared me for really tough design conversations and interpersonal relationships, the things you would deal with having a team, but I was totally wrong. What I realized breaking through this was that when we're at the studio and we had a client that was really difficult to work with, we would just drop them as a client. And when you have a team, you can't do that. You just have to work through it with people. So I went in with a lot of hubris that I knew how to work with other people, but I really didn't at all. So when I think about this project, my biggest takeaways were all the things I had to do to make it work with such a large group of people and still execute design. That meant elevating myself out of the pixels of design and focusing more on the outcomes of that design. So whenever I got stuck in a conversation about what we see, I would fail. And whenever I could get the conversation to talk about what design would help us achieve or help us do, we could move forward and progress. Working at the *Times* also taught me a lot about how to value my work and myself. Financially, it was more transformational than having my design studio. It allowed me to pay off my student loans, which is something I didn't think I would ever be able to do. So I got a lot out of it. But I had to give a lot, as I talked about, mourning

that loss of my identity as an independent designer and the loss of having a career goal, which was a big void, not having identity lists and goal lists. I set out to have a design studio, and now I don't know what to do, I guess I just work at this place. So I kind of let unintentionally the void be filled with the mission of the *Times* and the status of it, letting it become just as life consuming as it was to run a studio. I let it make me feel like a whole without examining the risks associated with that.

It made it so that nothing could feel or seem as important as the *New York Times* and what it was trying to do, especially after the 2016 election. So that was not sustainable for me to live and work that way. I worked there for six years, but I was still like "I'm gonna find something that actually mattered more than that. And, and oh shoot, I still need a goal! Why don't I have a goal? I need to figure out what I'm doing." I was sharing all these anxieties with a co-worker there, who's older and had a lot more experience and she gave me some advice that really stuck with me: careers are long. She said to me, "you've been working for 15 years. Well, guess what? You're going to be working for at least another 30 years. How are you going to do the same thing for that long?" That perspective just helped me realize that maybe I don't need to have a goal. And that's fine, I can just do what makes sense for right now. And in the course of the next 30 years, if I want to continue working in design, I can't burn out in all these different experiences.

So this is what led me to move to California and work at Dropbox. I'd been living in New York for 13 years running a studio or working at *The New York Times*, but I wanted to continue working in design without it completely taking over my life. I wanted distance between my work and myself. I was drawn to working in tech because there's a lot of younger designers there, and I get a lot of satisfaction out of helping designers grow by sharing my experience with them. I also wanted to work for a business that was clear how the business makes money. So at Dropbox, we offer you a service and you pay for it. We're not selling people's data. There's no advertizing involved. And then something that was important, but not something to lose sleep over. I wanted to make more money, if only for a short period of time, so that I could give myself more choices with what I decided to do next, not knowing what that is. I wanted to give myself the type of choices and privileges that I think Tibor had by selling Swatch watches. And I think through all those experiences I had, I knew the value that I brought myself and what I could get for it. And that's where I'm gonna segue into the one skill that I developed, which you can use no matter what path you choose: negotiation. If you want to work in a big company, or you work for yourself, here's some unsolicited, very specific advice about negotiation that I wish I knew early on. I think it's helpful for students now.

So, the first piece of advice is *to just to ask for it*. Just ask because you just might get what you're asking for. I think a lot of things keep people from asking for things like fear of rejection, fear of ruining a relationship, etc. Even if you do get rejected, like, what's the worst thing that can happen? I think more often than not, you just might get more things than you would just worrying that you won't get them. Women ask for what they want less often than men do and there is a double standard there where you could be perceived poorly for doing so. But I would just encourage women to ask even more often than you think you should. And when you ask for it, ask for a lot, because it can raise the perceived value of what you're asking for, and it allows you to graciously compromise and cut back on something which can make the other person you negotiate with happy. Everybody wants a discount. Everything is negotiable, almost. So don't be afraid to ask for something, even if you don't think you should.

NEGOTIATE OUTCOMES AND NOT DESIGN DECISIONS

This is one of the biggest lessons I learned from working at *The Times*. Whether you're seeking approval for your work, or buying for your work from a client, from a boss, from anyone, your teammates, frame it around what the design will do, and what will they see. So frame it around the value that you're providing, and not the actual thing that you're making. So if you're making a website, don't frame it around "this is a website" but around what the website actually intends to do. Your value is saving those providers time, not the apps that you're making to do that.

INTERESTS OVER POSITIONS

So story here: Consider the story of two men quarreling in a library. One wants the window open and the other one wants it closed. The bigger back and forth is about how much to leave it open: a crack, halfway, three quarters of the way, no solutions are satisfactory to them both. In comes the librarian, she asks why one wants the window open, and he says to get some fresh air. She asks the other man why he wants it closed, he says to avoid the draft. She thinks for a minute and then opens the window in the next room bringing in fresh air without a draft. So don't get mired in what I call the pixels of design, which is how much the window should be cracked and halfway open, but think about the actual outcomes or in this case, positions that you want to achieve. And we're all designers, so we're problem solvers. We're skilled at finding solutions for those as well.

SOME VERY SPECIFIC ADVICE ABOUT PRICING CLIENT AND FREELANCE WORK

Get information. Always ask for a budget. It could always be more than you're thinking and you never want to leave money at the table. Sometimes people don't want to share this, so I would just leverage silence as a tool to get people to share. Ask "what's your budget," and you don't have to say anything or justify it. Leave it hanging there till people fill it in for you. Your time is a very important factor in the costs. So if you think about pricing stuff by how long it will take you, that's one way to do it. But when you do that, you should factor in two things. One is the value that your design will provide for that client. A famous example, the Citibank logo that Paula Scher took on, she drew in the first meeting with the bank officials when talking about the logo. So even though she had sketched it in five minutes, it's a giant logo for a big corporation. It didn't matter how long she took to do it, although she'll say it's because of her experience that she was able to do it so quickly, which is true. But the value of the logo to that company was worth whatever the cost was. It didn't matter how

much time it would take for someone to create it. So the value it provides and not the time it would take you to make it is another factor. But also what would it be worth for you to have to do this? If just thinking about doing that design project is so painful to you, you should ask a lot for it, to make it worth it for you to do it. Have a good down payment, have a contract with a "kill fee," in case the client fires you, which can happen.

NEGOTIATING A JOB OFFER

They won't revoke the offer if you negotiate. People do an offer because they want you to work there, so you can feel really scared about asking for more, especially when something seems really generous, but you should always ask for a little bit more. And if they do revoke a job offer, you probably didn't want to work at a place like that. Ask for what your potentials are, not just your past experience. Your compensation is for your skills and experience that you are bringing to the role and *also what you have the potential to achieve in that role.* So don't lose sight of that. It's not just about where you are right now, and what you've been paid before, it doesn't really matter. You don't have to tell potential employers if they ask. In fact, in some states, I know in California, it's illegal for employers to ask candidates about their salary history. If they do ask, then ask them for their range. If they insist, you can say "this job requires XYZ based on my research. This is the range I'm expecting, is that in line with what you're offering." And then again, just ask for more. I said this like three times, but you don't even need a reason for it. You can just ask for more. I did this when I got my offer from Dropbox. When I talked to them on the phone, I said "this offer is very generous, I'm very excited about it. I have to ask, can I have more?" and they gave me $10,000 more, which is the easiest $10,000 I've ever made, by just asking for it. So always just ask.

If you can't get more money out of your effort, then ask for other things of value, like more paid time off, or different flexibilities at work or different things that are valuable to you that might not be monetary. Then always ask when your compensation will be up for review again, especially if you weren't able to get everything that you wanted in your initial job offer.

Renda Morton is Director of Product Design at Dropbox.

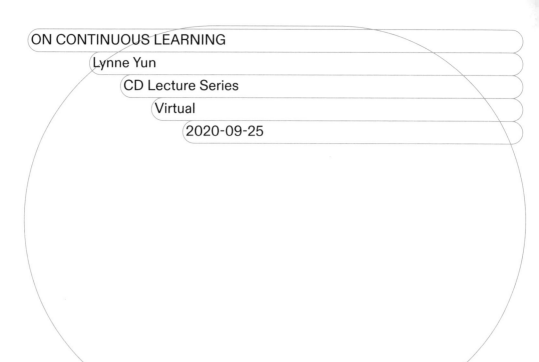

ON CONTINUOUS LEARNING

Lynne Yun

CD Lecture Series

Virtual

2020-09-25

The lecture title is loosely named "Chasing Inspirations, or They're Not Back Again, Yet". It's a reference to *The Hobbit*, since I'm a huge science fiction and fantasy nerd.

I always struggle with this idea of having a defined creative practice and also trying to find my place in the world as a designer, creative, whatever label that people give you these days as a professional visual designer. I was thinking about what I could share with you all, since this is a communication design lecture series, and I'm assuming that most of you who are watching are design students or people who are just starting out in the field. I think what I was always stressed out about when I was younger was the pressure to be creative. I think it seems like a very cliche thing—that we have to be creative or you have to be good creatives, whatever that means. It seems like a really wild word to me,

because even as a young student, it always felt like I needed to be creative with a capital C, as people say. These days, you need to be creative enough to get into a good art school, you need to be creative enough to get into a good company. And then after that, I'm assuming you want to be creative enough to be 30 under 30, 40 under 40, and so forth and so forth. But we can't live our lives like that day after day, right? You're not a gigantic company with some kind of northstar buzzword goals on a daily basis.

Over time, I've figured out that I just really like having a productive and happy day to day life. So, I figure out what I'm interested in, what I like to be doing in my spare time, and I think I've made peace with the fact that perhaps for me, this is my creative path. I know that learning new things doesn't really sound like a creative path, so I just wanted to share with you all what that has looked like for me. And of course, before I go on too far, I also wanted to show you a little bit of my background because I think for all of us, where we have spent time, places we've been, people who we've met, they all eventually define us in one way or another.

Here are some things that I've been involved in in formal capacities. I've worked for companies like Apple and Monotype. I went to the School of Visual Arts during undergrad, and I pursued a type design program at Type@Cooper. I later did a residency at the School for Poetic Computation, and I'm in the process of finishing up my degree at the ITP program at NYU. I think it's important to point out that you learn from all your experiences, even if you don't necessarily agree with them, like them, or even if you end up hating them afterwards. It still means you learn something. I think it's important to acknowledge the places that you've been.

So, the first job that I had straight out of school was working at Apple. I know you've heard a lot of things about Silicon Valley, especially back in the early 2010s. But I think the project that really defined some sort of marker in my life was making this "8" for iOS 8. I made that eight for I think two months, it was just non–stop drawing one figure 8, and it really wasn't good. I really cringe at this. But the lesson that I learned wound up online, there was this Twitter conversation asking, "Who drew that 8, the optical weight is off, blah, blah, blah." And then of course, after that, I was that person that said, "Oh, no, I made a terrible 8, I really need to go learn how to make an 8." And I ended up at Cooper Union's Type@Cooper program. There, I really learned how to draw letters as a type designer. Eventually, after I finished

the program, I still wasn't ready to commit to being a full time type designer. I think I was somewhere between this logotype designer and a graphic designer. I was making a lot of work for advertising companies just like this. This is a mural for a hockey team in Pittsburgh. Over time, I realized I just really liked drawing letterforms. I have a huge fascination about historical backgrounds and technology and all of a lot of these things. But what I really appreciate about letterforms is just my capacity to appreciate them, when I'm drawing it. It's kind of like having a go-to niche subject to be working on all the time.

Here are some paintings that I've done. Here is a sketch on the left side and the W, the Gothic looking W, is rendered in gouache on the right side. Here you see some other pieces of lettering that I was doing during this time, and I have to admit that the work that I was doing during the daytime in an advertising agency wasn't creatively fulfilling. I was running that path of doing something more interesting in the evenings in my own spare time to sort of offset that. I think I was the most productive in my own personal work when I was making a lot of rebate coupons for Sherwin-Williams paint cans for my day job...$5 off if you mailed this coupon kind of deal. So there are always glamour sides and unglam-orous sides to every single job. I often think that when you're starting out, it might seem like there's not a lot of outlets that you can pursue, but one of the things that you do have control over is your own free time after work. Obviously, a little bit of ambition as a young person definitely goes a long way for these kinds of things. Here, I was making a hand painted map of the United States, and you can see that's me on the top right side with a teeny tiny little paintbrush and jewelers glasses. These are magnifying glasses that you can put on your head. You can see that I made the crucial mistake of starting on the left side, on the West coast and then going to the East, so all the states are giant when it gets to the East. You can imagine my anguish as I kept going on towards the right. You live and you learn.

I think my interests are always changing over time. When I think about everything that I've done so far, it really comes out of a curiosity that I just really want to fulfill. And a part of this is what I was saying earlier about how I really wanted to be able to draw an eight in the proper way. So that led to me being more of a letterform specialist, and this is where my fascination with calligraphy starts. I think I was just looking at some logo or something. I don't remember exactly what but I distinctly remember seeing the A and the V next to each other, and I was thinking about how the A is thick on the right, but the V is thick on the left. I thought that this was really weird because it's not very self explanatory. So I started thinking about why this was and then I figured out that a lesson in calligraphy solves a lot of these problems. I figured out that with a pen and ink, the physicalities don't really allow you to have a thick stroke going up, up the hill is thin and then down the hill is thick. Eventually, this little foray into calligraphy led me to do a lot more calligraphy and then eventually incorporate it in my professional work.

Here are some drafts for the Lincoln Center that I was collaborating on with Small Stuff some years ago. What I also discovered was that being able to use multiple tools, digital or physical, really allows you to expand your way of thinking because I think there are a lot of limitations that the tool gives you that you're not really aware of until you start using different kinds of tools that let you break out of that mold. At this time I was using a lot of vector programs like Adobe Illustrator and so forth. Even though I got proficient later on with tracing paper and pencils, it really doesn't beat a calligraphy pen because in the time that it would take you to draw one letter, you've already done an entire word if you can use a pen and ink very well. Eventually, I started doing more and more doodling as I have a pen in my hand, and that leads me down this entire path of learning how to flourish. That's a whole other story for a whole another day. But eventually, I just kept going down this path, and at some point, as I was browsing eBay one late night, looking for manuscripts as bored calligraphers do, or maybe it's just me, but I found this little manuscript page. I think it was like $30. It was from the 1400s and because it has no illustration, it was extremely affordable for something from the 1400s. So I bought it. You can see from this quarter here, that it's actually really, really small. I really wanted to learn this style, so I was looking at it a lot and I was really trying to find if there was any calligrapher that would teach me the style, but it turned out that there wasn't. So I figured that if someone wrote it, I can probably also try to write it. This started an almost two year long, part-time of course, research into how to reverse engineer this script. The way I did this in an abbreviated format was that I scanned this; I did a lot of research into the type of manuscript that this was; I took tracing paper and then extracted the skeletal forms. Then the thing that I learned a lot is that there's a lot of physicality that goes into writing manuscripts, because there's the viscosity of the ink and the way that the human hand wants to write things. Fortunately, we all have a limited number of risks, and a limited number of, you know, joint flexibility, so it's kind of perceivable that my ability to write wouldn't be too different from a medieval scribe. But me not being a proficient medieval scribe, I started out in a bigger size, and then eventually, it transitioned to smaller and smaller sizes. I think at one point, I went down this rabbit hole of how to prepare manuscripts, so I got little pieces of vellum, and I was writing with a goose quill. Eventually, I just realized that this is all great, but I also live in the 2000s. And I can't be cutting up goose quills every single day. I also wanted to make it viable for me because it's great to have the ability to write a medieval manuscript, but also I want to be able to write this for myself with the modern tools that I have. Here is where I was learning how to write this hand, and eventually, as I got familiar with the hand enough, I could just write it out of muscle memory as opposed to trying to analyze every single letter. You can see here that I'm doing modern looking words that have words like an X, for example, that didn't exist back then. So, this is like another one of those hobbies that became a really deep, dark rabbit hole. Eventually, I taught workshops and things on this hand. Even though it seems that pursuing some sort of mildly weird interest you have seems like it'll lead nowhere, sometimes it does, and sometimes it's enjoyable, and often you'll have a lot of fun just getting there in the first place.

Eventually, these things seem to live in separate rooms in your head, but they do come together at some point because you're just one person. Here is an example where I was doing calligraphy, and I decided to make a lettering piece out of it. You can see the letters written with a calligraphy pen on the top left, and you can see it turning into a lettering piece, meaning that I was rendering all of them with a pen and pencil on tracing paper, and it started getting little nuances that you can't get from straight up a writing tool and ink. Then eventually, I vectorized it and then transformed it to a design that I could laser cut out of paper. Everything had to connect and not fall through. This is just an example of how knowing different kinds of processes can always merge together for you to be able to adapt it into different kinds of scenarios. Another recent project that I've been doing is a typeface that's inspired by calligraphy. Here, you can see the original sketch that I did with the pen up on top, and you can see that there's a lot of inconsistency every time I write the A, because I'm writing it with a physical tool, it'll be different. Here, you can see that I digitized it and I was slowly making it harmonize because the nature of a writing tool is very different from the nature of a digital font file that needs to work with every other letter in the alphabet. I was trying to reconcile those differences slowly but surely. I am a firm believer that without my ability to have experimented in the actual pen and ink, I probably would not have been able to get to the digital result. Here is just a random sample from a sketchbook that I was trying to sketch out letters in, and you can see that the process is different. If it was a pencil and marker sketch, maybe I would have made three and refined them over and over. But because this is pen and ink, I just kept writing more and more of them. Here, you can see that after I got to some sort of form that I wanted it to be. I was refining it with the pencil and that eventually it got brought on digitally. Then, of course, I was having a lot of fun with different kinds of ampersands.

This is the part where I just show you a couple of things that I've made for Monotype, which I used to work at full time for about two and a half years. I left last fall. Here you can see some typefaces that I was working on. This is a layered typeface, where I was working with three different styles that would layer on top of each other to make this dimensional form. I still tried to retain a lot of that experimentation that I do with the hand, and you can see here that even with something that seems as straightforward as a beveled design. There's really no such thing as it being straightforward. You can see the little minute difference in designs that I was trying out. These are typefaces that you would have layered on. It's funny when I'm making typefaces because I think about how my interests are just going more and more down this onion layer of information.

Let me unpack that for a second. So I was interested in design, graphic design as a whole. And then I got interested in typography. And then I got interested in type design. And then from there, I got interested in calligraphy, which is the historical background of type design. And then where do you really go from there? I was sort of stuck here for a little bit and eventually, I figured out that I was really curious about how fonts worked. So as a type designer, you make typefaces over and over again, they get packaged into little tiny font files that you can send out to people.

But what is a font file anyway? This is actually an interesting question because I was thinking about how, when I was growing up, I used to be able to hack things or build little things. I think when a radio wouldn't work, I would just get out a Phillips screwdriver and I would take it apart, hoping that I could put it back together in the state that it worked. I was definitely the really nerdy kid in school that was like trying to be "my video games are going to run so smoothly because I upgraded my RAM," that kind of kid. It was wild to me that I just didn't know how to take apart a font file because it's just on my screen or somewhere on my computer. And so I started to think "what if I could take apart a font file, just like I could take apart any other thing?" Now, of course, it seems like everything is sort of blocked in together, like when you see a phone, there's no little tiny screw holes in the back even though there used to be at some point. And when you download an app from the App Store, there's nothing physical, it just shows up on your phone, and you can't really open it up. So, I got interested in programming. Here is a slide where I am trying to express to you how I'm just really interested in this evolution of technology, and how people are building things. Here is a little diagram of little planets that I've been to so far. So, I was in graphic design, and that was type design. And now I'm getting into coding.

What I've discovered in my foray into technology is that type is also an onion layer of things. Type as a concept is a visual system, right? When you're trying to typeset something like a word, you expect the A to be similar to the T and E and so forth. Everything has a visual system. But when you start to look into it in a more detailed way, you notice that it's a modular system, right? If you've tried to dissect things in your typography class, you probably have realized that some parts are sort of reused, and you start to see that modular system behind it. So, when you're thinking about, let's say, an F, it probably seems like the E and the F are very similar, and the F looks like the E without the bottom bar and so forth. When you're learning type design, you learn that everything is a modular system, like little Lego pieces that you put together and take apart in order to make a bigger system. What I learned when I started to get into programming is that type is an instructional system. You can all do this. If you have a font file on your computer, you can just drag it into any kind of text editor, and you'll see that type is just a bunch of text and that there's little coordinates inside those files. What a font file is is a series of instructions that is letting the computer know how they should be drawn. We can talk about this for a very long time, since computers at their core are still very much a 0101. I'm getting too much into this. But what I realized was that typefaces were instructional. I also realized that it's very much possible to unpack these instructions that are inside a font file and to do something with it.

Here are some sketches that I was doing. At the time, I was going to the School for Poetic Computation, which I think is still in the West Village in New York City. Here is an exploration that I was doing in Zach Lieberman's class for Open Frameworks. This is Helvetica that I was trying to make into a three dimensional thing. I wasn't quite sure where I was going with that. But at the core of it, what the instructions on the left side are doing is that there's this little helicopter thing that's drawing lines as it's going around the parameters of an X. Then on the right side is a word inspired by Muriel Cooper. So, it has the word Cooper, and if a certain coordinate is inside the inner parts of a letter, it's bigger and closer to the viewer and the further it is, it's smaller, almost like a little grid star system. Eventually, I was wondering what it takes to have a parameter for time. Here you can see that the outlines are getting drawn for T, I, M, E, and the outlines are getting degraded over time, turning into little blocks.

Since then, I've been doing a lot more with technology and type, and I just wanted to share a few projects that I've done in relation to that. Here is a machine learning project, basically trying to teach a computer how to do something. So GAN stands for a generative adversarial network. If this all sounds like mumbo jumbo, don't worry too much about it because there is a really great platform called Runway that lets you start out machine learning, even with zero coding experience. It's really, really friendly. So to start out with machine learning, I was using Runway, and then I needed to collect data from somewhere because I wanted to work with letter forms. Although I could sit here and draw 1,000 letters, that would be really time consuming and it really wouldn't be crucial to what I was trying to do because I was trying to teach a machine how to draw letters. You can't always start from the granular step. Let's say sometimes I just want to go buy flour instead of growing crops and waiting a year. So, I discovered that MyFonts has an API, so MyFonts has a structure that lets you pull their data. What I did was that I pulled a lot of font images from the MyFonts API, and you can see that I had a gigabytes worth of images at some point. For this project, I set up a parameter for myself that I wanted it to be sans serifs because sans serifs seemed to have a very particular look that I could try to get the machine to draw for me. I downloaded more than 50,000 images from the MyFonts API and then I also had to manually feed 20,000. So sometimes, a lot of the work isn't collecting the information more than doing the actual thing itself. But I just wanted to point this out, because it's not some sort of magical algorithm from the sky that I was like "please give me a sans serif," and it happened. We're not quite there. But you can see that the original model was trained on human faces, so you'll see this uncanny valley of human faces turning into letters, and I was training them on the letter A. And it's not always perfect. This is my first try and instead of people's faces turning into letters, they turned into these weird penguin shapes. So nothing really happens in one shot, but eventually I was able to get it to produce A's that looked pretty sanserif-y. Then I trained it on a short word like A-S-H, because I figured an H was pretty standard and S was also a pretty standard shape. The AI already knew the A, so it just shimmied in there. You can see the word "ash" here. The machine clearly recognizes what the A-S-H should look like. Although there's more varia-tions in the A presumably because designs for the A vary a lot more than it would for the H for instance, you can imagine that for an A might have a little hat, it might have a little bit of a slant, maybe it has a round top, maybe has a pointy top, which is why it looks a little bit more shaky. And after I did this, I realized that this is

cool, but that's where my interest stopped because I said, "Okay, this is all great, but it's not as great as me just drawing it. There's none of these that I would look at and be like, that would be an awesome font and that I would want to use in all my projects."

Eventually I said, "Okay, what other ways could I try to get the machine to make a letter for me." So, the next thing that I tried was training a model called GPT-2, which specializes in generating text. And all of this is, just like Runway, available for you to train if you're so inclined on Google Colab. Here, you can see that I was using an existing notebook, as they call it, a platform that lets you run code in a certain specific order, which is why it's kind of like a digital notebook. Earlier on when I was trying to tell you that all font files at its core are just a series of instructions, this is where I live back to that concept. This is not a font file. This is an SVG that I opened up. But you can see here that on the top, it says, "This is the SVG version." Later on, it shows you what it's drawing. These are the instructions that this file is using in order to render this case on the left side. Let me make an analogy. Iimagine following a recipe that says "step one: you crack open an egg and mix it in a bowl. Step two: put sugar into this bowl." It's like that, but just with coordinates on this imaginary surface. So I said, okay, all a letter is a series of instructions. I'll get a ton of different K's, and I'll throw these instructions into a GPT-2 model and hopefully it will give me a K. I downloaded over 600 images of a K. I converted all of them to an SVG, and then I converted all the SVGs into a text file and ran them through the model. And guess what? Most of them didn't work. This is the best one that I got. Sometimes you have ideas, and it doesn't work. Sometimes you think this company is awesome, you go there, and it's actually not that great. But I think there's always something to learn from here, and because I tried this, it allows me to do other things. After I failed at this experiment, I could have thrown 10,000 more hours into this, but I said, "You know what, I'm going to try something new." The next thing that I did was making a computational tool where I had more input, because what I had learned from the previous two experiments was that I actually wanted to have more input just letting the machine draw 90% of the work really wasn't doing it for me. I was really inspired by Metafont. Metafont by Donald Knuth is a way a font could be rendered in multiple different ways. It has this skeletal form and then you can transform it into multiple different ways. I was inspired by that. Of course, you always want to start from somewhere, partially because I don't want to invent anything from the entire ground up, right? So I consulted with Allison Parrish, who I greatly admire. She's an amazing poet, programmer, and teacher. This is a library that she had for Python. So this is the first time where I was trying to create a standalone program in Python. So this is what I made, and I'll just talk over the illustration. So what's happening is that there is a program that will allow you to draw a skeletal form, and then it'll put clothes on top of it to the dimensions that you're specifying it. There's four colors that give you these skeletal forms, and depending on the stroke width that you want to have, you can input it underneath the color option. Every time you input it and refresh, it will show you that. For an entire set of typefaces, this might come in handy.

The advantage of me learning digital tools is that now I think of digital tools as something that is warm. When I was a student, I used to think of digital tools as cold, but I think part of it was that I didn't know how to use digital tools in a way that felt human and warm. But now I see the scripts that people have made, sometimes I know them personally, sometimes they're strangers on the internet, but now it feels like something more warm to me because it feels like something that can be built.

Lynne Yun is a type designer, educator, technologist, and partner at Space Type Continuum.

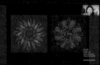

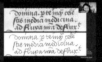

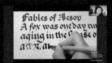

DESIGN PEDAGOGY: A CONVERSATION

Featuring Atif Akin, Taeyoon Choi, Rik Lomas, and Mindy Seu

Moderated by Juliette Cezzar

CD Symposium Panel, The Pedagogy of Design in the Age of Computation

Wolff Conference Room, Room D1103
Albert and Vera List Academic Center
6 East 16th Street

2018-05-15

In an increasingly homogenized inter-action design landscape, how can we continue to craft unique digital experiences? As designers, how do we retain agency and ownership over a process which has become progressively atomized?

The past several years have seen the rise of design systems and frame-works along with toolchains and build processes which have dramatically expanded the complexities of designing and developing for screen. Design and engineering roles have splintered and specialized, with large teams becoming the norm for producing digital artifacts at any scale. The net result has been a profusion of predictability—a continual rehashing of user experience tropes and patterns which define the visual form of most projects.

In this symposium, we attempted to unpack ways in which designers have been able to sustain their engagement with the materiality of screens and speculate on how we might maintain agency in a discipline which continues to stratify.

Juliette Cezzar
I want to thank all of our people who presented today. I think it's probably become obvious by the end of this that it's very deliberate that we chose people from very different worlds to come here, very different audiences. I have some burning questions too, so I do want to go ahead and dig into that. I have burning questions about all of it. I want to begin—despite our overly complicated title—with the whole question of whether design students, in particular, should be taught anything about code? There's been debates about it. The question, whether humans in general should be taught to code. Bloomberg had a big thing about how everybody should learn how to do it, and then we have

national coding days. If you're a third-grader, you're actually more likely to be taught coding than if you're in college, which I think is also kind of an interesting situation. So I wanted to open up and ask: who do you think should learn to code? And is the answer everyone? And is it creative people? Who do you think needs to know this?

Rik Lomas
I'll go first. I don't think anyone should. I don't think there should be something where it's like if you are in this industry or this kind of area that you should be doing this. And I think the people that we teach are very similar to the ones that you teach in terms of the designers, creative people, the artists.

I think there is that force. There's almost like an industry thing where it's like if you are a designer, you should learn to code. And I think that's almost wrong as people feel like they should learn to code because it actually helps them do the things they want to do. So if they're a digital designer, I think Linux code would be useful because they can upgrade their skills, they can work in the media of HTML and CSS or Processing or whatever it is. But I don't think anyone should be forced to learn.

JC
Is there a rebuttal in the panel to that or anybody disagree?

Taeyoon Choi
I just want to share a story. I got invited to talk at a high school in Chicago and I flew in and I went to a gym. There were about 100 teachers who were like physical education teachers, English teachers, and even chefs from the cafeteria. And we were trying to apply computational thinking to all the disciplines. And that was

what the whole day was about. And I felt like that's actually not necessary. Like there's kind of prioritizing tech over everything else. That computation is the center of human knowledge is quite wrong. I think it's a very useful tool. I think it's great to have as an option, and it leads to further understanding of disciplines and also understanding of different disciplines and potentially job-related skills. But I think it's bad to say that it's the only way.

JC
But then, Atif, in some of what you had talked about with early, especially foundational skills, you talked about teaching them computationally. How come?

Atif Akin
I think everybody codes. I mean, it's not the question: who should code? We'll always be coding. My grandmother was coding when she was knitting. She had a formula. She was just five red, one green, five red, one green and then you have a sweater at the end. She was a coder. And I think we had always been coding, but maybe there has been a divide with the computers, and then we had two classes of people like coders and non-coders. But I think putting things in order or putting things in a formula is a very natural defense mechanism of our perception. We want to group things like Gestalt. If you're creating some things, you want to create an order. And in terms of the basic design education, starting from Gestalt to Arnheim and to Bauhaus, I think there's a continuous order, necessity to code things. And I don't think we can create something on the computer or elsewhere without really coding. You can't knit a sweater without a code. You cannot tidy up your room without code. You cannot

cook—as Taeyoon does at the School of Poetic Computation—you cannot cook without a code. So I think coding is very innate to our human perception stability. So I think we need coding in different capacities. If you're spending quite amount of time on the computer, I think we should be coding that too.

Mindy Seu

I wonder if the question itself is a bit technologically deterministic. So to say that should everyone know how to code, does everyone need to know how to code? It's kind of what Taeyoon was saying, where we're putting the technology at the Center and if we don't know how to use this technology or if we do know how to make this technology, then we can save the world. It's like a kind of a form of evangelism. But I think what's more interesting in these settings is, yes, it is a tool just like you might learn InDesign or some other bookbinding strategy to implement your idea, but I think if we think of code as a type of media, then we should question what it's actually mediating. I'm more interested in why people want to learn how to code and what they want to make with it and for what audience, rather than just emphasizing the technical structure of the code itself.

JC

I'm interested in the question of should designers need to, want to, learn. All of you guys touched upon, maybe with the exception of Rik, the question of history and looking at historical precedents. We looked at the *Whole Earth Catalog*. We looked at information theory. Claude Shannon made an appearance a couple of times here with genetic codes. We're looking at all of these things and I think probably for a lot of people in this room, these are all things that get us excited. None of these things are things we teach in design history. So do you think that those are things we should be teaching in design history? And if so, how much? And if so, is it only to people who are interested in coding? Like how relevant is that history to us and how does that shake out? Can any of you respond to that more historical question?

TC

Oh yeah. That's a super fun topic. I think so. And I think history of craft and technology is a really great segue into computation because like Atif was saying the looms or other kinds of automatic machines were programmable even before electrical computers. So there's the history of textile designers such as Annie Albers or other types of practitioners who are applying computational processes to design objects.

I just want to say, this is sort of out of the blue, but I wish you all could teach designers without using any Adobe products. I mean, I think InDesign and coding are fundamentally different because you're working with a toolkit that is created for certain kinds of industrial mass production processes, which I fully respect. Like you need to use that if you're making books or making videos or whatever. However, as an artistic tool, a creative tool, for designers, I think it's fundamentally conditioning how you perceive the world. If you can only think about the representations through these interfaces that have huge inheritance to certain types of ways of thinking, I think you will just replicate the existing aesthetics. Say you learn ceramics, you don't use one brand of ceramics. You get to create your own clay, you get to understand different earth and minerals. And I just think how design education is so industry-focused and trying to get the students jobs after like four years of training, it's actually taking the design away from the possibility of it becoming a really rich cultural resource.

JC
So if you have the designer and you don't teach them code and you don't teach them Adobe software, what would you teach them?

TC
I think I'll teach code and I'll probably tell them how to hack Adobe software, but not like hacking to not pay for it but to create different iterations or kind of uses.

AA
It's decentralized a little bit; I agree on that. Like nobody uses Dreamweaver anymore.

JC
Speak for yourself.

AA
I just thought about it once you brought it up. I'm thinking really in the last three or four years, I haven't been requiring any Adobe software. Maybe Acrobat for PDFs? But on the other end again, I'm not sure if it is helping liberating. I don't know if it is helping because then they're a little smaller companies and then they're being bought by other companies. Of course, we are at some point tied up to a capitalist system, if not Adobe.

MS
I also wanted to add that my former boss at 2×4, Michael Rock, would say that ideally, the things that you're learning in a school setting should stick with you 50 years or throughout your entire career. So if we are just focusing on InDesign, which I did not mean to conflate with coding, but

rather just as a mechanism to create something.

JC
A tool.

MS
Yeah, a tool. Then if these tools then become outdated, if for whatever reason Adobe no longer exists and we only know how to think within that platform, then what will we actually be doing later? So I think critical thinking, historical references, what you mentioned about space-time continuum, I think that's much more valuable.

JC
So other than historical things that you guys have mentioned—and that I was delighted to see *Post-Digital Print*, which is possibly one of my favorite design books, mentioned twice—what do you think designers should know that we don't normally teach? Especially when it comes to historical references, what are the references that all designers should know that you have run across, and you're like, "Wow, why didn't I know about that? Now everything makes sense!"

AA
I didn't know who's teaching all the time. That's why I cannot speak on behalf of everyone, but I feel like there's some effort to put into decolonizing the curriculum a little bit. For instance, I'm looking at my syllabus every year, and I'm seeing it's lacking at diversity, but this diversity not in terms of identity politics, not that I don't have so and so in my curriculum. But I don't know, maybe getting to travel more and getting to learn more about the craft. I think we're missing craft a little bit in terms of teaching the design history. I mean, again, Taeyoon brought up the

Cartesian model, but actually, that idea has been broken by the Polynesians with their stick charts so they totally skipped the Cartesian history of wayfinding. They had stick charts which were adaptable to the ocean conditions because the ocean could never be mapped because there was no one solid reference point. So while I was teaching data and working on mapping, I decided to bring it in—this oceanic view when there's actually no solid ground, there is no Cartesian system, but yet they can depart from Polynesia and land in Hawaii after six months and on the same day using the same stick chart. So I think it's important to look into wider craft history.

RL
And I think as well, especially teaching young designers, to know what is bullshit or not. If you look at most developers, they look like me: white guy with a beard generally. And I think there's that kind of thing in design where it's like they like to follow trends, and there's that kind of Magpie Effect if you look at anything on like Dribbble or Behance. There's a lot of stealing. And I think as you get a senior as a designer, you kind of start to work out what is bullshit and what is just copying and what is just following what everyone else is doing. I think it comes back to things like decolonizing design and things like that as well. What are those designers interested in and why they're interested in that and kind of like telling them almost like the history of that and going away from the grain of what everyone else is doing as well.

JC
I don't know if anybody's familiar with the book *Life in Code* by Ellen Ullman. She's a developer who wrote what I think is an excellent memoir, and she opens the whole thing by talking about taking a Python class online and how the two guys who are giving the class. She did a whole sampling of stuff, and she's like, "I already knew how to code Python, but I just wanted to see how it was done." And the first 10 minutes of class, like all they do is make jokes about how Python came from *Monty Python*, and they start making *Monty Python* jokes. They're talking about all of these kind of coded references to a very specific culture. And she's pointing out that at 10 minutes in, anybody who did not know the five or ten references that are meant to make a lighthearted class would have been gone at that moment. So how do you all think about being able to open up? This is an issue we've always had here at Parsons too. It's like you have a student who comes into the class, and they take one look at the guy teaching the class and they're like, I'll sit through this, but this is not for me. So what are ways that computation in the design classroom can become accessible to everyone—craft being one of them—but do you have other ideas for us to make it something that is like for me when I walk into that classroom.

TC
I think the most important thing that we've learned over the years at School for Poetic Computation is that coding is essentially a series of rules that are abstracted in some sort of agreement between people. So C++ or JavaScript, those are all built on top of different systems that have been agreed by a larger group of people. And so there are discrepancies and there's disagreements about what to call certain functions. And those are all imaginable, meaning that there are people like Ari Spiegel who works on a feminist

programming language where there's no patriarchal structure such as master and slave. And those are all definable. I think giving that as a beginning point and having students design the languages they want. And people like Ramsey Nasser who made an Islamic programming language that is not based on the [Latin] alphabet. So these are all possible. And I think if we just focus on JavaScript or Python, which are industry standard languages, we end up creating the very same content. And we have a student make a programming language from sponges because sponges have a black side and a white side, or for scrubs and then it's binary so you could have a programmable code inside of sponges. So those are imaginations. And I think, the ability to imagine should be the first thing that we empower students with.

RL
And I think as well, it's like pushing those people's work afterwards as well so you're showing off the great work of women, basically not white guys. So something we try to do is heavily push people of all different backgrounds and show the work that they can do to show it's not just a white guy thing, learning to code.

JC
Can I ask some big questions to you guys? Can you teach curiosity?

MS
I'm not going to answer that directly, but I will say now that I've gone back to school and I'm currently in grad school, I've had this sinking feeling that the more that I learn, I realize the less that I know. On the one hand, it's exciting and it makes you more curious to go into these wormholes, but on the other side, it brings you into this state of insecurity because

there's just so much more that you could learn. I don't know if that will actually teach curiosity, but I think exposure to new ideas and tools and people is kind of the best way to expand or just reveal everything you don't know. And ideally, I think humans are naturally curious and want to know what they don't know.

TC
I think curiosities can be stolen away from an individual when there's discouragement or peer pressure in a toxic way.

MS
How so? Explain more.

TC
I think people including myself lose curiosity when I feel like I can't do it or I feel less equipped than a student next to me. And in technical courses, it's very easy to create a dynamic in which the star student who probably has done that technical exercise before ends up getting the most attention or most respect from the class. And we try to revert that by creating hallmarks that are equally challenging for advanced and beginner students and that opens up dialogues between students. So for example, we have an assignment that shows how binary numbers work like zeros and ones and the assignment is to create a game in which you teach another person how the binary number works. So that's challenging for advanced and beginner students because it's more about under-standing and applying that under-standing to pedagogical processes in which that could be transferred to other people. I think the best you can do is not to kill the curiosity.

JC
I'm going to ask one more question and then I'll open it up to everyone

else because this is another one of these big questions and it comes up in all teaching of technology. Can you teach autonomy? Can you actually teach somebody to be able to say I don't know how to do this, now how am I going to figure it out and then come up with a way to figure it out? Is that something that's teachable or is that just like a natural quality that people have?

RL
I think it's definitely teachable. I think there's obviously lots of tools online that people can Google and find, basically that read the docs almost. But I think it's kind of telling people how the underlying things work and where to find that information as well. So for instance, if we teach in JavaScript, there's sites that show you what kind of JavaScript you should use. And we were talking about the docs in the talk earlier. It's those kinds of methodologies of saying like, if you're doing this language or you're trying to do this, this is where you'd look and don't look here because this is out of date and look here because this is the new stuff. I think you can teach that. And I think people can run with that as well.

AA
I think it is possible to teach how to model a problem. I think that's the first step to the solution. I think in an academic setting, the best one can do is basically help them, drawing from different disciplines like science or nature or social science at least to like defining a problem, and model the problem and then I guess the solution is that it can autonomously be solved.

MS
So I also want to add that whether you can teach someone autonomy or not, again maybe it's not the right

question, but rather why do we want to solve problems by ourselves? I think it's trying to work with people around you who know more than you do and vice versa so you can work together to create whatever project you're trying to implement. But going into a tutorial hall online to do something on your own, I don't know if we actually need to do that. We're trying to build collectives and communities I think, and maybe that's more meaningful than trying to do something on your own, even if it's possible.

TC
Really quick, I think the best thing that we can do for design students is to help them respect engineering as a field and also be able to communicate with engineers in a sophisticated manner, respecting their craft and their time and asking the right question because in the industry I think most of the work it's divided and is delegated, but there's a lot of conflict between designers and engineers and product managers. It's a source of modern drama today. And I think it comes from lack of under-standing and lack of respect for each other. I've had experiences with students who just say like, "I don't think I'll become an engineer, but I have a much better relationship with my engineering friends, collaborators, and team."

JC
So should we open up to questions? Any questions from over here?

Audience Member
You said something about people copying each other, and I was wondering if you think there's some kind of wisdom that comes out of this whole culture of people copying each other, is there some kind of wisdom

that comes out of this sort of collective copying off of each other?

RL
I think there definitely is when people try to copy those trends, it's almost like they can see where the technique comes from. But I think doing it for just a stylistic purpose doesn't always make too much sense. And if you look at trends from the last 15 years of the web or digital media, you've got things like Web 2.0, very flat design right now. So it can lead people into kind of dead ends I suppose. Like, this is my style because I like this style because someone else did it. From an education point of view, I think it's quite good for a junior to know how things are done, but I think based in your whole kind of graphic design practice around that, it doesn't make too much sense, and it's almost like trying to find where did that style come from and who originated that style is probably more important than just lazily copying something from Dribbble for instance.

Audience Member
So we talked about the demographics of students. How has that actually changed or is that the basis for new types of learning?

RL
I can go first. For us, we have students in 80 countries, and the gender split is relatively good. Obviously, we have lots of competition online, and most of their gender split is actually a lot more heavily skewed towards male. We're trying to move it away from that kind of stereotype a little bit more and trying to move it away. I think we're both trying to do similar stuff and like not making it code is this white guy thing like how it's shown in the kind of advertisements that you get online. And I think when you can make a kind of worldwide thing and make it a very cross demographic kind of thing, I think it just makes it a lot more accessible to anyone wanting to get into those industries as well.

AA
In terms of demographics, I don't mean race or gender or age, but I think it's very important or responsible to show what you do, like what the visual landscape is like, what's the cultural context. And when I first moved here and started teaching at Rutgers, we mostly get, obviously, New Jersey residents and suburban families. We still get them, but now I've started feeling and observing that the students who are applying to our program are interested in what the others did before. It's hard to explain, but I have a visual landscape of what's happening at SFPC, I have a visual landscape of what's happening here. I think it's the responsibility to show what is going on. And then the demographics, of course, it's affected by many different factors and from where you are, a lot of different factors. But I think it's the pedagogic responsibility to show what the others did and I think that defines the demographics, if not by race and gender.

MS
I also wanted to add, this isn't necessarily about demographics, but I feel like we hear this phrase decolonization quite often and I don't have an answer for this, but it's just a question I've been grappling with, but is that actually the right word? Because it's a very, very heavy, deeply historical political word. So there's this great essay by Eve Tuck and Wayne Yang that claims that decolonization is not a metaphor. That's the title. So while it's extremely important to open up the canonical figures that

we talk and teach about in schools, I'm just worried about conflating the term and I don't have an answer for it, but it's just something that I've been thinking about, which I think is related to demographics in a sense.

JC
Well, there's also the argument that demographics, in general, are changing too. One of the critiques of the movement to teach everybody how to code is that it's actually a conspiracy effort for companies to make sure that the price that they pay for coders goes down. But I'm going to ask one question: speaking of platforms taking over our lives and the question is, how do you think the gap between what we learn from school about coding ethics and how we implement technology in the business world? What mindset should one have when in that dilemma? What is your advice to people who are going to work at Palantir or whatever, like what do you think that they should do? And what do you think, us in the classroom, who are struggling to just explain what a folder is, at what point do we actually open up that whole question of what it means to work at YouTube? What would you like to tell people to do basically about that?

TC
I think about this a lot actually because I have students who have worked at giant tech companies, and they're escaping it. And then there's also people who are coming from the arts and literature and try to find a more employable career where they could actually have some reasonable salary because being an artist is really hard financially. And I think those boundaries are very porous. The ones who are on one side of capitalism and the others. I think it's a false binary actually. For example, I have some

students who come from underprivileged communities or people with disabilities, whose access to coding skills is a way of connecting with the world, connecting with the communities and having financial freedom, and being empowered to be themselves. I respect their decision. I think their decision to work in giant tech companies are justified in my perspective. And I want them to have a really good position in those places because I believe they can change it from inside. And I've seen young engineers who climb up the corporate ladder and make policy changes. The Google walkout was a few months ago, and I knew people there. I think it's always a struggle and resistance from inside and outside. So I don't criticize people for working at certain companies except those who are explicitly evil or doing harm to people. But I think that's a really tricky conversation that we try to have at the school. And so far the conversations are ongoing, and it happens even within small collaborative settings. I think that's what made our community a more rich place where people could come without having to confront their decision about their career choices.

RL
Yeah, to kind of echo exactly the same thing, I think one thing that we say it's like it is of the student in the end, it's their decision. But similar to who are making the AI for things and what power do you actually have within that company is kind of a secondary thing that we ask them as well. Like, do they know what they came into when they're at this company? I think that's kind of an important thing to bring up to a student. Do you know what your role is at this company and what you can do and can't do? And

where can you change that in the future too?

Audience Member

Design is a discipline that always is connected to the usage of a tool. Do you think that coding is also a tool? If not, what do you think that coding opens up or restrains? Do you think that it's just a tool or if more, what is more for you?

RL

I would say it is a tool, but there is great power with those tools, as well. Like you can make anything that you want with code in a digital way. That's very important for people to realize. What is the power behind the stuff that you're making with Photoshop and Adobe tools? It's almost not real and it's not out there in the world, whereas with code, it's like you're switching something on and it's out there and on a URL that someone can link to. And there's almost that kind of discussion I suppose with this tool, similar to a hammer. You can use a hammer for hammering nails or you could go around killing people with a hammer. But it's the same kind of thing. It's the same tool.

AA

I don't think it is a tool. It becomes part of the body really. It's like a sailor, you cannot say it's a vessel. It's different from the cap, right, for a sailor. It's like a different thing. At some point, you make an emotional connection with that and then also physically, if you're sailing, your body begins working with it. And I don't think that divide is not like hammer and nail and hand. So I think of course it's a very intellectually engaged profession. And then I think that they're not really tools. And coding is not a tool either. It's just the thinking method.

JC

If it is a way of thinking, then isn't it worth it to learn how to do it, even if you don't use it as a tool to make design?

AA

Yes, I think it's worth it to learn how to do it. It's like being bilingual, trilingual, like apparently out of people, if you can speak more than one language, if you think in another language, in a literal language, you can have a more multidimensional thinking skill. And I think coding, in one way or the other, I think it's important. Not for making, but at least for thinking. But also for design, I don't think any design tool that a designer uses to produce something that is beloved to them is not a tool. It's like a sailboat that at some point you fall in love.

Audience Member

Organizations are kind of a product of their communications structure and are kind of destined to reproduce the structure of their organizations in the tools that they make. I'm wondering since it is a designer's role to shape these tools and because you are at a school as an organization that creates some kind of information structure to teach students, how do you see that progression in creating an environment that teaches students and then students make tools? Where do you as teachers place yourself in that system?

RL

For us, we make tools as well as teach. A lot of the students that we have, have already tried to learn to code in lots of different ways so things like Codeacademy or just tutorials online. I think when they come to us and they find the tools, they're still doing the same thing. They just have this kind of different thought process on top of what they were trying to learn. I think that makes them think a bit more about how to make other things a bit easier, almost like user experience I suppose.

But how do you go through the hard process of learning this stuff? It doesn't take eight weeks or ten weeks or however long it is. It's a long time to actually feel comfortable with code. I think if you can basically engineer around the experience rather than kind of saying like, "hey, here are all the tools that are out there that aren't for you." Most coding tools are aimed at intermediate and advanced level people, and they're not aimed at beginners and there's barely any tools aimed at beginner coders. And it's something that when we were trying to teach, we just couldn't find anything at the time so we had to build our own and really think, how does this work? How do you even teach this stuff when no one's in the room with you? What can we add in here that will actually make people's lives easier?

AA
Totally the opposite answer because apparently I will speak from the privilege of teaching at a research university in which it's like a church. Like we don't guarantee if you come to church you'll go to heaven. So we just produce the knowledge, and it's our job to make research around the discipline and design is my discipline. I'm trying to produce knowledge around that and make sure that this knowledge is available, first to the students, then to the larger audience, to the public. We cannot guarantee that you're going to get a job after it. We cannot guarantee that you're going to have to go to heaven because you came to church. But we are responsible for the ethics of the discipline, and we're responsible for

the research. And the tools, I don't think we really make tools, but we create an environment as they're trying to do at SFPC, in a way.

TC
I think something that we didn't really talk about is the price of education, which is a big part of why students need to get a job right after because they have huge loans, and institutions are putting students in debt that is just huge. Like that's an ethical dilemma of teaching in institutions large and small. And part of the founding principle of SFPC was accessibility and inclusion and having fairness among those who pay and those who get paid. So still a balancing act right now. But what I found is that through a more trans-parent model, we can actually gain the trust of the community much more easily. So we publish all of our finances online in the hopes that other people who are trying to start schools could replicate that model or learn from our mistakes and make something better. And we also hire our alumni to teach and organize sessions and there's projects like the Code Societies, which is a three-week session run by Melanie Hoff, who was our student and a teacher.

And I think seeing her take on a more leadership role over the two years' period has been very rewarding. And that's a way of flipping the classroom to become a platform in which students can grow. And I think the cost is a huge barrier in traditional and especially private universities because you can't flip that role because you can't just start paying your students to teach in the same tuition that you charge them. I have a lot of friends who teach at universities who say I cannot afford the tuition of my university where I cannot pay for my kid. So I think this is where code becomes an interesting topic because it's seen as like this golden horse to make our students more employable. I think that's where there's pressure to make this like the skill set actually comes into play.

Audience Member
One of the things I really liked about Taeyoon's description of the poetic part in societies is that he said code is very good for two reasons. One reason is that code itself is a poetic expression as a language. The other one is that you can use code to create very poetic effects. So I think that captures code in two ways: one as a language, the other as a media. And I think historically if you look at things such as letterpress or photography, the advance of the tools actually helps a lot in shaping how the media came into being. So my question is that thinking for a larger scale, what would you think would be some of the important things or important tools that people should design to help more people to learn how to code?

TC
There's a book that you could download online called *People's Guide to AI*. It just got published and it's free. I think that's great because we don't know what AI is, nobody knows. Nobody's telling us. Like that's a great question. I think demystifying technologies and discourses around it and making it accessible is great, and I think generally code could be used for social justice and empow- erment of any people. I just think if we change the narratives around code, I think that those effects will be possible.

RL
I also think there's a lot of tools that definitely could change that we're still using as well. So it's not just code

editors, but things like command line tools that some people have to use and all of the tools that people make. It feels like it's getting more complex to start to learn to code, and it just feels like it's backwards. Why are these tools so hard to use? It's like they're aimed at creating things, and they're getting harder rather than easier. It just makes me angry.

MS
I also wonder if instead of trying to make new tools, we can also consider how to break the ones we currently have. So there's a media theorist and writer named Wendy Wei Xiang Chan, and she talks about how if you consider the society that we have as a grammar and then data as kind of like a piece of that written structure, then we can kind of exaggerate or use fiction to amplify or talk about the problems within the system. So instead of if you think of data scraping, our natural inclination is to say maybe privacy and surveillance is what we should be talking about, but instead, maybe we can just exaggerate the way we use these certain platforms. Like for example, are we using Google Maps? Like, yes, we know how to use Google Maps in the way that's intended but is there a way to kind of tweak the structure that's currently there to figure out what the breaking points of this thing are? People use it as like a narrative structure, for example, to tell stories through Google Maps. I think it's quite interesting to think about, to use tools in ways that weren't actually their intended use.

Audience Member
Do you think that there are certain values that exclude particular people or students from learning about coding and design, and what are those values? Ultimately I'm inter-

ested in what the values that exist both in an academic context look like, and also what the value systems look like in industry because I think that part of the driving factor for students while they're in school, the aim is to go out and get a job and make money, that their focus while they're in school and how they're learning code is really impacted by that.

TC

That's a great question. I think when we say we're teaching code, we are actually hiding what's essential to computation, which is mathematics, logic, and being able to read and write. So I teach young people code, like middle school students, and you can see the people who have understood geometry and those who have not. And I see that with college-level students and adults, as well. So coding is a way of getting into that math where math meets language. And I think, just going a step deeper, it will be physics. To understand physical qualities of electronics. Those are the parallel things that you are touching on. I feel very passionate that coding is just one of the top layers, the most visible layer, in which what we are talking about sits on.

RL

What makes good designers and good coders is empathy for the user and making those tools so it's not selfishly for yourself. When you're thinking about all these other people using these tools, I think that actually improves things like design and code. I think they're not too dissimilar, design and code. I think they're making things, and I think empathy is a big part of making things in general.

MS

I'm not going to answer the question, but I just want to pose another one because we've been dissecting words so much today, but is user actually the right word we should be using?

JC

I do want to tell the anecdote of one of the most head-scratching things when I was directing the program here in 2011. Students would come into my office week after week saying that they shouldn't be forced to learn Processing because Processing wasn't a program that they were going to use in their job. It was always very difficult to kind of unpack and then repack and we've changed and re-changed the whole code curriculum here somewhat in response to that. They were like, "I paid $40,000, you can't make me learn this." And it was really weird. It was like a logic that I had never anticipated. So I guess I'll turn that into a question. Given that, as somebody sitting in front of you who tells you that, how would you respond to them?

TC

If you can only see yourself as an employable subject, you just want to obtain the skill set in which that could be traded for certain types of currency. But this comes back to what Mindy was asking about the user. Do we want to think about our audience, our people, as users and content creators? Do we want our people to be considered a coder, not like an inventor or like people who are technologists who are able to imagine different ways of using physical qualities of the things that we have for it to do something else? Those are magical things that we have capacity to do, but I think we are just limiting ourselves to this employable metrics which could be calculated through salary rates or hourly rates. And I just think it's the neoliberalization of education itself that we should be talking about.

Audience Member
Can I ask one other quick question? Again, not to go back to value systems, but I'm curious then these incentives for certain students and to potentially go out into the workforce, that if they are sort of considering how they see themselves in a space beyond school, if they're coming in already with a certain agenda, I don't know if there's a way that we can necessarily break that as an educator?

JC
Let's say it's our job to break that.

Audience Member
Can I ask one question, kind of piggy-backing on that conversation that was happening? As we discussed, coding is like the gateway to this whole other universe, especially to my students in many cases. And I keep thinking about what is the right way to do it and the right way meaning what is the most effective way, what is the correct way, what is the most responsible way that I can do this? And I'm just curious, do you guys have any thoughts on that? Are there any tips and advice in that regard?

TC
I think it comes down to thinking about what you the teacher is getting out of this relationship. And I hope that most teaching is this emancipatory experience for students as well as the teacher where it's a reciprocal trade of ideas and experience and friendship and solidarity. I mean, it's all very idealistic, but without that, it becomes a transactional exchange between the ones who have the knowledge or access to grading and those who need that. And I think marginalized communities or people

who need to have this access to technology as a human right, they should have equal access to explore the creative side of technology as well. So I know people who are activists who are working with refugees and trying to get them to become a coding professionals, and I respect that because I think that access should come before our very liberal notion of creativity, access to water, and technology. But at the same time, I think if we just had them work in a certain capitalist system, I think we'll just continue to recreate the systems of precarity that we're trying to prevent them from entering into. So yeah, I think in our school, we try to make sure that the teaching is R&D for the teachers in practice and make sure the curriculum reflects their own interests and that students influence the teacher's back.

Audience Member
I'm thinking about the way that in some of the comments and discussion, there seems to be some equating the practice of coding and computational thinking, so I want to maybe decouple them for a second and maybe think about the title of the event, which I have no problems with. I'm thinking about the work of Alan Turing and Ada Lovelace, which was theoretical, right? It was about conceptual machines and the need to tackle the issues that we have now in our technological landscaping in society. Do you see value in teaching computational thinking without coding in order to facilitate maybe designing critical systems or social relations but without the syntax of coding?

TC
That's very exciting to think about it. There's a whole lot of people doing exactly that either through game

mechanics or either through performative activities. For example, in Japan, there's an institution called Yamaguchi Center for Art and Media where they have a digital playground where the young people can design their own rules to govern their playground. And they have adult's assistance who program it so that the playground reacts differently after the young people decide. And I think metaphors are really important. However, I think the practice of coding or working with computers in a much more intimate way is still very important. Like if you open up a terminal and make the machine do the things that it's not supposed to do, you have this transformative experience with a computer where you feel more empowered to fix it. And I still think that hands-on experience leads to more responsible behaviors with technology, which leads to better society.

AA

I think in the arts, there are a lot of historical examples. The closest one to us is Fluxus, which was totally procedural and instructional. Every place has its own sort of Fluxus history. I think there's amazing pedagogical value but also some sort of libertarian value in thinking about coding without the computer. But then if you're spending two and half hours a day in front of the computer, you'd rather use that too.

RL

I think the best example that I've seen is there was a program for kids learning to code, and I put code in air quotes because what we do with the parents is basically give them instructions to kind of get around a maze. And the parents could only read the instructions one by one. So it was basically forcing the kids to do these commands that made their parents like robots. So walk four paces forwards, turn left. Walk four paces forwards, turn right. And it would make them go around the maze almost like having this computational thinking by proxy that they're kind of doing it in a completely different way. And I think like metaphors as well, I think that is really important, but I think that was the best example I've seen for children, was basically forcing them to go away from the computer and think about how a robot would work and the robot was the parent instead.

JC

Great. So with that, we will end here. I thank you guys all for coming out on a Friday afternoon. Thanks to our panel.

Atif Akin is an artist, designer, and Associate Professor at Rutgers University. Taeyoon Choi is an artist who works with drawing, painting, computer programming, performance art and video. Rik Lomas is the founder of SuperHi. Mindy Seu is a designer and Assistant Professor at Rutgers University. Juliette Cezzar is an Associate Professor of Communication Design at Parsons.

STUDENTS

The following is a list of graduates based on degrees conferred across all Communication Design programs over the past decade. The first MPS Communication Design students graduated in 2018. The first AAS Communication Design students graduated in 2020.

2020–21 BFA Communication Design (123 graduates)

Falilat-Abike O. Adedotun Abeshinbioke, Sung Hyun Ahn,
Hazal Sena Aysel, Vivek Bajaj, Sunayana Bali,
Elliot Erik Bohlen, Madison Paige Brang, Allison Bynum,
Emily Jing Sum Chan, Rachel Chang, Lilliana Checo,
Jizheng Chen, Leqi Chen, Minxi Chen, Raghav Chhabra,
Shreya Chittaranjan, Christopher Garrett Chu,
Chih Hsuan Chuang, Calen Chung, Hannah Mae Craford,
Chengcheng Cui, Rebecca Ann D'Agostino,
Danielle Ann Delossantos, Nika Diomidovskaia,
Aira Patricia M. Dolfo, Maya Miriam Eapen, Yaron Erkin,
Xiaoke Fei, Bernadette Fernandez Figueroa, Shih-Ju Fu,
Michelle D. Gamble, Chenxi Gao, Sierra Rose Glicker,
Danielle Beatriz Dizon Go, Danielle M. Gomez,
Qing Ying Guan, Peiru Guo, Siyu Hang, Trudy Tran Hoang,
William James Howell, Wenqing Huang, Charis Lee Huling,
Sana Faek Jamali, Aeva Germaine Karlsrud,
Lake L. Kennedy, Byunghyun Kim, Su Yeon Destiny Kim,
Yeji Kim, Young Ji Kim, Zen Koo, Padmaja Rajiv Kothari,
McKayla Kathleen Lankau, Hyunseung Maddie Lee,
Jade Young Ja Lee, Jiwoo Lee, Juna Lee,
Victoria Nagaño Lee, Emma G. Lepore, Emily Hue Foo Li,
Scarlet Yuan Li, Sunny Li, Sohyun Lim,
Chuhan Stephanie Lin, Misty Lin, Yu Tong Tiffany Ling,
Lilian Ying Liu, Hoi Yi Phoebe Lo, Charlotte Jane Lomas,
Kevin Loumeau, Wen-Hsin Lu, Dirmawan Luawo,
Peiyun Luo, Youran Mao, Ana Clara Marques Furtado,
Imani Danae Mcintosh, Rebecca Mesonjnik,
Velimar Arianna Molina, Louis Sebastien Motte Dit Falisse,
Gavin Patrick Mullally, Syalsabila Karissa Munaf,
Michael Mungai, Sanjana Navar, Aileen Pan,
Chanjoo Tiffany Park, Namjoon Park, Storey Pearson,
Mariel Quadrino, Simran Rao, Felitasari Widya Rekso,
Elizabeth Anna Richards, Yasmin Binti Rozmee,
Rainier Alexander Salas, Julia Rose Sams,
Eva Blanca Serrano Reisner, Anvita Anand Shah,
Suditi Shah, Amal Masood Shaheedi, Jingjing Shi,
Samantha Costabile Simotas, Hyunji Song,
Carolina Stierli De Abreu, Niharika Sundarigari,
Rachael Tomaszewski, Svasti Ujagar, Camila Ullauri,
Ariana Ushiki, Diana Victoreen, Wenpei Wang, Yiqi Wang,
Zheng Wang, Jasmine Wei, Savannah Kelsey West,
Summer Elizabeth Wojtas, Jacquelyn Wu, Ricky Xie,
Connie Xu, Jiayi Xu, Jacqueline Wen Qian Yang,
Xirou Yang, Emily Yun, Monique Zeitouny,
Cecilia Runxi Zhang, Cheryl Zhang

2020–21 MPS Communication Design (24 graduates)

Mari Al-Midhadi, Gandhali Bapat, Kaitlyn Brown,
Cheuk Ying Cherie Chan, Ching Chang,
Roseanne Ruo Xi Chao, Meijia Deng, Kebing Han,
Sejeong Hwang-Yoo, Defne Kaynak,
Mohammed Maher Labban, Regina Mary Ann Itchon La O,
Chengran Li, Zhenliang Li, Yijun Liang, Seo Ho Moon,
Xue Shan, Kaiwen Tao, Qing Wen, Kara Elizabeth Wilson,
Jessica Yang, Qiuyi Yu, Haiyi Zhao, Xiaoyu Zhou

2020–21 AAS Communication Design (28 graduates)

Akane Aigase, Cristina Alves, Christopher Michael Barrett,
Jacob Joseph Berstein, Emily Ellen Bluedorn,
Isabel Gianna Campbell, Yi Chen, Xueyi Cui,
Abigail Paige Dahl, Dannis Fu, Rebecca Marie Greubel,
Nani Rachel Harakawa, Allison Joy Kobren, Leslie Kay Lim,
Annachiara Maffezzoli, Nittika Mehra, Denise Mylonakis,
Rafia Elizabeth Rehman, Nicola Andrea Enrile Roxas,
Denisa Sadocco Haas, Brooke Arden Shapiro,
Gabriel Mark Smoller, Julia Grace Sullivan,

Lucia Velasco Gomez, Jennifer S. Wang, Jia Cheng Wang,
Jaemin Yoon, Sydney Ariel Stamm Zeldis

2019–20 BFA Communication Design (136 graduates)

Estefania Acosta Dume, Kamaldeen Kolade Adisa,
Sakshi Agarwal, Sejal Aggarwal, Geddes O. Alexander II,
Kaitlyn Charisse Amable, Emily Sofia Maud Baro,
Emily Ann Bergerson, Xiujie Bi, Sonja R. Briney,
Dahee Byun, Idil Celik, Kimberly Wai Kay Chan,
Krish Kamlesh Chandiramani, Julie Yu Chen,
Xingman Cheng, Habin Cheong, Ho Yau Chik,
Olivia Lauren Chow, Paloma Isabel Corrigan,
Jessica Dantas, Misha Danielle Dhanoolal, Wing Ki Fan,
Maria Fe Rosa Farah Tenorio, Evelin Susan Fung Zhong,
Vincent Garcia, Christina Heather Gordon,
Maria Fernanda Guardazzi, Gideon Tobias Gulko,
Esra Gumrukculer, Aanya Gupta,
Carolyn Alexandra Haitz Olaguivel, Arani Halder,
Bobby Isaiah Hill, Jinghan Hu, Olivia Megan Hunter,
Se Jung Hwang, Jyudeh Maximilian Russ Jarrett,
Sulamita Edelweiss Javier Balanutsa,
Madison Barrett Jennings, Won Kyung Jung,
Inga Natalie Kan, Suji Kang, Ayse Yaren Kaya,
Prithi Khalique, Polina Khvostova, Shanjida Kibria,
Celine Kim, Seowon Kim, Suah Kim, Youjong Kim,
Rasheka Krishan, Eli Strauss Lederberg,
Grace Ann Ledoux, Alicia Kayoung Lee, Hyunseo Lee,
Ngar Man Natashia Lee, Rachel Joohee Lee, Yoo An Lee,
Sik Hang Tiffany Leung, Sinong Li, Qiyao Lin, Jiayi Liu,
Sichao Liu, Sophia Marinelli, Julia L. McGillicuddy,
Sarah Elizabeth Mcnutt, Sanika S. Mehta,
Eleni Rosa Mentis, Vincent Antoine Noel Merle,
Yehia Abouseif, Anthony Muchai Muiruri, Daniel Mullins,
Meredith Brooke Nelson, Ruowen Niu, Catalina O'Connor,
Hyun Sun Ohm, Lorna Marie Oppenheim,
Kyle Anthony Palma, Anastasia Papakonstantinou,
Brendon Park, Ji Min Park, Lee Jun Park,
Sanha Saeyoung Park, Tommy Park, Holly Katherine Parkin,
Tunchanok Patana-Anake, Sean Phan,
Olimpia Pignatti Morano Campori, Delaney Hunter Poitras,
Vincent Maxwell Privitera, Jhoenny Ramirez,
Taylor Sade Raschillo, Zhen Ren,
Militza Asuncion Rodriguez Charr, Rachel Heller Rudolph,
Lily Sun Yun Saeli, Leoder A. Sanchez,
Maria Agustina Sanchez, Simone Sciacovelli, Shreya Shah,
Seth Sharbono, TongRun Shi, Mei Tsen Shih,
Avni Shivkumar, Arunima Sinha, Shivam Sinha,
Dominic Gabriel Syjuco Siy, Jason Decker Sloves,
Bailey Elizabeth Storms, Demi Isabela Straulino, Tingyu Su,
Yuchen Su, Katartouch Tobunluepop, Kiana Toossi,
Shivani Toshniwal, Morella Tovar Mancera, Ha Anh Tran,
Kyle Luke Tranquilli, Valerie Alyssa Trisnadi, Yi-Chieh Tsai,
Kayla Jean Van Der Byl, Manasi Vashi,
Emil Thomas Waldron, Jingyi Wang, Xinyi Wang,
Yuzheng Wang, Ziqing Wang, Sophie Marie Westfall,
Jiapei Wu, Xinyi Wu, Jun Hyuk Yang, Kyle Austin Yu,
Xinchen Zhang, Yujing Zhang,
Evgeniya Aleksandrovna Zykova

2019–20 MPS Communication Design (15 graduates)

Luenne Yasmin Albuquerque Neri, Zuyuan Fan,
Zhaojing Feng, Jing Gu, Yu Ri Ha, Rajlaxmi Jain,
Elif Karakose, Ching Tien Lee, Xuerui Li, Stephany Madi,
Sanchi Sanjeev Oberoi, Shiyuan Peng, Jessie Yao,
Yifu Zhang, Shuqi Zhu

Nafisa Afrin Iqbal, Daniela L. Al-Saleh,
Yasmeen A. Alayoub, Maria Michelle Badasian,
Evan Cyrus Badr, Jennifer Maccarelli Barroll,
Jaire Xavier Berkel, Bhavika Prakash Bhatia, Leehe Bok,
Lauren April Brady, Maria Elisa Bustos Schmutzer,
Gabrielle Cantamessa, Joseph Michael Castanon,
German Castellanos, Cristina Cepeda Thielmann,
Madeline Cericola, Vicky Chau, Tiange Chen,
Yingyou Chen, Dahee Choi, Carol Hee-Jin Chong,
Matthew James Chu, Lily Eve Clempson,
Analuisa Corrigan, Gaurika Milan Dalal, Sylvia Ana Epstein,
Jamie Shi Ying Fong, Mariana Gaviria,
Constantine Georgiadis, Baruch Bentzion Goldman,
Shagari Guity, Sarah Jane Hennessy,
Irene Belen Hernandez Gaona, Sara S. Hilany,
Justina Hilsenrad, Marielle Holland, Allen Hu,
Gufeng Huang, Julia Isman, Erika Nicolette Jaquez,
Andrea S. Jassir, Moonnyung Jo,
Adam Wei-Loong Johansen, Souraya Jureidini,
Cynthia Toshie Kamata-Banks, Suranart Kasitipradit,
Anastasia Shahla Khadivi,
Peggy Southaphone Khammanotham, Ji Won Kim,
Minhae Kim, Sarah Eirene Kim, Soyeon Kim, Soyeon Kim,
Esther Louise Klingbiel, Rose Zaza Kramer,
Clare Elizabeth Lagomarsino, Julia A. Lassen, Jahyun Lee,
Nicole Danielle Lee, Sunghee Lee, Ye Eun Lee, Leqi Liang,
Chia Ying Lin, Chih-Yi Lin, Eric Jacob Lish,
Clarissa Emilia Losciale, Eileen Lu, Cobey Scott Lusinger,
Maria De Guadalupe Magnani Blanco, Kristiana Marcon,
Miguel Marcos, Iyana Martin Diaz,
Gaebrielle Jade Mcintosh, Mitali Mehta, Ana Sofia Murillo,
Dahao Y. Ni, Mitali Arvind Nopany, Eugene Ong Bang Jun,
Diana Yunhee Pak, Seongjin Park, Annika Nicole Phillips,
Marie Anne Brigitte Poncin, Jin Qian, Jea Hyun Reece,
Jack Rieger, Kenisha Bijoux Mora Rullan,
Joshua Gates Ryan, Bushra Sarker, Amy Elizabeth Schultz,
Vitoria Schweitzer Fiore, Leah Nicole Slava,
Limmie Michael-Joshua Snoddy, Rebecca Leila Speiser,
Anisha Subberwal, Erica Brooke Tagliarino,
Elisa Emma Tordjmann, Elizabeth Tsai, Yasemin Varlik,
Varun Vig, Diana Vivar, Yifei Wang, Yuqi Wang,
Coco Brigitte Wohrle, Evelyn Z. Wu, Angela Chu Lin Yang,
Stella Ting Yen, Tiffany Choi Yung Ying, Ingrid Yiu,
Celestine Jieling Yuan, Seoyoung Yun, Maria Zabolotnaya,
Amanda Nicole Zaldivar, Yinglin Zeng, Junhao Zhang,
Lingya Zhang, Haitong Zheng, Karolina Anna Zuchowski

Shefali Agarwal, Victoria Tam Duong, Yu Fu,
Clemence Juliette Houede, Eunjung Kim, Nataly Klajner,
Katherine Claire Leisy, Anh Hong Mai, Zachary Ian Perkins,
YuFei Sun, Rijk Antonie Van Zanten, Yu Lun Wang,
Sherley Soraya Wijaya, Jiawei Yan

Maxine Joy Almendra, Amon Dario Appelt, Shruti Ashok,
Whitney Badge, Ingrid Bonetti Veloz, Victoria Boyd Duran,
Madison Bozinoff, Malulani Marie Bria,
Kaylin MacKenzie Brown, Rachel Brownjohn, Lian Chao,
Amber Chen, Yuan Chen, Wendy Ching, Emily Cho,
Connie Chu, Channon Chung, Leonardo Cilmi,
Emma Theresa Conway, Nicole Amanda Corso,
Talia Cotton, Qamile Margarite Dani,
Magdalena de la Torre Suárez, Amanda Jasmin Ericson,
Daniel Louis Feldman, Anna Feng, Natalia Flores,
Peter Frasco, Maria Lucia Garza,
Olive Pearlgrace Golyakov-Burd, Grant Engelman Gulla,
John Connor Hammond, Aimee Vera Hedman,
Mike M. Hefez, Adrianna Marie L. Hinsey,
Avinash V. Hirdaramani, Grace Erin Hong, Surkho Hong,
Pauline Olympia Maria Hotelier, Dylan Hughes,
Jiyoung Hwang, Sonali Jain, Christina Joan Jenkins,
Maria Jessica, Erin Johnston, Javarius Travon Jones,
Myles Jones Montano Mendoza, Yea Ji Jung, Rachel Kahn,

Anastasia Kharchenko, Jonathan Haojaq Kho, Alexa S. Kim,
Da Won Kim, Sang Eon Kim, Somin Kim, Yoonji Kim,
Kyungmin Ko, Sidney Law, Hyeon Beom Lee,
Joungyeun Lee, Matheus Dal Santo Lewis,
Hannah Marshall, Kruti Ketan Mehta, Gabriel Mester,
Charlotte Ellen Dryden Miller, Mintra Marion Morrison,
Tamir Moses, Kaisha Murzamadiyeva, Nghĩa Hữu Nguyễn,
Alaina Nowak, Satoe Onizuka, Steven Orts,
Lauren Ouaknine, Owen Caverly Pace, Carly Page,
Tatyana Palacios, Herin Park, Olga Pavlova,
Maria Luisa Peralta-Esquivel, Lindsay Caroline Petricca,
Camille P. Petricola, Constanza Pinto Barreyro,
Shreya Razak, Costanza Reiser, Vincent Riportella,
Bateel Saber, Ahana Seth, Sage Smith,
Cristina Soberón Hernández, Natalia Elaine Spotts,
Sabrina Steck, Lauren Nicole Stein,
Johnnie D. Stephenson Jr., Richard Supriano,
Shivalika Tandon, Jissaura Taveras Hernandez,
Nathalia Giselle Tello Arias, Brinna Thomsen,
Eden Touil Tartour, Altyn Nurbek Turdukulova,
Amena Abeezar Tyebji, Gabriela Marie Vieira,
Juan Diego Villegas Currea, Yi Ge Wang, Jessie Yao,
Crystal Yin, Yue Zhang, Jiayi Zhou

Husani Barnwell, Carolyn Jane Keavy Berry, Jinyue Chen,
Sheila Cheng, Samia Ahmed Husari, Vidya Keshavan,
Diana Mejia, Nikhil Misra, Patricia Robinson,
Sonali Anuradha Sampat, Danielle Santucci, Patrick Serr

Selwa Abderrazak, Mariam H. Abutaleb,
Jason Andrew Agus, Ameer Akbar, Moriaki Akiho,
Orhan S. Awatramani, Mercedes Kimi Beach,
Mrinal V. Bhatia, Yaël Bienenstock, Olivia Noelle Brodtman,
Adomas Bruzga, Holly Renee Burt, Kiana Caesar,
Robert Capaldo, Elizabeth Jayne Capreol,
Christian Jon Caraballo, Alyson Cardenas,
Gabriela Carnabuci, Marjorie Chamberlain, Vanna Chan,
Sachi Chandiramani, Leslie Carolina Chavez, Sarada Chen,
Katherine Cheng, Linette Cheong Yeak Yeow, Hyeree Choi,
Soomin Choi, Eva Marie Cruz,
Dorothy Elizabeth Cruz Perdomo, Katherine DeAngelis,
Nicole Jane Debler, Mariana Del Nogal, Dominique DeVito,
Megan Dias, Theresa Elisabeth Duemler,
Michelle Chelsea Eguia, Sherifa El Alfi, Audrey Farnsworth,
Myesha Evon Gardner, Maria Gabriela Garuz,
Stella Maria Giavos, Alijah Gilbert, Daniela Godard Rangel,
Jin Ju Han, Perla Herrera, Mckenna Elle Hogue,
Lauren Michelle Horsman, Zhiyan Huang, Ji Hea Jang,
KyungJun Jang, Urvita Jhaveri, Cheryl Kao,
Phoebe Kennedy, Chewon Kim, Han Sung Kim,
Jung Yeon Kim, Sanggyun Kim, Thomas Sang Gul Kim,
Ye Ji Alice Kim, Yi Hui Teresa Koh, Likando Kumoyo,
Josh W. LaCalamito, Kyung Sun Lee, Soo Ji Lee,
Yunjoo Lee, Meijun Li, Alice Lim, Junya Lin, Yuchen Liu,
Kimberly Rose Lombardi, Natalia Malik,
Roisin Ciara Marie McNulty, Simen L. Meyer,
Nikoletta Mitsopoulou, Juan Francisco Morales Egas,
Alexandra Morton, Chloë G Murray,
Sofia Olarra Rodriguez, Clarissa Ong, Kamila Ortiz,
Ji Hyun Park, Yeon Soo Park, Sara J. Pena,
Melissa S. Peralta, Sander L. Phoenix, Lisa Sakai Quinley,
Cyrus Ra, Urvi Raghbeer, Andrew Ramirez, Brianna Saba,
Stephen Salomon, Julianna Amelia Santolucito,
Raida Saveree Sarwar, Ritika Shah, Shui Shan, Jisoo Sim,
Pei Yu Sun, Laura Tien, Karina Madelin Tristandy,
Joel Tschong, Paula Volchok, Dih Jiun Wang,
Shangwei Wang, Taylor Anne Wasikonis, Junlu Xie,
Marie Yamamoto, Yang Yi, Jasmine Zhang

Nicolas Abreu, Seung Hyun Ahn, Aviva R. Atri,
Katharine Lee Atwood, Miles Andrew Short Barretto,

Ana Cecilia Barros Thompson Motta, Ambroise Bellec,
Lili Marie Bravi, Supisara Ngaovithunvong,
Carla Campos-Rodriguez, Jiaying Cao,
Janet Cecilia Chan Chen, Hanna Chang, Purwa Chauhan,
Jiayi Chen, Kuanling Lynna Chen, Patrick Chen,
Eunsil Choi, Sung Ji Choi, Yerang Choi, Morgan Connellee,
Veselin Cuparic, Brittany Ellen Cutrone,
Arianna De Gasperis-Brigante,
Amanda Lauren DeGiuseppe, Paola Delucca Velilla,
Rubina Melati Diran, Ann Dwyer, Dilan Emre,
Douglas Escalante, Joe Louis Evans,
Juliana Marie Luchkiw, Mark Foss, Marius Franc,
Ceilidh Fraser, Anais Freitas Elespuru, Jiayi Ge,
Perri Axler Ginsberg, Meher Goel, Jessica Clare Griscti,
Alyssa Michele Gruber, Yu Bean Han, Hsiao-hui Ho,
Jasmine Hong, Tzu-Chieh Hsiao, Hyun Sun Hwang,
Louise Pei Foong Hyde, Sanghyun Ji, Kathleen M. Kehres,
April Kim, Eun Rae Kim, Lisa Kim, Sharon Y. Kim,
David Klein, Liberty Rebekah Leben, Jae Jun Lee,
Jiyoon Lee, Lauren Elizabeth Lee, Stephanie Sumin Lee,
Dana Li, Mengdi Li, Haowei Lin, Caroline W. Liu,
Lucas Long, Lisa Nicole Looye, Zongliang Lou,
Ankita G. Menon, Lauren Melinda Miller,
Katherine Minchak, Isabela Natalie Montalvo,
Nathalie Moreno, Regina Morgan Munoz,
Natalia Barbara Mrozek, Samah Mudasar, Shirin Muradova,
Gabriela Nisenbaum, Inyegumena Nosegbe,
Zoe Jena Oleshansky, Anna Wright Peditto,
Xing Hai Effy Piao, Pamela Pombo Rodriguez,
Josephine Rahadi, Simone Roark, Rick Rodriguez,
Ana Julia Rodriguez Penfold, Maria Fernanda Romero,
Hannah Sawyer Rosen-Hamilton,
Ivana Roumiantzeff-Pachkevitch, Taylor A. Russo,
Ariella Liliane Saragossi, Christian Schofield,
Nengneng Shen, Kripa Sial, Gaya Sirmabiyik,
Matthew Sporzynski, Mariusz Stankiewicz, Kurt M. Stives,
Minji Sung, Vanshika Swaika, Peter Toh,
Ujvala Abirami Vemparala, Yue Wang, Kevin Wen,
Yingmeng Xu, Anna Yamoto, Jiawei Yan, Vivian S. Yang,
Xiao Qing Yang, McLayne Bradford Ycmat, Brenden Ying,
Emily Yu, Jingyao Zhang, Xuan Zhang

2014–15 BFA Communication Design (103 graduates)

Carolina Acosta, Carina Danielle Adijanto, Kathryn Adkins,
Che Ying Au, Elizabeth Bakacs, Nadia Bakst, Kevin Ballon,
Roy Edison Bedingfield III, Evan Bender, Jan-Luca Berger,
Elizabeth Bergesch, Gabriel Berrios, Bianca Rose Bono,
Zoe Sarah Bortz, Margot Bravi, Harlie Rose Brindak,
Christopher S. Brody, Shamma Buhazza,
Lily Kathleen Campbell, Daniela Milagros Casado Fortique,
Da Hye Chang, Alicia Wen Wei Chen, Yu-Hua Cheng,
Taylor Nicole Childers, Sanjana Chimnani, Yun Hee Choi,
Caroline Elizabeth Chriss, Gina Marie Costa,
Karen Cristina Cruz, Rachel Darmody,
Roderic Eugene David, Brittany DiPeri, Phoebe Feng,
S.K. Finnegan, Maryann George, Camille Gervais,
Amanda Brooke Goldstein, Sarah Lynn Gonzalez,
Christa Ann Herchek, Albert Lawrence Hicks IV,
Deja Mone Holden, Carolyn Anne Hume,
Zachary David Hurley, Anushae Hussain,
Thanh Cong Huynh, Lama Marwan Kaddura, Green Kim,
Hyerin Kim, Ji Hyun Kim, Sul Kim, Sunghoon Kim,
Felicitas Emilie Kofler, Joan Koo, Hannah Lee Kramer,
Taiji Kuroda, Stephanie Kwan, Jasmine Faye Lam,
Alexandra Lardaro, Adrian Lee, Jayne Lee, Victoria L. Lee,
Yongmin Lee, Stephanie Jean Leone, Crysta Leong,
Sara Li, Liza Littlefield, Michelle Luo, Briana Lynch,
Rachel Wai Yan Mak, David Jose Marte Olivares,
Andrea Fiorella Martinez, Ellen Charlotte McDade,
Kelly Merole, Marie Mhina, Riho Monica Mineta,
Jiwon Myung, Caroline Elizabeth Newton,
Adrian Ortega Pedraza, Yasemin Pars,
Rusbeny Pichardo Castillo, Maria Setiamuliati Putri,
Nancy J. Rivera, Emalis J. Robateau,
Mian Hussain Feroze Salahuddin, Ariel Vittoria Saura,
Taleen Setrakian, Wren Elizabeth Sieber,
Erinn Elizabeth Springer, Elizabeth Drinkwater Stankus,

Phuong Tran, Hilary Ellen Tunstall,
Rafael-Maria Vazquez Cordoba,
Gosbinda Vizarretea Rodriguez, Claudia Von Hillebrandt,
Marcus Anthony Washington, Jr., Elisa Winograd,
Jocelyn Wu, Jasmine Yacoub, Immanuel Paula Yang,
Sara Yonas, Kirsten Young-Clark, Sophia Marie Zell,
Christelle Yuanyuan Zhang

2013–14 BFA Communication Design (127 graduates)

Christos Anthony Adamopoulos, Sarah Salah AlFulaij,
Yasmine Amish, Michael Jesse Anderson,
Darwin Andrango, Leonardo Alexander Araujo, Atif Azam,
Rachel Leigh Bernstein, Diana Ashley Blau,
Matthew Scott Boblet, Glenn Boozan,
Mallory Jane Brennan, Noelle Elisabeth Campbell,
Victoria Jane Censits, Fang Ting Flora Chan,
Julie Hanna Chea, Wanyu Chen, Kar Shing Justin Cheung,
Xue Lin Sherylene Chew, Seoyeon Lisa Cho,
Paul Jay Choe, Mehr Chopra, Lu Chuang, Yoo Min Chun,
Hae Soo Chung, Key Peum Chung, Tyler Cohen,
Vernicia Colon, Gabriela d'Amato,
Ambar Adriana Del Moral, Taryn Melody Dooley,
Anthony V. Duong, Laura Robin Eirinberg,
Patricia Encarnación Contreras, Evelee Estevez,
Virginia Leigh Farrell, Enrique Paul Ferreyros,
Jane Helen Gardner, Constantine John Giavos,
Stephanie Elyse Gonzalez, Danielle Nechama Gorodenzik,
Natasha Griego Villarraga, Gabrielle Ann Guglielmelli,
Elda Taline Hadajian, Joy Han, Emma Lee Hanson,
Ileana Hernandez Ramos, Jacob Peter Hernandez,
Julio Hernandez, Jennifer Holt, Chris Yunki Hong,
Yung-Chu Hsieh, Xinle Huang, Samantha Hutchinson,
Anthony Iciano, Sukjin Jang, Jussi Johansson,
Wesley Thomas Johnson, Polina Kadkina, Byoungok Kim,
Esther Kim, Ga Hyun Kim, Gena Kim, Hyo Taek Kim,
Jaeyoung Kim, Jane Kim, Ji Won Kim, Lindsey S. Kim,
Tiffany Kim, Andrea E. Latimer, Jina Lee, Ji Yun Lee,
Seul Bi Lee, Iris King Lam Li, Léopoldine Liechtenstein,
Chai Wen Joanne Lim, Manuel Lora, Rebecca Low,
Odile Aurora Martinez-Santamaria,
Caroline Rose Mathews, Gerald David Morin,
Nadine Sameh Muhtadi, Burak Nehbit, Seema Nisar,
Alexa Marielle Ouaknine, Tephany-Lou Casino Padreganda,
Boram Park, Sungwon Park, Patty Valentina Pherson,
Brenna Kirsten Pladsen, Ellie-Ann Quynh Pohl,
Cody J. Pumper, Regina Maria Laura De Joya Puno,
Konstantinos Riginos, Sarah Rim, Young Hee Ryu,
Sylvia Saborio, Camille Marie Charlotte Salvador,
Emilio Sanchez, Rebecca Rose Sandy, Katherine J. Santos,
Joely Saravia, Amber Rose Chantal Seppi,
Jennifer Hyon Shin, Pauline Jiyoung Shin, Anjana Singhwi,
Renee Michelle Sluzhevsky, Meghan Christina Smart,
Noelle Amber Smith, Chrystal Angella Soegandhi Gan,
Wannina Somboonvechakarn, Junghwan Son,
Soo-Ho Song, Kwan Tung Charmaine Sum,
Natasha Sumant, Naomi Sundberg, Hiu Ying Rachal Tai,
Lisa Thieffry, Natashia Tjandra, Francisco Vivar,
William O. Warner, Ashley Wayne, Boyun Yang,
Kanny Yeung, Jody Zhiding Zhou, Biyin Zhu,
Michael Francis Zoppo

2012–13 BFA Communication Design (104 graduates)

Amel Afzal Khan, Jeongkyun Ahn, Ogoby Asencio,
Cynthia Bacall, Shravika Upendra Bothra,
Benjamin Thabo Boustred, Zipporah Rose Burman,
John Albert Bussiere, Isabel Castillo Guijarro,
Susana Castro, Angel Manuel Ceballos,
Nathan Andrew Cepis, Yi-Shan Chang, Tai Jung Chou,
Jihye Chung, Caitlin Clingman, Evon R. Coleman,
Larissa Colon, Rachel Cutler, James Czyz,
Krystal Mae Decena, Stephanie De Jesus,
Jonathan De La Rosa, Carlos De León Duverge,
Suzy Deroyan, Dawa Dolma, Ryan Duenas,
Erica Efstratoudakis, Alexis Dawn Ely,
Kristen Ashley Erdelyi, Beril Esin, Sofia Margarita Falcon,

Lia Fernandez, Nika Simovich, Lindsey Elise Flood,
Erik Matthias Freer, Ying Fu, Ermioni Giakou,
Britton Alexandra Karin Hack,
Axel Hammarskioeld Spendrup, Shaobo Han, Paulina Ho,
Lauren Marie Hodges, Kimberly Hogan, Ping-Chien Huang,
Maria Daniela Huiza Blanco, Jessica Anne Hutchison,
Joanna Rose Izzo, Hasita Kamlesh, Elizabeth Kenney,
Michelle H. Kim, Natalie Kim, Sojung Kim, Max Kuhn,
Min Jung Kwon, Alleson Meghan Lai, Sharon Lee,
Siyel Lee, Soo Yen Lee, Yejin Lee, Michael Leng,
Suzanne Li, Nils Teodor Jacob Lindell,
Amanda Jean Maduri, Jenni Maria Maellinen,
Tara Rifkinson Mann, Jennifer Martins,
Anna Vendeland McKendrick, Bryan Michael Meador,
Melanie E. Mencarelli, Julio Angel Montás Hernández,
Hoang My Nguyen, Jacqueline Shinyoo Oh,
Melisa Zehra Ozkan, Caroline Partridge, Richard Péan,
Carlos J. Pion, Chun Hei Charis Poon, Stephanie E. Porzio,
Jonathan Ramirez, Robert August Riegert III,
Joelle Dianne Riffle, Cesar Rodriguez,
Elizabeth Guadalupe Rodriguez, Camilla Yvonne Romano,
Hanna Julia Sender, Shelly Seroussi, Betty Xiaoyan Shang,
Leslie Mary Shapiro, Ashley Mei Shen,
Jennifer Haesoo Shim, Andrew Shimasaki,
Robin Ivy Silevitch, Brittany Ede Tapsall,
Sabina Telagis Temesheva, Azalea Vaseghi, Thi Lone Wan,
Anita Wong, Chu Yi Wu, Min Xu Wu, Giselle Nari Wynn,
Katherine Suzanne Yaksich, Kyungwon Yang,
Alexandra Callan Zulkoski

2011–12 BFA Communication Design (111 graduates)

Mollie R. Ableman, Shoug Alghunaim, Vera Antebi,
Pierre Mandela Bagwell-Green, Chelsea Baken,
Ashlee Ruth Beggs, Lucas J. Benarroch Monsalve,
Tanya Benet-Ebtehaj, Mariel Eve Bennett, Simoni Bhansali,
Eva Isabelle Bochem-Shur, Karl Alexander Bulloch,
Sophie Marie-Madeleine Margaret Butcher, Anna Cai,
Phillip Ambrose Campion, Emily Elizabeth Cappa,
Sean Catlin Cauley, Wen-Ting Julie Chen, Eun Gi Cho,
Woon Hee Choi, Rachel Lee Chung,
Carolyn Isabel Ciccotelli, Charles Clark,
Gabrielle Marie Cuoccio, Natan Daskal, Caitlin Davis,
Reynaldo Emilio DeJesus, Karla Sofia Despradel Dargam,
Hannah Lea Dykast, Emy Eriksson, Ming Fang,
Anna Ferrier, Alexander Gregory Fisher, Nora Jane Gecan,
Zhi Xiang Goh, Cordarro Gordon, Aashika Gupta,
Ernesto Gutierrez Lezama, Danielle Hall, Erina Ho,
Sharon Ho, Yi-Ting Ho, Min Jung Huh, Seung Won Hur,
Sabahattin Sinan Imre, Mark C. Jensen, Hyun Jung Joo,
Woo Ri Jun, Mutiara Kasih, Carrie Elizabeth Kawamura,
Da Hyun Kim, Elizabeth Kim, Stephanie Sungeun Kim,
Anna Kochman, Jyotsna Anand Lakhiani,
Cherry Juliet Chor-Ting Lam, Donnihe Amin Lauando,
Taietsaronsere G. Leclaire, Hobin Lee, Hoon Lee,
Tina Aram Lee, Cindy Liang, Ju Wan Lim, Justin Lucey,
Simon Lugassy, Stuart Lyle, April Gem Macaraeg,
Veronica Emilia Maitin Alvins, Pratima Prakash Mani,
You Sun Min, Janvi Mody, Charrel Di Montalbo,
Taylor Evans Moore, Diandra Talisa Muléy,
Karina Nova Rancier, Joanne Margaret O'Neill,
Elijah Seongchan Park, Sarah Meredith Piper-Goldberg,

Rashida T. Prattis, Adam Richard Rodriguez,
Jordan Romanoff, Samuel Eric Rossel,
Mariana Varenka Ruiz, Josefina Santos Urzola,
Francine Ilana Shamosh, Ji Heui Seo, Supriya Nirav Shah,
Nakiska Shaikh, Annie Shen, Haejin Jean Shim, Na Ri Shin,
Sarah Elizabeth Smith, Meagan Molloy Steinkamp,
Anastasia Strizhenova, Melanie Ichigo Sugiura,
Michael Suh, Alev Takil, Michael Joseph Tully,
Yoon Joo Um, Nicholas Mark Vidovich,
Alexa Gabrielle Vignoles, Radhika Wadhwa, Alyssa Wadley,
Scott Liam Walker, Sharmaine Yanntel Wilson,
Joan Ning Wong, Stephanie Wenyu Xing,
Esther Eun Jin Yang, Jenny Yieh, Donna Zitelli,
Charlotte Marie Du Pont Zoller

2010–11 BFA Communication Design (111 graduates)

Prerna Agarwal, Sung Jun Ahn, Tomoyo Akaishi,
Vicen Aipohaku Akina, Djinane Alsuwayeh,
William Andrew Anderson, Irina Anisimova,
Regina Maria Arnadóttir, Aya Baeshean,
Jacquelyn T. Molendyke, Dawn Michelle Balhorn,
Joanna Behar, Roxanne Bello, Jonathan Michael Billick,
Curtis Bryant III, Soo Jin Byun, Erik D.W. Carter,
Caruba Benjamin, Ho Ki Derek Chan, Tiffany Chang,
Vivian Cheung, Wai Kitty Cheung, Sang-il Chin,
Alexander Chi-Han Chou, Hei Yoon Sally Chung,
Zuri Chung, Allison Patricia Cruzado,
Cory Samantha Dahlen, Selene Diaz, Ivan Dutton,
Geraldine Sy Dy, Nicole Elizabeth Dymant, Sarah Erickson,
Briana Sinead Fahey, Melissa Feijoo, Rhiannon Fox,
Tara Ghazanfar, Gayatri Gopal, Yu Kyong Han,
Thomas John Hayes, Shirley Hernández Ticona,
Ryan J. Hines, Jean Hong, Whitney House,
Christine Hsiang, Savannah Lynn Hughes,
Joanna Luyang Jiang, Minji Kang, Sunghye Kang,
Arunee Kasemphaibulsuk, Parneet Kaur, Jasmine Kim,
Ji In Kim, Judy Kim, Michelle Jung Kim, Sung Eun Kim,
Susan Chong Kim, Ella Kivinen, Stefan Knecht,
Amanda Catherine Konopko, Tanya Kumar,
Alice Eunsuh Park Lee, Jessica Lee, Joo Yeun Lee,
Soomin Lee, Alda Constance Leung, Jin Ha Lim,
Prin Limphongpand, Valentina Lopez de Haro Gonzalez,
Christopher Louie, Peter Lung Lum, Dana Lynn,
Cristopher Ramirez Malonzo, Joseph R. Mango,
Christopher Anthony McLaughlin,
Cynthia Nicole Medranda, Erick Melendez Medina,
Erin Oh, Liran Okanon, Anastasia Orlov, Sin Hae Park,
Elena Georgieva Paunova,
Eduardo Miguel Ramirez Holguin, Ariel Redmond,
Ryan James Riegner, Sabrina Santander, Sonia Ling Scarr,
David Earl Sealey, Amaya Odyl Segura, Staci Semper,
Alfonso Sjogreen III, Jessica Stango, Kinsley Stofft,
Pui Shan Sze, Sarah Nicole Taverna,
Alejandra Temprana Giraldo, Kimberly Jane Thorpe,
Carlos Torres, Varvara Tsepkova, Yasmiyn A'aida Tyler,
Christine Meryl Vedros, Alexandra Velasco Gonzalez,
Katherine Cheever Willmann, Chen-Hsuan Wu,
Takayo Yamazaki, Sarah Youngae Yi, Daniel Jae Yoo,
Jin Young Yoon, Miki Cristina Yoon, Gillean Fay Yuen,
Sevgi Zeynep Zarbun

STUDENT NATIONALITIES

Countries represented as well as a cumulative listing of languages spoken in the Communication Design student body over the last decade are indicated.

Countries	From 2011–12 to 2020–21
Australia	
Austria	
Bangladesh	
Belarus	
Brazil	
Brunei	
Canada	
Chile	
China	
Colombia	
Dominican Republic	
Ecuador	
Egypt	
France	
Germany	
Greece	
Hong Kong	
Iceland	
India	
Indonesia	
Israel	
Italy	
Japan	
Kenya	
Korea, Rep. of	
Lebanon	
Mauritius	
Mexico	
New Zealand	
Norway	
Panama	
Peru	
Philippines	
Russia	
Singapore	
Spain	
Sweden	
Switzerland	
Taiwan, R.O.C.	
Thailand	
Turkey	
United Arab Emirates	
United Kingdom	
United States of America	
Uruguay	

Languages Spoken
Albanian
Amharic
Arabic
Azerbaijani
Bangla
Belarusian
Bengali
Cantonese
Croatian
Czech
Dominican Creole French
Dutch
English
French
Georgian
German
Greek
Haitian Creole
Hebrew
Hindi
Icelandic
Indonesian
Italian
Japanese
Kazakh
Khmer
Korean
Latvian
Lithuanian
Macedonian
Malay
Malayalam
Mandarin
Mauritian Creole
Mongolian
Myanmar
Norwegian
Oromo
Oshiwambo
Persian
Polish
Portuguese
Punjabi
Romanian
Russian
Spanish
Swahili
Swazi
Swedish
Tagalog
Thai
Turkish
Urdu
Vietnamese

COURSE GROWTH

The total number of Communication Design students have steadily increased over the past decade. Their relative numbers are highlighted in white from the 2013–2014 academic year when Communication Design separated from the Design & Technology program.

2011–12: 166 classes, 15 student average per class

2012–13: 172 classes, 15 student average per class

2013–14: 111 classes, 15 student average per class

2014–15: 128 classes, 15 student average per class

2015–16: 134 classes, 14 student average per class

2016–17: 154 classes, 14 student average per class

2017–18: 171 classes, 14 student average per class

2018–19: 176 classes, 14 student average per class

2019–20: 209 classes, 15 student average per class

2020–21: 178 classes, 16 student average per class

COURSES

Over the past decade, Communication Design courses have become more standardized across the BFA (PUCD), MPS (PMCD), and AAS (PACD) programs. Electives (PSAM) are generally shared and open to any Parsons student. Required, core classes are marked in white.

2011–12 PUCD

- 2025 Type: Core Studio
- 2026 Type: Core Lab
- 2110 Display Lettering
- 3095 Topics: Art Direction
- 3095 Topics: Information Design
- 3095 Topics: Interaction
- 3095 Topics: Motion Graphics
- 3095 Topics: Narrative
- 3095 Topics: Print Studio
- 4205 Senior Thesis 1
- 4210 Senior Thesis 2
- 2010 Print Design
- 2013 Letterpress
- 2031 Business Practices for Media
- 2060 Print Design 2
- 2120 Calligraphy
- 3010 Advanced Typography
- 3020 Intro to Information Design
- 3030 Book Design
- 3035 Book Cover Design
- 3040 Corporate Design
- 3050 Package Design 1
- 3050 Package Design I
- 3060 Advertising Concepts
- 3120 Corporate ID & Packaging
- 3170 Editorial Design
- 3200 Typeface Design
- 3300 Spatial Graphics 1
- 3300 Spatial Graphics 1: Urb Brand
- 3900 Independent Study
- 3900 IS: Information Design 2
- 3900 IS: The Future of Packaging
- 3901 Professional Internship
- 4030 Publication Design
- 4040 Promotion Design
- 4050 Package Design 2
- 4060 Print Campaigns
- 4071 Exhibition Design
- 4090 Experimental Typography
- 4111 Designing for Non-Profits
- 4132 Brand Experience Design
- 4144 Advertising & Marketing
- 4145 Advertising & Marketing

2011–12 PUDT

- 1203 Creative Computing
- 2100 Interaction: Core Studio
- 2101 Interaction: Core Lab

2011–12 PSAM

- 1070 Typography and Visual Design
- 1500 Typography and Visual Design
- 2500 Imaging for Designers
- 3500 Commercial Storyboarding
- 3800 Photo Editorial
- 5600 Currents: Interactive Books
- 5600 Currents: iPad Prototyping
- 5900 Independent Study
- 5900 IS: Datamyne
- 5900 IS: Urban Bike
- 5900 IS: Urban Research Toolkit

2012–13 PUCD

- 2025 Core Studio: Typography
- 2026 Core Lab: Typography
- 3095 Topics: Art Direction
- 3095 Topics: Information Design
- 3095 Topics: Interaction
- 3095 Topics: Motion Graphics
- 3095 Topics: Narrative
- 3095 Topics: Print Studio
- 3095 Topics: Typography Studio
- 4205 Senior Thesis 1
- 4210 Senior Thesis 2
- 2010 Intro to Print Design
- 2031 Business Practices for Media
- 2033 Contemporary Brand Concepts
- 2060 Print Design 2
- 2090 Intro to Information Design
- 2120 Calligraphy
- 3010 Advanced Typography
- 3013 Letterpress
- 3030 Book Design
- 3035 Book Cover Design
- 3040 Identity Design
- 3050 Package Design 1
- 3060 Advertising Concepts
- 3120 Modernism, Identity, Packaging
- 3170 Editorial Design
- 3200 Typeface Design
- 3300 Spatial Graphics 1
- 3300 Spatial Graphics 1: Urb Brand
- 3900 Independent Study
- 3900 IS:
- 3901 Professional Internship
- 4030 Publication Design
- 4040 Integrated Promotion Strategy
- 4060 Advertising Campaigns
- 4071 Exhibition Design
- 4090 Experimental Typography
- 4111 Designing for Non-Profits
- 4132 Brand Experience Design
- 4144 Integrated Advertising Lab
- 4145 Integrated Advertising Lab 2

2012–13 PUDT

- 1203 Creative Computing
- 2100 Core Studio: Interaction
- 2101 Core Lab: Interaction

2012–13 PSAM

- 1070 Typography and Visual Design
- 2500 Imaging for Design
- 3500 Commercial Storyboarding
- 3800 Photo Editorial
- 5570 Applied Research
- 5600 Currents:

2013–14 PUCD

- 2025 Core Studio: Typography
- 2026 Core Lab: Typography
- 3095 Topics: Advertising
- 3095 Topics: Branding
- 3095 Topics: Editorial Experience
- 3095 Topics: Information Design
- 3095 Topics: Motion Graphics
- 3095 Topics: Narrative
- 3095 Topics: New Genres
- 3095 Topics: Typography
- 3095 Topics: Web/Mobile Product Design
- 4205 Senior Thesis 1
- 4210 Senior Thesis 2
- 2090 Intro to Information Design
- 2120 Calligraphy
- 3010 Advanced Typography
- 3030 Book Design
- 3035 Book Cover Design
- 3040 Identity Design
- 3050 Package Design 1
- 3060 Advertising Concepts
- 3200 Typeface Design
- 3300 Spatial Graphics 1
- 3300 Spatial Graphics 1: Urb Brand
- 4030 Publication Design
- 4030 Publication Design: Workshop
- 4040 Promotion Design
- 4071 Exhibition Design
- 4090 Experimental Typography
- 4111 Designing for Non-Profits
- 4132 Brand Experience Design
- 4144 Integrated Advertising Lab

2013–14 PUDT

- 1203 Creative Computing
- 2100 Core Studio: Interaction
- 2101 Core Lab: Interaction

2013–14 PSAM

- 2033 Brand Concepts
- 2070 Editorial Concepts

Communication Design and Design & Technology (PUDT) courses are offered until the end of the 2013-14 academic year when the programs separated.

2014–15 PUCD

2025 Core Studio Typography
2026 Core Lab Typography
2035 Creative Computing
2125 Core Studio Interaction
2126 Core Lab Interaction
3095 Topics: Advertising
3095 Topics: Branding
3095 Topics: Editorial Experience
3095 Topics: Information Design
3095 Topics: Motion Graphics
3095 Topics: Narrative
3095 Topics: New Genres
3095 Topics: Typography
3095 Topics: Web/Mobile Product Design
4205 Senior Thesis 1
4210 Senior Thesis 2
3010 Advanced Typography
3030 Book Design
3035 Book Cover Design
3040 Identity Design
3050 Package Design 1
3200 Typeface Design
3300 Spatial Graphics 1
4030 Publication Design
4030 Publication Design: Workshop
4040 Promotion Design
4060 Advertising Campaigns
4071 Exhibition Design
4090 Experimental Typography
4132 Brand Experience Design
4144 Integrated Advertising Lab

2014–15 PSAM

1020 Calligraphy
1070 Typography and Visual Design
2031 Business Practices for Media
2033 Brand Concepts
2060 Advertising Concepts
2070 Editorial Concepts
2090 Information Design Concepts
3011 Designing for Non-Profits
3050 Collab: Design for Literacy
3050 Collab: Future of Publishing
3050 Collab: Soc Activism & Print
3050 Collab: Speak Music & Design
3050 Collab: Tourism, ID & Memory
3050 Collab: Univ Design Studio
3050 Collab: Visualizing Pub Policy
3060 Currents: Design Social Change
3710 Collab: Univ Design Studio

2015–16 PUCD

2025 Core Studio Typography
2026 Core Lab Typography
2035 Creative Computing
2125 Core Studio Interaction
2126 Core Lab Interaction
2130 Advanced Typography
3095 Topics: Advertising
3095 Topics: Branding
3095 Topics: Editorial Experience
3095 Topics: Motion Graphics
3095 Topics: Typography
3095 Topics: Web/Mobile Product Design
4205 Senior Thesis 1
4210 Senior Thesis 2

2015–16 PSAM

1028 Web Design Basics
1070 Typography and Visual Design
2033 Brand Concepts
2050 Package Design
2060 Advertising Concepts
2070 Editorial Concepts
2090 Information Design Concepts
2440 Motion Concepts
3005 Experimental Typography
3010 Typeface Design
3011 Designing for Non-Profits
3030 Spatial Graphics
3035 Book Design
3040 Identity Design
3044 Integrated Advertising Lab
3050 Collab: Art, In Living Context
3050 Collab: Design for Literacy
3050 Collab: Future of Publishing
3050 Collab: Making Astor Place
3050 Collab: MicroHabitats
3050 Collab: Streetscape: NY/Detroit
3050 Collab: Univ Design Studio
3059 Brand Experience Design
3060 Currents: Computational Form
3060 Currents: Design in Context
3060 Currents: Design Social Change
3060 Currents: Digital Painting
3060 Currents: Experimental Publish
3060 Currents: Interact Video/Sound
3061 Advertising Campaigns
3070 Publication Design
3070 Publication Design: Workshop
3071 Exhibition Design
3075 Promotion Design
3210 Web Advanced: Javascript
3210 Web Advanced: Mobile Design
3441 Advanced Motion Graphics

2016–17 PUCD

2025 Core Studio Typography
2026 Core Lab Typography
2035 Creative Computing
2125 Core Studio Interaction
2126 Core Lab Interaction
2130 Advanced Typography
3095 Topics: Advertising
3095 Topics: Branding
3095 Topics: Editorial Experience
3095 Topics: Motion Graphics
3095 Topics: Web/Mobile Product Design
4205 Senior Thesis 1
4210 Senior Thesis 2

2016–17 PSAM

1028 Web Design Basics
1070 Typography and Visual Design
2031 Business Practices for Media
2033 Brand Concepts
2050 Package Design
2060 Advertising Concepts
2070 Editorial Concepts
2090 Information Design Concepts
2120 Web: Interaction
2440 Motion Concepts
3005 Experimental Typography
3010 Typeface Design
3011 Designing for Non-Profits
3030 Spatial Graphics
3035 Book Design
3040 Identity Design
3050 Collab: Design for Literacy
3050 Collab: Future of Publishing
3050 Collab: Literature and Race
3050 Collab: Speak Music & Design
3050 Collab: Univ Design Studio
3059 Brand Experience Design
3060 Currents: Alt Publishing
3060 Currents: Computational Form
3060 Currents: Future of the Poster
3060 Currents: Resonant Encounters
3060 Currents: What Makes a Village
3061 Advertising Campaigns
3070 Publication Design
3071 Exhibition Design
3075 Promotion Design
3210 Web Advanced: Javascript
3210 Web Advanced: Mobile Design
3441 Advanced Motion Graphics

2017–18 PUCD

- 2025 Core Studio Typography
- 2026 Core Lab Typography
- 2035 Creative Computing
- 2125 Core Studio Interaction
- 2126 Core Lab Interaction
- 2130 Advanced Typography
- 3095 Topics: Advertising
- 3095 Topics: Branding
- 3095 Topics: Editorial Experience
- 3095 Topics: Motion Graphics
- 3095 Topics: Web/Mobile Product Design
- 4205 Senior Thesis 1
- 4210 Senior Thesis 2

2017–18 PMCD

- 5000 Type & Interaction 1: Skills
- 5001 Typography & Interaction 1
- 5002 Typography & Interaction 2
- 5101 Major Studio 1
- 5102 Major Studio 2
- 5200 Visual Culture Seminar
- 5300 Methods & Practices

2017–18 PSAM

- 1028 Web Design Basics
- 1070 Typography and Visual Design
- 2033 Brand Concepts
- 2050 Package Design
- 2060 Advertising Concepts
- 2070 Editorial Concepts
- 2090 Information Design Concepts
- 2120 Web: Interaction
- 2440 Motion Concepts
- 3010 Typeface Design
- 3011 Designing for Non-Profits
- 3030 Spatial Graphics
- 3040 Identity Design
- 3050 Collab: Branding for a Journal
- 3050 Collab: Design for Literacy
- 3050 Collab: Future of Publishing
- 3050 Collab: Reading without Pages
- 3050 Collab: Speak Music & Design
- 3050 Collab: Writing and Chapbooks
- 3059 Brand Experience Design
- 3060 Currents: Computational Form
- 3060 Currents: Contemp Art Direction
- 3060 Currents: Design Fiction
- 3060 Currents: Poster Future
- 3071 Exhibition Design
- 3075 Promotion Design
- 3210 Web Advanced: Javascript
- 3210 Web Advanced: Mobile Design
- 3441 Advanced Motion Graphics
- 3715 University Design Studio
- 5600 Currents: Building in Practice
- 5600 Currents: Feminist Internet

2018–19 PUCD

- 2025 Core Studio Typography
- 2026 Core Lab Typography
- 2035 Creative Computing
- 2125 Core Studio Interaction
- 2126 Core Lab Interaction
- 2130 Advanced Typography
- 3095 Topics: Advertising
- 3095 Topics: Branding
- 3095 Topics: Editorial Experience
- 3095 Topics: Motion Graphics
- 3095 Topics: Web/Mobile Product Design
- 4205 Senior Thesis 1
- 4210 Senior Thesis 2

2018–19 PMCD

- 5000 Type & Interaction 1: Skills
- 5001 Typography & Interaction 1
- 5002 Typography & Interaction 2
- 5101 Major Studio 1
- 5102 Major Studio 2
- 5200 Visual Culture Seminar
- 5300 Methods & Practices

2018–19 PSAM

- 1028 Web Design Basics
- 1070 Typography and Visual Design
- 2033 Brand Concepts
- 2050 Package Design
- 2060 Advertising Concepts
- 2070 Editorial Concepts
- 2090 Information Design Concepts
- 2120 Web: Interaction
- 2440 Motion Concepts
- 3005 Experimental Typography
- 3010 Typeface Design
- 3011 Designing for Non-Profits
- 3030 Spatial Graphics
- 3035 Book Design
- 3040 Identity Design
- 3050 Collab: Brand a NYC Bike Club
- 3050 Collab: Design for Literacy
- 3050 Collab: Future of Publishing
- 3050 Collab: Network Interfacing
- 3050 Collab: Speak Music & Design
- 3059 Brand Experience Design
- 3060 Currents: Activism in Motion
- 3060 Currents: CD Workshop
- 3060 Currents: Digital Dialect
- 3060 Currents: Library of Babel
- 3071 Exhibition Design
- 3075 Promotion Design
- 3210 Web Advanced: Javascript
- 3210 Web Advanced: Mobile Design
- 3441 Advanced Motion Graphics
- 3715 University Design Studio
- 5857 University Design Studio

2019–20 PUCD

- 2025 Core Studio Typography
- 2026 Core Lab Typography
- 2035 Creative Computing
- 2125 Core Studio Interaction
- 2126 Core Lab Interaction
- 2130 Advanced Typography
- 3095 Topics: Advertising
- 3095 Topics: Branding
- 3095 Topics: Editorial Experience
- 3095 Topics: Motion Graphics
- 3095 Topics: Web/Mobile Product Design
- 4205 Senior Thesis 1
- 4210 Senior Thesis 2

2019–20 PMCD

- 5001 Typography & Interaction 1
- 5002 Typography & Interaction 2
- 5101 Major Studio 1
- 5102 Major Studio 2
- 5200 Visual Culture Seminar
- 5300 Methods & Practices

2019–20 PACD

- 1010 Design History & Practice
- 1100 Core 1: Typography
- 1110 Core 1: Interaction
- 1200 Core 2: Type & Interaction
- 1500 Prof Practices & Portfolio

2019–20 PSAM

- 1028 Web Design Basics
- 1070 Typography and Visual Design
- 1085 Digital Tools for Layout & Imaging
- 1130 The Visual Archive
- 2033 Brand Concepts
- 2040 Advanced Digital Tools for Layout & Imaging
- 2050 Package Design
- 2060 Advertising Concepts
- 2070 Editorial Concepts
- 2090 Information Design Concepts
- 2120 Web: Interaction
- 2160 Advanced Typography
- 2440 Motion Concepts
- 3005 Experimental Typography
- 3010 Typeface Design
- 3011 Designing for Non-Profits
- 3030 Spatial Graphics
- 3035 Book Design
- 3040 Identity Design
- 3050 Collab: Design for Literacy
- 3050 Collab: Future of Publishing
- 3059 Brand Experience Design
- 3060 Currents: Activism in Motion
- 3060 Currents: CD Workshop
- 3060 Currents: Context = ½ the Work
- 3060 Currents: Digital Dialect
- 3060 Currents: Generative Books
- 3060 Currents: Library of Babel
- 3071 Exhibition Design
- 3075 Promotion Design
- 3210 Web Advanced: Javascript
- 3210 Web Advanced: Mobile Design
- 3441 Advanced Motion Graphics
- 3715 University Design Studio
- 5857 University Design Studio

2020–21 PUCD	
2025	Core 1: Typography Studio
2026	Core 1: Typography Lecture
2035	Core 1: Interaction
2125	Core 2: Interaction Studio
2126	Core 2: Interaction Lab
2130	Core 2: Typography
3095	Core 3: Topics
4205	Core 4: Thesis 1
4210	Core 5: Senior Thesis 2
2020–21 PMCD	
5001	Typography & Interaction 1
5002	Typography & Interaction 2
5100	Major Studio 1: Lecture
5101	Major Studio 1: Lab
5102	Major Studio 2
5200	Visual Culture Seminar
5300	Methods & Practices
2020–21 PACD	
1010	Design History & Practice
1100	Core 1: Typography
1110	Core 1: Interaction
1200	Core 2: Type & Interaction
1500	Prof Practices & Portfolio
2100	Core 3: Capstone
2020–21 PSAM	
1028	CD Foundations: Interaction
1070	CD Foundations: Typography
1085	Digital Tools for Layout & Imaging
1130	The Visual Archive
2033	CD Studio: Systems for Brands
2040	Advanced Digital Tools for Layout & Imaging
2050	CD Studio: Now in Production
2060	CD Studio: Stories ⇄ Platforms
2070	CD Studio: Multiple Editions
2090	CD Studio: Dynamic Content
2120	CD Studio: Digital Products
2160	Advanced Typography
2440	CD Studio: Motion Graphics
3005	CD Studio: Word as Image
3010	CD Studio: Typeface Design
3011	CD Studio: Social Impact
3030	CD Studio: Experience in Space
3035	CD Studio: Books and Archives
3040	CD Studio: Signs and Symbols
3050	Collab: Design for Literacy
3050	Collab: Future of Publishing
3060	Currents: a-generative-web
3060	Currents: Black Visual Culture
3060	Currents: CD Workshop
3060	Currents: Context = ½ the Work
3060	Currents: Design with Archives
3060	Currents: Memory as Practice
3071	CD Studio: Experience in Space
3210	CD Studio: JavaScript

Course names in the Communication Design programs were refreshed in 2019 and again in 2020.

Faculty are selected from across the discipline who represent a cross-section of contemporary methodologies and practices. Virtually all maintain active professional practices while teaching in the program. Each white box indicates an academic year a faculty member has taught in the program over the last decade. Current, full-time Communication Design faculty are highlighted.

Each row shows ten academic years from 2011–12 to 2020–21. A white box (■) marks a year taught; a hatched box (·) marks a year not taught.

Name	1	2	3	4	5	6	7	8	9	10
Rebecca Abbe	·	·	·	·	·	·	·	·	■	·
Josef Abboud	·	·	·	·	■	·	·	·	·	·
Alison Abreu-Garcia	·	·	·	■	·	■	·	·	·	·
Aarati Akkapeddi	·	·	·	·	·	·	·	·	·	·
Peter Alfano	·	·	·	·	·	■	·	·	·	·
Chris Allick	·	·	·	·	·	·	·	·	·	·
William Anderson	·	·	·	·	·	·	·	·	·	■
Andre Andreev	·	·	·	·	·	·	·	·	·	·
Dwight Armstrong	·	·	·	·	·	·	·	·	·	■
Chelsea Atwell	·	·	·	·	·	·	·	·	·	·
Carly Ayres	·	·	·	·	·	·	·	■	·	·
Benjamin L. Bacon	·	·	■	·	·	·	·	■	·	·
Kees Bakker	·	·	·	·	·	·	·	·	·	·
Justin Bakse	·	·	·	·	·	·	·	·	·	·
Urshula Barbour	■	·	·	·	·	·	·	·	·	·
Emily Barnett	·	·	·	·	·	·	·	·	·	·
Suzanne Baron	·	·	·	·	·	·	·	·	·	·
Edward Baumgarten	·	·	·	·	·	·	·	·	■	·
Mark Beasley	·	·	·	·	·	·	·	■	·	·
Eliot Bergman	·	·	·	·	·	·	·	·	·	·
William Bevington	·	■	·	·	·	·	·	■	·	·
Marc Blaustein	·	·	·	·	·	·	·	·	·	·
Brad Blondes	·	·	■	·	·	·	·	·	·	·
Nathan Blowers	·	·	■	·	·	·	·	·	·	·
Stephen Blue	·	·	·	·	·	■	·	·	·	·
Matthew Bohne	·	·	·	·	·	■	·	·	·	·
Jason Booher	·	·	·	·	·	·	·	·	·	·
Thomas Bosket	·	·	·	·	·	·	·	·	·	·
Michael Bowser	·	·	·	·	·	·	·	·	■	·
Kevin Brainard	■	■	■	■	■	■	■	■	■	■
Claudia Brandenburg	·	·	·	·	·	·	·	·	·	·
Aaron Brashear	·	■	·	·	·	·	·	·	·	·
Sam Brenner	·	·	·	·	■	·	·	·	·	·
Daniel Brewster	·	·	·	■	·	·	·	·	·	·
Adam Brodowski	·	·	·	■	·	·	·	·	·	·
Beverly Brodsky	·	·	·	■	■	·	·	·	·	·
Keri Bronk	·	·	·	■	■	·	·	·	·	·
Jennifer Brook	■	·	·	·	·	·	·	·	·	·
Chris Bruffee	·	·	·	■	·	·	·	·	·	·
Emma Bruml Norton	·	·	·	·	·	·	·	·	·	·
Anthony Bryant	·	·	·	·	·	·	·	·	·	·
Luke Bulman	■	■	■	■	■	■	■	■	■	■
Clara Bunker	·	·	·	·	■	·	·	·	·	·
Grace Burney	■	·	·	·	·	·	·	·	·	·
Edward Byfield	·	·	·	·	·	·	·	·	·	·
Agnes Cameron	■	·	·	·	·	·	·	·	·	·
Callil Capuozzo	■	·	·	·	·	·	·	·	·	·
Paul Carlos	·	■	·	·	·	·	·	·	·	·
David Carroll	·	■	·	·	·	·	·	·	·	·
Luke Carter	·	·	·	·	·	·	·	·	·	·
Juliette Cezzar										
Natasha Chandani	·	■	·	·	·	·	·	·	·	·
Agnes Chang	·	·	·	·	·	·	·	·	·	·
Evan Chang	·	·	·	·	·	·	·	·	·	·
Tina Chang	·	·	·	·	·	·	·	·	■	·
Marcos Chavez	·	·	·	·	·	·	·	·	·	·
Belinda Chen	·	·	·	·	·	·	■	·	·	·

Name	1	2	3	4	5	6	7	8	9	10
Irwin Chen	·	·	·	·	·	·	·	·	·	·
Dennis Cheung	·	·	·	·	·	·	·	·	·	·
Yiye Cho	·	·	·	·	·	·	·	·	·	·
Marc Choi	·	·	·	·	·	·	·	·	·	·
Minnie Choi	·	·	·	·	·	·	·	·	·	·
Ingrid Chou	·	·	·	·	·	·	·	·	·	·
Virginia Chow	·	·	·	·	■	·	·	·	·	·
Matthew Chrislip	·	·	·	·	■	·	·	·	·	·
Emily Chu	·	·	·	·	·	·	·	·	·	·
Ariel Churi	·	·	·	■	·	·	·	·	·	·
Libby Clarke	·	·	·	·	·	·	·	·	·	·
Lorenzo Clayton	·	·	·	·	·	·	·	·	·	·
Steven Clunis	·	·	·	·	·	·	·	·	·	·
Carl Collins	·	·	■	·	·	·	·	·	·	·
Elliott Cost	·	·	·	·	·	·	·	·	·	·
Inva Cota	·	·	·	·	·	·	·	·	·	·
Talia Cotton	·	·	·	·	·	·	·	·	·	·
Alexis Cuadrado	·	·	·	·	·	·	·	·	·	·
Pedro Cuni	·	·	·	·	·	·	·	·	·	·
Simone Cutri	·	·	·	·	·	·	·	·	·	·
Jonathan Dahan	·	·	·	·	■	·	·	·	·	·
Luiza Dale	·	·	·	·	·	·	·	·	·	·
Andy Dayton	·	·	·	·	·	·	·	·	·	·
Cecilia Dean	·	·	·	·	·	·	·	·	·	·
Stephen Decker	·	·	·	·	·	·	·	·	·	·
Sarah Deford	·	·	·	·	·	·	·	·	·	·
Marvin de Jong	·	·	·	·	·	■	·	·	·	·
Onno De Jong	·	·	·	·	·	·	·	·	·	·
Will Denton	·	·	·	·	·	·	·	·	·	·
Ben Denzer	·	·	·	·	·	·	·	·	·	·
Garrett DeRossett	·	·	·	·	·	·	·	·	·	·
Olivia de Salve Villedieu	·	·	·	·	·	·	·	·	·	·
Eric Doctor	·	·	·	·	·	·	·	·	·	·
Neil Donnelly	·	·	·	·	·	·	·	·	·	·
Ojus Doshi	·	·	·	·	·	·	·	·	·	·
Graham Douglas	·	·	·	■	·	·	·	·	·	·
Thomas Doyle	·	·	·	■	·	·	·	·	·	·
Kevin Dresser	·	·	·	·	·	·	·	·	·	·
Debra Drodvillo	·	·	·	·	·	·	·	·	·	·
Sarah Dunham	·	·	·	·	·	■	·	·	·	·
Ben Duval	·	·	·	·	·	·	·	·	·	·
Kori Dyer	·	·	·	·	·	·	·	·	·	·
Michael Dyer	·	·	■	·	·	·	·	·	·	·
Lukas Eigler-Harding	·	·	·	·	·	·	·	·	·	·
Axel Esquite	·	·	·	·	·	■	·	·	·	·
Ellen Evjen	·	·	·	·	·	·	·	·	·	·
Clayton Ewing	·	·	·	·	·	·	·	·	·	·
Hicham Faraj	·	·	·	·	·	·	·	·	·	·
John Farrar	·	·	·	·	·	·	·	·	·	·
Megan Feehan	·	·	·	·	·	·	·	·	·	·
Ben Fehrman-Lee	·	·	·	·	·	·	·	·	·	·
Alonzo Felix	·	·	·	■	·	·	·	·	·	·
Lina Fenequito	·	·	■	·	·	·	·	·	·	·
Dylan Fisher	·	·	·	·	·	·	·	·	·	·
Jack Henrie Fisher	·	·	·	·	·	·	·	·	·	·
Nika Fisher (Simovich)	·	·	·	·	·	·	·	·	·	·
Greg Foley	·	·	·	·	·	·	·	·	·	·
Alison Forner	·	·	·	·	·	·	·	·	·	·

Audrey Fox
Erik Freer
Dinah Fried
Barbara Friedman
Daniel Frumhoff
Jarrett Fuller
Sam Galison
Suny Gao
Rosalie Garlow
Katy Garnier
Benjamin Gaulon
Isaac Gertman
Rebecca Gimenez
Yuri Gitman
Kelli Ann Glancey
Pascal Glissmann
Julia Gorton
Jonathan Gouthier
Andrew Graber
Minda Gralnek
Cybele Grandjean
Steven Grant
Jennifer Langdon Graves
Hilary Greenbaum
Michael Greenblatt
Isaac Green Diebboll
Remina Greenfield
Brendan Griffiths
Tom Griffiths
Katarzyna Gruda
Yotam Hadar
Matt Hallock
Geoffrey Han
Berton Hasebe
Donald Hearn
David Joseph Heasty
August Heffner
Jacob Heftmann
Krystyn Heide
Erica Heinz
Kristian Henson
Molly Herman
Nitzan Hermon
Andrew Herzog
Aaron Hill
Daniel Hill
Jerry Hoak
Tiff Hockin
Jeanette Hodge-Abbink
Jinu Hong
Mies Hora
Allen Hori
Jacob Hoving
Eric Hu
Shawna Huang
Laura Huaranga
Allyn Hughes
Pat Iadanza
Ekene Ijeoma
Shira Inbar
Jessica Irish
Carol Irving
Matt Jacobson
Faiyaz Jafri
Brian James
Christina Janus

Dawoon Jeon
Jerel Johnson
Glendon Jones
David Justus
Jake Kahana
Earl Kallemeyn
E Roon Kang
Lev Kanter
Peter Kaplan
Alvin Katz
Steven Kennedy
Jonathan Key
Lynn Kiang
Dana Kim
Elle Kim
Hoon Kim
Jieun Kim
Minkyoung Kim
Alexander King
Christopher King
Sean King
Willis Kingery
Peter Kirn
Ernesto Klar
Zak Klauck
Pamela Klein
Andrew Kner
Azusa Kobayashi
Kathryn Koch
Kellie Konapelsky
Robby Kraft
Seth Kranzler
Dmitry Krasny
Mara Kurtz
Hyo Jung Kwon
Caspar Lam
Scott Langer
Francis La Rocca
Eric Kwan Tai Lau
Veronica Lawlor
Cynthia Lawson
Dan Leatherman
Andrew LeClair
Jon Lee
Min Hee Lee
Tony Lee
Jurg Lehni
Wendy Letven
Andrew Levinson
Meg Lewis
Astrid Lewis Reedy
Ivy Li
Kan Yang Li
Yan Sze Li
Zhongkai Li
Prin Limphongpand
Alex Lin
Drew Litowitz
Jackie Liu
Jonathan Lu
Jon Lucas
Lynda Lucas
Tracy Ma
Lisa Maione
Tamara Maletic
Sankho Mallik

David Marcinkowski
Paul Marcus
Joe Marianek
Martin Mazorra
Robert McConnell
Conor McGlauflin
Colin Mclain
David McManus
Thomas McManus
William McNamara
Pablo A Medina
Rafael Medina
Mary Meehan
Ken Meier
Antonino Mendolia
Stephen Metts
Dan Michaelson
Leigh Mignona
Chad Miller
Luke Miller
James Montalbano
Christine Moog
Wael Morcos
Joseph William Morrisey
Eileen Mullan
Mark Mullin
Frederick Murhammer
Joel Murphy
Jena Myung
Michelle Nahum-Albright
Thomas Naughton
Charles Nix
John Noneman
Ben Norskov
Alexa Nosal
Eric Nylund
Patrick O'Neill
Annaka Olsen
Laimah Osman
Paul Paauwe
Michie Pagulayan
YuJune Park
Chun-wo Pat
Marcus Peabody
Asad Pervaiz
Tuan Pham
Alma Phipps
Jane Pirone
Matt Poor
Alexandra Portis
Jeffrey Powers
Domenick Propati
Kate Proulx
John Provencher
Ryan Joseph Raffa
Leah Raintree
Jesse Reed
JiEun Rim
David Robinson
Michael Robinson
Jacob Romer
Janine Rosen
Eli Rousso
Chuck Routhier
Ryan Rowlett
Chris Rypkema
Damien Saatdijan
Joseph Saavedra
Richard Salcer
Mark Saltz
Timothy Samara
Nic Sanchez
Junko Sassa
Daniel Sauter
Nick Schaden
Derrick Schultz
Laurel Schwulst
Jeffrey Scudder
Anezka Sebek
Jesse Seegers
Leslie Segal
Zack Seuberling
Patrick Seymour
Fred Shallcrass
Anna Sharp
Paul Shaw
Andrew Shea
Maurice Sherman
Sam Sherman
Elizabeth Shim
Pat Shiu
Soomin Shon
Zeke Shore
Zeke Shore
Hua Shu
Andrew Shurtz
Pascual Sisto
Emily Skillings
Jeremy Smith
Kevin Smith
Lisa Smith
Marian Smith
Rory Solomon
Robert Spica
Matthew Sporzynski
Ashley Stevens
Holly Stevenson
Jessica Svendsen
Beata Szpura
Madhava Tankha
Corey Tegeler
Ramon Tejada
Lucille Tenazas
Pan Terzis
Dimitry Tetin
Jonathan Thirkield
Sally Thurer
Crystal Tong
Dustin Tong
Justin Travis
Robert Trostle
Mike Tully
Édouard Urcades
Tu Uthaisri
Mary-Jo Valentino
Henk Van Assen
Polina Vasilieva
Janice Veksler
Noah Venezia
Jeanne Verdoux
Jon Vingiano
Ben Wagner

Jonathan Wajskol
Jeffrey Waldman
Michael Waldron
Edward Walter
Kelly Walters
Ping Yi Wang
Wei-Hao Wang
Emily Wardwell
Julia Wargaski
David S Warren
Devin Washburn
Mike Wasilewski
Brian Watterson
Jessica Weber
Stefanie Weigler
Bryant Wells
Nicholas Weltyk
Davey Whitcraft
Alex White
Lydia White
Michael Wiemeyer
Jesse Wilbur
Luke Williams

Bryce Wilner
Gabriele Wilson
Katherine Witherell
Michael Wolf
Audra Wolowiec
Desmond Wong
Willy Wong
David Lance Wyman
Krissi Xenakis
Janice Yamanaka-Lew
Ilya Yavnoshan
Sean Yendrys
Helen Yentus
Allan Yu
David Yun
Lynne Yun
Carmile Zaino
Gary Zhang
Liyan Zhao
Maxim Zhukov
Or Zubalsky
Roy Zucca

EXTERNAL CRITICS

External critics have regularly been invited to provide feedback to students within classroom and end-of-year contexts. Each white box indicates an academic year an external critic participated in Communication Design activities.

Name	From 2011–12 to 2020–21
Jeannette Abbink	
Mike Abbink	
Nida Abdullah	
Rachel Abrams	
Roanne Adams	
Sean Adams	
Jennifer Ahern	
Atif Akin	
Jason Alejandro	
Robin Andersen	
Chelsea Atwell	
Sophie Auger	
Mark Aver	
Justin Bakse	
Bijan Berahimi	
Rachel Berger	
Anne Berry	
Kim Bost	
Jamar Bromley	
Keri Bronk	
Malcolm Buick	
John Caserta	
James Chae	
Flora Chan	
Abby Chen	
Alicia Cheng	
Hyung Cho	
Yoonjai Choi	
Ingrid Chou	
Virginia Chow	
Archie Lee Coates IV	
Matias Corea	
Talia Cotton	
Glen Cummings	
Ian Dapot	
Rodrigo de Benito Sanz	
Meaghan Dee	
Anthony Deen	
Sarah Deford	
Barbara deWilde	
Iyana Martin Diaz	
Keetra Dean Dixon	
Michael Donovan	
Graham Douglas	
Lyanne Dubon	
CJ Dunn	
Tony Dunne	
Victoria Duong	
Michael Dyer	
Aliza Dzik	
Logan Emser	
Minsun Eo	
Allan Espiritu	
Simone Fabricius	
Megan Feehan	
Ben Fehrman-Lee	
Dylan Fisher	
Nika Fisher	
Lauren Francescone	
Jeffrey Franklin	
Erik Freer	
Dinah Fried	
David Frisco	
Timothy Gambell	
Javier Garcia	
Rosie Garschina	
Harry Gassel	
Greg Gazdowicz	
Njoki Gitahi	
Barbara Glauber	
Jeff Glendenning	
Daniel Goddemeyer	
Elizabeth Goodspeed	
Minda Gralnek	
Hilary Greenbaum	
Michael Greenblatt	
Dylan Greif	
Lisa Grocott	
Peter Hall	
August Heffner	
Kristian Henson	
Enrique Hernandez	
Albert Hicks IV	
Aaron Hill	
Tori Hinn	
Lucinda Hitchcock	
Hanah Ho	
LaiYee Ho	
Pablo Honey	
Paul Hoppe	
Allen Hori	
Eric Hu	
Allyn Hughes	
Cindy Hwang	
Gaia Hwang	
Matt Ipcar	
Jonathan Jackson	
Moon Jung Jang	
E Roon Kang	
Jenny Kang	
Justin Thomas Kay	
Ian Keliher	
Bo-Won Keum	
Meena Khalili	
Anoushka Khandwala	
Lynn Kiang	
David Kille	
Nicole Killian	
Jane Kim	
Minkyung Kim	
David Klein	
Molly Lafferty	
Jeff Lai	
Penina Acayo Laker	
Caspar Lam	
Brian LaRossa	
Cynthia Lawson	
Andrew LeClair	
Christopher Lee	

Jon Lee
Jonathan Lee
Min Hee Lee
Kate Leisy
Melissa Levin
Briar Levit
Min Lew
Alexandra Lezberg
Beverly Liang
Alex Limpaecher
Prin Limphongpand
Alex Lin
Yenwei Liu
Elaine Lopez
Andrew Losowsky
Renald Louissaint
Hoshi Ludwig
Elisa Maezono
Tadeu Magalhaes
Joe Marianek
Bobby Martin
Michael McCaughley
Tadeu Mighales
Manuel Miranda
Sigi Moeslinger
Emile Molin
Elliott Montgomery
Carlos Moore
Wael Morcos
Michelle Morrison
Renda Morton
Nontsikelelo Mutiti
Jena Myung
Lisa Naftolin
Igal Nassima
John Niedermeyer
Erin Nolan
Inye Nosegbe
Eric Nylund
Justin Ouellette
Juan Carlos Pagan
Maziyar Pahlevan
Deroy Peraza
Jeremy Perez-Cruz
Asad Pervaiz
Daniel Peterson
Isabel Urbina Peña
Eric Price
Chris Pross
Robert Rabinovitz
Fiona Raby
Jesse Ragan
Shem Rajoon
Ana Realmuto
Sam Renwick
Josef Reyes
Anna Rieger
Tim Ripper
Ryder Ripps
Juan Carlos Rodriguez Rivera
Chris Ro

Rebecca Ross
Julika Rudelius
Andrew Rutledge
Louise Sandhaus
Daniel Sauter
Paula Scher
Laurel Schwulst
Jeffrey Alan Scudder
Jesse Seegers
Mindy Seu
Lucas Sharp
Andrew Shea
Jonny Sikov
Andrew Sloat
Elizabeth Carey Smith
Emily Smith
Josh Smith
Lisa Smith
Tina Smith
Paul Soulellis
Sebastian Speier
Jon Sueda
Jin Jin Sun
Ethan Sung
Jessica Svendsen
Mariko Takagi
Erika Tarte
Ramon Tejada
Justin Ternullo
Jackie Thaw
Richard The
Jennifer Thibault
Carolyn Thomas
Preston Thompson
Lauren Thorson
Aggie Toppins
Ka-Man Tse
Rich Tu
Masamichi Udagawa
Kay Unger
Julia Vakser-Selzer
Karen Vanderbilt
Keith Venkiteswaran
Federico Villoro
Robert Vinluan
Paul Vlachou
Jeffrey Waldman
David Jon Walker
Jessica Walker
Michael Waltzer
Cap Watkins
Travis Weber
Vance Wellenstein
Lydia White
Ida Woldemichael
Willy Wong
Chris Wu
Xin Xin
Forest Young
Stephanie Yung
Jeremy Zilar

NETWORK

The collective experiences of the Communication Design faculty and external critics are listed below. Places where two or more individuals in the Communication Design community have overlapped are highlighted. Information is based on self-reported, online data.

Undergraduate Schools Attended

Adelphi University	Georgia Institute of Technology	Natcol Institute of Technology	Seoul National University	University of Cambridge	University of Oregon
Arizona State University	Gerrit Rietveld Academie Amsterdam	National Taiwan University	Skidmore College	University of Chicago	University of Pennsylvania
ArtCenter College of Design	The Glasgow School of Art	Nebraska Wesleyan University	Southern Adventist University	University of Cincinnati	University of Pittsburgh
ArtEZ University of the Arts	Hastings College	The New School	St. Stephen's College	University of Colorado Boulder	University of Southern California
Bard College	Haverford University	New York University	State University of New York College at Plattsburgh	University of Hartford	University of Southern Mississippi
Barnard	Hongik University	North Carolina State University	Stony Brook University	University of Hawaii at Manoa	University of Texas
Bath Spa University	Illinois Institute of Technology	Northeastern University	SUNY New Paltz	University of Houston	University of the Arts
Berklee College of Music	Indiana University Bloomington	Notre Dame University	Swarthmore College	University of Illinois at Urbana-Champaign	University of the Philippines
Bezalel Academy of Art and Design	ISIA Urbino	Occidental College	Technische Universität Dresden	University of Kansas	University of Wisconsin-Madison
Binghampton University	James Madison University	The Ohio State University	Temple University	University of Maryland Baltimore County	Virginia Commonwealth University
Bowling Green State University	The Johns Hopkins University	Ohio University	Tufts University	University of Massachusetts Amherst	Virginia Tech
Bringham Young University	Kansas City Art Institute	Oregon State University	Universidad de Los Andes	University of Michigan	Washington University in St. Louis
Brown University	Karlsruhe University of Arts and Design	Otis College of Art and Design	Université des Sciences Humaines	University of New Mexico	Webster University
California College of the Arts	Kean University	Penn State University	University of Applied Sciences Düsseldorf	University of North Carolina at Chapel Hill	Wellesley College
Calvin University	Keene State College	Pepperdine University	University of California, Berkeley	University of North Texas	Wesleyan University
Carnegie Mellon University	Konkuk University	Philadelphia University	University of California, Davis	University of Northern Colorado	Wheaton College
Central Academy of Fine Arts	Korea University	Portland State University	University of California, Los Angeles		Williams College
College of the Holy Spirit Manila	Kutztown University	Pratt Institute			Yale University
The College of Saint Rose	La Sierra University	Princeton University			York University
The College of Wooster	Lehigh University	Purchase College			
Columbia College Chicago	Long Island University	Reed College			
Columbia University	Louisiana State University	Rhode Island School of Design			
Columbus College of Art & Design	Maryland Institute College of Art	Rice University			
The Cooper Union for the Advancement of Science and Art	Massachusetts Institute of Technology	Rochester Institute of Technology			
Corcoran College of Art + Design	McDaniel College	Royal Academy of Art, The Hague			
Cornell University	Memphis College of Art	Royal College of Fine Arts			
CUNY City College	Michigan State University	Royal Melbourne Institute of Technology			
Dartmouth College	Middlesex University	Rutgers University			
DePaul University	Minneapolis College of Art and Design	San Francisco State University			
Drew University	Moore College of Art and Design	Savannah College of Art and Design			
Drexel University	Moscow Printing Institute	School of the Art Institute of Chicago			
Ecole cantonale d'art de Lausanne	Nanyang Technological University	School of Visual Arts			
Emerson College		Scripps College			
ENSAAMA					
Ewha Womans University					

Graduate Schools Attended

Academy of Media Arts Cologne	Lewis & Clark College	Royal Academy of Art in The Hague
ArtEZ University of the Arts	Maryland Institute College of Art	Royal College of Art
Bard College	Massachusetts Institute of Technology	School for Poetic Computation
Bowling Green State University	Milwaukee Institute of Art & Design	School of Visual Arts
Brown University	The New School	Technische Universiteit Delft
California College of the Arts	New York University	Temple University
California Institute of the Arts	Otis College of Art and Design	University of California, Irvine
Carnegie Mellon University	Pratt Institute	University of California, Los Angeles
Columbia University	Princeton University	University of Cincinnati
The Cooper Union for the Advancement of Science and Art	Rhode Island School of Design	University of the Arts
Cranbrook Academy of Art	Rice University	Vassar College
General Assembly	Rochester Institute of Technology	Vermont College of Fine Arts

<table>
<tr><td>Virginia Commonwealth University</td><td>Yale University</td></tr>
</table>

Places Worked

15-Five
18F
2×4
Aaron Brashear Design
Ada
Adobe
ADURO, inc
AIGA
AIGA Eye on Design
AIGA New York
Aleda for Council
Alexander Wang
Allbirds
Alright Studio
Anomaly
Antenna Design
Antidote Games
Apple
Architecture Magazine
Architecture Research Office
Area of Practice
The Art Institute of New York City
ArtCenter College of Design
Arthackday
Artists Space
Artstor
Artsy
Aruliden
Assemble Brands
Associated Press
ATypI
Austin Peay State University
AUTHENTIC
Avenues
Avid Reader Press
Away
B-Reel
Balcony Magazine
BAM
Bank Street College of Education
Barton F. Graf
Base Design
Bates Hori
BBDO
Behance
Betterpath
Bloomberg
Blue State Digital
Bone Design
Brand New School
Bright Polka Dot

Brooklyn Academy of Music
The Brooklyn Rail
BustBright
Buzzfeed
CAB Productions
California College of the Arts
California Institute of the Arts
Casper
Catalog Press
Caveday
CBRE Build
Cdxs L.L.C.
Central Saint Martins, University of the Arts London
Champions Design
Channel Studio
Channel
Chobani
Chronicle Books
Chung & Trostle
CJ Type
CLANADA
Cleveland State University
Clunis Creative
CoinBase Design
Collins
Columbia Records
Columbia University
The College of New Jersey
Commercial Type
Common Name
Compass
Condé Nast
Cooper Hewitt
The Cooper Union for the Advancement of Science and Art
Cooperative Editions
Cornell Tech
The Creative Circus
Crossbeat
Datadog
DC Comics
Dearest Creative
Designlounge
designwajskol
Deutsch LA
Dome
Doshisha Women's College of Liberal Arts

Dowland
DraftFCB
Dreamers & Doers
Dress Code NY
Droga5
Dropbox
e.a.d. design corp
ENGN
Essential Herbs, Natural Remedies & Other Oddities
Etsy
Everything Studio
Experimental design agency
Facebook Connectivity
Fake Love
Fashion Institute of Technology
Ferdinando Verderi Studio
Field Series
Figma
First Church Torrington
FISK
Fjord
FlyLeaf Creative
Foreign Objects
Frank Collective
Franklyn
FreemanXP
Frere-Jones Type
The Frick Collection
Frog
Funeral
Future-of
Gabriele Wilson Design
General Assembly
Gigster
Givewith
Go High Signs
Google
Grilli Type
Guggenheim
Hacker School
Haha Services
Hardworking Goodlooking
Harry's
Haus
Hearst
Heavy Meta
Herman Miller
The Hillary for America Design Team
Hoffman Creative
Hofstra University
Hongik University

Huge
Hunter College
HvADESIGN
Hyperakt
IBM
IDEO
Incredible Machines
Independent
India China Institute
Instagram
Instrument
Interbrand
Jam3
Jeanne Verdoux Studio
Jessica Weber Design
Jet.com
Jon Lucas Office
Jones Knowles Ritchie
Kallemeyn Press
Kay Unger Design
KC Witherell Design
Keri Bronk
Kinesso
L+L Design
Labud
Lance Wyman Ltd.
Landor
Language Arts
LEAP
Libby Clarke Design LLC
Lido Studio
LiftLab
Lightscale Labs
Linked by Air
Little Spoons
Local Projects
Lore
Mailchimp
The Martin Agency
Martiniburger
Maryland Institute College of Art
Math Practice
McCann Erickson
McCann Worldgroup
McKinsey & Company
Medium
Meisei University
Mekanism
Method
MetLife
Metropolis Magazine
The Metropolitan Museum of Art
MGMT
Microsoft

Minda Gralnek & Compay
The Mintz Group
MIT Media Lab
MMP
Mod Op
MoMA
Monotype
Morcos Key
Mornings
Mother
MTV
MTWTF
Muse and Company
Museum of Contemporary Art Antwerp
Nahum-Albright Associates
NBC Universal Media
Neil Donnelly Studio
Neue Galerie
New Museum of Contemporary Art
The New School
New York City College of Technology
New York Film Academy
New York Magazine
The New York Times
New York University
Nexxus Design Company
Nike
No Ideas
No Plans
Noë & Associates
Noneman and Noneman Design
Notion Studio
NS Board
NYC
O-R-G
Observational Lab
OCD
Office of Luke Bulman
The Office of PlayLab
Ogilvy & Mather
Ojus Drawing Co.
OKFocus
oldthings-newplaces.com
Order
Organization for Spatial Practice
Other Forms
Other Means
Pagan & Sharp
Paperless Post

Paul Shaw Letter Design
Penguin Books
Pentagram
PepsiCo
Permalight
Pitchfork
Place+Make / Place+Code
Pleasure
Policygenius
Portland State University
Porto Rocha
Pratt Institute
Primary
PROPS.Supply
ProPublica
Protiviti
Prudential Financial
PS1 Printshop
Purchase College
Pure+Applied
QuickBooks
Quirky
R/GA
Radical Media
Rabbit Ear
Rational Beauty
Razorfish
Red Antler
Red Scout
Remake
Rhizome
Rhode Island School of Design
Ro&Co
Rockwell Group
Rokkan
Rona Represents
Room Studio
Rumors
Runyon Design
Rutgers University
Rutgers University-Camden
Safari Sundays
Samsung
San Jose State University
Scholastic
School for Poetic Computation
School of Visual Arts
Schoolhouse.World
Sesh
Shake, Inc.
Shawna X INC
Sibling Rivalry Studio
Siegel+Gale
Silicon Graphics Incorporated
Simon & Schuster

Simone Cutri Design
SimpleReach
Small Crowd Brand Consultants
Small Studio
Small Stuff
Smart Design
Solomon R. Guggenheim Foundation
SONY
Space Type Continuum
Sparkle Labs
Spire Integrated Design, Inc
Splash Worldwide
Spotify
Spring Studios
Spring, Inc.
Square

Squarespace
SSENSE
Standards
Stink Studios
Strategy Studio
Studio Art Work
Studio fnt
Studio Galison
Studio Ijeoma
Studio Lin
Studio RYTE
subcologne
Sudden Industries
Sum
Sunday Afternoon
Superbright
Superficial
Superliminal
Synoptic Office
SYPartners
Talk Magazine
Target / McCann

Tata Consultancy Services
Teachers Pay Teachers
Telfar
Tenazas Design
Terminal Design
This is Our Work
Time Inc
TODA New York
Triboro
Triple Canopy
Try The World
TV Land
twenty-six.design
TwentyToNine
Type Directors Club
Type/Code
The Unemployed Philosophers Guild

Uniqlo
Uniswap Labs
University of Europe for Applied Sciences in Berlin
University of Georgia
University of Miami
University of South Carolina
University of Tennessee at Chattanooga
University of Texas
V Magazine
Van Cleef & Arpels
Vantan Design Institute
Verizon

Viacom
Vidcode
Virginia Commonwealth University
Virginia Tech
Visionaire
Vistaprint
Vox Media
The Wall Street Journal
The Walt Disney Studios
Warby Parker
Wardwell Design
Washington University in St. Louis
WAX Studios
We Have Photoshop
We're Magnetic
Webflow

Webrecorder
WeShouldDoItAll
West
WeWork
Whitney Museum of American Art
Why Not Smile
Wide Eye
WITH creative, llc
Wkshps
Wolff Olins
Wondersauce
Work & Co
Work-Order
World Famous Electronics llc
XXIX
Yale University
Zaino Design
Zero Studios
Zut Alors!

EVENTS

The CD Lecture Series and the CD Symposia, produced and hosted by the Communication Design department, are highlighted. Other events are hosted by the Communication Design department but are sponsored and produced through partnerships with AIGA New York and the Type Directors Club.

CD Symposia

2020–21	Symposia suspended due to COVID-19
2019-05-15	Authenticity Moderator: Kelly Walters, Assistant Professor of Communication Design, Parsons Lukas Eigler Harding, Independent; Elaine Lopez, MFA Candidate, RISD; Andrew Shurtz, We Have Photoshop
2018-12-07	The Pedagogy of Design in the Age of Computation Moderator: Juliette Cezzar, Assistant Professor of Communication Design, Parsons Atif Akin, Associate Professor in Design, Rutgers; Taeyoon Choi, Co-Founder, School for Poetic Computation; Rik Lomas, Founder and CEO, SuperHi; Mindy Seu, Fellow, Berkman Klein Center for the Internet and Society
2018-05-15	Digital Materiality in the Age of Design Systems Moderator: Carly Ayres, HAWRAF Anil Dash, Glitch; Jacob Heftmann, XXIX; Tiff Hockin, Bloomberg; Laurel Schwulst, Critic, Yale School of Art; Allan Yu, Wilson.fm

CD Lecture Series

2021-04-23	Renda Morton, Director of Product Design, Dropbox
2021-03-26	Nikki Gonnissen, Founder, Thonik
2021-03-05	Andrew Shurtz, Founder, We Have Photoshop
2021-02-19	Jon Key, Partner, Morcos Key
2021-02-05	Susana Rodriguez de Tembleque, VP of Design, IBM Research
2020-12-04	Shira Inbar, Senior Designer, Pentagram
2020-11-20	John Provencher, Founder, Haha Services
2020-11-06	Kim Bost, Work & Co; Wes O'Haire, Dropbox; Kyra Price, Work & Co; Bruce Wilnen, Public Mechanics
2020-10-23	Paul Carlos, Principal, Pure+Applied
2020-10-09	Jon Sueda, Chair, Graduate Design Program, California College of the Arts
2020-09-25	Lynne Yun, Partner, Space Type Continuum
2020-09-11	Ramon Tejada, Assistant Professor, RISD
2020-02-21	Carly Ayres, HAWRAF
2020-02-07	Isabel Urbina Peña, Independent
2019-12-06	Hyo Kwon, Independent
2019-11-22	Chris Lee, Assistant Professor, Pratt Institute
2019-10-25	Luke Bulman, Office of Luke Bulman
2019-10-11	Rachel Berger, Chair of Graphic Design, California College of the Arts
2019-09-27	Tala Safié, Independent
2019-09-13	Thierry Blancpain, Grilli Type

2019-04-23	Tracy Ma, The New York Times
2019-04-08	Tamara Maletic, Linked by Air; Dan Michelson, Linked by Air; Eric Nyland, Linked by Air
2019-03-25	Paul Soulellis, Associate Professor, RISD
2019-02-12	Neil Donnelly, Independent

CD Virtual Field Trips

2020-12-11	Hemlock Printers: Facility Tour
2020-10-16	Poster House: Swiss Grid Exhibition

In Partnership with AIGA New York

2020–21	Onsite events suspended due to COVID-19
2020-02-27	AIGA NY Job Fair Hosts: Caspar Lam; Janet Esquirol; Jarrett Fuller
2020-02-25	Designing for 2020 Moderator: Victor Ng Bobby C. Martin Jr., The Original Champions of Design; Ben Ostrower, Wide Eye Creative; Deroy Peraza & Logan Emser, Hyperakt; Meena Yi, Creative Director for Cory Booker 2020
2020-01-29	Self-Love: Adam J. Kurtz & Eric Hu Eric Hu; Adam J. Kurtz
2020-01-22	Screening: Los Ultimos / Endless Letterpress
2019-12-12	Designing a New MoMA Moderator: Perrin Drumm, Eye on Design Ingrid Chou, Creative Director, MoMA; Shannon Darrough, Director of Digital Media, MoMA; Rob Giampietro, Director of Design, MoMA; Elle Kim, Associate Creative Director, MoMA; Damien Saatdjian, Art Director, MoMA
2019-11-21	Type x Graphic Design: Global Typography Moderator: Ksenya Samarskaya, Samarskaya & Partners Caspar Lam & YuJune Park, Synoptic Office; Wael Morcos, Morcos Key; Chris Wu, Wkshps
2019-10-28	Type x Graphic Design: Emerging Global Practices Moderator: Jason Alejandro, Assistant Professor of Graphic Design, The College of New Jersey Pragun Agarwal, Graduate, MICA; Ivy Li, Graduate, VCU; Breatiz Lozano, Graduate, University of Michigan
2019-10-24	Studio Transformation: Mythology + Pattern Moderator: Jessie McGuire, ThoughtMatter Emmett Shine, Pattern; Anthony Sperduti, Mythology
2019-10-14	Steps to Design Leadership Ariba Jahan, Director of Innovation, The Ad Council; Jinjin Sun, Senior Experience Designer, Adobe

2019-09-23	Branding the Tangible: Base Design + Jones Knowles Ritchie Moderator: Sarah Williams Min Lew, Base Design; Taylor Childers, Jones Knowles Ritchie; Tosh Hall, Jones Knowles Ritchie; Esther Li, Jones Knowles Ritchie; James Taylor, Jones Knowles Ritchie
2019-09-12	First Generation Conversation: Benjamin Evans of Airbnb Benjamin Evans, Airbnb
2019-06-07	Fresh Grad 2019: Part 2 Hosts: Meg Beckum; Caspar Lam Laura Scofield Cardoso, SVA MA in Design Research, Writing & Criticism; Emily Chu, Parsons, MS Data Visualization; Mitchell Johnson, SVA MFA Design; Ivy Yixue Li, Virginia Commonwealth University, MFA Graphic Design; Brenden Lovejoy, Cranbrook MFA 2D Design; Site Ma, MICA MFA Graphic Design; Annaka Olsen, RISD MFA Graphic Design; Heather Snyder Quinn, VCFA MFA Graphic Design; Zack Robbins, Yale MFA Graphic Design
2019-06-06	Fresh Grad 2019: Part 1 Hosts: Meg Beckum; Caspar Lam Natalie Alcide, The City College of New York Media & Communication Arts (BIC); Ilana Bonder, NYU, MPS in Interactive Telecommunications; Andy Kang, SVA MFA Interaction Design; Nobi Kashiwagi, Cooper Certificate Type Design; Kate Leisy, Parsons, MPS Communication Design; Lindsey Peterson, SCAD MFA Graphic Design; Michael Shirey, SVA Masters in Branding; Aditi Verma, Pratt MFA Communications Design
2019-04-24	Design Observer: Culture is Not Always Popular Moderator: Jarrett Fuller Ashleigh Axios; Michael Bierut; Jessica Helfand; Steven Heller; Karrie Jacobs; Thomas de Monchaux
2019-04-17	Panel Discussion: The Part-Time Professor Moderators: Janet Esquirol; Caspar Lam Neil Donnelly; Dan Kawasaki; Lynn Kiang; Sasha Portis
2019-03-27	Type x Graphic Design ~ Relationships & Collaboration Elizabeth Carey Smith; YuJune Park; June Shin; Lisa Smith; Nina Stössinger
2019-03-20	Work Wife: Erica Cerulo and Claire Mazur Speakers: Erica Cerulo; Claire Mazur Panelists: Melissa Deckert; Kendra Eash; Nicole Licht; Kelli Miller
2019-02-27	Co-creating a Customer Experience: Uber and Wolff Olins Moderator: Tori Miner Peter Markatos; Forest Young
2019-02-19	The Great Contentment: Tina Essmaker Tina Essmaker
2019-02-15	AIGA NY Job Fair Hosts: Janet Esquirol; Caspar Lam
2019-01-28	The Aesthetics of Joy: Ingrid Fetell Lee Ingrid Fetell Lee; Debbie Millman
2018-11-29	Branding the Alexandria Ocasio-Cortez Campaign: Tandem Tandem
2018-10-25	Brand by Hand: Jon Contino and Julia Rothman Jon Contino; Julia Rothman
2018-10-17	Emily Cohen: It's Your Fault! Emily Cohen
2018-09-27	Dori Tunstall: Decolonizing Design Dori Tunstall
2018-06-08	Fresh Grad 2018 #02 Moderators: Meg Beckum; Aaris Sherin Lucas Albrecht, Cranbrook, MFA 2D Design; Cara Buzzell, RISD, MFA Graphic Design; Katja Fluekiger, MICA, MFA Graphic Design; Todd Hilgert, VCFA, MFA Graphic Design; Celina Lacaze, Parsons, MFA Transdisciplinary Design; Anja Laubscher, SVA, MA in Design Research, Writing & Criticism; Krongporn Thongongarj, SVA, MFA Design; Bryce Wilner, Yale, MFA Graphic Design
2018-06-07	Fresh Grad 2018 #01 Moderators: Meg Beckum; Aaris Sherin Amy Ashida, SVA, MFA Interaction Design; Samia Husari, Parsons, MPS Communication Design; Hayeon Hwang, NYU, MPS in Interactive Telecommunications; Cheryl Johnson, SVA, Masters in Branding; Lauren King, Cooper, Certificate Type Design; Laura Ruiz de Gamboa Peres, Pratt, MFA Communications Design; Shruti Shyam, SCAD, MFA Graphic Design
2018-05-30	ModMag: The NY Edition Hosts: Jeremy Leslie, magCulture; Liv Siddall, Riposte & Redundancy Radio Kirsten Algera, MacGuffin; Gail Bichler, Design Director, The New York Times Magazine; Perrin Drumm, Founder, AIGA Eye on Design; Emily Oberman, No Man's Land; Michele Outland, Creative Director, Gather Journal & Bon Appetit; Omar Sosa, Creative Director, Apartamento; Alexander Tochilovsky, The Lubalin Centre; Justinien Tribillon & Isabel Seiffert, Migrant Journal; Richard Turley, Mushpit and Civilization
2018-05-01	Rules of Engagement: Brand Building & Social Media Moderator: Matthew Schneier, The New York Times Mike Eckhaus, Eckhaus Latta; Parick Janelle, Spring Street Social Society; Babak Radboy, Telfar
2018-03-20	One in Ten: Gender Equality in Design Moderator: Tina Essmaker Jessica Brillhart; Stella Bugbee; Ariella Gogol; Renda Morton
2018-02-08	2018 Job Fair
2017-11-20	Meet The Moderns: Midcentury American Graphic Design Introduction: Debbie Millman Speakers: Steven Heller; Greg D'Onofrio Panelists: Richard Danne; Tom Geismar; George Lois; Rudi Wolff
2017-10-30	The Game Studio Moderator: Steve Milton Dan Gray; Patrick Moberg; Cody Uhler; Ross Wariner
2017-09-26	Paul Sahre: Why Be a Designer? Introduction: Paula Scher Paul Sahre

2017-06-21 Paula Scher and Unit Editions: 522 Pages and 41 Years
Paula Scher; Adrian Shaughnessy

2017-06-09 AIGA/NY Fresh Grad / Edu Talks 2017
Hosts: E Roon Kang; Joe Marianek
Moderators: David Frisco; Aaris Sherin
Panelists: Keetra Dixon, Assistant Professor, Rhode Island School of Design; Tyler Hartrich, UXDI Lead Instructor, General Assembly; Lara Penin, PhD Director Transdisciplinary Design Graduate Program, Parsons School of Design; Mark Addision Smith, Assistant Professor, Art Department, The City College of New York Students: Aldrena Corder, VCFA, MFA Graphic Design; Cem Eskinazi, RISD, MFA Graphic Design; Eric Freer, Yale, MFA Graphic Design; Christopher Lopez, Parsons, MFA Transdisciplinary Design; Andrew Peters, MICA, MFA Graphic Design; Michael Stone, SVA, MFA Design; Molly Woodward, SVA, MA in Design Research, Writing & Criticism; Qingyu Wu, Cranbrook, MFA 2D Design

2017-06-08 AIGA/NY Fresh Grad / Edu Talks 2017
Hosts: E Roon Kang; Joe Marianek; Aaris Sherin
Ariane Beauregard, Pratt, MFA Communications Design; Mathura Govindarajan, NYU, MPS in Interactive Telecommunications; Dave Mahmarian, SVA, MFA Interaction Design; Sam Vickars, Parsons, MS Data Visualization; Memoli Ward, SVA, Masters in Branding; Sihan Wu, SCAD, MFA Graphic Design

2017-03-29 The Hillary for America Design Team
Introduction: Michael Bierut Moderator: Jennifer Kinon, OCD Co-founder, Hillary for America Design Director
Chelsea Atwell; Laura Bernstein; Shar Biggers; Maggie Bignell; Erica Deahl; Eric Hartman; Kara Haupt; Hanah Ho; Allyn Hughes; Cindy Hwang; Steve Merenda; Victor Ng; Meg Vazquez; Monina Velarde; Ida Woldemichael

2017-02-23 Real Talk about Design Systems
Moderator: Daniel Burka, Design Partner, Google Ventures
Emily Brick, Product Designer, Buzzfeed; Diana Mounter, Product Designer, GitHub; Viktor Perrson, Staff Designer, Material Design, Google

2016-12-14 New Narratives in Motion
Moderator: Alex Moulton, Executive Creative Director, Trollbäck + Company
Beat Baudenbacher, Co-Founder, LOYALKASPAR; John Colette, Professor of Motion Media Design, Savannah College of Art and Design; Michelle Higa Fox, CEO, Slanted Studios; Adam Mignanelli, Design Director, VICE Media; Hélène Park, Designer, Google Chrome UX

2016-11-02 Christoph Niemann: Sunday Sketching
Christoph Niemann

2016-10-27 Servicing Tech: SF x NY
Moderator: Forest Young, Wolff Olins
Tom Crabtree, Manual; Linda Eliasen, ueno; August Heffner, Work & Co

2016-09-29 Day in the Life: SF x NY
Sarah Cooper, Ex-Googler / Writer & Comedian; Tom Harman, Product Design Manager, BuzzFeed; Danny Jones, Designer, Google VR; Karla Mickens, Product Designer, Facebook; Jeremy Perez-Cruz, Senior Design Manager, Uber; Jing Wei, Brand Illustrator, Etsy

2016-06-13 Fresh Grad 2016 #02
Hosts: David Frisco; Joe Marianek
Shazeeda Bhola, SVA, MPS Branding; Derek Love, SVA D-Crit, MA Design Research, Writing & Criticism; Marc-Andre Roberge, 30 Weeks Program; Pat Shiu, NYU ITP, MA Interactive Telecommunications Program; Christiana Theophanopoulos, Pratt, MS Communications Design; Jonathan Thirkield, Parsons, MS Data Visualization; Misha Volf, Parsons, MA Design Studies; Lynne Yun, Type@Cooper, Post-Graduate Typeface Design

2016-06-06 Designing the Future of Design Education
Moderators: Juliette Cezzar; Bryn Smith
Rachel Berger; John Caserta; YuJune Park

2016-06-02 Fresh Grad 2016 #01
Hosts: David Frisco; Joe Marianek
Matthew Bambach, MICA, MFA Graphic Design; Megan Dombeck, SCAD, MFA Graphic Design; Kelsey Elder, Cranbrook, MFA 2D Design; Laura Rossi Garcia, VCFA, MFA Graphic Design; Tyler Henry, Parsons, MFA Design + Technology; Aya Jaffar, Parsons, MFA Transdisciplinary Design; Qiong Li, Yale, MFA Graphic Design; Xinyi Li, Pratt, MFA Communications Design; Alexander Martin, VCU, MFA Graphic Design; Gabriel Melcher, RISD, MFA Graphic Design; Roya Ramezani, SVA, MFA Products of Design; Josh Sucher, SVA, MFA Interaction Design; Sarah Wilson, SVA, MFA Design

2016-05-10 A Sense of Place, How Graphic Designers Make Cities too
Introduction: David Frisco, AIGA/NY Treasurer; Manuel Miranda, AIGA/NY VP Moderator: Laetitia Wolff, AIGA/NY Program Director
Alicia Cheng, AIGA/NY Board Member and Principal, MGMT Design; Lauren Coakley-Vincent, Director, Neighborhood Development Division, NYC Small Business Services; Alexandria Sica, Executive Director, DUMBO Business Improvement District; Vanessa Smith & Megan Marini, Principals, 3×3 Design; Jodi Terwilliger, Creative Director, HUSH

2016-05-05 Design x Fashion
Moderator: Piera Gelardi
Greg Foley; Kristen Naiman; Nicola Formichetti

2016-04-27 Tall Tales From A Large Man
Aaron James Draplin

2016-03-24 In The House with Tumblr & Pinterest
Moderator: Jonathan Lee
Zack Sultan, Tumblr; Scott Tong, Pinterest

2016-02-24	Design for People: Chapter 13 Moderator: Willy Wong Rachel Bozek, Copy Chief, Design for People; Chappell Ellison, Editor, Design for People; Karrie Jacobs, Essay Writer, Design for People; Martha Kang McGill, Book Designer, Design for People; Bryn Smith, Editor, Design for People; Scott Stowell, Director, Design for People
2016-02-08	The Worst Thing I Ever Made: Part 2 Renda Morton Kim Bost; Antonio de Luca; L&L; Ksenya Samarskaya
2015-12-16	Kelli Anderson: The Hidden Talents of Everyday Things Kelli Anderson
2015-10-28	Is the Expansion of Design a Triumph or a Tragedy? Jeremy DiPaolo, Global Director of Brand Design Strategy, PepsiCo
2015-09-30	It's Not Just About the Money, It's Not Just About the Art Paul Barnes; Christian Schwartz
2015-06-10	Fresh Grad 2015 Hosts: David Frisco; Agnieszka Gasparska Najeebah Al-Ghadban, SVA, MFA Design; Leah Cabrera Fischer, Ashley Graham, Chisun Rees, Parsons, MFA Transdisciplinary; Alon Chitayat, NYU ITP; Gabriel Gianordoli, Parsons, MFA Design + Technology; Monique Grimord, SCAD, MFA Graphic Design; Katrina Keane, MICA, MFA Graphic Design; Eric Nylund, Yale, MFA Graphic Design; Philippe Ostiguy, SVA, MPS Branding; Eduardo Palma, Pratt, MFA GradComD; Amanda Pickens, RISD, MFA Graphic Design; Anke Stohlmann, SVA, MFA IxD; Jesen Tanadi, Cranbrook, MFA Design; Justin Zhuang, SVA, MFA Design Criticism
2015-04-22	Design x Fashion Moderator: Greg Foley Garance Doré; Piera Gelardi; Patrick Li
2015-03-26	In the House Museum Moderator: Juliette Cezzar Mike Abbink, Museum of Modern Art; Hilary Greenbaum, Whitney Museum of American Art; Peter Kaplan, Museum of Arts and Design; Emile Molin, Metropolitan Museum of Art; Lorraine Wild, Los Angeles County Museum of Art
2015-02-26	Louise Sandhaus: Earthquakes, Mudslides, Fires & Riots Moderator: Alexandra Lange Barbara Glauber; Louise Sandhaus; Lucille Tenazas
2015-01-28	Natasha Jen: Fresh on the Boat Natasha Jen
2014-11-03	Dan Friedman: Radical Modernist Chris Pullman
2014-09-17	Tobias Frere-Jones: In Letters We Trust Tobias Frere-Jones
2014-06-11	My Dog & Pony: Fresh Blood V Hosts: Juliette Cezzar; Jesse Ragan Chiara Bajardi, SVA Design; Amy-Nicole Dosen, Cranbrook Academy of Art; Sameer Farooq, RISD; Su Hyun Kim, NYU ITP; Alejandro Largo, SVA Branding; Or Leviteh, Parsons Design & Technology; Martha McGill, Yale; Anne Quito, SVA D-Crit; Emma Sherwood-Forbes, MICA; Alexander Todaro, SVA IxD; Lauren Wong, Parsons Transdiciplinary; Diego Zaks, Pratt Communications Design
2014-04-22	Sesame Street the Longest Street in the World Theresa Fitzgerald; Nadine Zylstra; Philip Toscano
2014-04-17	Nicholas Blechman: Food Chains Nicholas Blechman
2014-03-27	In-The-House IV: Culture, Connectivity and Content. Moderator: Debbie Millman Renda Morton; Joe Marianek
2014-01-29	Boom: A Conversation with Irma Boom & Debbie Millman Irma Boom; Debbie Millman
2013-11-14	Fonts for the Web with Jonathan Hoefler Jonathan Hoefler
2013-10-03	International Perspectives: It's Nice That: Championing Creativity Across the World Alex Bec; Will Hudson

In Partnership with the Type Directors Club

2020–21	Onsite events suspended due to COVID-19
2020-01-23	TDC at Parsons Lecture Series: Judges' Night Hosts: Liz DeLuna; Douglas Riccardi; Juan Villanueva Maria Doureuli, Contrast Foundry; Greg Gazdowicz, Commercial Type; Rebecca Gimenez, IA Collaborative; Laura Meseguer, Type-O-Tones; Wael Morcos, Morcos Key; Silas Munro, Poly-Mode; Dori Tunstall, OCAD University; Eva Wendel, Neue Gestaltung
2019-05-08	Type x Graphic Design ~ Craft & Originality Naomi Abel; Jennifer Kinon; Charles Nix; Ksenya Samarskaya; Christian Schwartz
2019-01-24	Judges' Night: Karin Fong and Kristyan Sarkis Karin Fong; Kristyan Sarkis
2018-06-14	In Letters We Trust: Tobias Frere-Jones + Journey to the Dark Side of Contrast: Nina Stössinger Tobias Frere-Jones; Nina Stössinger
2018-06-13	Type & Time: Neville Brody Neville Brody

1 Year

Department Profile	MPS CD: Class of 2021
216	347
BFA CD: Class of 2021	AAS CD: Class of 2021
219	367
	Data Traces
	387

WHO WE ARE

Communication Design at Parsons is an international community of technologically-inclined, socially-minded, and future-focused individuals. We work and learn in interdisciplinary ways to advance our understanding of how ideas and experiences are systematically created through visual and textual form.

WHY WE MAKE

Communication Design addresses an enduring need for human beings to express themselves through language made visible and ideas made material. We believe design is a negotiation between material form and its evolving methods of production. The generative meanings that arise through context and criticism shape our networked culture and expand our ability to comprehend increasingly complex, visual environments.

WHAT WE DO

The Parsons Communication Design program is the oldest undergraduate program of its kind in the United States. Located in the center of the nation's design capital and housed at a progressive university, the program provides an ideal environment for students to direct their imagination and intellect to engage the world: both to address its ever-changing challenges and to celebrate the delight of human creativity.

Our approach to the discipline is grounded in the study of typography, the visual shape of language, and interaction, the causal relationships among people and digital experiences. These two areas run through our STEM curricula with the intention of initiating students on their life-long journey towards personal agency and a mastery of craft. Our students work in increasingly expansive contexts to systematically plan, project, and convey meaning experienced in a single moment or sustained over time. From drawing typefaces and making books to creating exhibitions and designing digital products, they develop the capability to use design to reconcile competing demands into a coherent whole.

Students engage with design practitioners of the highest caliber. They work across a diversity of conditions—from technology giants to independent studios—with differing aesthetic attitudes but united in an uncompromising conviction in the value of design to deepen our collective capacity to see.

AREAS OF STUDY

Undergraduate Programs of Study	Graduate Programs of Study	Adult, Professional, and Continuing Education Programs
BFA Communication Design	MPS Communication Design Digital Product Design	AAS Communication Design
Communication Design Minor	MA Communication Design[i]	
	MFA Communication Design[i]	

	Related Graduate Programs of Study at The New School	Related Adult, Professional, and Continuing Education Programs at The New School
	MS Data Visualization	Certificate in Infographics and Data Visualization
		Certificate in Graphic and Digital Design
		Certificate in User-Centered Design (UX/UI)
		Certificate in Web Design

CD Courses Support	CD Courses Support
BA in Journalism + Design	MA in Creative Publishing and Critical Journalism
	Psychology & UX/HCI[i]

RESEARCH & INDUSTRY

Centers of Research	Industry Partnerships
Center and Archives for Global Typography[ii]	American Institute of Graphic Arts New York
Publishing Imprint[ii]	Type Directors Club / One Club for Creativity
	Alliance Graphique Internationale

STUDENT SUPPORT PROGRAMS	ACADEMIC PARTNERSHIPS
CD Lecture Series	Cornell Tech Program
CD Symposia Program	
Teaching Fellowship Program[ii]	
Lance Wyman Scholars	
CD Tutors Program	

i. Under Consideration
ii. In Progress

Design is intensely solitary in execution but extraordinarily public in its dissemination and dialogue. Designers learn to work between these antipodal modes through a cyclical practice of making, critique, and reflection. For over a year now, these activities have been reorganized by conditions brought forth by a global pestilence. The Class of 2021, and indeed all designers, have rediscovered how vital community is for the discipline to flourish.

The challenges of the past year have also shifted and reconfigured our collective sense of materiality: the knowledge and feeling of how formal properties can be flexed and molded. Many in this year's class experienced a profound loss when access to common tools of the trade like paper and printing were denied. For everyone, pandemic life has been an accelerated encounter and re-familiarization with the materiality of the screen. The opportunities and challenges of representational imagery, thus, became a central and vexing issue. What is a physical artifact if it is only seen through the screen but never felt and never experienced? The last year has shown what life would be like to design and live solely through this medium.

It comes as no surprise that this year's class has responded to these challenges in a myriad of ways. Many have leaned into the opportunities afforded by the web while others have defied expectations by turning their rooms into makeshift print studios. Questions about identity, memory, representation, and future are foremost in their minds. But looking more closely, these questions are related to perennial questions about the qualities and concerns of the human person. Rather than being a set of projects meant solely for consumption in the "next thing," these projects stand as an archive of thousands of conversations about what matters to these specific students in 2021 virtually connected to each other through their decision to study at Parsons.

The thesis begins with a question, problem, or dilemma, and responds with design. Over the course of a year, students practice research, ideation, prototyping, iteration and presentation in the service of something that matters to them. A successful project does not only show a capable designer, but also someone who has the curiosity to learn independently about a subject outside of design, as well as the tenacity to learn whatever it takes to convey a message or solve a problem.

For those who continue to see making as a way to learn rather than just a means to an end, design is a lifelong framework to see the world and their place in it. Our strongest hope is that students will take with them a habit of wonder, tenacity, and learning. Their thesis projects are the first proof that they can.

EVERYDAY NAIJA
Dotun Abeshinbioke

Ankara prints, also known as African prints, are native fabrics to most of West Africa, mostly worn as everyday clothing and clothes are popular amongst West Africans and the origins of many are unknown. Ankara was originally developed by the Dutch for the Indonesian Textile Market however they gained more interest in the West African Market due to the colors and tribal like patterns

and Vlisco is one of the only and longest manufacturers of this fabrics. When it gained interest in West Africa a lot of the patterns designed were pivoted to keep up that interest but adorning the patterns with objects and motifs that would be recognizable amongst Africans. Africa's most popular textile is made by the Dutch.

Everyday Naija is a series of patterns and prints inspired by the everyday beauty of Nigerian culture from our food to culture to

household products. The patterns directly reference and are inspired by the design aesthetic of ordinary products, the goal of this project is not only to highlight the beauty in the ordinary and everyday but also to create a sense of nostalgia and encourage conversation on what African Print can be and story-telling through patterns. This catalogue is organized by theme and the patterns are contextualized through images of the everyday items that inspired them.

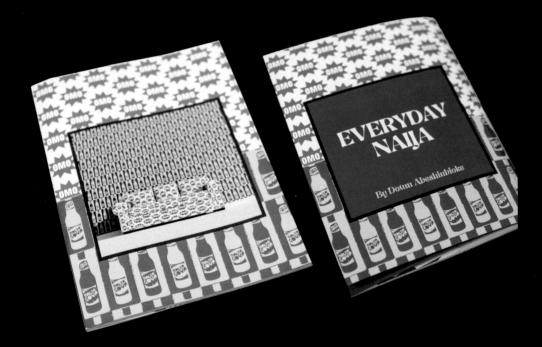

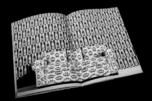

→ doseofdots.co/everyday-naija
→ doseofdots.co

220

WHAT WE ARE MADE OF
Darina Abuzarova

What We Are Made Of tells a story of an alternative history of Russian culture and society. The center of the book is Russian youth and their subcultures that began to appear in the USSR during Ottepel (1950 - 1965) and Perestroika (1980s). The book seeks to tell not only the history, but also the development of concepts such as freedom or creative expression behind the iron certain. Another important factor of this book is different design objects that illus-trates the time, they show the uniqueness of Russian design, music, and production.

Generations of Russian people grew up in the subcultures covered in this book, and also formed them. In chronological order, the book shows how one can see entire movements grew out of underground and even sometimes forbidden clubs. We are familiar with Hippies, Dudes, New Wavers, Breakers, Punks, Rockers, Skaters and Ravers, but we would never guess that their appearance came out of protest and desire of change. Most of them did not orient themselves towards foreign analogs at all, rather they perceived and translated them in their own way. I wanted to show that in Russia and in the USSR, just as all around the world, there was cultural progress even during this period.

The book has bilingual typesetting, in order to tell a story of the important cultural changes to a wider range of readers. All the information in the book were found in contemporary or archival sources, including photographs by Igor Mukhin and others.

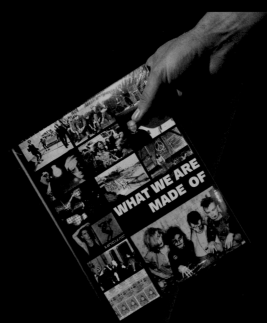

→ whatwearemadeof.cargo.site
→ abuzd452baa6.myportfolio.com

UNWIND
   Sung Hyun (Julie) Ahn

We are not born with a mindset. We have to practice a certain mindset we want to acquire, and our mindset develops as we age. Being mindful and in focus are critical skills that not many people have nowadays with the constant distractions from social media and technology.

Consequently, I wanted to question how we might create a platform or a fun way of instilling mental mindfulness at a young age so that it would become habitual and natural to help them be more focused in the present and better cope with stress? To answer my question, I came up with a possible solution which is an analog interactive game called Unwind. The target audience is aged 8–10 because studies have reported that habits would take root by the age of 9. This game is to practice mindfulness with the little ones, friends, or alone. The entire game box is used for the game. Both the assembling and disassembling of the box are an activity that can be shared with the little ones. The box contains a set of five mindful books: Breathe, Focus, Imagine, Move, and Relax which includes twelve different exercises to practice in the respective categories. There will be a mat attached to the box for the child to sit on, a spinner on the bottom to choose a category and two dice to pick an exercise. In conclusion, I hope that the young-aged population would build a healthy mentality through mindful activities.

→ sunghyunahn.com
→ sunghyunahn.com/work/unwind

ASSIST

The field of mental health has seen many changes in the past decades, be it from the shift in its approach from isolating the mentally ill to focusing on community healing, or the major change in people's attitudes and prejudices towards mental disorders and the seeking of treatment. However, certain important aspects of the mental health industry such as supporting resources like skills worksheets and patient safety plans continue to be overlooked. In addition to that, these existing resources lack an aesthetic value, which as a result makes them less helpful and leads patients to utilize them less in their recovery. My aim in this project was to research how different design approaches and elements can influence human emotion and use my findings in redesigning existing mental health resources.

I created the website Assist to provide a platform that can house different tools that patients suffering from depression and anxiety disorders can use to aid their recovery. Assist consists of an AI that checks in on the patient's current well-being and progress with therapy. Additionally, it helps patients with daily journaling and encourages the use of helpful skills through several prompts. Finally, it provides a new approach to skills worksheets as it creates a more interactive learning approach that deviates away from the basic print handouts.

SOFT PERSUASION OF NEW INSECURITIES
Hazal Aysel

The early 20th century marked a great shift in the social and cultural ethos of American culture, slowly giving way to a new set of values and building the powerful roots of consumerist culture. Following a long history of change and reinvention, advertising in the United States remains as the most influential tool in commodifying insecurities as a promising route to self realization.

While the direction toward which the mirror faces between society and advertisement is often broadly questioned, their relation is in reality dichotomous. Popular culture is ever-changing and advertising has continuously adapted itself to shifting paradigms. It is crucial to acknowledge that advertising cannot be considered and evaluated in isolation. There is semiotic and social meaning behind all choices made in advertising and everyday consumption.

Soft Persuasion of New Insecurities approaches American advertising and popular culture through a critical lens, exploring the ever changing insecurities baited by the consumerist happiness machine while questioning its future within a neoliberal context. Each chapter, with its own designated color, chronologically addresses an era defined by its new insecurities. Historical nostalgia and a speculative future unite in a strive to unveil persuasive methods. Through the study of theories such as the Therapeutic Ethos and Conspicuous Consumption this book explores the history and future of insecurities that are the instruments and byproducts of American Consumerist Culture.

→ hazalaysel.persona.co/403450
→ hazalaysel.persona.co

In the age of nostalgics, we are surrounded by art that originates from the past. Nostalgia OS focuses on the role of nostalgia in contemporary culture and aims to question and understand its purpose. Due to the internet boom, our society is able to interact with each other in a way never imagined before. Hyper globalization has lead to a rise in social media and in turn consumerism. We are so used to instant gratification and rapid change.

In these conditions, nostalgia can be used as a device to offer a notion of permanence and identity, owing to its ability to transcend cultural barriers like language. Nostalgia OS is an attempt to explore the role of nostalgia in contemporary culture and design. Adopting cultures from both the past and the present, the project takes two forms: a website and a book. Although the mediums are different, both of them are designed in a similar fashion, with the use of modular forms and shapes that call back to the early computer era. The typography alludes to the relationship between humans and computers, employing the first typeface recognizable by both. The book serves as a guide to under-standing nostalgia, while the website functions as a more inter-active medium, and serves to convey the meaning of the project through its interaction.

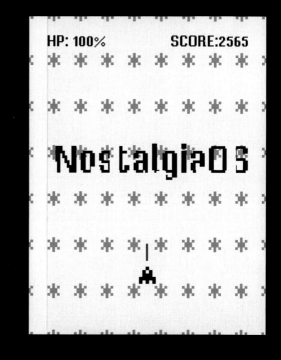

DEVI SAYS
Sunayana Bali

In India, goddesses are worshipped as a source of power and inspiration. Each deity is associated with a different trait that defines their unique characteristics. Today, we see the patriarchy worshiping goddesses but discriminating against women—while women in the past were active members in decision making, many are now restricted to family roles. The goal of this project is to explore the role goddesses play in our society and

whether they can be a positive model for women.

Devi Says is catered towards young and striving Indian women that are being challenged by society's moral standards and expectations. The seven traits captured in Devi Says are derived from stories of women that achieved great heights and proved patriarchy wrong. Devi Says takes the form of a seasonal magazine that compiles stories of women past and present and an app that challenges patriarchal expectations. The magazine gives insight into the many traditions celebrated to worship Hindu goddesses,

juxtaposed with stories from women speaking about their experiences and beliefs. The app is designed to challenge women with various activities that they might have been discriminated "not" to do.

The aim of Devi Says is to change mental perception and build a community where women can enjoy the benefits of their rights and overcome boundaries set by the patriarchy. Jawaharlal Nehru once stated that the status of women could determine a nation's worth. To see change, we need to act.

QUEERING COMPUTATION
Elliot Bohlen

Queer theory is rooted in failure and non-normativity, which are two concepts this project embraces. This analysis is centered in the rejection of compulsory norms such as capitalism and heteronormativity. By being identified as a failure in a system, one's existence becomes an act of resistance against these "protocols," becoming glitches, bugs, and errors. There is a strong link tying queer theory to non-normative computation, which I will now refer to as "queer computation," as both are opposing the system. Normative uses of code, determined by strict protocols, demand websites to become seamless tools that discourage critical and emotional engagement. This homogeneity leaves little room for deviation. Queer computation creates opportunities for deviation, and is a place where I feel confident resisting. By exploiting and breaking the web's protocols when creating digital work, I feel that I am embodied as a queer individual who is constantly "othered."

Deviating from these norms allows for valuable opportunities for play, resistance, and engagement. I created a collection of single serving sites that utilize queer computational techniques and notions of embodiment. The web is regarded as a neutral space but, in these sites, I imbued the medium with emotion, physicality, and identity. I paired this with a book titled 404: Page Not Found which contextualizes the ambiguities presented in each site, as it is a place where I display and annotate my source code. I hope to propose an alternative to normative computation in favor of one that is more human and engaging.

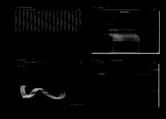

THE RESISTANCE PLATFORM
Madison Brang

With devastating environmental and social realities, there is activism, legislation, and resistance. The Resistance Platform is a letter-generating tool that promotes change by giving everyone a voice, starting conversations, and connecting the public sphere to the industrial sphere to petition against environmental and social injustices. Focusing on 'Cancer Alley,' St James Parish, Louisiana, the Resistance Platform holds Formosa plastics, the Taiwanese petroleum manufacturing company, accountable for

environmental racism and targeted hazardous waste.

Cancer Alley is a predominantly Black community in St. James Parish, Louisiana, bordering large industrial petrochemical plants. It is coined Cancer Alley because of the increasing toxicity in the air due to the industrial plants' intentional proximity near the residence.

The Resistance Platform directly connects the user to major contributors and supporters of Formosa Plastics' newest $9.4 billion project, The Sunshine Project, through letter generation. The Sunshine Project has the potential of doubling the toxicity of the air in St. James Parish. The

Resistance Platform will educate the user and allow people, including St. James Parish residents, environmentalists, frontline workers at Formosa Plastics, etc., to place accountability and directly contact policymakers and corporate entities involved in the promotion of The Sunshine Project. The mission is to provide an accessible, intersectional platform for conversation between the ones affected and the ones who can create change within environmental and social justice movements. It follows the ideals of transparency, reliance, and accountability by placing responsibility on large industries creatively and purposefully.

→ resistance-platform.com
→ madisonbrang.com

CENTER STAGE
Allison Bynum

In grade school art classes, students rarely learn about people of color in the art industry in non-specialized classes. European or white male artists and designers are taught about and deemed to be the greats of their art movements. From my experience, as a young aspiring artist in high school, I grew tired of learning about the same artists in every art class. The picture painted by the information given about the standard set of artists was a linear story. It wasn't until my first art history class in college that I began to learn a more diverse perspective on art history, and the linear art history I'd known became a web of creative people of all colors. This project was inspired by my desire to share this experience with other young aspiring artists. Representation in the art industry for children of color is important, so Center Stage, the African-American artist cards, are meant to supplement the art history curriculum to bring that representation. The cards include a mix of African-American artists and designers living and deceased. The living artists and designers give children people to look up to, while the passed artists add African-American artists and designers to their art history knowledge.

AUME ACADEMY
Rachel Chang

Our world isn't necessarily designed for the minority, and most products released today don't consider using inclusive & accessible design. I found in my research that existing resources - specifically for children with autism, can be outdated and aren't designed using accessible UX/UI principles because the educators making them don't have a design background. In other words, existing resources could very much be adding further implications and discomfort to their learning environments.

My thesis attempts to solve this problem, creating a resource called Aume Academy that is specifically designed for children with autism in mind. UX/UI principles used that support accessibility/inclusivity include: supporting sensory overload, using a typeface supporting dyslexia, reducing color intensity, no scrolling, use of labeled buttons to navigate pages, muted color palette, use of hierarchy to show importance, etc.

Aume Academy is the joint partnership between educators that work with kids with autism and inclusive design principles to create a cohesive resource for children ages 5-9, equipping them with fundamental knowledge for what life will bring. My thesis is presented through an illustrated square book with exercises after each lesson, and a website app that both unlock different types of sensory experiences. The book is a square format that offers tangible interactions, and the app incorporates accessible UX/UI principles and supports sound. When creating Aume Academy my goal was to create an intentional, safe, and comfortable learning environment for children with autism, to equip them with whatever they need to help navigate the world.

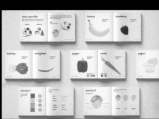

DECOLONIZATION IS A REFUSAL TO CONFORM
Lilliana Checo

"History repeats itself, first as a tragedy, second as a farce." —Karl Marx

My thesis consists of a compilation of contemporary writing that continues the long, ongoing conversation of decolonization in a few of its aspects and how excerpts of this conversation are lost in translation. To visualize this disruption, I chose pull quotes that in my opinion hold the essence of the message yet bring it out of context. Straining them further out of their context, I physically disrupt the pages by the means of marking, scratching, and creasing. Despite the rupture of the pages, I believe is important to be presented with these ideas today when our societies are, relatively, more open to the idea of reform. Though the idea is not the act, this is a pivotal moment to read these manifestos and pick and choose from them the ideas that might help us in the future. History repeats itself, for better or for worse.

MOVIES AND COMMENTS
Jizheng Chen

Companies are all transferring their working mode today from offline to online, including film companies. They are more and more bonded with the internet as it keeps developing. My past working experience in the film makes me wonder what I can do to help the progress of filmmaking to be more efficient. And I found that the low opacity of actor costs and inconvenience of finding actors are big problems for directors and producers. So I want to create an app that helps video directors and producers to find the actors they want by just searching on the platform. I used Adobe XD to design the prototype of the app. I want it to have a complete user journey, put in everything that I can imagine and I believe is necessary for this app. The style of this app will be creative but also clear and practical.

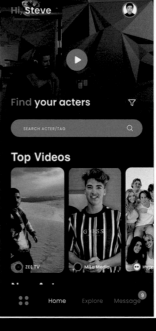

ANTIQUES OF THE PRESENT
Lena Chen

What would humanity and culture shift from 2021? How do we document the current moment? How would future people remember us? It's as important for us to talk to our younger generations ahead of time as we talk to each others now. The way we document the contemporary, the way our era is recorded, should be thoughtfully designed.

Work-from-home allows us to pay more attention to surrounding things: what I'm using in a daily basis and what I'm throwing away. In fact, due to the stunning pace at which scientific technology develops, we rarely notice how fast things are upgrading while other things are becoming obsolete. Ordinary objects are falling into disuse and replaced by innovations everyday.

Antiques of the Present is a bold exploration in terms of both physical scale and time range. It's a website archive of objects which we consider to be antiques in the near future. Objects are cleaned, disinfected and sealed in vacuum bags. The initial collection consists of 18 objects, but it's open for people to add to it over time. It's a never-ended project.

→ leqichen1228.github.io
→ chenl213.wixsite.com/lenachen/antiques-of-the-present

ur early experiences with our mily-of-origin have a major fluence on how we see urselves, others, and the world, nd how we behave in our daily ves. However, the influence can ometimes be toxic and negatively fect who we are when we grow .

Through the Crevice is a ook comprised of transcriptions om an interview-based video that llects four people's traumatic

experiences with their family and how they impact their adulthood, and documentation of a virtual exhibition—a reproduction of my childhood home that displays the artworks inspired by my own traumatic family memories. The artworks are placed in the rooms where specific incidents took place in order to restore the authenticity of memories, while the furniture inside the exhibition is left without materiality and color with the intention of creating an obscure and cold, yet familiar environment. The recollections

behind each piece are hidden inside the folded pages of the book. By tearing them open, readers encounter the personal narratives of the traumatic incidents.

This project is a personal exploration of traumatic memorie through various situations in whic family brings negative influence o us that might seem subtle and invisible, aiming to alert the audiences who find themselves in similar situations, no matter the role they play in their family—parents or child.

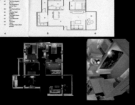

DIGITAL ACCESS
Raghav Chhabra

Digital design makes content on the web more attractive and easier to understand for many people. However, design can create major barriers for people when it is not accessible. Digital Access was born with a mission to provide equal access to digital content for everyone.

Digital Access aims to provide a platform to designers that help them learn more about making their designs more accessible. The platform provides tools, tips, and resources for designers in a clear form without overwhelming them. The website is easy to use, engaging, and has been built keeping its audience in mind.

It covers vision impairment as well as physical, hearing, and reading disabilities. Digital Access offers information about best practices for navigation, text size and weight, color and contrast, appearance, motion, and audio. The website itself is ADA and WCAG compliant and allows users to adjust their experience of using the website according to their needs.

→ accessibility.wiki
→ raghavc.design

LOVE

Shreya Chittaranjan

Hollywood has convinced us that love is unconditional and that it is the path to happiness. The way that it is portrayed is unidimensional. These movies show you "love" until the credits roll, but no one knows what happens after. This is because love does not have one definition and one function. Love is based on more than just a superficial attraction of two beautiful people in the movies.

During my research stage, I stumbled upon Plato's Symposium, a text that encompasses seven different types of love, discussed by ancient greek philosophers. The thesis explored these definitions and placed them besides modern day themes. This led to creating a coming of age series with three books. The first book is in the form of a story for young children covering the theme of affection. The second, for teenagers, covering various topics under friendship, lust, flirting, and

self-love. The last book, for young adults, covers the ideas of committed married love and unconditional love through the original text from the Symposium. The way we understand love affects how we form and perceive our relationships. It is important to question such abstract concepts from a young age so that we aren't confined by boundaries we set up for ourselves through fixed definitions.

EXPLORING THE POST-
STREAMING NARRATIVE
LANDSCAPE
Christopher Chu

During the first month of lockdown in New York City, when information was sparse and anxiety high, many turned to comfort through screens. The escapism that narrative entertainment provides through melodrama, surrealism and absurdity is an important part of people's lives. This love led to the beginning of the project, an examination of the narrative system in general, and the various designs that comprise it. Language is a centerpiece of the project, and often can accomplish the medium of a narrative alone. By creating mashups of situational and trope-based language, the result is abstract gestures of a scene or action. Each "gesture" is then written on posters with simple type and colorful backgrounds, called "The Commandments." This also began the digital transition of the project due to quarantine circumstances. The web offered an opportunity to reinforce how limited tropes are through randomization and an ever-evolving level of absurd language.

The final catalog of the project directly parodies these limitations by riffing on the trends of cinematic universes. Using Georges Polti's "36 Dramatic Situations" as a base, the website personifies the disillusioned state of the narrative system, and ultimately takes on a cyclical (and cynical) role. Integrating web interactions, animation and CG, the "36 Situation Universe" also emphasizes graphic design's role in perpetuating narrative tropes. While it will always be a reliable method of escapism, the narratives we love seem to return again and again, but with increasingly delicate standing. We already expect the unexpected.

THE 36 SITUATION UNIVERSE

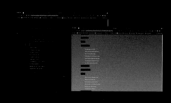

→ chuc036.github.io/portfolio/landing.html

CHANATION
Shenny Chuang

Tasting plays a significant role in Chinese tea culture. Chinese people believe that tasting tea is not only a way to show respect and friendship, but also provides an emotional satisfaction that allows people to enjoy the tea itself. There are six kinds of Chinese tea: yellow tea, oolong tea, green tea, dark tea, black tea, and white tea. Each variety tastes different and has different benefits for health, helping manage stress, with weight loss, and by lowering the risk of diabetes and more, that are worthwhile for people to discover.

Chanation is a teashop that brings tea lovers together and allows them to create their own cups of tea and share their recipes with others. The entire project applies soft colors and a legible sans serif typeface in order to be accessible and approachable to everyone who's interested in tea tasting. Through Chanation, I aim to make Chinese tea culture stand out and expand the tea community by introducing and promoting different kinds of Chinese tea to audiences who are not familiar with Chinese tea, especially young people in the western hemisphere. I want to encourage more young people to not only try, but also enjoy, drinking and learning about different types of Chinese tea in an engaging way.

FACING THE FACTS
Calen Chung

By definition from the 115th Congress of the United States, AI appears to be working for the people, for it is "designed to act rationally." If AI is to act rationally, can we give it the power to take over impressionable jobs like policing our cities?

Facing the Facts is a collection of web experiences that informs the public about the racial biases in facial recognition programs. Not many people realize that cities have implemented AI systems into their police departments. Predictive policing uses facial recognition to give police officers tips on locations, people to be attentive to, and people to prosecute. Machine learning analyzes recurring patterns and makes predictions based on previous data. This data is historical—meaning it is inherently racist.

"What Would I Score," tells the story of a victim being wrongly accused by an algorithm. It places the user in front of the camera to force them to look at themselves, reflecting on what the percents placed over their faces means for them and others. "Facing the Facts," is an interactive experience of research gathered over the past year. The 3D helix includes interactive websites and videos that advocate for the removal of facial recognition in policing. We have a right to privacy and equal opportunity. If we can learn how it's being obstructed, we can make a change.

ESCAPE
Mae Craford

It will most likely not come as a shock that human beings love to escape reality. As we have witnessed over the past few years, when days grow dark and threats loom people take a break from reality and turn to entertainment or fantasy for comfort and relief.

For some it might be as simple as a song, others may turn to drugs, still others turn to religion. The issue is not how one escapes but rather the degree to which they are escaping. Instead of learning how to adapt to the environment people find themselves in, they tuck tail and dive head first down a rabbit hole of relief.

The archive website I have designed and curated over the last six months seeks to display the range and degrees of escapism which people subscribe to. Through the use of early website design aesthetics I aim to guide the viewer through an explorative experience. Juxtaposing the simple fantasy tv show you watch before bedtime to the cult which sought to leave Earth in a UFO. Escapism is something which happens but is never acknowledged. In displaying the endless accounts of ways people escape in one central location, I hope to wake people up to the plague of ignoring reality.

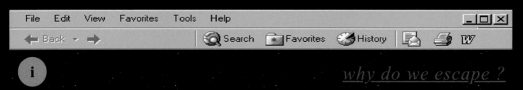

→ escape-to-salvation.webflow.io
→ maecraford.github.io

LIMINAL SPACE
Chengcheng Cui

In a time where art, music and technology are integrating rapidly with one another, a space is needed to bridge artists in all forms. How can an identity be inclusive, extensive and dynamic for a multidisciplinary art space?

Liminality in its literal meaning is the experience between the "past" and the "future." It is the transitional phase where the old world is able to fall apart, and the unknown world is revealed. Focusing on cultural production, the aim of Liminal Space is to merge the traditional and the experimental to discover a new realm of artistic expression. The place consists of an art studio, a music studio and a gallery space that allow artists in all forms to create, collaborate and exhibit their works on one platform.

The logo in motion reflects the idea of "transitional phase." While hundreds of iterations of the logo seem entirely independent from one another, they are all generated through the same process of change. This concept seeks to elucidate Liminal Space's vision by which reflects the inclusivity and variety of its practice.

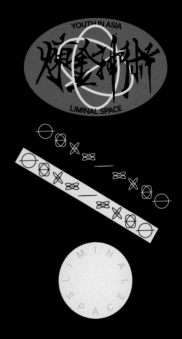

→ chengchengcui.com/liminalspace
→ chengchengcui.com

Trauma is something that happens more often than we think. Often when we think of trauma, we tend to only imagine things that are catastrophic on the surface, but trauma can happen in small, hidden ways too. People are scared to admit when they have experienced trauma, because we have been conditioned by society to think that we shouldn't complain or that "it could have been worse." This is a dangerous mindset to have because it prevents people from healing properly, many times causing cycles of trauma to repeat.

No Trauma Too Small works to create a space that welcomes all kinds of stories and traumas, no matter how "small." Inspired by talk therapy and personal experience, this work book leads users on a journey towards healing. This work book includes guided journal prompts that help users identify what their trauma may be rooted in and how it may be effecting them day to day. This work book acts as a helping hand and listening ear for users who feel alone and unheard. Using mindful design strategies, it manages to welcome all audiences and provide both a tone of empathy and empowerment.

As long as we understand that we have all experienced hard things and provide validation and compassion to every story, we could all feel loved and cared for in this dark world. I hope that with the help of this work book, people could learn that they are heard, loved, and worthy of true healing.

THE ART OF REMINISCING
Dani de los Santos

As we survive through an unprecedented health crisis and experience major political and social events, we all experience collective trauma. One can't help but think about the past or "what could have been" if certain things never happened. In a city that is no stranger to resilience, New York residents are especially ruminating on the past as the present rapidly evolves around them. For many, nostalgia is the prominent coping mechanism for both young and old. Many consider nostalgia a healthy tool for escapism because it establishes self-worth through past experiences and cultivates hope for the future. My thesis asks the following: how can we escape and cope in healthy ways, and why is it important to relish past delights?

The Art of Reminiscing is a campaign that searches for moments of respite in a fast-paced world. The project gives past and present residents of New York City an outlet for relief through nostalgia as we share stories of our past and chase moments of delight. Sharing memories helps us grow closer as a community and encourages us to make even more. The warm fuzzy feelings we chase from time to time are brought to life through brand identity and world-building. The Art of Reminiscing lives within New York City itself through branded applications and merchandise that promote why New Yorkers love the city.

VISUALIZATION OF SOUND
nika diomidovskaia

Sound is something that can't be seen by the human eye, however it is a material thing that can be represented visually by both humans and nature. I have always been interested in the perception of sound. It is very intriguing to me the way one sound can be interpreted visually in so many different ways.

The focus of my thesis is the visualization of musical pieces. I have studied different methods of visualizing music, and I discovered multiple principles that are best for visualizations. In my experimentations, I have limited myself to only two of these principles at a time. I have used arrangement principle, the placing of type and objects on a page, and combined it with typeface, weight, color, spacing, scale, form, and image. This approach has forced me to explore each principle in detail, and was very useful for my personal design growth. I have created a book that summarizes my research and shows my visual explorations. I have written two songs for my first part of the research. For the final part, I have chosen a song by Billie Eilish, "bad guy." I wanted to experiment with a very popular song that everyone could recognize, and music that people have never heard before.

I hope this project will demonstrate to whoever is looking at it how limitation can actually help you discover new ways of creativity. This research is a tool for people to creating musical representations such as cover art.

FILIPINO REMEDIES
Aira Dolfo

Today, wellness surrounds us in forms of vitamin supplements, clean eating ads and juice trends. At the same time, we are surrounded by junk food marketing and processed foods. Both industries use branding and overused, friendly verbiage to lure consumers. Modern diets and the commercialization of wellness create a conflicting environment for consumers to make healthier choices for themselves.

Prior to these trends and topics, people practiced traditional home remedies and cultural health practices. Traditional healing is ingrained in Filipino culture with documentation dating back to pre-Spanish colonization. People may often be skeptical of home remedies. However, they do contain cultural significance and have been successful for people. How can we highlight and share traditional health practices and remedies today?

Filipino Remedies is a resource designed to share traditional Filipino remedies as a response to mainstream health trends and the commercialization of food. An online platform and printed newspaper were created to showcase this information both in a digital and analog format. The website was launched and newspapers were distributed at a local Filipino store in New Jersey. Information such as taste, step by step instructions and time duration were included to help users find the right remedy for them. These remedies are not intended to replace professional medical advice but serve as an alternative natural resource. The goal of this project suggests a return to natural processes and remedies which allow people to be more intentional about their consumption of food and health choices.

CULTURAL ATTACHMENT AND ADAPTATION
Maya Eapen

The influx of western influences and globalization in India have increased the popularity of English as a spoken language among the urban, Indian youth. English connotes status. As a result, many young Indian, including myself, have grown up without learning or practicing our mother tongues. My typeface, Bangalore Display, questions whether typography can change the attitude of the Indian youth and inspire them to learn and speak their regional languages.

Bangalore Display is a playful, and bold Kannada (a South Indian Language) typeface inspired by the hand lettered street signs scattered across my childhood home of Bangalore, India. The friendly and bubbly appearance of the typeface intends to appeal to a younger demographic and make the language accessible to them. It is displayed on an interactive microsite that breaks down the nuances and stylistic choices behind the typeface to help users appreciate the details that went into the design. The typeface is accompanied by a type design compendium that documents my process of learning the language Kannada while designing the typeface. It includes personal reflections about experimenting with different materials followed by deeper conversations with type experts. By making the language accessible to young Indians, I hope the project inspires them to appreciate the beauty of Indian languages and encourages them to engage with their mother tongues.

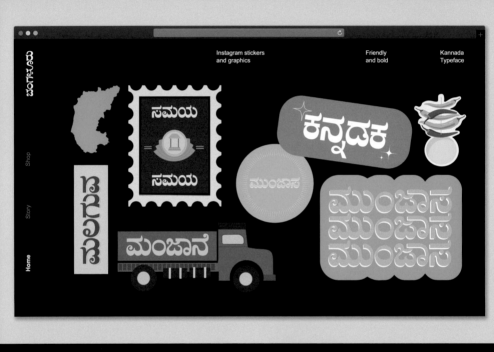

→ mayameapen123.github.io/BangaloreDisplay
→ mayameapen.com

THE USER AGREEMENT
Yaron Erkin

Intangibility, This is our condition. We are tangible, but our digital selves are not. As we move further online we are losing the importance of tangibility. As I become my Tinder bio, my Zoom screen, and my Facebook comments I (or my body rather) begin to disappear. Simultaneously as my emotions become more dictated by the digital boxes within which I exist, there is a reverse effect; these intangible spaces are pulled into reality. The flattened world is sucked into three dimensions. Existing in a digital space is inter-active intangibility. How do you explain the third dimension to a second-dimensional being? How can I show myself who exists in my phone what it's like to eat an orange, touch a flower, stub my toe?

My project interrogates intangibility within the space between digital and physical. The User Condition blends physical and digital objects and environments to create an ambiguous space which leads us to become vessels in this contradictory liminal space. Transitioning from one to another we are able to recognize and dissociate ourselves from the perceived limitations of tangibility. Presented through a website this state is shown through a collection of images and scans with the addition of a webcam to acknowledge the users interaction with this state.

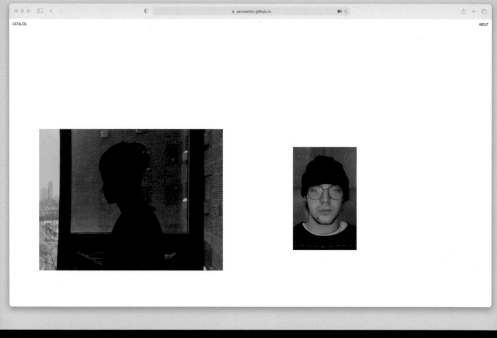

The window is incredibly multi-faceted. It is a connection between interior and exterior, a hole in the facade of a structurally sound construction, an opportunity for ornamentation upon a repetitive surface. I sought to explore the window as a means of visual art and graphic identity while dissecting themes of repetition, structure, and form.

Windows is a series exploring the window as a visual system. I do this by capturing flat, observational images and then treating the image until the "background" fades away, leaving only the frame of the glass within the window. This allows the viewer to examine the intricacies of the window form. 'Blocks' is an experiment (realized through two major projects) capturing a city block in the same observational format. The website component consists of a scrollable image of a city block and a hover feature that reveals the glass in the windows and the activity behind them; and the subsequent "Proposal for Space" cards explore my role as a graphic designer interested in architecture.

F_RM is a variable brand identity for a gallery that draws a graphic identity from my past research. By extrapolating the glass forms from the window images, I was able to create shapes resembling O, A, and I glyphs. I then substituted these shapes within the term F_RM, and created logo marks with the words Form, Farm, and Firm. Solo exhibitions are housed under the label FORM, duo exhibitions under the label FARM, and group exhibitions by the moniker FIRM.

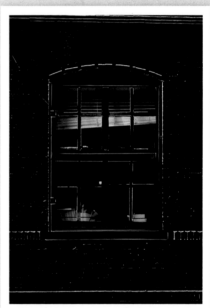

GUSHI

Xiaoke Fei

People often thought about the signature takeout box and the fortune cookies when we talk about Chinese food. And when we thought about the taste of Chinese food, people coming from a different country and different cultural backgrounds will have different answers. The reason is that "Chinese food" in Western countries will feature the ingredients people popularly eat in their countries. People seem to care less and less about the originality of the recipes nowadays. This phenomenon makes people ignore the value of the ingredients and eventually leads to a misunderstanding of one's culture.

Chinese traditional food culture consists of eight cuisines with different styles. The diverse climate, geomorphic features, and agricultural produce from each region make the eight cuisines distinct. "This division reflects regional culture, which is gradually reduced due to the modern economic globalization." Over time, there are more and more people who are not familiar with this disappearing tradition. People who have deep relations and their home's memory with the food culture feel that they have been constantly abandoned.

Gushi is an app designed to let people learn about Chinese regional cuisines' history and cook the dishes according to the traditional recipe. It also helps to bring back the disappearing food tradition and memories, provides people a space to communicate and learn about each other's regional food culture.

→ feix026.wixsite.com/portfolio/gushi
→ feix026.wixsite.com/portfolio

Bernadette Figueroa

There's no denying the impact communication technology has on our everyday routine —but it's become an extension of our lives without our conscious consent. This project encapsulates a critique of social media, a technology that has affected how we value emotion and the ways we interact in our society.

My design response is a visual soundscape. Narrated by sound, a set of images and short clips reminiscent of the 21st century information landscape: dirty pop-up ads, reality tv snippets, ads that enforce subtle propaganda, juxtaposed against the formation of an embryo, a new life symbolizing innocence. Through the fusion of these two extremes I hope to spark critical thinking in viewers, to reconsider the technologies in our day-to-day life and how they affect us. The jaggedness and chaotic nature of the video represents a certain anxiety tied to social media, specifically Instagram, in regards to how influential it is and how it affects the youth.

While this approach might seem acidic, the tactics social media use to monetize the attention of its users, while compiling large sums of data on them for their own ulterior motives, is worse. These communication tools have been developed to erase the lines between artificial and the real world, in order to create a more pliable and easily-influenced user.

UNDECIDED
Shih-Ju Fu

The relationship between China and Taiwan has always been very complex and controversial. While both sides are mainly Han Chinese, the Chinese civil war created a division in 1949, and the Kuomintang fled to Taiwan while the Communist party remained in mainland China. Growing up Chinese and Taiwanese, many times, embracing my Taiwanese identity meant dropping my Chinese one, vice versa. These two places are the same and different, culturally similar, political opposites. How do I make peace with two opposing political cultures of my own?

Undecided is a double-sided daily tear-off calendar proposed to address the political hostility of China and Taiwan and showcase the shared cultural roots of these two places. The calendar is separated into two sides, where one side represents China, and the other represents Taiwan. Upon using the calendar, one will have to choose a side to begin and end the calendar year with. Each page features a political event that has happened on the day, it can be anything, policy changes, protests, anything that could have altered either side's position today.

→ shihju.design

GROOVEMAP
 Ana Furtado

We are always trying to find our place in the world. We use cartography to figure out where we are physically as well as astrology to understand who we are. There are thousands of different types of maps that give us this comfort of sense of self, physically as well as psychologically. However, something we are surrounded by that doesn't have a map (or at least a well known one) is music.

I believe that what we listen to can inform one much more than any coordinates or star placement. Music has the power to fill uncomfortable silences, alleviate feelings of loneliness, and relieve boredom. We use it as a mechanism to explore feelings of joy to grief. GrooveMap is an exploration that defines the placement of different genres of music according to BPM. The colors relate to wavelength and the wavelength is related to the BPM. Colors with a slower wavelength signify a slower BPM while colors with a higher wavelength signify a faster BPM. With the map, a series of applications were created to explore the functions of the map.

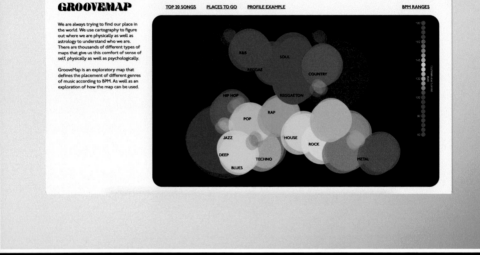

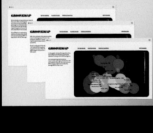
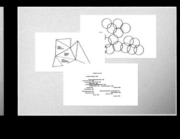

→ anacfurtado.github.io/groovemap
→ furtadodesign.com

ABANDON IN TIME
Martina Gallo

What does it really mean to be abandoned? At its core, it is a relinquishing of responsibility that changes the status quo. It destabilizes what was once known, sending people through emotional and physical withdrawal. The lingering, fragmented emotions make up the pieces of a disassembled puzzle. In examining our own abandoned spaces through time, care, and attention, we can learn to heal.

Such a method appears in writing. Communication is the acknowledgment of emotion and thought. As such, I created Abandon In Time, a journaling book with the intention to help those sorting through their emotions of abandonment and loneliness. Each page features an interactive prompt to provoke memories and encourage documentation. Activities include: drawing, writing, or collecting—all tools that are used in art therapy. This derives from Emotion-Focused Therapy, which proposes

the centrality of emotion in meaning-making and adaptive behavior. In search of community and kinship, this project should naturally live online as well. I created a website that centers around collecting, displaying, and distributing the materials and stories of other people. Here, those interested can read into stories of solace, pain, and emotional validation. Whether they be positive, negative, or anything in-between, the simple act of being heard can help mitigate the distress caused by abandonment.

→ readymag.com/u176904144/2706042
→ bit.ly/3qjiM5u

FLOATING IDENTITIES
Chenxi (Lisa) Gao

Identities are qualitative and quantitative. The construction of one's identities are a reciprocating process between one's self and the specific social contexts. Identities are the result of the externalizations of internal reflection based on social interactions. As graphic designers, we are hired to create visual identities for people. So the questions lingering in my head are: what is identity? What is my identity? With my feeling of wandering growing up, I always find it difficult to clearly define my own identity.

Floating Identities is composed of three projects: an animated collage, a set of business cards, and a passport, which I explored the formations of my various personal identities through them. The animated collage unfolds my various identities through flashing photography. It shows how my physical attributes change as my perception and recognition of myself is evolving as I experience things in life. Business cards, as an interpersonal communicative tool, function as introduction of one's self to others. It can be seen as the images one wishes others to perceive of oneself. By designing a series of business cards, I'm in control of how others perceive my identity. A passport is a proof of identity that can take you to travel from one place to another. This passport takes the audiences to travel through the various identities of mine. Unlike business cards where you present the role you wish people to know. Passport is mandated essential documentation of one self, but is it the true self?

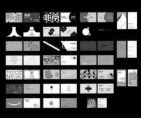

→ lisagao.squarespace.com

THE GOLDEN DOOR
Sierra Glicker

In the early 1800s, people celebrated immigration, and the idea of the United States becoming a melting pot for all cultures provided people with a positive outlook. Unfortunately, today, this is seen negatively due to the impacts it has on our nation overall. I believe that changing this perception can occur best by sharing personal experiences and stories through historical visual aids. We all come from diverse families with our own unique cultures and values and can benefit when shared and celebrated.

In my book, The Golden Door, I want to start a meaningful narrative to showcase different cultures and backgrounds. This would be accomplished by sharing stories of those who came to the United States from across the world and historical artifacts such as postcards, poetry, and stamps. I focused on immigration stories throughout various periods to showcase the transitions within this topic and how their lives changed due to the opportunities The United States offered them. This piece will spark a conversation and aid the movement that has already begun surrounding immigration with positive values. We as a nation need to continue to celebrate different backgrounds and offer an acceptance towards immigration by showcasing the positive aspects of people being in one location worldwide.

CORE EMPATH CORP
Danielle Beatriz Go

Empathy is not only placing oneself into another person's perspective, but similarly it is the ability to understand other people's experiences. Because of the resemblance between a personal identity and a brand identity, brands have the capacity to empathize and create personal connections with their customers. Though brand empathy can seem disingenuous, when done transparently with the interest of catering to the needs of the community and the planet, it has the power to cultivate social change and have consumers do the same.

Core Empath Corp is the first benefit corporation that identifies empathetic businesses and certifies them as Core Empaths. The OTA-bound brand manual contains collected brand user interviews that explore what it means to be an empathetic brand and what brands can do to be more empathetic. It is brought to life with bright, softened gradients to represent brand empathy in a positive light. Typography is used to differentiate itself from the B-Corp, with enlarged text signifying a call to action that encourages readers to ask these questions themselves; or, free-form text that suggests energetic movement and the visual identity's ability to take on various forms.

Core Empath Corp sheds light on the need for greater empathy among company leaders, designers at brand agencies, and, above all else, within oneself. Mindful acts of empathy can inform conscious consumption: how money is spent and in whom it is invested. An investment towards the planet is an investment towards people—ourselves and future generations to come.

KEEPING ANXIETY IN CHECK
Danni Gomez

For this thesis project, I've created a personalized digital space for those struggling with anxiety to record and keep track of their feelings, symptoms, and general experience. This project is aimed specifically at those who are unable to afford or attend therapy. This app creates a peaceful acknowledgement of their experiences in the hopes that they can improve their day-to-day experience while being informed with their personal data. This app also includes a guide and minor exercises to assist with anxiety issues on a daily basis. Track, learn, and take a break from anxiety in a customizable space.

DISSECTION
QingYing (Mimi) Guan

What would it look like if I uploaded my brain to the web? This was the question I started to think about as the pandemic shifted our collective relationship to technology, mediating our communications and controlling our desires through predictive algorithms. Perhaps, as futurist Robin Hanson proposes, our memories and personalities will one day be uploaded to the cloud too?

Dissection is a project exploring the concept of a hyper-personalized space on the internet. Housed within an inter-active website, the workings of my mind are represented as links to symbolic dreamscapes. The style used throughout the site is a strange mixture, integrating medical illustration, psychedelic art, doodles, and childhood snapshots.

I can never see the chaotic flux of my own mind because it is impossible to find a neutral vantage point from which to view

it. All I can do is build a working model, which may or may not be useful. While Freud's taxonomy of id, ego, and superego is meant as a universal structure, Dissection is specific only to me. I organized my personality into a series of inter-connected zones based on my memory and experiences throughout my life relating to my upbringing in Australia & China and 2000s memorabilia.

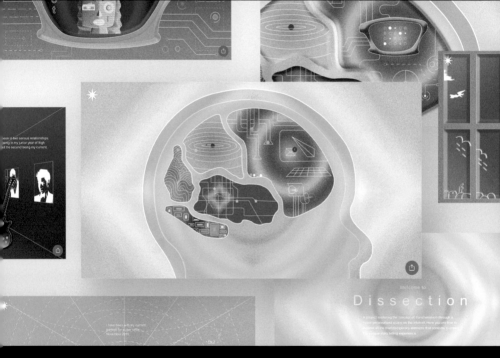

SLOW-PACED COMMUNICATION
Peiru Guo

We live in a fast-paced communication environment with text messages and video callings, communicating through texting a few words with fast responses. Fewer people are willing to spend time waiting for answers, so it causes the phenomenon that people don't cherish relationships. However, keeping our inner calm is a communication attitude that we should hold. I hold a habit of sending postcards with my friends several times each month to communicate our daily interesting things. We all enjoy the experience of the postcard and cherish our relationship. Therefore, I want to transmit the concept of slow-paced communication under the fast-paced communication environment, making people value the importance of waiting in social communication through experiencing a hybrid of traditional communication with digital technology: digital postcards.

It's not a typical social communication app: postcards take time to be delivered. Users need to experience writing a postcard seriously instead of rushing text messages, and then waiting for the delivery of postcards. The concept of slowness is displayed in the time of writing and delivering the postcards. Unlike Twitter, Instagram, and many existing communication media, the app has nothing to do with people's appearances, so there are no personal images in the profile, but more emphasis on slow-paced communications between two souls.

Challenging current fast-paced connections, through slow-paced communication experience of writing postcards seriously and waiting for the arrival of postcards in the app, people will understand that having communication with another person should be cherished and taken into serious consideration of the relationship.

→ behance.net/peiruguo

HI, MOM
Siyu Hang

As a Chinese woman in my twenties, this project begins from the contradiction between my mother and me, and is interested in deeply exploring the generation gap between the current generation and the previous generation. The generation gap in China is not only the product of historical development and the external cultural environment but also the result of interactions between subjects of different generations. In the past, due to the orderly succession of generations, the offspring followed without deviation from their elders. However, the new generation is trying to break the balance of intergenerational inheritance.

Hi, Mom is an illustrated book based on the exploration of the generation gap and an in-depth understanding of the older generation society from the perspective of the younger generation. It takes us back to the 1960s when mothers grew up, observing and discovering the influence of their environment, life experience, and educational background on them, using the method of comparison to explain the differences in lifestyle, consumption, and relationships in contemporary Chinese mothers and daughters from different families.

The book expresses that even though the incompatibility between the two generations lies in the different eras they live in, we must give both sides enough respect, accept differentiation, give to each other understanding, and independent space in life. This project is dedicated to all mothers: Thank you for your patience and company as the greatest mom, and I'm sorry I drove you crazy sometimes... And I love you mama.

LOST GALLERY
Trudy Hoang

When you think of art, what do you think of? Many people think of the Mona Lisa or the Starry Night. Art is typically defined by Eurocentric movements, however, Europe wasn't the only place in the world creating art. The non-western world is filled with art that is lost from history, its land, and our collective consciousness.

Lost Gallery is an interactive website where people can uncover and learn about art by people who are underrepresented in Western conversations about art history. It challenges the idea of what a gallery is and celebrates art that has been "lost." Each page is titled with a question or statement that leads the experience of each activity. Participants can start by participating in a land acknowledgement that the website will perform for them. A link is generated to encourage the user to do their own research through Google on art that's about and made by the Indigenous people whose land they are on. Participants can also interact with fun activities that feature curated art, such as old art from different cultures and contemporary art by artists of color. Through these activities, participants can question what they've been taught about art and expand their knowledge by opening up to new art and artists. Then, participants are encouraged to continue decolonizing their biases about art and visual culture through further learning. There is a one-page mini zine which participants can print out and use as a guide to critical thinking at any art museum.

4 FUTURE REFERENCE*
Will Howell

4 Future Reference* is a project that explores Will Howell's identity and the introspective space he has remained in for the past year. The first part of this project explores the history of the Black design aesthetic over the past 100 years in America in the form of a visual zine and coded website. The second part of the project takes these references as a starting point while reflecting on the current zeitgeist and year of isolation caused by Covid-19. Will's next concept was to venture into new territory by designing a capsule collection of garments that would embody this year of Covid-19 provoked isolation and self-reflection. Embedded in the design of the garments, contains subtle gems hinting at transparency in self and personal trauma healing. Will's design process differed from previous projects by embarking on the notion of starting from zero and generating lists. Some of these themes embodied in this collection include therapy, music, time, reality, and escapism. Instead of displaying in a regular retail space, Will made the decision to have these garments on display in The MoMA along with a temporary curation which would allow further opportunity to dive into these personal references. Altogether, this project serves as an exploration of personal design aesthetics, as well as a public call to action. With the intention of acknowledging previous Black contributions in design, and showing through my own actions, how one might explore their personal design aesthetic by pulling from experience.

ACIDIC ATMOSPHERE
Annie Hua

Acidic Atmosphere is a colloquial lab report focused on air quality. The purpose of this publication is to facilitate public understanding on this global health challenge by providing comprehensive context to its pertinent determining factors. Though the design approach is academically formatted, the overall visual spectacle is aesthetically driven in order to stimulate viewer's experience. By utilizing the methodology of design as the basis for communicating a scientific topic, the goal is to create a tactile report that is more interesting for public engagement. The final deliverables include the physical report in addition to a supplementary instagram page as a container for promotion and distribution to a wider audience.

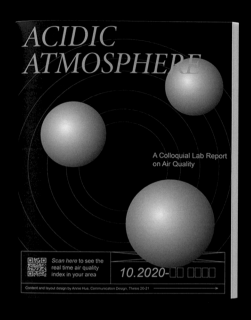

HOW DO WE IMAGINE THE UNKNOWN FUTURE?

Wallis Huang

Our interpretation of "unpre-dictability" evolves as we grow up and potentially reflects our state of mind during different life stages. With the current U.S.-China geopolitical tensions, how does Gen Z, with bicultural identities and at the stage of transitioning into adulthood, express and

identify their skepticism regarding the future?

This website showcases a collection of responses from 25 Gen Zs, who were born in China and either move or study in the U.S., about what they've envisioned about the future—as a view from the past, and the present time. The responses are illustrated through 50 collabo-rative artworks based on my inter-pretations of the content provided

by each participant, adding new opinions and forming a collective perspective.

Centered around the question "How do we imagine the unknown future?" this online platform encourages open conver-sations and reconvenes the viewers to rethink about "unpre-dictability" from various points of view.

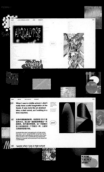

→ wallishuang.com/How-do-we-imagine-the-future-Website
→ wallishuang.com

Charis Huling

Playlists are a cultural phenomenon. Making a collection of songs that feels right together and creates a mood—what could be more powerful? The original High Fidelity (2001) discusses the significance of mixtapes while the reboot modernizes the story through playlists: "Making a playlist is a delicate art. It's like writing a love letter, but better in a way. You get to use someone else's poetry to express how you feel." Someone might not have the words to say, but playlists have the power to take on a voice of their own. It's knowing someone in a different way, pinpointing their preferences and the way they think. It's a form of intimacy unmatched by anything else.

Mix Theory is a project that invites people to submit playlists, which are then curated according to different moods ranging from broad to hyper-specific. Through each collection, it is possible to see a small microcosm of the music people turn to when they feel a certain way. The Internet is an archive in itself and with a website, it is possible to collect these playlists as an archive of its own. By creating a zine to accompany the website, those listening online can read simulta-neously, understanding the effort that goes into each playlist while also approaching the subject matter through a more personal perspective. Drawing on late '70s post-punk aesthetics and the DIY punk ethos, Mix Theory highlights the universality of playlists as a lasting cultural form.

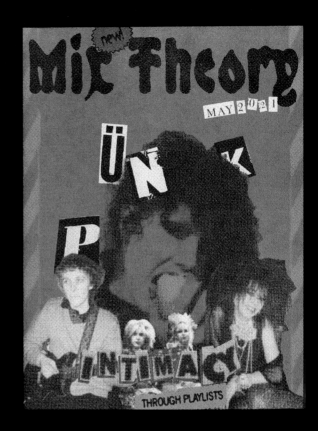

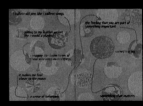

BEIRUT BAYTI
Sana Jamali

What does it mean to be Lebanese and be able to live as an outsider, far away from the chaos? Lebanon has been experiencing crisis after crisis. As a result of years of corruption, the Lebanese pound took a major dive and lost 80% of its value plunging the country into a deep economic crisis. In response, hundreds of thousands took to the streets demanding for an end to political injustices. In the midst of the protests, an explosion at the port of Beirut stripped many Lebanese families from their homes, as the injured flooded unprepared hospitals greatly increasing the magnitude of the crisis. Lebanese citizens became victims of political oppression, economic crisis and an uncontrolled COVID outbreak leading to extreme loss of lives, livelihood and pain.

Beirut Bayti uses raw and unfiltered photography, taken by the Lebanese citizens in their darkest moments, revealing the trauma and sorrow of heartbroken citizens, to change the attitude of the Lebanese government and raise awareness of the damages caused to the Lebanese community. I designed seemingly endless sequences of associatively related photographs. A make-up of intuitive combinations, that aim to encapsulate the series of tragic events mirroring the never ending distressed caused to the Lebanese citizens, because the subject itself is too intense, and beyond one's grasp. This visual narrative enters a polarity to form an actual work affirming chaos of all the facts and gestures that have transpired all across Lebanon. The work becomes part of a stance in pursuit for justice.

→ sanajamali.com/beirut-bayti
→ sanajamali.com

SIMULACRA AMBASSADOR
Aeva Karlsrud

The contemporary world requires young creatives to market themselves as designers and as individuals to gain employment as well as social capital. Postmodernity—which, according to media theorist Jean Baudrillard, is a form of hyper-reality, or a state in which signs and symbols that represent reality replace reality itself, has distilled personhood to a digital presence. As media has become social, every successful person has become an ambassador of their own "brand": a mix of tangible symbols and intangible attributes. But how does one become an ambassador of self?

The trickiness of crafting one's public persona is tied up with the task of figuring out who you are on the inside. Branding has become intimately personal, involving a simultaneous becoming and marketing of self. Simulacra Ambassador is a personal brand book that borrows from 1980's media theory and aesthetics to address the contemporary intersection of branding and personal identity as they coalesce in navigating the professional and philosophical narrative landscape. Part reference manual and part self-help workbook, Simulacra Ambassador bridges the psychic gaps between the curation of the inner self and the public persona.

Simulacra Ambassador aims to dissect and diagram the ideals that we perpetuate in creative work and life as digital-age designers. It injects the branding manual with an element of the absurd, designed to both celebrate and question the designer's conception of the ideal and the real as they unite under the modern (and morally ambiguous) hypothesis that authentic nature is a source of profit.

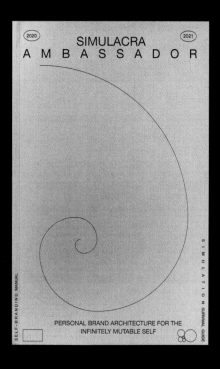

→ aevakarlsrud.com/editorial/simulacra-ambassador
→ aevakarlsrud.com

ABLEISM IN HIGHER EDUCATION
Lake Kennedy

The higher education system is inherently ableist, built on a history of eugenic experimentation and celebrating the hyper-able student. Due to this, students with disabilities are often seen today as a threat to the academic status quo or as a liability. Universities project a strong stance for progress and equity, all the while making their coursework inaccessible to people with disabilities—highlighting wider implications towards the use of performative activism towards the disability community. Inevitably, this attitude not only creates an ableist learning environment, but also instills each student with internalized ableism. This thesis aims to empower the disability community and educate able-bodied individuals who have the privilege of not needing accommodations.

This thesis critiques the current education systems and administrations in universities. The education institutions which present themselves as an equity of experience and access, should and can do more to support and plan for disabilities, in order to provide a better education experience for all.

→ laurenlourdeskennedy.com/project/ableism-in-higher-education
→ laurenlourdeskennedy.com

INTERNET STANDARD CHALLENGE
Byunghyun Kim

Throughout the last couple of years, the internet has made so much impact in the last two decades and people are now almost inseparable from online activities, especially with the help of fast computer technology development. Being one of billions of consumers dwelling on the internet, I have come to the conclusion that most of the people have become adapted to the "usual" functions and designs on the internet that it has become more of an internet "instinct." Though it brings comfort to people learning the internet by keeping these basic functions and aesthetics written on stone, it also makes mold in which designs and concepts could become very limited.

As a graphic designer, I want to challenge users facing functions and designs that they are very familiar with, yet could come off as frustrating, confusing, or even discomforting when they do not come off as they "should." I want to recreate websites and elements that people will attempt to navigate through using functions they are used to, yet all of these will be quite peculiar and odd from the original and do things that are not "normal." Not only does sudden change make people feel confused and uncomfortable, but it will also make people realize that not everything has to follow the internet norms. As the final outcome, I am hoping to see people break the mold that designers and internet users have set on stone, and become more adaptable to many more different elements the internet could offer.

→ strawberrycookie.github.io/enduponfear.github.io/
internetstandardchallenge.html
→ welcometobryan.portfolio.com

(PRIVATE) SEASONS
Destiny Kim

Just as the earth experiences four seasons, there also are seasons in our lives. Like spring always comes after winter that never seemed to end, there comes bright and hopeful days after difficult and suffering times in life. (Private) Seasons reflects on the time of 2020, which was exceptionally difficult and confusing due to the Covid-19 pandemic. To remember resilience against adversity, it looks at the theme of four seasons from the perspectives of nature and life.

Have you ever experienced local tangerine farms in Jeju Island, South Korea? Many visitors travel to Jeju Island to enjoy its natural beauty and coastline. Bong is an AI bot and your tangerine farm booking agent. The name "Bong" is inspired by a type of tangerine called "Halla-bong," Jeju's representative fruit. The app's primary purpose is to allow tourists to enjoy Jeju and support local farmers economically by promoting sustainable tourism and agritourism. The target audience includes both locals who have tangerine farms and tourists who want to travel to Jeju. When a user signs up for the app, they create their own custom tangerine avatar that serves as the main interface for the app. Based on the research, most tourists in Jeju come from different countries, so they don't have a chance to communicate directly with the locals because of the language barrier. Bong helps you chat with locals and other users through auto-translation. Many local farm owners want to promote their tangerine farms and products to satisfy consumers' tastes and expectations. Bong provides specific information about local farms, local products, and outdoor activities. Users can make reservations about farm activities by discovering local farms. This app will help tangerine farm owners financially and allow tourists to have memorable experiences in Jeju Island.

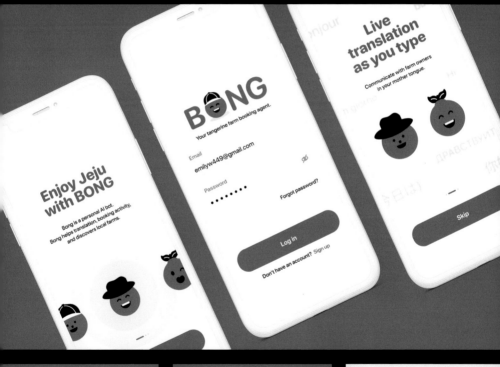

CHINESE GASTRONOMY
Zen Koo

As an essential part of Chinese culture, Chinese cuisines are originated in diverse regions throughout the country. The main Chinese cuisine principle is that the flavors should mix and textures should alter, emphasizing the color, smell, and taste of food. However, overseas, Chinese food is still undergoing a great change because it is always considered delicious but portrayed as identical and cheap fast food. Introducing the Chinese food culture through the eight major regional cuisines, the website shows a wide range of flavors and textures to explain the complicated aspects of Chinese cuisines and elevate Chinese cuisine to reform the audience's understanding and appreciation Chinese food.

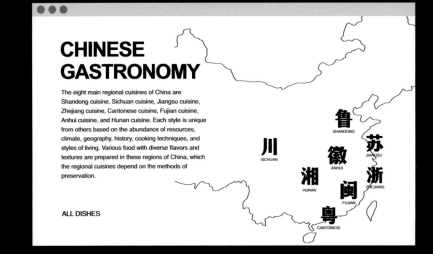

NUSHKA
Padmaja Kothari

A lot of brands promise to be cruelty-free, phthalate-free, sulfate-free—free of everything. They have clunky packaging and too many ingredients. Through my thesis, I created a beaut yand wellness brand that provides a sustainable alternative to chemical-laden skincare products. Nushka is an amalgamation of a variety of "Ghar ke Nuskhe" (homemade remedies) made using household ingredients. The more natural the ingredients are, the more reliable they can be in terms of having a lower ecological impact. The inspiration behind Nushka is my grandmother's skincare recipe book that has been passed down for genera-tions. As a designer, I want my work to be accessible and relatable to a large audience which will give a platform to showcase the themes and topics that are important to me. For my brand Nushka, I created an app that consists of all the skincare recipes as well as daily tips from my grandma's book. The app will help build a community for people interested in clean skincare. To reinforce my brand, I have also created content for social media to help promote the app as well as the brand. Nushka stands for all-natural and organic ingredients so I wanted my design to reflect the same. I created an organic pattern picked an earthy muted palette, and used a rounded typeface.

_BLANK
McKayla Lankau

Social media is a huge part of people's lives today. This is especially true for younger generations using apps like Instagram, Tiktok, Twitter, Facebook, and Snapchat, among others. It is a wonderful resource that is often used to share documentation of society's most pressing issues.

However, these platforms are impacting social change in ways beyond how they were initially designed. Endless scrolling makes it easy to quickly pass what's important. The overload of drastically different types of content makes it hard to focus on one at a time. The mere placement of banal pop culture in the same space as meaningful information dilutes the gravity of it. This is how we become desensitized. These platforms intend to keep our attention for as long as possible, and they profit from preventing focused action. The more we scroll, the more money they make.

_blank is a digital experience that contributes to this contemporary conversation about social media consumption. The editorial website was made with video editing, animations, and interactive features. It uses the viewer's webcam to place their own live video in the space. It also exhibits documentation of a complementary physical installation.

The _blank experience ultimately suggests to the audience that they need to be mindful of their online habits and relationships to technology. Overstimulation leads to overwhelm, and sometimes it's better to do nothing than to do nothing on your phone.

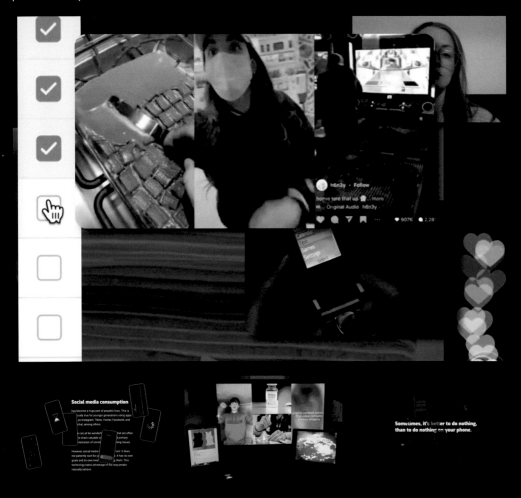

→ mckaylalankau.com/projects/_blank.html
→ mckaylalankau.com

SEE THE UNSEEN
        Hyunseung Maddie Lee

See The Unseen is a collection of web experiments designed for people who internalize their traumas. Through my thesis, I explored a group of people who are suffering from traumas especially in cyberbullying and anti-Asian issues. I selected the issues that I can personally sympathize with well as I have been witnessing and experiencing

so far. Suicide rates due to Social media, especially in teenagers sharply increased during the late 2000s. In terms of anti-Asian issues, those in the United States have been reported long before the 1900s historically, but the current Atlanta spa shooting triggered so many people in AAPI communities. While the suicidal rate and the number of violence cases are increasing, it is hard to understand those cases from an individual level and get resources

that are catered to victims internalizing traumas. The website showcases these "unseen" narratives in real-time. It suggests the next step and provides resources for the audiences to overcome their trauma together as a community. The website provides an open space to share personal narratives, make their voice heard, and take action. See The Unseen aims to encourage disconnected communities that lack social support.

DISRUPTING PUNK
Jade Lee

As society changes, our customs and expressions follow, yet while these aspects of mainstream culture fall in and out of fashion, a counter-culture persists. One particular sector of counter-culture that has been especially influential over the past 60 years has been punk. When hearing the term "punk" at first, one might think of the stereotypical elements: distorted aggressive music, ripped clothing, mohawks, and anything considered "underground." As I developed research on the punk influence in contemporary culture, I discovered that undergrounded-ness, was the most critical part of punk's survival. The punk ethos is formed around beliefs such as non-conformity, anti-authoritarianism, anti-corporatism, a do-it-yourself ethic, anti-consumerist, anti-corporate greed, direct action, not "selling out." By this definition, punk-ness must be conceived and acted out independently, by each person.

With this in mind, I decided to challenge how we, as a society, perceive contemporary punk-ness. I quickly realized that this could not be done through traditional graphic design and that in order to best communicate my argument, I had to become uncomfortable, taking on a punk mindset to guide my actions. Storytelling became the most important aspect of my project and these accounts, best told in video format. In these biographical videos, three different "punks" are unconventionally interviewed and edited into short videos. Using this punk lens, my thesis is a visual communication of the roughness and fractious complexities to be found in the punk ethos.

Disrupting Punk
Disrupting Punk
Disrupting Punk
Disrupting Punk
Disrupting Punk

→ jadeylee.org/portfolio/senior-thesis
→ jadeylee.org

MS. BUDDY
Jiwoo Lee

Firstly, I wanted to create a mobile application that improves the quality of women's daily lives. I had to think about the target audience, the purpose of the application, and the proper design that would suit the concept. Then I thought of the MBTI psychological test, which is popular among the MZ generation in Korea (a pairing of two groups—Millennials and Generation Z—these days. The MZ generation is active in expressing themselves and tries to identify what type of person they are and show themselves on social media. Therefore, MZ generation women can find out who they genuinely are and through this application and care of themselves. In this application, the main character is "Ms. Buddy" and she collects user data every day through daily and personal questions. It builds intimacy with users by asking them various types of questions such as "What are some things that make you nostalgic?" and "What kind of snack are you craving for before the menstruation?" This helps it easier and faster for users to understand their tastes and personalities and provides a medium for MZ generations who are still confused about who they are and what they like.

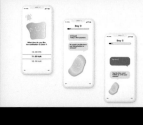

→ leej263.wixsite.com/my-site/ms-buddy
→ leej263.wixsite.com/my-site

THE JOURNEY
Juna Lee

I like games. I especially like boardgames where people need to communicate to truly enjoy. What I like the most about board game is that it creates a topic to talk about and build a joyful relationship between people. From this concept, I started experimenting with how a game can build relationships and solve a lack of communication.

I created a card game for multiple people who are not close to each other, especially those who are experiencing a language barrier. The result was a set of cards with abstract illustrations that let users guess their meaning. There is no words on the card, so users can play without language.

I also created an exchange diary for two people who are already close but would like to know more about each other. As a result, I made a diary for two

people. The users alternatively answer the questions written in the diary which leads them to understand themselves deeper. By passing this diary between themselves, they read each other's handwritten thoughts about one another, record the feelings about the moment they were together, and through this experience would build better and more thoughtful relationships. Working on this journal, users can walk through an emotional journey together.

THE FREELANCER'S JOURNEY
Victoria Lee

What is the atmosphere behind most material that teaches you about freelance design? Is it intimidating? Who does it include and exclude? In my thesis, I am creating a community resource that horizontally educates and shares information about what it takes to be a freelance designer. I want this resource to feel welcoming, exciting, and accessible. I want to challenge the status quo of what the face of design often looks like, and create

a space that designers of color can turn to for advice that looks and feels like us.

Through this project, The Freelancer's Journey, I want to make the freelance design space more approachable to beginners. Especially students of color, queer students, and low-income students, who often already deal with high levels imposter syndrome, lack of mentorship, and networking opportunities.

In the book and website that I created for this project, I use warm and welcoming colors alongside soft and rounded fonts

to make things feel less harsh and clinical. The aesthetics of this project are especially important because it not only shares information that has traditionally been gatekept, but allows the reader to feel that they are in a welcoming space to learn that information. I know from experience that a guiding voice or helping hand that would have saved me so much frustration when I first began to freelance. I want folks in the future to be able to have that and utilize their talent to its full potential.

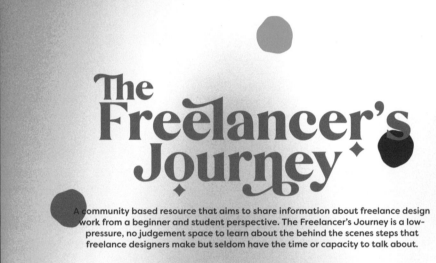

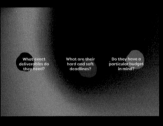

→ buoako.com/the-freelancers-journey-website
→ buoako.com

BACK TO OUR FUTURE REMIX
Emma Lepore

Reflecting on my personal brand as a designer, I find that I gravitate towards colorful, noisy, spunky, and formative compositions. At one point during my time at Parsons, I wasn't fearless about my love for these styles, I thought that others would perceive it as silly or "bad design." However, a confidence had grown in me over the years as I met professors and peers who celebrated my design style and saw the joy and friend-liness that such compositions evoked. I best express myself through color, pop, and maximalism, and I can now embrace the noise and quirk that defines me, in and out of Adobe Suite.

For these aesthetics and inspirations, I can give many thanks to the visual pop culture of the 1980s, an era that is glorified and a lot of graphic design harps on. We are truly living in the shadows of the 80s, as everything since that decade informs what we do today. This is supported by David Sirota's text, Back to Our Future, which discusses this exact idea, that everything we do in our current pop culture, politics, and entertainment is influenced by this time period. For my thesis, Back to Our Future Remix, I am directly using Sirota's text as a vehicle to explore and celebrate the realm of formative design, repurpose 80s' retro inspired imagery, and challenge my wit and personality as a designer. I aspired to let the pages of this book be unapologeti-cally 80s and effortlessly me.

Scarlet Li

Why are we so emotionally attached to objects? This question stemmed from a moment I shared with my roommate, who showed me these love letters that she had kept from her elementary days. It was so fascinating to see her find so much emotional value in them after all these years.

It has become apparent that almost everyone builds some type of relationship with the things around them. We seem to find emotional value in these objects, because they act as extensions of ourselves. They become manifestations of our emotions, feelings, memories, etc. Whether they're physical or not, these objects around us manage to form bonds with us in ways that are quite phenomenal.

Self— is a digital archive of stories that reflects the bonds we build with objects. Through this archive, visitors will gain a deeper perspective on how their thoughts and memories are being reflected through the objects that they are attached to. Stories are interlinked with others, creating an endless web of interconnected experiences, further affirming that everyone has experienced this phenomena to a certain extent. It strives to be an ever growing archive, allowing all visitors to share their own stories. As the archive grows, a greater variety of stories will be added, further expanding the web of experiences, no matter what kind they are.

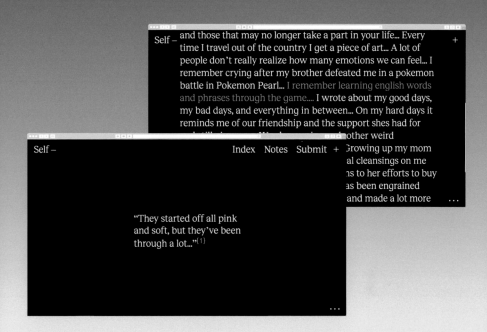

What is time? This question has been asked throughout history, but no authoritative explanation has been offered. People have tried to measure it more accurately or to calculate it as a physical quantity, but we are still individually unaware of the nature of time. This project asks, if we could better appreciate our personal experience of time, wouldn't we have a better comprehension of its general nature? The concept of time is too abstract for us to use language to describe it accurately,

so the best way to understand it is to feel it.

In the first experiment, I redesign timing methods, making a video to measure different durations subjectively, unlocking minutes and hours from the standard clock. Measuring it differently only gives me a new perspective; to give others a new perspective I need to display it differently. The second part redesigns the "display method" to show the time system of our lives through a motion graphic. The first part is explanatory, describing the essence of the standard time system based on cosmology,

showing how a second can be used to measure a minute. Further interactions synchronize the audience's temporal perception with the real-time actions of the video, gently moving the viewer into a more and more intimate experience with their perception of time. The third part of the project takes these observations and applies them to an interface for interaction between two mobile phone screens. These connect the users spatially and temporally to synchronize their experiences.

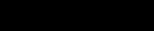

00:33:45:10 ›

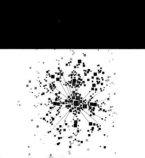

MY PANDEMIC KIT
Sohyunn Lim

With the number of coronavirus patients rising around the world, children are being exposed to covid-19 misinformation from many sources. Due to the coronavirus, many children spend lots of time at home and hard to express their feelings. So, I want to make a pandemic kit for kids 6–8 years old. This is a 14-day fun daily activity kit for them during covid-19. This kit has a coronavirus activity book, postcards, stickers, and paper crafts. The book has kid-friendly information on the coronavirus, what it is, and how can you prevent the spread of the virus. The drawing activity parts help them to relieve their stress and anxiety by drawing. It has an emotions journal part to express their everyday feelings to record. It can be a safe place where they can vent their emotions. kids are missing out on some socializing. So, making drawing postcards and send to their friends, will help them to share their feelings and feel more connected. This entertaining kit will give accurate information about coronavirus and an outlet to their emotions in a creative way through both writings and drawings.

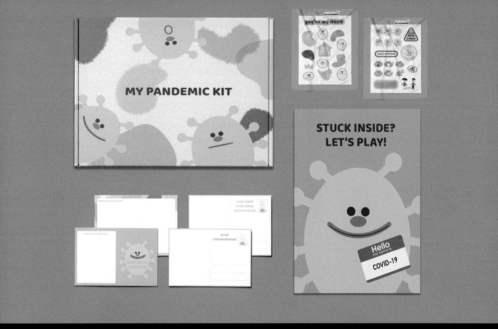

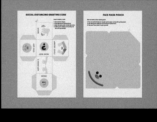

To You

Misty Lin

Nowadays it is difficult to have meaningful conversations with others. The pandemic challenged people to balance their personal life with their career work, all from their own home. This leaves us feeling drained and disconnected. We struggle to maintain the relationship we have with ourselves, along with the relationship we have with other people. Although sending a text message is an easy way to get in touch with someone, it lacks intimacy. Mail is a more intimate method of communication. There is a special feeling when opening the mailbox to find something specifically written for you.

As a communication designer, I want to create a website that combines the convenience of technology with the warmth of writing to someone more personally. To You is a website that allows people to create their own postcards meant to be sent to someone. The user is able to select their own image to use, customize the postcard, and choose the prompt they wish to answer on the back. At the end the postcard is downloadable and can be emailed directly to someone. The goal of this project is to encourage people to communicate more often, more personally, and maintain the relationships they have with others.

WAYS OF WRITING
stephanie lin

Chinese, the written language, has over 50,000 characters and is well known for its complexity and hieroglyphic features. It has remained a prominent status in East Asian languages. Over thousands of years, traditional Chinese characters have evolved from hieroglyphic and cuneiform writing. Through the last century, they were condensed into simplified Chinese and is currently practiced in mainland China. From ancient to modern, Chinese characters leave a profound mark on human culture.

In this exhibition, Ways of Writing, I have designed a series of artifacts that explores the characters as an art form using a combination of visual expression and semantics interpretation. The exhibition is divided into four sections in chronological order to examine how Chinese characters have progressed from collections of calligraphy relics to contemporary calligraphy art. Old-fashioned and rigid are the common impressions of Chinese calligraphy. Through this exhibition, my intention is to introduce this evocative modus operandi to the rising generation and transfigure their stereotypes.

From hieroglyphics to traditional and to the now simplified Chinese, we march towards simplicity and functionality but lose the richness of its artistic visual form. In a ridiculously impatient world, Ways of Writing is an appreciation to an ancient yet exquisite system of writing could evokes patience and a thrill of joy.

GROOP: GATHERING STUDENTS TOGETHER

Yu Tong Tiffany Ling

The internet has reduced interaction between people, and the global pandemic has even increased interpersonal distance and reduced communication through social distancing. This project began by observing the behavior of peers. Due to the pandemic, people's social circles are relatively limited by online applications, and they cannot meet other like-minded strangers through school and hobbies.

Groop is a mobile application that facilitates offline interaction for US college students during or after the post-pandemic era. Users can create or join study groups through their courses, and they can also create or join after-school activities based on their interests. With the help of this application, college students can enrich their campus life. The core theme of this application is a drop of water as a metaphor for a single user. The assembly of water drops becomes flowing water, which symbolizes the vitality that occurs when people are gathered together. The entire application is designed in bright colors with round containers and simple forms.

The emergence of the epidemic prompted the birth of this application, which fills a void in the market. This application will serve college students by helping them break through their comfort zones and alleviate their social fears.

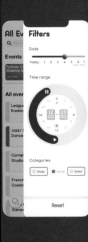

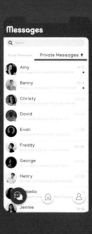

"HOME" COOKED MEAL
Lilian Liu

Art has a powerful language of bring people of different backgrounds together in celebration of what is being spoken of or for. That can't be said for the access of art through fund greedy institutionalized establishments. Public displays, in particular murals, break the traditional viewing of art in confined gallery spaces to the public eye where it can be viewed for all. The language of murals have been traditionally used to convey political messages to the public. In today's day and age, murals are used to help bring awareness of the surrounding communities by having people be drawn to aesthetic art photos. A mural created by the community takes the idea of the everyday viewer into an active participant, becoming the artist themselves.

"Home" Cooked Meal is a public mural that illustrates the diversity of Asian American cuisines in Atlanta, Georgia.The mural itself is a community based project in a sense where the people from the Atlanta community become the artist themselves. By having people join in creating a piece of work, it brings a sense of accomplishment and fulfillment that members from different communities can come together to create a work of art. In the recent event of all the Asian hate crimes occurring all over the world and especially in America during this time of the Covid-19 Pandemic, this mural will stand to be the beginning conversations and explorations of the Asian American identity in the American South and for all of America.

→ readymag.com/LilianLiu

QUARANZINE! AN ISOLATED TIME CAPSULE
Phoebe Lo

"If I could have an instruction manual on how to conduct conversations in the first awkward empty minutes of joining a new zoom call, I would be forever grateful."
—Paraphrased from a zoom call with a friend

In modern times, especially in this era of self-isolation, how do we as humans engage in communication effectively through virtual means? While spending my senior year taking my classes via zoom, quarantine and self-isolation—in an age where we are more connected than ever before, yet feeling lonelier than ever—made me realize that modern loneliness is a pandemic in itself. Quaranzine! is a comprehensive brand identity that aims to explore the idea of taking this strange "new normal" and the feelings that come with it by presenting it in a tangible form. How can the bittersweet memories of 2020–2021 and the feelings that come with it become not only physical objects, but also a witty sense of humour that feels like an inside joke that the entire world is in on? In the midst of a pandemic, what we need most is another reason to smile. Quaranzine! includes multiple elements, such as infographic postcards, "stay at home" concert posters, word search wine bottles an enneagram flowchart quiz, strangely scented candles, bingo sheets, and other branded merchandise that comes together as a satirical time capsule.

THE CURE FOR LONELINESS
Charlotte Lomas

Loneliness is a powerful and confusing emotion that most people can have difficulty processing, especially as a result of this pandemic. People have often done crazy things in an attempt to 'cure' the feeling of loneliness as they spend extended periods of time in isolation. Exploring the ethical boundaries surrounding AI, how far are we willing to go to find our perfect companion and what do the qualities we seek in others say about ourselves?

Corps (pronounced core) is a grow-your-own friend, managed from an app in your phone. Inspired by the little 2000's gag gifts given as a joke to those considered "lonely." This hypothetical company specializes in AI robotics creating endless possibilities in what defines companionship; with all elements of your friend customizable to your liking. This project focuses on each persons complex needs in our relationships and our own human need for interaction and connection. In a new era of speed dating apps and reality television shows, is the future of compatibility matching and relationships artificial?

Corps questions the human experience and what drives our need to be close to one another in a time where it is nearly impossible. It reimagines what intimacy and closeness can look like in a world without "human" contact. Through its simplistic and warm design, it invites us to explore our deepest human desires when seeking in others what we need from ourselves.

→ charlottelomas.com/corps
→ charlottelomas.com

THE WAITING CO.
Kevin Loumeau

Nobody likes to wait, but somehow we always find ourselves waiting for something. Whether it's for an appointment, a table at a restaurant, or for your vaccine shot, the time spent sitting around usually increases your anxiety. The Waiting Co. is an app designed to make waiting a little less stressful.

Designed around a simple interface allowing users to book appointments, keep their spot in line, track waiting time, and everything needed to stay on top of your calendar. With a simple swipe on the home page, you enter a personal waiting room that can be completely customized to your liking. Change everything from the seat, the mood color, the lighting, to the objects around you. Feeling fidgety? Your waiting space is interactive, so go ahead and spin the chair around, turn the lights on and off, or even knock the plant over, we'll clean it up. With all the chaos around you, take time to relax with The Waiting Co.

→ loumeau.design/the-waiting-co
→ loumeau.design

MEMORY
Wen Hsin Lu

Ever since I was a child, I started to write diaries. Sometimes I look over my diaries I wrote in elementary school, and those good or bad memories flash back into my mind. Looking at those old memories often inspires a solution when I'm feeling low. They are something that keeps me motivated and growing.

This book is a collection of people's memories. I have divided it into three parts. The first part is about significant objects that I collect from people around me. I let the people demonstrate what memories each object represents. This section is in chronological order by the year they got the object. The second part of this book is about food memories. What is one food that lets you remember a person, or a story? The last section is a little different than the first two chapters. It is about unforgettable anecdotes.

Through this book, I want to express those memories that represent ways of feeling, which people hold on to through different methods. Some of these methods can be hearing a song, seeing a photo, writing a diary, sniffing a scent, or missing a person. This project preserves a few of those formats and a few of those memories.

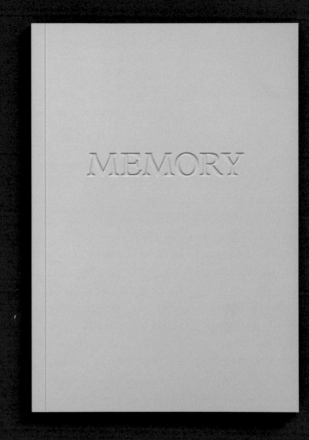

INDO-GRATE
Dirm Luawo

Growing up in an immigrant culture isn't easy. Oftentimes, the home culture and the host culture conflict and creates an uneasy, unwelcoming community that can be a burden, especially to the children of immigrants. As a first-generation Indo-American, our experience growing up in America while being raised under our Indonesian parents creates a unique culture and experience in itself: we're not entirely Indonesian nor American, and this creates a culture clash, an identity crisis. This dissonance was something I explored in this project, considering our experiences and documenting them to solidify our place in the world.

The passport form acts as a personal critique on oneself in a hands-on, printed approach. The pages of the passport plays on visual representations of both cultures while expanding on various themes of history. The function of the passport are supported with satirical stickers that mimic travel stamps, which are questions to be responded to into the book, as well as additional cues for participants to interact with this passport. Its small form allows it to act as a journal, documenting experiences while visually appearing like something familiar. In creating this project, I aim to gather the Indonesian diaspora into my project, collect experiences, and strengthen a healthy relationship with our community here in the States.

→ dirmluawo.github.io/portfolio

Peiyun Luo

The problem I am trying to address is how to give non-binary people a platform to make friends that truly understand them. My own research has shown that people of binary genders tend to have a lack of information and understanding of those of non-binary genders. Non-binary people are more likely to feel alienated in social interaction and mate selection than binary people. Currently, there is a public need to provide information, general data, and a space tailored to people of non-binary gender. The way I tackle this issue is by creating a mobile application named Niji.

Besides non-binary groups, the targeted audience also includes those who are confused about their gender identity. Users can freely and boldly fill in all kinds of information about their gender identity through this app while sharing their stories, asking questions, getting to know and date people just like them.

The app begins with a registration process that customizes a user's gender identity, using a percentage bar that represents a gender spectrum instead of a binary choice. After the initial profile is completed, it will match the user with other users that are deemed most suitable by the algorithm. To aid users' understanding of their own identity, the more time people spend on the app, the more complete their profile becomes. Aside from the above, it also functions as a traditional social media platform. Through this simple and easily used app with a fresh-looking UI, non-binary people can make friends without any constraints.

→ pennyluo.com/niji
→ pennyluo.com

LISTEN, SPEAK
Youran Mao

Around the end of the year 2020, a news report caught the attention of many netizens in China. It was about a 14-year-old middle school student jumping to his death after being publicly slapped by his mother for playing card games in the classroom. Although the discussion about youth suicide in China had always been taken seriously, this new increase of attention initiated more reflections on youths' academic stresses, family relationships, and mental health. According to Annual Reports of China's Education, family conflicts took the highest ratio in the main causations for students' suicides.

With a focus on this social issue of parent-child communication in China, and an attempt to help relieve this difficulty, this project includes a set of workbooks that aids a positive communication process between teenagers or young adults and their parents who have had difficulties previously. It guides both youths and their parents to sit side by side, reintroduce and open up themselves to each other, equally and respectfully reflect upon past conflicts, learn to understand the changes in their own emotions during a communication process with each other and express them in a clearer and non-violent way. With this set, families will also have access to helpful resources and be able to keep future communication experiences on the record.

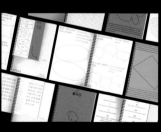

The popular phrase "Jamaica No Problem" saturates the country's tourism industry and paints Jamaica as an ideal, unproblematic world. However this facade is highly curated and palatable to the tourist who takes advantage of the "best" that Jamaica has to offer. Foreign Eyes Foreignize is a critique and personal exploration of the role of the tourist who visits Jamaica, and highlights the irony of the phrase. The tourist is centered within the problems faced by Jamaicans on an everyday basis, illustrated by spreads inspired by hand painted signage in the country, highlighting issues of skin bleaching, gun violence, domestic abuse and lotto scamming, while at the same time confronting the tourist as a part Jamaica's problems as well.

The book showcases my own artistic exploration of a monstrous character that embodies the tourist as I try to invade the tourists "No Problem" bubble by using items that they would typically surround themselves with. Patterns are used to create various pieces of clothing that allude to the issues featured in the typographic explorations as a way to surround and make the tourist aware of these issues as they wear the pieces. My book offers a critical perspective on who the tourist is and questions the way the tourist navigates as an outsider, to subvert the idea of "Jamaica No Problem."

A BRIEF HISTORY OF AMERICAN MYTHS

Rebecca Mesonjnik

What makes America? This is a question I ask myself constantly. As a child of immigrants I am always being pulled in two directions, either I must honor my parent culture or assimilate into American society. In the first half of my thesis, I explore what "being American" means on a personal level. I investigate how immigrants fit into our national identity, and why we categorize them as "other" while fetishizing their narrative.

Drawing on personal experience and interviews with other children of immigrants, I attempt to debunk the Bootstrap myth (the success of immigrant generations decreases the longer they live in America). In the process I pose questions about who shapes our collective identity and what it means to aspire to the American dream.

This personal experience with American myth-making inspired the second half of my thesis project. A Brief History of American Myths investigates the source of American identity,

inspired by my own experience of blindly accepting everything I read in history books, only to later find out that there was much more to history, and what we were taught as children purposefully omitted the stories of marginalized groups. After speaking with others whose experiences mirrored my own, I wanted to know what untruths we may have internalized and regurgitated as fact. Through this book I hope to encourage others to begin the process of uncovering the truth.

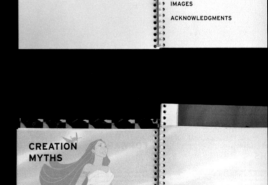

>>For the master's tools will never dismantle the master's house. They may allow us temporarily to beat him at his own game, but they will never enable us to bring about genuine change.<<

- Audre Lorde

CREATION MYTHS

MOTION & EMOTION
Velimar Molina

There is power in expressing emotion. Motion and Emotion is a kinetic experiment of typography that explores the visual forms of type in movement. What does type look like when it's moving? How can type be manipulated to express emotion? I designed a virtual space that uses the browser as the canvas. In Motion and Emotion the computer is my tool and social media my exhibition space. Through moving forms and typography we are connected.

Motion and Emotion gives a new meaning to the browser where we spend so much time in and connects people through motion graphics depicting emotions or complex desires. The emotions I chose to include are inspired by what many people felt in lockdown–feelings like claustrophobia and agitation to desires like dancing, kicking or playing. This digital universe acts as an optimistic antidote through typography and motion graphics. The type used on the motion graphics is meant to support or give more life to each emotion by restating each emotion. Motion and Emotion allows us to return to appreciating graphic design online for the sake of it, even when we feel saturated and overwhelmed by the digital world. We invite artists, graphic designers, students and people interested in exploring the endless possibilities that exist when manipulating type to join our movement.

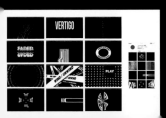

The Craigslist Missed Connections page serves as a playground where the hopeless can anonymously confess their feelings. Whether you are actively looking for yourself, writing about a lost chance at love, or just scrolling through, the Missed Connections page is undoubtedly a source of entertainment for both the lonely and cuffed. Each post feels personal and almost sacred as the writer's voice is so clear and decisions such as word choice, formatting, and spelling can make the experience of reading these feel like an overstep into a stranger's personal life. However, this overstep is also what lends these posts to have a unique charm, pulling readers into daydreaming about moments in stranger's lives for hours.

Given the current state of the world, our longing for human connection might be higher than usual and we find ourselves with more hesitation when put in social situations. These posts live on a platform that is under designed and stripped down to its most basic form. As a designer, I want to humanize these stories so they are presented in a way that reflects their content. I play with color and illustration to compliment the liveliness these stories possess. Additionally, I want to take these stories and turn them into something that can be physically posted in a community or shared through the web. Creating a series of colorful posters and digital animations, I hope to create something that brings life to these stories and helps strengthen
human connection.

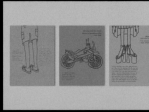

→ matildesofiamonti.cargo.site
→ matildemonti.com

THE SEPARATION ISSUE
Gavin Mullally

Within the Covid-19 pandemic, many artists, designers, photographers and ordinary individuals have been forced to adapt to a shift in the creative industry and find means to present, translate and problem solve ideas through the complexities given within an uncertain social landscape. My biggest question and overall theme my project intends to address is, how does one visually represent the idea of physical separation while displaying unity in graphic design? For my thesis project I have created the

Separation Issue, a print intended publication that combines personal interviews that addresses and dissects the idea of adaptability and how creatives pushed forward during this uncertain time. The publication also consists of secondary articles that tackle notions of adaptability within the fashion industry during Covid-19, while displaying aspects of isolation within the design structure. The treatment of imagery within the design framework, was crucial in order to further emphasize my concept of separation. Within these articles, I referenced the Zoom window size and formed a grid based off of

these dimensions to display detachment. In the spreads I have created, I utilized the combination of type, imagery and sequence to showcase the presence of separation and how these individuals have coped through barriers on a personal and emotional level. Visually, a primary theme to communicate the idea of isolation effectively was the presence of negative space and the use of lines to contrast separation and connection. In the interview articles, it was important for me to ask raw authentic questions.

WORK IN PROGRESS
Syalsabila Karissa Munaf

Work in Progress is a podcast that is interested in the ways design students talk about their own thesis projects. It aims to create a space for students to have critical dialogues and discussions around design; a forum where ideas are being exchanged; a place where conversations can live and grow; a platform where I can shine a spotlight on them because I believe students have important things to say. The conversations center on the subject matter, but they also touch on research, process, and untold stories. By sharing these conversations widely across channels, listeners gain insights into the topics that each student covered and learn from the way this generation of designers thinks and solves problems. Choosing an audio format for the podcast allows me to create in-depth and intimate conversations. The use of a contemporary visual language—electric blue and a bitmap typeface—speaks to my energy as a host and the relevance of the topics. Throughout this project, I learned that we may feel insecure talking about our own work or afraid of sounding too much like an expert, but when I created a space and shined a light on us, we owned the floor.

NDOME

Michael Mungai

Who gets to own history? Western colonialism resulted in the loss of a large part of the heritage of many cultures around the world through the "acquisition" of cultural artifacts. Today, many of these artifacts are housed in Western collections, and with ever increasing globalism, the ideas of ownership and provenance have come into question.

As a graphic designer and member of the Kikuyu tribe of Kenya, I wanted to explore this topic by focusing on one artifact in particular—the ndome—through which I can actualize some form of repatriation of these objects, and reclaim a lost part of Kikuyu cultural heritage. In this, I want to follow the tenants of Afrofuturism: to reevaluate the past and present of people of African descent, in order to reimagine our cultural heritage and re-imagine a new future which we have written.

The ndome is a ceremonial shield boys during their coming-of-age ceremony and features many intricate designs on both sides. It is a symbol of familial heritage, and is often passed down from generation to generation.

My project, Ndome, is an interface where users can create their own ndome using designs and patterns I have extracted from existing shields. The interface allows for many different variations of designs, through which Africans and people of African descent can create their own shields, and reclaim a part of their cultural heritage.

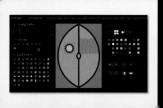

DESIGNING FOR THOSE WHO ARE OFTEN NOT CONSIDERED
Sanjana Navar

Empathy is an emotion that many learn through experience. Designers often have to be empathetic, especially when designing experiences for others. My thesis is a book and app experience that aims to build empathy for people with disabilities and their difficulty with digital products through learning and designing solutions for different inaccessible experiences. The book utilises AR images to allow the reader to experience what individuals with different disabilities see, feel, and think. By

scanning QR codes in the book, the user enters the app to create solutions to the problem spaces discussed.

Those with disabilities experience a lack of empathy through our everyday designs. Whether it may be the inability to buy jewellery for a spouse on Valentine's Day because the contrast between text and background on the website is too low, or being unable to watch videos with friends at gatherings because there are no captions; all these pose limitations to the overall quality of life for many individuals.

Many of these problems come from those involved in the

product creation process not being knowledgeable, empathetic and understanding of individuals with different abilities. It is not necessarily because of ignorance, but lack of awareness. How can designers develop empathy and understanding for those with disabilities while simultaneously learning how to design accessible digital experiences?

This project hopes to contribute to the accessibility conversation by having more people "doing" than just "talking" and encourage conversations around the experience of those with disabilities in an increasingly digital world.

THE CHANCE ENCOUNTER OF A SEWING MACHINE AND AN UMBRELLA ON AN OPERATING TABLE

Katelyn Paik

Great surrealist thinkers have always challenged ideas of consciousness and composition through the practices of prose, thought, form and aesthetic. Working within the discipline of graphic design, I co-opted the agenda of André Breton's 1920s Surrealist manifesto to explore these concepts through unusual juxtapositions. My process started with compiling examples of composite imagery, nonsensical objects, and I also went through a process of creating word puzzles and aimless mind maps. As these pieces began to come together—juxtaposed spatially and formally—I found myself making unexpected connections and finding overlapping meaning within these normally unrelated things. I began to realize a certain beauty in these "chance encounters"—moments of duplicity, and systems of organization.

It is said that our reality is organized along an axis of binary opposition: black/white, good/evil, highbrow/lowbrow, typography/image, form/content, and so on.

The act of juxtaposition also revealed more of the strange space that lies between the categorizations through which we live and orbit. In response to these concepts, I have curated and juxtaposed various surrealist works with the composite experimentations I conducted. I also incorporated a pictographic typeface I made that overlaps mundane objects with the alphabet, creating a glitch-like experience in the text. Through these outcomes, I aim to deconstruct these polarities and perhaps find something interesting, perhaps even humorous, in the grey areas between them.

REFASHIONING: KIMONO REFASHIONED
Aileen Pan

Kimono Refashioned was an exhibition at the Asian Art Museum of San Francisco. It is a collection of work from 1980s Japanese avant-garde designers deconstructs traditional Japanese clothing, the Kimono. The exhibition reveals the materials, forms, techniques, and decorative motifs that inspired designers for more than 150 years. After the exhibition tours, the museum provides artistic production for kids at the Experimental Learning

Center. However, it closed due to the pandemic.

Refashioning: Kimono Refashioned, an educational program for kids, aims to relieve the pressure from the pandemic on the museum by designing inter-active fashion-related products for kids to continue their education journey at home. The project centers around a kit to get kids in touch with knowledge on Japanese textiles. Kids create their own textile design with the highlighted motifs and sample patterns provided in the kit. A pattern generator on both the web and a kiosk in the museum helps

kids with their final artistic production. Kids can use the generator to create and print their designs on products, including T-shirts, tote bags, and mugs.

The goal of this project is to help kids to learn and to create innovative work with the knowledge they learn from the exhibition. The tactile-making process helps kids to be creative and to explore art knowledge. It supports museum's mission of art education as they adapt to the pandemic crisis, and it demon-strates a way for museums to interact with their audiences and introduce kids to fashion. |

ARCHIVAL
Chanjoo Tiffany Park

How can we restore energy in 2021? Me time, meaning time spent relaxing on one's own as opposed to working or doing things for others, is seen as an opportunity to reduce stress or restore energy.

Archival is a mobile app that helps digital natives hold "me time" by archiving images and text of personal interests. Built upon

the philosophy of staying focused, Archival allows users to ensure time aiming at growth in activities for their enjoyment to meet their needs solely. We sometimes need a break from our responsibilities, tasks, news, and externalities in the outside world. Many platforms out in the world allow people to consume information that is happening outside of themselves. However, there is no platform specifically designed for us to secure an archive of our interests.

Time for self-nourishment is vital for the modern digital ecosystem. We need a place where we can ultimately be free from external influences or work or even life—being entirely liberated and pay attention to what purely excites our curiosity or holds our attention. When we forget to take care of ourselves, it could result in a mental or physical state such as burnout or fatigue. Archival helps to secure "me time" by archiving personal interests.

FORMAL STUDIES
    Namjoon Park

My thesis project harnesses the most basic design principles to articulate the global catastrophe that unfolded during my senior year. Formally, it recalls the vernacular of International Style Modernism, but unlike the optimism that characterized that historical movement (a belief in the perfectibility of systems), my project is in many ways about failure and disintegration.

When the crisis began, I frantically booked my flight back to South Korea to escape the chaos of New York City. Upon my arrival, I began my 14-day quarantine session, and my initial fear was supplanted with laziness, procrastination, and depression. I needed an outlet to keep me sane and productive, and this project could be described as a kind of therapy.

    Formal Studies organizes design fundamentals into categories such as Scale, Hierarchy, and Balance. Like the

canonical design manual of a figure like Armin Hoffman, I limit myself to a palette of black and white, stressing aesthetic cleanliness and objectivity. However, the captions that run alongside my illustrations narrate the messy realities of pandemic living. This book is an archive, an artwork, and a journal that holds the record of my unforgettable senior year.

PHANTOM'S BAZAAR
Storey Pearson

Phantom's Bazaar is a card game designed to emphasize how individuals' "purposeful choices" are actually the product of chasing after meaningless values. It's designed for young adults who are susceptible to aimless scrolling, and technology-minded adults. The project is comprised of a card game and a website. The website is an introduction to the project both providing additional context as well as a "What celebrity are you?" quiz which users will find their choices to be unrelated to the result. Phantom's Bazaar is visually obnoxious to communicate to users the unrealistic perception presented online.

Your choices matter. The consequence of choices—from accepting a job offer, deciding whether or not to support Jeff Bezos, or eating a spicy chicken sandwich from Chick-Fil-A®, goes beyond a split-second decision. Sometimes the weight of these choices is too difficult to bear so we silence them by escaping to our devices; a place that appears to be better than our reality. Unknowingly, we give time—and occasionally money—away to algorithms and influencers who are carefully built to appeal to a wide audience. The project was created to encourage players to take an honest accounting on how they chose to spend their time. It's difficult to be alert about these issues even when they're front and center. However, the consequence is seeking everything online; and becoming isolated from real-life experiences.

→ storeypearson.com/phantomsbazaar
→ storeypearson.com

FINDING CATHARSIS AS A COMMUNITY
Mariel Quadrino

I am using design as a means to explore catharsis and relief in a public setting. New York City can feel lonely at times and the pandemic has made it even harder to create a sense of community. Catharsis, an emotional release of unconscious conflicts, can help improve mental wellbeing. We spend a lot of time interacting with social media and digital spaces, so I made something more tangible and direct.

I created a series of inter-active posters that I put up around the neighborhood of Tompkins Square Park with simple prompts such as "What's your deepest secret?," "What makes you angry?" and "What's your deli order?" These prompts invite strangers to share their thoughts, feelings, and secrets anony-mously, creating an asynchronous conversation within the community.

The small radius of about five blocks aims to connect people living directly in my neighborhood. Once the posters fill up, I collect them back and combine them into a printed zine. While the posters themselves are not up for very long, they are transformed into a zine, making them into a permanent, but still informal, form of documentation. I created an Instagram account for the project (@anonymous.posters) that documents the process from the posters to the zine.

The cycle of making posters and zines will continue. Eventually, I will compile them into a book, produced annually, that extends the longevity of the project and creates an archive of the continual progress.

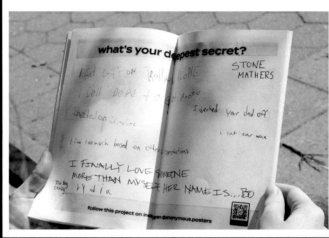

→ marielquadrino.com/featured-project-thesis
→ marielquadrino.com

RELIGION REALIGNED
Simran Rao

Religion has been a defining factor in people's lives for several hundred thousand years. Religion is ubiquitous across the globe, and virtually everyone has had to contend with it in one way or another. My opinion stems from witnessing the violence and division caused by the Hindu and Muslim communities in India.

This thesis, Religion Realigned, aims to explore religion through three distinct projects that look at the subject from different critical perspectives. The

Unsung Manifestos are a series of books that urge its readers to see all religions in an open-minded and equal way. It takes away the pedestal that only grants very few religions, respect, and gravitas.

The Sanctum is a website that explores the material objects that reflect a religion in their places of worship and asks the viewer how important they truly are in representing the space. Religion can be divisive and prejudicial, so in response, The Sanctum allows users from around the globe to experience an unfamiliar place of worship in its purest essence.

The Indoctrination Inactivity Book aims to expand the minds of young adults who have inborn religious views and opinions, due to their communities or upbringings. It encourages them to explore their biases, thoughts, opinions and hopefully allows them to broaden their mindsets about topics they might have previously been certain on. Through these projects, Religion Realigned hopes to start conversations about the detrimental effects of religion and inspire curiosity and open-mindedness in regards to religions they might be unfamiliar with.

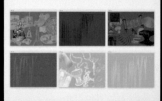

→ sanctum.world
→ simranrao.in

THE INJUSTICES OF CHINA'S UYGHUR CAMPS
(Red)

Taking an inward look into what I am most passionate about, I used design to enable, spread, and bring awareness to a very close-to-home Human Rights issue.

Thinking about the overarching theme of Chinese Propaganda, specifically into China's Uyghur concentration camps and their injustices; I've cheaply produced and distributed informational packets, inspired by Samizdat Books and emphasized through anonymity (for my own safety). These booklets and pamphlets contain leaked information, annotated propaganda and various stories and interviews from former detainees of China's Uyghur camps. I've also been anonymously circulating a video documentary, in order to communicate to young activists about the injustices of Uyghur camps.

I took advantage of the natural distribution methods from existing published materials (i.e newspapers) and the internet (i.e anonymous forums). Disguising my findings within newspapers and throughout the internet is essential to communicate to a broader audience, anonymously. This way, the information is not limited to young activists in NYC, but to all over the globe.

You will run into one of these copies soon. Meanwhile, please dig deeper into China's Uyghur camps. As designers, we are held accountable for our design decisions and what we choose to put out there for the world to consume. Let's communicate in a meaningful way and call for societal change against China's Uyghur camps.

→ youtube.com/watch?v=L9-Il5htksc

INFRASTRUCTURE WORKBOOK: JAKARTA EDITION
Felitasari (Tata) Rekso

How do we see infrastructure from different angles? Infrastructure surrounds us, yet we don't fully understand it. According to Oxford Languages, Infrastructure is "the basic physical and organizational structures and facilities (e.g. buildings, roads, power supplies) needed for the operation of a society or enterprise." From its definition, infrastructure can be viewed as the set of rules of a system or a game.

That's where a workbook comes into play. A children's workbook is set up similarly to infrastructure. They have a set framework for the questions that are answered within them. Additionally, the format makes the challenging topic accessible and approachable, while it highlights the problems and shows new possibilities.

My project, Infrastructure Workbook Jakarta Edition, investigates the topic through twelve workbook activities that focus on transportation, communications, energy, waste management, and water management. These categories make Jakarta up and are vital to keeping the city functioning, but common problems such as floods and traffic get in the way. This workbook will allow people to relearn their environment and become less ignorant. It will also showcase new ways of navigating and living in Jakarta, becoming more appreciative, and noticing the small details like the colors of signages and electrical transformers. Through better insight into a city's infrastructure, people would better understand their living conditions and the system—becoming more critical o what has existed.

SEND LOVE, WITH ME,
Yasmin Rozmee

In times of quarantine, I was left by myself with my own thoughts more than usual, confined to my own space. I realized how crucial reaching out and communicating and keeping the strengths of relationships with loved ones are. But how do I approach that?

I decided to explore the notion of language, through the possibilities of tools of communication. Themes of intimacy, longing, and loneliness were explored. The projects are concerned with tackling the idea of intimacy and proximity through different ways of expression. A reflection on different ways to communicate.

Send Love, With Me, explores the notions of messaging loved ones while also allowing people to reflect through my journey of exploring these themes through these tools. Send Me a Postcard Sometime explores traditional forms of communications such as postcards in digital space while also being prompted ideas on what to say. Tone of Voice explores how language is conveyed through typography and how that can be utilized visually.

Alone Together takes in the content of sent text messages from various people. Common keywords amongst the messages are then isolated to highlight an atmosphere of intimacy and loneliness.

Send Love, With Me is a great form of putting puzzling pieces together of my own mind, that allowed me inputs to express and process how I speak but also gave me the opportunity to reflect on what it means to really listen to myself and how I want to communicate to loved ones.

→ send-me-a-message.glitch.me
→ yasminrozmee.co

DIAGNOSIS: A NEW LIFE
Rainier Salas

Everything in our bodies has purpose, yet we continue to go about our daily lives without realizing its importance. One in four adults in the United States are living with a disability that restricts their ability to do normal everyday tasks. Some develop a sickness sometime throughout their lives, This has a huge impact on the mental health of those who are affected and may find it hard to get out of this mindset. Those who

are diagnosed with a disability become acutely aware of the inner workings of their bodies. They know the marathon that is run each day to support the act of simply existing. You have to adjust your lifestyle in accordance to your treatment, and appointments. Most of the disabled population live a majority of their daily lives at doctors offices and hospitals. Some submerge into the darkness of a poor mental state, fearing the journey ahead.

The brain is the main control center that regulates the body, but

once you experience a mental and emotional change it's hard for you body to focus on healing. As a result, a cycle begins causing people to develop new symptoms in response to their new mental state. To make this process less formidable, I designed a book that can be used as a tool to guide you through your process of your diagnosis, From being diagnosed, to treatment plans, what to expect keeping track of your health and mental health, and to remind you that you are not alone.

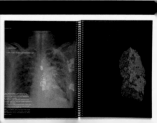

Julia Sams

Taking care of our only home, the land we come from, and the land we will go back to, should be at the center of our lives. The Industrial Revolution marked the beginning of an ecological epoch known as the Anthropocene, in which human activities accelerated the rate of species extinction and recklessly altered the environment. My thesis project is a campaign centered around The Universal Declaration of the Rights of Mother Earth, which was put together by indigenous groups around the world. This document outlines the guidelines we must follow to restore a healthy (pre-industrial) relationship with Mother Earth.

Thus, the aesthetic of my campaign is rooted in the tactile, the analog, the lovingly handmade. The homespun process of my project is an important feature of the message I am communicating. As the global north tries to disconnect ourselves from our roots, the analog form is important to continue to learn and pass along. While in Pennsylvania with limited resources around me, I used what I could find, starting with my hands and paying attention to the details of my environment. The touch of a physical object can hold so much power. The intention put into the design is rooted in the object, even if it isn't explicitly stated. The human hand is imperfect, messy, but can create strength with community. The Home campaign is about bringing people together with nature, or rather, realizing that we are one and the same.

→ mundane.page/thesis
→ mundane.page

61 LAWS: ALL INSTANCES OF GOD IN THE U.S. CODE
Eva Serrano Reisner

Christianity and democracy in the United States have had a close relationship since the country's conception. 61 Laws presents this relationship by creating a handwritten book of all the instances of "God" in the United States Code of Laws.

The method of recording the text was inspired by medieval manuscripts that incorporate hand calligraphy on large pages with larger margins. This was done to juxtapose the time period of the relevancy of these laws with the archaic form in which they are written and to evoke a grand and powerful feeling when holding the book. The filming of the book's production adds a performance element to the project by bringing emphasis to the number of laws written through the amount of time taken to write them. Because of the nature of the book's creation, the setting for the book is seen in an art gallery or installation. A website was created as well in order to make the content more accessible.

Through this, 61 Laws aims to ask "how does current American democracy prevent a true way of living under one's own morals?" The project presents these ideas without a predisposed voice. Information is power, and this book strives to use design to inform instead of offering preconceived solutions. By bringing awareness to this question,

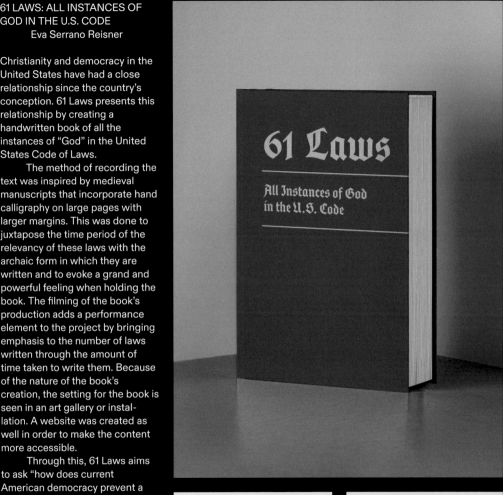

the developmental years of our lives, such as connecting the dots or coloring inside the lines, this project challenges the prospect of

like app uses a simple graphic aesthetic where every digital interaction is linked to a more physical and perhaps forgotten interaction—pulling a lever or rolling a

inputs are actually our own, and how we would like to move forward with changing our thinking.

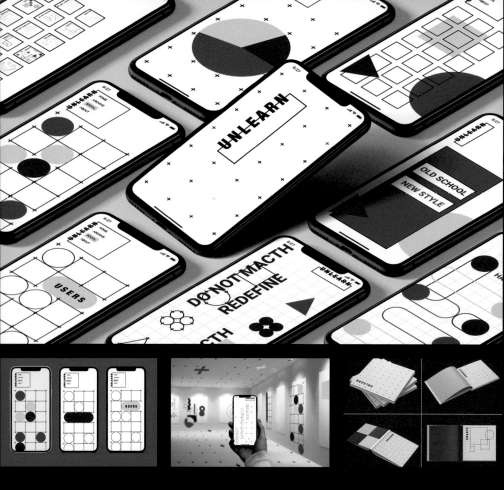

→ anvitashah.myportfolio.com/unlearn
→ anvitashah.myportfolio.com/work

DATAPOLY
Suditi Shah

Datapoly is a redesigned version of the popular board game Monopoly. It aims to make audiences of all age groups experience the incessant data transactions occurring on the internet. We live in a highly connected society. The widespread internet access and enmeshed networks have allowed humans to connect with one another and also communicate with things. This sort of networking require's one's smart devices to access their personal and public·data, in real time. For example, one's smart fridge may detect that they are running out of groceries and automatically contact the grocery store to have the food delivered to their house.

Human data is constantly being collected by companies within every industry and this is resulting in a downfall in human communication on a global scale. What is the future of human relationships if such technologies become mainstream? How can one's data be used for or against them? How does one measure the value of Data?

These questions don't have straightforward answers and thus Datapoly aims to create a playful experience that triggers one's thought process in this direction. The game comes with a Play board, Chance and Community Chest cards, Player tokens, Companies as property, Data as currency, and a User Manual. The User Manual provides a deeper insight on how emerging technologies in different settings use personal data. Like most Monopoly games, Datapoly players may end up in a quarrel, however this time its a fight to secure one's data!

→ suditishah.com/datapoly
→ suditishah.com

BAGHAWAT
Amal Shaheedi

Baghawat is a print/web archive that challenges false female representation and stereotypes within Pakistan. Through my work, I aim to bring to light the feminist movement, that has been underway since the birth of the country.

Renowned female activists Farida Shaheed and Khawar Mumtaz describe the journey of a Pakistani woman as "One step forward, two steps back." This is the struggle that is overshadowed by the male-dominant narratives prevalent within the society. Women of Pakistan are often painted as "conformists" who exist to serve in the roles of "sisters", "mothers" and "wives". Baghawat gives voice to a community that has been silenced over time.

By analyzing newspapers and other direct sources of past representation, one can question narratives surrounding women and how they came to exist. How has censorship altered the stereotypes around the female identity? The goal of this archive is to showcase an accurate portrayal of Pakistani women, in order to form and revive our own history. In doing this, I will be bringing forward the work of female activists through a web archive and a personal reflection- the Baghawat zine. This web archive will serve as a historical reference for their works, while the zine offers direct insight into the struggles shared by us women.

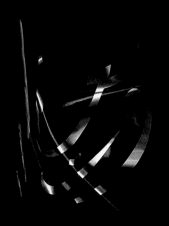

→ amalsportfolio.net/home/baghawat
→ amalsportfolio.net

OBJECTS, MEMORIES, DEATH, US.

Joyce Shi

Objects,
(What things have we encoun-
tered in our life?)
Memories,
(What do these things leave
behind?)

Death,
(Shall it be the end of the time and
bodies we occupy?)
Us.
(And...how do all of these above
affect the way we approach and
know ourselves?)

Things don't change, we do.
One day I dug out a pack of
old family videos, discs of past
decades technologies, from a box

that has been untouched for years.
I played the videos, looking at the
laptop screen as if I was looking at
the life story of someone else, felt
so far away.
Then I recall a quote, Nature loves
to hide.

Is it that nature hides from
us? Or is it that we misinterpret
nature, as we've become such
different people?

→ joyceshidesign.com/Objects_Memories_Death_Us.html
→ joyceshidesign.com

CAPITALISM: THE VISUAL IDENTITY OF AMERICA
Samantha Simotas

America's form of capitalism has molded society, culture, and politics in this nation and has enabled an elite fraction of the population to prosper disproportionately relative to its whole. In the 20th-century design became a valued tool for corporate America, creating brands, packaging, and marketing for consumer goods, graphic designers became an integral part of the free market system by contributing to the creation of wealth in society. Today, the primary focus of American design is through the lens of capitalism. The designer is valued more as a business asset to champion the merits of a corporation's wares to its target audience than as a contributor to cultural progress. American business's relentless pursuit of the next sale has led to design in America constructing and influencing the visual identity of the American experience through which we live and navigate.

My thesis aims to document the ways in which capitalism has built the visual identity of America. This book guides you through this nation's commitment to the economic systems in place to build wealth and the extent that the function of design is used to accomplish this task. Compiled in three broad themes, privatizing the public sector, designing the American landscape, and the exponential consumption of goods. Capitalism: The Visual Identity of America, highlights the most common and mundane design artifacts that we encounter everyday in the United States, including the subway system, billboards, malls, suburbs, and products.

→ samsimotas.com

MODERN EDUCATION 2021
Claira Smith

Education in American has essential remained unchanged for he past 100 years. Our current system of education was designed n the Industrial age mainly to turn out blue collar workers. At present, We have an extremely standardize system where all students are taught the same things in the same manne. How can we create an educational assets that conform and respects the individual learning experience rather than the collective?

This thesis aims to assist learning through design, which taps into all modalities or ways of learning whether it be hands on, creative, or visual learning. My aim is to design a better learning experience for 4th Grade students, using the input from my interviews, research, and investigations with teaching professionals.

FOODBIAS
    Hyunji Song

Foodbias is an app specially
designed for people who have
food phobias/ aversions—who are
afraid to eat certain foods related
to the texture, smell and flavor.
The app encourages people to
overcome the fear of food and to
have a healthy relationship with
food. Types of food phobias,
health benefits, food recommendations, healthy recipes, open
chat, all in one place. Let's
overcome food phobias
with Foodbias!

THE MODERN PROTEST GRAPHIC AND SOCIAL MEDIA
Carolina Stierli de Abreu

Protest Graphics have always been an integral part of social movements and as activism has evolved so have they. They have shifted in medium and have gone from posters to mostly digital graphics that live on social media which nowadays is often the first point of contact from which we get our information, express our opinions or find communities so

its content is often indicative of the conversations being held at a global level.

The feminist protest graphics currently dominating the conversation across social media platforms are all mostly similar in that they have taken complex feminist theories and boiled them down to short one liners in order to fit a certain aesthetic and appeal to a wider audience.

Although social media in its nature can't effectively hold all the information needed for the viewer

to fully understand complex feminist theory it can be the starting point for these complicated conversations about complex topics. I want to find better way to communicate these complex theories and ideas online by creating experiments that directly address the issues and frustrations I have with graphics currently circulating on social media.

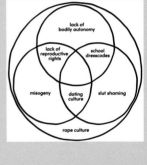

OUR PHONES TELL STORIES
Niharika Sundarigari

We live in a world where every facet of our life is influenced by social media. The information social media provides us, often-times excessive and intrusive, paints a person's life story through their pictures. But is this story an accurate depiction of their real life? The answer is no.

Initially, diving deeper into my followers' pictures on their phones allowed me to conclude that 90% of people don't reveal their actual selves to the internet by hiding their emotions through a happy facade. These pictures posted online are almost always filtered, edited, and curated to look perfect. At the beginning of 2020, I conducted polls and surveys on Instagram and found that 85% of my followers filtered out the hard times they were facing due to the pandemic while updating their social media. 2020 was one of the most difficult years for most people and has driven people away from platforms like Instagram. So where can you get a glimpse of people's real-life in 2020?

Flowto is an app that takes your emotions into account by promoting a healthy relationship with social media. It normalizes sharing stories however sad, dark, or deep; not everything needs to be perfect. The app excludes likes, comments, followers, and filters, temporary forms of validation we seek to feel good about ourselves. The app allows you to filter what you would like to see and allows you to express yourself freely by bringing light to the real stories of our lives.

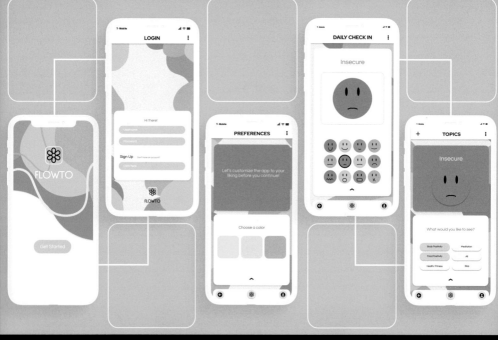

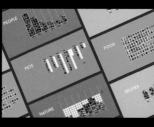

→ sundn199.myportfolio.com/Thesis
→ sundn199.myportfolio.com

324

MELITE

Rachael Tomaszewski

My thesis explores language and identity through the lens of Maltese colonization, divided into two parts. First, I created a bilingual book, in English and Maltese, that explores post-colonial Maltese identity. The book is divided into three sections: an introduction, Defining Identity, and a conclusion. The introduction provides historical context, the Defining Identity section addresses a series of responses from personal interviews I conducted with Maltese people, inquiring about their individual perspectives regarding their cultural identity, and the conclusion re-contextualizes the interviews, highlighting the generational shifts in identity as Malta repositioned from an occupied nation to a free one. British colonization significantly impacted our identity and the way we view ourselves, as well as our culture.

Curious to explore Malta's identity pre-colonization, I created a Maltese display typeface for the second portion of the project. The typeface, Melite, is inspired by pre-colonial Maltese culture and the megalithic structures Ħaġar Qim, Mnajdra, and Ġgantija. Featuring both English and Maltese glyphs, it was applied to the bilingual book from the first phase of the project. Melite features blocky, geometric elements, referencing the rigid limestone blocks commonly found in Maltese temple architecture. From the interview responses, I found that while the sense of identity varies among individuals, the most common identifying factor is the language, which is what links the two portions of this project.

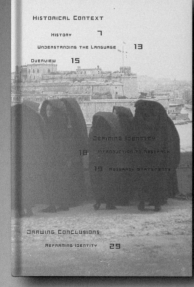

Space: In Two Parts is an interpersonal investigation of our relationship to the idea of "space," not in a physical sense, but the one that exists in ourselves and the many moments to come when we inhabit inside them. My aim for this thesis is to let us view and feel the ways others imagine their comfort outside of the physical spatial sense. I want to help the reader grasp the ephemerality of space which changes the instant time passes.

The Survey Booklet is a tool to meditate and imagine the possibilities of what "safe space" can be, presenting a transparency of my inquiry on space. Through responses curated from a series of questions I created, such as "What colors" "shapes," "smells," "objects," "living organisms," "words are in your ideal safe space?" and "What existing," "movies," "music inform your safe space?", the booklet puts to words the underlying concepts which make up the nuances of intimate, safe space further explored in the second book.

Good Space Journal is a book about experiencing spaces that are intimate, meaningful, looking at the memories that remain long after viewing and feeling them. Featuring writing, visual art, and interactive exercises, Good Space Journal captures elements of personal good space, evoking the readers own associations with good space in this book. The ultimate question this book seeks to answer is how can one capture a fleeting moment or memory of a space

→ tongtiffany.cargo.site/Space-In-Two-Parts
→ tongtiffany.cargo.site

Recollection is a memory app that I created that allows one to input text about their memory, and auto generate a visual collage that would accompany it, enhancing a journaling and memorabilia experience. The user may swipe through their curated memories, in a completely randomized order, much like the way our minds surf through memories, or, the user may choose to view their memories according to date, much like diaries or journal entries.

Living and dwelling often go hand in hand. We live our lives in reality, but we may often find ourselves dwelling on the past, present, or even the future. This is most found to be true during pandemic musings. We may sometimes revisit the same memories over and over again, or enter a rabbit hole of memories.

If you pay attention to your memories, you may find that it may not necessarily form a linear storyline. Our memories represent fragments of our thoughts, sensations, and feelings, all reconstructed and strung together to be

housed in our minds. One mere fragment of a memory can lead you into remembering something entirely different, but that's just the way memory works. Many document their memories in the form of pictures they take on their phone or on social media, and some like to keep a journal. However, the art of journaling may be a dying form in the presence and development of technology. How can we preserve, and digitalize the art of curating our memories? Recollection may be the answer.

→ svastiujagar.com/recollection
→ svastiujagar.com

YOU'RE WORTH THE ROOM
Ariana Ushiki

In the wake of the COVID-19 pandemic, I spent a fair amount this year examining the physical and emotional relationship of people to their spaces. The pandemic has abruptly changed our relationship to our spaces; being home once felt more like a home base, but now become our entire world. Our communities are often seen as prisons to escape one day rather than areas can appreciate at this moment now. Our bodies and our shelters are prisons rather than a place of peace. I'd like to challenge this phenomenon and see if there's a way to embrace our extended times in our most immediate spaces.

You're Worth the Room is a game made of three decks meant to challenge different layers of space humans to interact with on a daily basis; the community, the home, and the self. In this thesis, my goal was to explore the idea of "taking up space" and using space as a tool to heal during this time of stagnation. Rather than being stuck in our spaces, we can grow and begin to understand and reflect on the spaces we take up.

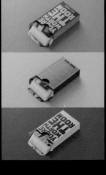

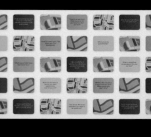

→ arianaushiki.com

328

TOOLS FOR MAXIMUM PRODUCTIVITY AND EFFICIENCY

Diana Victoreen

How do we determine what is valuable and worthwhile? When we're so used to discussing value in abstract terms like currency, the concrete things represented by these abstracts are easily lost on us. Value governs all of the choices that we make in life, so what happens when we can't determine value for ourselves? When values are aligned with the success and profit of corporations rather than the wellbeing of people and communities the result is waste, inequality, and suffering in the name of efficiency and productivity. This is neither efficient nor productive.

Tools for Maximum Productivity and Efficiency is an ever expanding suite of tools for those who are new to the realities of full time labor and financial independence–or really anyone who needs a fresh perspective on value. tfmpe.com currently hosts two animated series, Phone a friend: conversations about value with various guests, and Question Time: a series that answers big questions like "what is value" in terms simple enough for a child to understand. The platform also offers a browser extension which converts any mention of currency on the web into metrics of the user's choosing.

The ever growing collection of tools available on tmfpe.com provides users and viewers new entry points into the discussion of value, and creates space for people to define value for themselves and live efficiently and productively as a result.

→ tfmpe.com
→ dianavictoreen.com

Yiqi Wang

The current fresh produce sales model is monopolized by large companies. Many small farms have limited sales channels and are suffering from economic deficiencies. According to USDA, farms with direct-to-consumer (DTC) type of sales channel have a much greater chance of surviving than farms that practice traditional methods. However, now there is a lack of online platforms for selling local fruits and vegetables. Before the pandemic, people have always tended to buy in the farmer's

market, but the impact scale is microscopic. Moreover, after the pandemic, everyone is scared to shop at traditional markets where people usually gathered. To help farmers escape the current dilemma, I created a service that assists local farms and small family businesses in selling their products through live streams and virtual shopping.

The project, Enliven, is composed of an app and a branding package. Enliven helps not only farmers but also consumers to get fresh groceries from local farms near their house and be able to communicate with

the real people who are growing them. With the live streaming technology, the consumer will know every detail of their food while purchasing them, which brings transparency to the once opaque process. By introducing the service, I also want to create communities that connect the local producers and customers. I hope that people will choose to buy less processed and packaged food sent from thousands of miles away and instead pay more attention to local farmers just within reach.

→ yiqiworks.com/enliven
→ yiqiworks.com

THE LOST AND FOUND
Yutong Wang

What makes us who we are? How do we distinguish ourselves from others? These questions regarding identity have bothered me all the time. We are different in the clothes we wear, the way we talk, and the objects we possess. However, identity is beyond that. It is an intricate web woven from the experiences we've had, the choices we've made, and the lifestyle we are living. Presented in a book, the first part of the project is an investigation transforming identity into a physical presence. Several participants selected three objects that they thought best reflected their identity, interests, and personality. Following interviews with each object-owner on their objects, observations from others on the same objects were gathered revealing the differences between self reflection and objective observation. Besides the physical forms of objects, how do we find ourselves? The second part of the project consists of an animation on a self-reflection poem, The Lost and Found. Portrayed in illustration, a protag-

onist confronts different kinds of emotional struggles during the process of self realization. A series of these animations are collected to create a website which offers the site-users a variety of protagonists to explore, each of whom has different experiences and feelings about their life struggles. The online platform, a shared space that creates a variety of paths for communication, outlines an expansive picture of what one can eventually find as one wakes up to who they truly are.

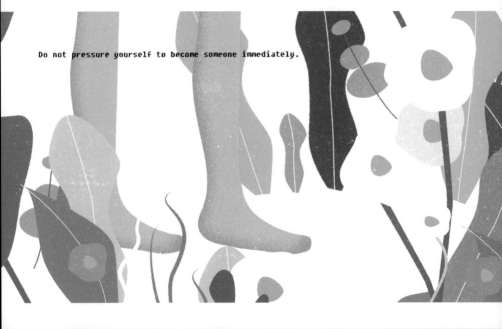

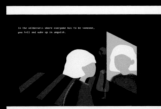

→ wangy882.wixsite.com/portfolio

HUMAN BODY OPERATION MANUAL
Zheng Wang

The history of humanity is the evolutionary chronicle of tools. This project focuses on our body which is the very first tool we have ever adopted as human. We learnt how to use our limbs and other body parts through a non linguistic way from our parent when we were young. Human body is so primitive that we often ignore its limitation and how the human body's form restrain oneself as a tool. So I decided to emphasize human body's attributes as a tool by using a modern method through a systematic media. I choose adopting the form of operation manual, pretending that we have never used our body before and explanatorily intro-ducing the human body as a brand new product.

Human can only observe and interact with surroundings by using various types of tools. Thus, what kind of tools we use and how we use them determine what we think about the world and where do we position ourselves in this world. If so, then how does the relationship with those tools as a whole influence our consciousness and cognition towards reality? To answer that, I broke down the idea of tool into segments, and I found the pattern that each time as we developing and adopting a new tool, we are losing the complexity of reality and alienating the essence of surroundings. And as for this work, it is a small but sincere attempt by me under this colossal topic.

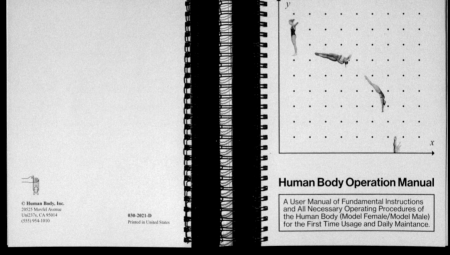

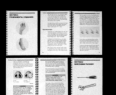

PRESENT PERFECT TENSE
Jasmine Wei

Since the start of the pandemic, Taiwan has started to be seen by the world of how well we managed Covid-19, yet except for our political background, not many people know the beauty of Taiwan or want to visit Taiwan for tourism. As someone who was born and raised in Taiwan, I've experienced the cultural diversity, the breath-taking natural sceneries, convenient transportation, and welcoming nice people. As a Taiwanese, I wanted to stand out and create an app that helps tourists to discover this beautiful island in a more in-depth way.

History makes us who we are. To fully know the ground we stand on, it is key to understand the past, and also be mindful about the future. Users simply go anywhere and take a picture of a place, then they will be provided with past, present information, and future plans within that space. The pictures that are taken will be used as assets for site information for others to view, too. There are more functions like most popular desti-nations, background information, and personal visited sites. In this way, tourists would be able to explore Taiwan in a more in-depth and convenient way.

→ jasmine-wei.com/portfolio-2/present-perfect-tense
→ jasmine-wei.com

METAMORTHESIS
Savannah West

The products of graphic design are to be found everywhere, in the form of logos, publications, websites, and targeted social media advertisements — yet despite the ubiquity of design, the forces that shape the visual landscape remain a mystery to the general public. Oftentimes designers are trained and not born out of pure skill or talent. Their creative rituals have, more likely than not, been passed down from generations of teachers and mentors before them. This inherited design process has perpetuated a cycle of predictable uniformity in both form and process. New forms cannot be discovered with outdated or trained processes. Metamorthesis explores the notion that a new kind of graphic design might be possible if we broaden the discourse beyond the preoccupations of "high design."

The book contains a collection of 11 interviews from a group of diverse individuals outside of the design community. The structure entailed asking participants to think like a designer. Each interviewee was asked to pick one or two of the following subjects: representation, memory, identity, environment, communication, and information. Then the following questions were asked: Why are you passionate about your subject(s)? Is there a problem you observe within your subject(s)? How would you begin to solve that problem? What advice might you give? This series of questions closely mimics a conventional process, but without any designer interference. Instead of the default starting point of research and collection, the design can start and end with visual execution.

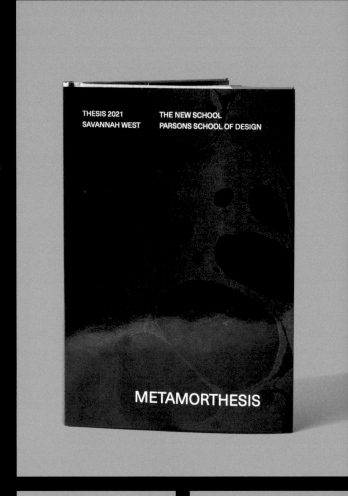

DOES EVERYONE IN AMERICA HAVE ANXIETY?

Summer Wojtas

This book explores the growing prevalence of anxiety in America. Through a series of writings and images sequenced to simulate the varying emotions and ups and downs of having anxiety, the author processes her own journey with mental health. Each design decision was made intentionally in order to evoke a feeling of anxiety. Spacing, size, hierarchy, and color all contribute to this feeling. Pages with full blocks of text, or big letters with barely any spacing, function to overwhelm the reader. A page with only a few words or a full spread image gives the mind a rest.

Intentionality is something that is important to mental health recovery, as is awareness. Recovery is learning who one is and what one likes to do because one can finally see out of the thick fog of anxiety. It's being intentional about how life is lived and how time is spent. These two things go hand-in-hand, and these principles guide design, as well as life. The purpose of creating this book was not necessarily for anyone else besides myself. However, I hope that by putting what I have learned and processed about my own mental health out there, people will inherently understand something about themselves from that vulnerability and from the design that provokes those feelings.

AQUEOUS HEADSPACE
Jacquelyn Wu

Living with mental illness(s) is unarguably a grueling experience. The road is bumpy and never linear. For those experiencing it, their state of well-being may fluctuate with many ups and downs. And in some cases, a painful slippery slope occurs as one condition branches and develops to several others. Mental illness can feel like an endless loop, with moments of elation coupled with dispair. Specifically, bipolar disorder and its vicious cycle of mania and severe depression is an example of this experience.

In the mainstream, the discussion mainly focuses on the negative aspects of living with a condition. In a lot of these conversations, "struggling", "battling" and "coping" with symptoms is a common choice of diction. It contains a connotation that individuals will need to exhaust themselves in intense competition against their illness to achieve an imitation of perceived normalcy. This assumption creates additional stress to a mind that's already in turmoil. Consolidating narratives such as being able to make peace with your condition is rarely mentioned.

To console and uplift people with mental illness, this motion graphic project wishes to encourage that equilibrium is achievable when managing symptoms in mental health. It serves as a screen saver, providing comfort, meditation, and a sense of tranquility. The metaphor of water is utilized to represent symptoms and emotional fluctuations. Like water, mental illness is terrifying because it promises destruction, chaos, and causes us to drown within them. However, water also nurtures, soothes, and allows one to be afloat.

VIRTUAL OFFICE
Ricky Xie

While working from home has its benefits, delineating boundaries between work and life can be challenging without the nine-to-five office workday. At home, a space used for working tends to double as a space for leisurely activities, such as a dining table or bedroom, which can leave workers indolent from constant distractions or burnt out from persisting in a working mindset all day.

Fortunately, it is possible to relieve the productivity and mental health impairments caused by working from home. Virtual workers may find more work satisfaction by separating regions in their homes by function, i.e. work or leisure, or establishing the separation by time, to simulate the lost transition from home to office and vice versa.

Virtual Office is a speculative app that aims to help workers reattain this work-life balance by designating work spaces in their homes and building a habit of using the appropriate spaces for work and leisure.

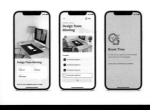

→ rickyxie.ml/project/virtual-office
→ rickyxie.ml

MARY BLUE
Connie Xu

This work focuses on images
generated with Facebook
DensePose, an open-source pose
estimation tool. Pose estimation
uses computer vision, which trains
machines to identify and classify
objects, to detect and track the
location of human figures in visual
material. DensePose exceeds
basic object recognition; it detects
human bodies in images and
constructs a 3D surface-based
model of the body. Also public is
DensePose's training image set of
50,000 people. Typically, the
application of the tool is trans-
porting one body's texture onto
another's pose. The outputs in this
project are instead reconstruc-
tions of a singular body onto itself.

Images were taken from e-
commerce entries for swimwear
and run through two tools: the first
identifies the body and flattens it
into a texture of segmented body
parts, and the second recon-
structs the model based on the
body's position. In the resulting
output, image, surface, and body
are placed onto a plane where
their characteristics clash, but are
also indiscernible from one
another. The effect of the
technology emerges in the cracks,
mistakes, and lost data of these
generated bodies.

Treating the bodies as
images, they are projected onto
prefabricated swimwear patterns
and output and sewn by a print-
on-demand company. The material
of swimwear is mutable, synthetic,
and body conforming; the inter-
twining of swimwear and body
shows the divisions and overlaps
between synthetic and natural
form. A live video presentation of
the swimsuits, in which a model
moves through poses, shows her
struggling, obeying, indulging, and
refusing in front of us.

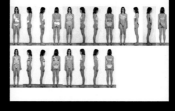

THE MANY IMAGERIES
Karrie Xu

The purpose of many words is to remind us of things rather than to announce things. In poetry, visual elements of some kind are often present between lines. Moon, silver, dust, roundelays... poetic wordings like these create a series of visual links and gift the discourse a range of non-visual attributes that are sensuously suggestive. These attributes collectively build a strong conceptual image for the audience.

However, this nuanced notion of the image is often hard to put into words, and the interpretations of a single piece of poetic writing can be discursive due to the bifurcation of readers' previous association with the elements presented and their new response to the aesthetic relationships established by the poets. Attempting to unravel a poem's imagery, The Many Imageries traces the braiding of images around which the poem is built. It reproduces and visualizes the ongoing cognition and the discursive imaginative space where each audience explores a stretch of poetic discourse.

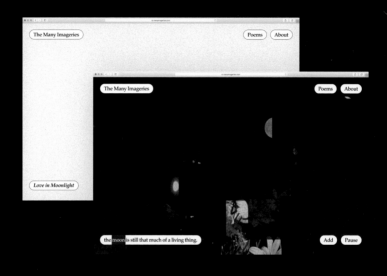

→ thttp://manyimageries.com
→ karriexu.com

Memory House is a project exploring the emotional feelings and memories people have on their belongings. The project begins with sending surveys to friends and anonymous online users from Chinese public forum, asking people to share their unique memories and feelings of one object they keep and upload images of it. The stories and images collected are organized and re-arranged into a book transferring abstract feelings into visual design. The Memory House also has different forms of design functions differently. For example, the serial postcards allow the audience to share their experience and mail to others, the web is for keep collecting information so it can be a long-lasting "memory gallery."

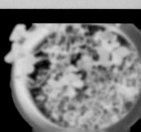

UNBOXING
Jacqueline Yang

Everyone and everything is inherently masked in some way. What we see is merely a projection of how people want to be perceived as. Large corporations also take a part in this action through branding.

This realization inspired my project: Unboxing. Unboxing is a trend in the twentieth century where influencers would record their process of revealing their purchase and the items from their packaging. There is often a mysterious uncertainty and surprise that comes along with the action of unboxing. However, what is inside sometimes is unexpected that deviates from viewers' initial expectations. I interpret unboxing as unfolding the surface and revealing the truth underneath. The action that shines a light on what is disguised and concealed underneath the beautiful packaging.

My research aims to conduct in-depth investigation on some of the most renowned brands in the world: Zara, Apple, Amazon, Popmart, United Airline, and Wells Fargo to reveal the contrast and connection between their beautiful surface and their underlying unethical problems. The research is delivered in the form of packaging design and as the packaging boxes unfold, the truth is unboxed. The outer packaging is branded to match with the aesthetic of the companies. This creates a stark contrast with the interior design where the surface is filled with dense text of the unethical practices of the industry and how they are affecting the world environmentally, socially, and economically. As the boxes unfold, the truth is unboxed.

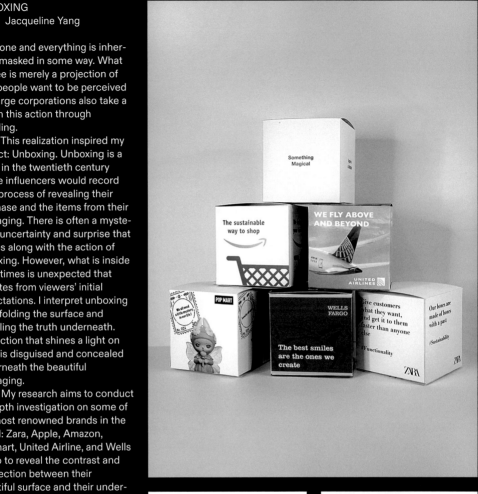

CULT OF CUTE
Emily Yun

Why is America so obsessed with all things petite, Asian, and domesticated? What are the critical notions behind cuteness and, through its globalization, how has it evolved through mass consumption? These questions drove my personal investigation into a visual and semantic exploration of cuteness.

Cult of Cute encourages dialogue on the matter, as an aesthetic so harmless in nature becomes equally concerning. It uncovers contextual research that exposes this impulse as a form of escapism, indulgence, and the subversive tools of soft power. Cult of Cute looks into two cultural conceptions of the idea both Western and Kawaii as well as the globalization and consumption of this phenomenon. Inspired by past research, personal writing, and images, this project set out to create a sense of eeriness to reveal cute's darker undertones.

As a designer, I want to generate a conversation on cute politics by adding tension to the matter. Through full spread images that include various types of cute objects, the book was made to feel like a journal, with kitsch as its factor to play into its easy consumption. Simultaneously, as viewers are lured in, they may also question their own relationship to cute's attractive appeal. What is offered is a more critical perspective on this ever-popular aesthetic, promoting mindful reflection upon cute's overconsumption in capitalism, its oversaturation in our media, and sometimes its harmful incorporation into identity politics.

Every designer has a different process in order to create their desired end-product. We primarily focus on form, functionality, and meaning. As a painter, color is my essential tool to explore these fundamentals. I choose colors meticulously when designing so that the piece will look and feel a specific way. Color selection is a subjective process and entails different results depending on who is making the sampling decisions. How is the outcome of an artist's color sampling different

In order to understand how subjective the process is, I had three different people sample five colors, from images I took, that they felt represented each image as a whole. The images were taken in several different cities from around the world. The first selector is myself, the second is Billy, a mechanical engineer. The third is Jack, a business major.

What I wanted to know was how could we begin to create color palettes objectively? To answer this, I developed a python code to remove the subjective

dominant colors of any image based on pixel count and to represent them proportionally in an information graph. My subjective selections seemingly have more emphasis on hue, while the computer generated selections on value. Using both of these tools for subjective and objective sampling, two different city identities were generated for each location and collected in a book along with documentation of the process.

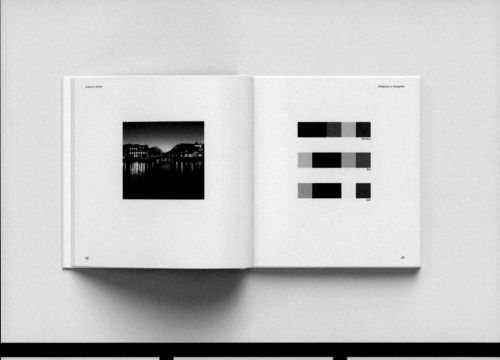

→ moniquezeitouny.wixsite.com/portfolio/thesis
→ moniquezeitouny.wixsite.com/portfolio

In the past two decades, Wikipedia has gone from an underdog, unpromising experiment to the world's largest and most widely accessed encyclopedia. It started as an empty platform and evolved into millions of articles purely from volunteer participation and an ambitious vision of free knowledge. The site is a labour of love, one that is built from community, from humor and thoughtfulness. It is no less a feat than a termite mound, built individually, one edit at a time.

"It's a misconception people work for free," stated Jimmy Wales, the founder of Wikipedia. "They have fun for free." This kind of fun is all over the meta pages of the site: talk pages, commentaries, wiki-newspapers„ in-person meetups and beyond. There is a passionate, robust community of Wikipedia editors working together tirelessly behind the scenes to make everything happen, not unlike a massive multiplayer video game.

Wiki:pedia Zines, a series of freely distributed magazines, presents a deep dive into the culture of Wikipedia. Each issue focuses on a specific topic, from Wikipedian policies, to humor, to language, to author bias etc. Questions like: who edits Wikipedia? What content is allowed? Why are people so passionate about the site? are all questions that are addressed in the zines. Each zine hopes to bring both a critical and joyful lens in viewing Wikipedia; rooted in the understanding that behind each article, is a passionate and imperfect volunteer, dedicating their time towards the ambitious pursuit of free knowledge for all.

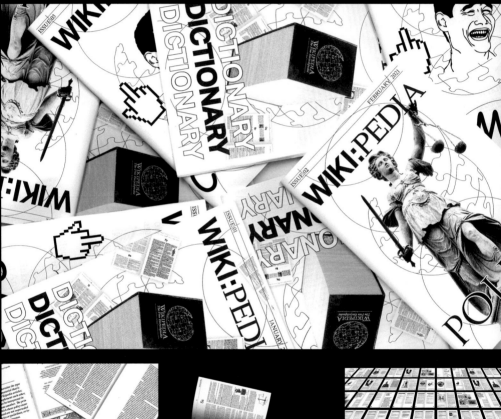

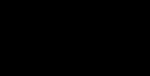

→ ceciliazhang.work/wikipedia
→ ceciliazhang.work

LOOKING BEYOND AND BEHIND TEA

Cheryl Zhang

Tea is the most consumed beverage in the world, just after water. Tea drinkers are on the rise as they begin to see numerous benefits in tea. More people are including tea as part of their daily routine. However, as a tea drinker, I have noticed that people often only see how wonderful and tasteful tea is. We rarely hear and talk about the opposing side of tea as the truth is that not only tea production is violating human rights, destroying our environment, and causing loss of biodiversity, but tea has also widened social classes and triggered conflicts in history. Every story has two sides to it. Same for tea. When we look beyond to recognize our experiences with tea, we should also look behind to acknowledge some of the harms tea has brought now and in the past.

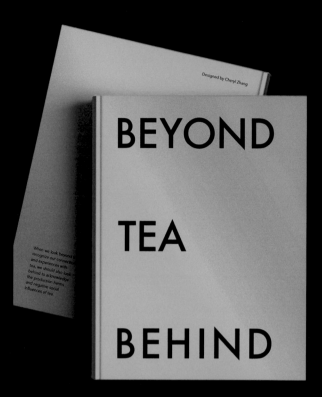

The book will allow people to reflect their journey with tea through reading survey responses I collected. It also emphasizes the destructive impacts of tea and its severity so that tea drinkers as a collaborative group can adjust daily trivial acts to avoid directly funding the concerning issues and to prevent the ways people used tea in the past. Tea is more than a beverage. It is a subject that can urge self-reflection, evoke senses, and spark conversations. This project is aimed to push people to explore the other side of the story and to make trivial changes as a collective group for the bigger causes behind.

→ cherylz.com

RECIPES FOR COMMUNITY
Claire Zhang

Recipes for Community is a project sowed from a simple concept: sharing recipes to bridge distance. The book documents an email chain I started in March 2021, connecting 6 people of Asian diaspora living in America, some of whom had met individually but have never come together as a whole. Through the cultural medium of cooking, Recipes for Community seeks to apply the essence of "cooking for one another" as a concept beyond cooking, one that can be applied to any form of connectivity and community. By having the participants share recipes, stories, pictures from their childhoods, and more, Recipes for Community unfolds beyond a "cookbook," transforming into an exploration of space, memory, community, and family, while building exactly that—a family.

Ostensibly, this book documents a community started as a space to provide healing for Asian Americans and Pacific Islanders during a year when the veil of model minority was pulled back to reveal how truly vulnerable we are and have always been to the violence of a perpetually foreign existence. However, I want this project to be a seed to grow more intimate, healing communities across digital and physical boundaries, not only for AAPI, but other marginalized communities as well.

Recipes for Community is both an object and an invitation—a way of reminding others the solidity of the communities we create, and an open invitation to join our table.

→ clairezhang.net/recipesforcommunity
→ clairezhang.net

Launched just four years ago, the Master of Professional Studies program in Communication Design was built to serve early and mid-career designers seeking to augment their practice with a specialized course of study. Students spend nine months engrossed in the world of Digital Product Design, learning how to design for and think critically about the interfaces which increasingly permeate our lives. The culmination of this effort is the production of a fully realized product conceived of and produced from scratch by each graduate of the program.

It's often said that design is never done (and this is particularly true in the realm of digital products), and thus the work you see here isn't the end point of a project but rather a snapshot of an idea which was germinated in the time these students spent with us. With candidates entering in the fall and graduating already in the spring, each year runs as a little experiment, unique in its own way, and the class of 2021 was of course no exception. As we shifted to a fully remote model with 29 students distributed across six time zones, this group of graduates responded with the kind of resilience and perseverance which will carry them far in this nascent corner of the discipline.

Design is a curious subject to professionalize. There are no licenses required to practice, no bar exams to pass, nor residencies to complete. And as the scope of what we do continues to grow, even notions of what is or isn't design have become contentious and blurred. In the end, perhaps the only test of a designer is the work, and the projects presented here demonstrate the breadth and depth of a cohort of practitioners ready to operate amongst the best in our industry.

STOOPING NYC
Mari Al-Midhadi

One person's trash is another person's treasure. STOOPING NYC is a web app that marks free stuff on the streets of New York City through crowd-sourced information, promoting sustainability, adventure, and community. This project is an extension of @stoopingnyc, a popular Instagram account that reposts photos and locations of furniture left on the curbs and stoops of NYC. The account has 150K+ followers and has built its own community from the uniquely New York experience of finding rare and often still usable furniture on the street. The account, run by two professionals with full-time jobs, receives thousands of submissions a day. With people constantly moving in and out of apartments, the influx of posts can be overwhelming, and a lot of submissions end up not being posted. STOOPING NYC streamlines this process by allowing submissions from users that are automatically posted, enabling them to browse and be notified of free things near them. Users can post an item with ease and mark the exact location of the item. All posts expire in 24 hours due to the time-sensitive nature of these items. Most importantly, people can mark an item as taken, saving time and greatly enhancing the experience of stooping.

stooping[1]
/stOopiNG/
verb

gerund or present participle: stooping

1. **Finding and taking an item home from the street.**
"He stooped that pink couch on mott street!"

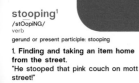

FIND FREE FURNITURE AND STUFF NEAR YOU

NUI
Gandhali Bapat

In an increasingly cashless world, Nui is an app designed to empower users to know the best credit card to use for any transaction. The app also helps users quickly make payments, understand their savings, recuperate annual fee costs, and see available credit card offers. Nui means plentiful in Hawaiian and Maori languages.

→ gandhalibapat.com/work/nui
→ gandhalibapat.com

ORANGE SUNSHINE
DAYDREAM MUSIC AND FILM
FESTIVAL
        Katie Brown

Orange Sunshine Daydream is a
weekend of morning to night
psychedelic experiences, intended

to reveal the power of psychedelic
music and film on the human
consciousness. Expect live music,
film screenings, live music
recordings, food, and dance.
Orange Sunshine Daydream
Music and Film Festival is a
celebration of the late 1960's

psychedelic era and aims to
engage and inspire fans of all
ages. OSD strives to bridge the
gap with generations of psychedelic enthusiasts and bring people
together through music and film.

DINO

Cherie Chan

Dino is an engaging educational platform that crowdsources assignment projects for school teachers and builds a community full of amazing teaching ideas. The platform simplifies communication and integrates features needed by teachers and students in digital education. At Dino, teachers are creators. They can create school projects, assign them as homework, give live instruction,

and check submissions all in one place. Dino simulates the best student engagement inside and outside the classroom, highlighting the value of hands-on activities. This version focuses on the teacher's interface and emphasizes the range of media that could be included to make teaching plans more engaging.

Kowai Kawaii is a wayfinding system directing visitors to historical sites in relation to Yōkai (妖怪, "ghost", "supernatural beings" in Japanese). The history

of Yōkai spans across two millennia, from ancient to modern Japan through literature, folklore and visual arts. Learning about local mythologies helps one understand the multiplicity of Japanese history and culture. The system has the potential to be a city based series that will eventually capture all the Yōkai and their narratives throughout Japan. The current edition focuses on Kyoto and consists of five signs and a booklet.

ROOTFUL
Roseanne Chao

community-engaged manual
contact-tracing app.

Stay rooted and mindful of your
surrounding. Rootful is a

By clicking on a location, you get to see live details about it. Swiping up provides even more information, if there is a disturbance sighting reported by you/somebody there.

REVI

Sejeong Hwang-Yoo

Over the last few years, the fast fashion market has been growing exponentially. As a consequence, clothing waste has been a major environmental issue. Along with the retailers and manufacturers, consumers are looking for ways to wear and dispose of their clothes in responsible ways. Buying less and buying valuable clothes is a first, but in order to bring clothes back into the cycle, consumer participation in the post-consumer market is crucial. Revi is a mobile experience focused website that guides users to resell, donate or recycle their unwanted clothes in the post-consumer clothing industry by providing information and incentives for keeping clothes out of landfills.

LLEY
Defne Kaynak

Making plans for a trip can be especially difficult with a group. Fleet is an app that provides travel groups with the tools to make the location discovery, decision making, and itinerary creation processes easy for a smooth trip. Users can start a new trip, take a questionnaire for personalized location suggestions for their travel group, view each other's interests, use polls for decision making, and create an itinerary together. Fleet is travel planning made easy.

CHITCHAT
    Regina La O'

Shifting to virtual workspaces has meant that engagements between coworkers have become hyper-scheduled. Chitchat aims to create more opportunities for sponta-neous interactions to help teams build meaningful relationships beyond just work. The desktop app is a space for remote team members to gather freely throughout the day away from where work is being done. In doing so, the platform is designed to take the planning and sched-uling away from how we engage with our coworkers to recreate more of those spontaneous conversations that have become almost non existent in their virtual workspaces. It also reimagines the video chat experience to reduce cognitive load and facilitate conversations beyond small talk.

ATTND.
Mo Labban

Attnd. is a live event platform where artists and businesses to live stream their content for people to enjoy from any location.

The goal of this project was to identify a problem that was brought on by the pandemic. I chose to tackle music and theatre events in a post-pandemic world where some would probably be skeptical about attending large-scale events. My solution was to

create a mobile app that allows users to watch shows while also interacting with the artists from any location. In addition to the mobile app, I chose to design a TV app where it is more comfortable for the user to watch shows on a big screen.

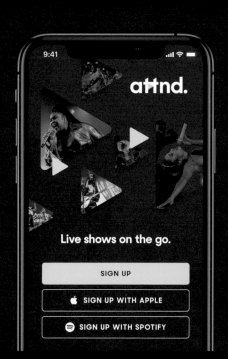

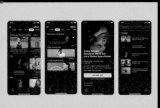

MINDBOOK
Anita Li

College mental health was already a severe issue before the pandemic, and it is worse now. After conducting desk research, we identified three major problems:

1. Students do not know what is happening when negative emotions affect them.
2. They do not know how and where to seek help.
3. Lots of students are not willing to ask for help for complex reasons.

We want to help students recognize when they need help, encourage them to ask for it, and eventually find it in a quick and low-stress way. Mindbook is an app that provides an informative platform of mental health resources with daily mental self-care methods and mental health education in a private and easily accessible.

Mindbook

Anita Li

Goal

Create a mobile app for all college students, faculty and alumni, aiming to provide an informative platform for mental health resources from on and off-campus with daily mental self-care methods and mental health education in a private and easily accessible way.

Meta insights

Lack of mental health education.
Lack of necessary information.
Stigmas & constrains in reality.

Resources

Self-Care

IMMERSART-IMMERSE IN ART APP

Imogene Liang

Immersart is a mobile app that brings connections between artists and art fans digitally. Users can easily match interests, collect artworks, share projects, and curate virtual exhibitions.

immersart

—

Immerse in Art

Immersart is a mobile app that brings connections between artists and art fans digitally. Users can easily find interest, collect artworks, share projects, and curate virtual exhibitions.

Curate at Anywhere You Want.

Curate at Anywhere You Want.

CURA

Sofia Moon

Cura is an AI-powered telehealth solution that improves patient care through simplified workflows and quality interactions. The solution contains two parts: a provider-facing desktop app that focuses on helping providers save time and complete tasks efficiently and a patient-facing mobile app with features focused on receiving care and connecting with providers.

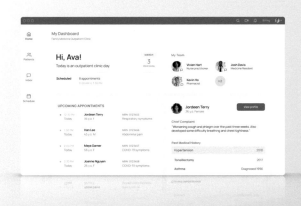

Cüra

Delivering care and connection

DESKTOP APP

A provider-facing desktop app focused on saving them time.

MOBILE APP

A patient-facing mobile app focused on connecting with and building a provider network.

PEAPOD
    Yina Shan

"Like peas in a pod." Peapod is an app that helps roommates get along. Of the 79 million U.S. adults who live with roommates, 40% are not satisfied with their living arrangements. Everyone has their own living habits which may disturb others that don't live the same way. After rounds of research and interviews, I realized the most positive impact on roommate relationships can be made in the beginning. If everyone can get on the same page about how they will be sharing the home, a lot of issues can be prevented entirely. However, such conversations can feel awkward and unpleasant to bring up.

How can Peapod help? We provide a questionnaire for users covering all aspects of roommate life. A group living together can compare everyone's honest answers and predict potential areas of conflict. The app then facilitates discussions of potential conflicts and encourages users to come up with a solution together. I believe living with roommates can be a great experience, and I hope Peapod can help users communicate and empathize with their roommates, as well as normalize and facilitate fair discussions around rules and expectations.

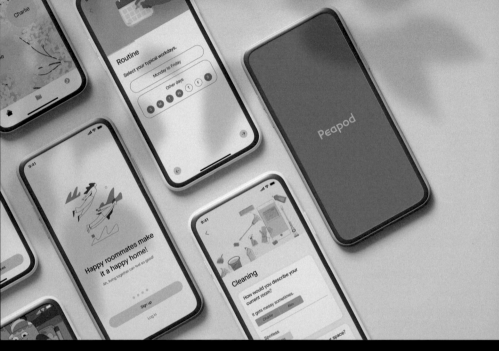

→ yinashan.com/peapod
→ yinashan.com

WORKING REMOTELY
Kaiwen Tao

This project tries to solve problems when people work remotely. Because of COVID-19, more and more people started to telework, and it causes a bunch of questions, not only for efficiency but also for mental health. This project focuses on those who work remotely in a team and tries to help them solve daily problems. These challenges include understanding a new group of people and conducting UX virtually instead of physically.

Kaiwen Tao / MPS Communication Design   UX/UI Project

Working Remotely

Role: Product designer

Problem: How to improve the efficiency when people work remotely with groups?

Challenge: Understanding a new group of people appear based on the pandemic and doing UX virtually instead of physically

Since the pandemic started, people began spending more time cooking at home. Studies suggest that "cooking fatigue" has become a problem. The main reasons that cause cooking fatigue include: cooking for one or even two people is not efficient; following

recipes is not relaxing or fun, and people miss the pleasure of cooking food for friends and family. The goal for my design is to create a digital product that helps make cooking more efficient and allows users to share their cooking experience through an engaging experience. The final outcome is the Chef's Diary app. Through AI support, users only need to

choose the ingredients, and the app will create a fast, simple, and healthy recipe for them. The app helps users to share their own recipes and discover new recipes among friends and family members. I hope through Chef's Diary, users can rediscover the fun of cooking and share the pleasure of cooking with friends and family.

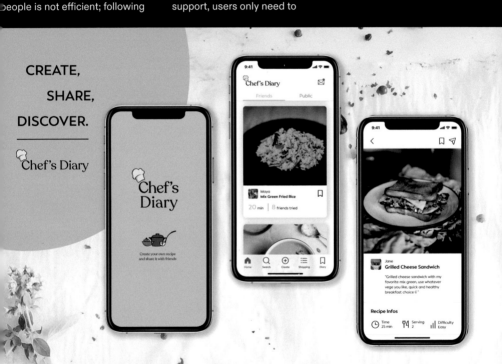

CREATE,
SHARE,
DISCOVER.

Chef's Diary

WHAT'S LEFT?
Qing Wen

The pandemic has brought changes, with dining out being the most prominent one. Due to safety concerns, it is safer to cook at home over dining out. For a cooking enthusiast like myself, this is a good time to explore and try new recipes. In the meantime, I realized that there could be various types of challenges associated with cooking at home.

This app is designed to assist with ingredient management within your kitchen. It serves as a gateway to efficient and affordable cooking. Grocery shoppers and home cooks can take advantage of this app to navigate shop visits, plan for the next meal, and elevate their personal culinary experience.

I started with the desire to elevate people's experience of cooking and dining at home. Through research, I found the problem that I was going to solve:

the ingredient management of ingredients. In fact, there could be numerous discrepancies between the groceries that we buy and recipes that we use, or between the receipts and our cooking schedule. I had encountered a similar situation many times when I opened my fridge to find a rotten tomato or an expired bag of pasta. With this problem in mind, the app What's Left was born.

DINNER PARTY: A MORE MEANINGFUL TAKEOUT EXPERIENCE
Kara Wilson

The restaurant model has shifted dramatically over the past year, forcing restaurants to jump through hoops to reinvent their business or otherwise close down. Dinner Party is a resource for restaurants to offer ticketed and curated take-home meal experiences. It connects customers' desires to support their favorite local restaurants with a platform that elevates the restaurants' existing operational systems. Dinner Party is a solution to optimize the takeout experience through delight and experimentation.

PRESSDONE
   Jessica Yang

Pressdone is a communication and management tool that helps users to be more productive and better organized. Pressdone offers users a centralized platform for streamlined communication and workflow. Pressdone has a desktop dashboard and three main sections: Tasks, Contacts, and Calendar. Its goal is to directly link the user and contacts to their shared tasks and meetings. Pressdone is an all-in-one tool for both remote and in-person work.

Pressdone

GREENITY
Xiaoyu Zhou

Climate change includes global warming driven by human emissions of greenhouse gases and resulting large-scale weather patterns. Since the mid-20th century, humans have had an unprecedented impact on the Earth's climate system and have caused change on a global scale. Therefore, it has become very urgent to control climate change caused by human behavior. Through user research, I found that people have some awareness of climate impact, but life conditions always limit their actions. However, from online research, I found that "...when people see their neighbors taking environmental action like conserving energy, they feel more compelled to act." The quote suggested that there is opportunity to influence each other to do more behaviors. The problem I want to solve is how to help people learn environmental knowledge and how to motivate them to become more environmentally conscious.

My solution is a community app for people to organize and participate in environmental activities with their neighbors to influence each other. Users can arrange environmental activities, invite people to join, share experiences, and post problems and eco-friendly solutions together.

AAS Communication Design Students join our community with a diverse mix of previous life experiences. They are practitioners in fields like biology, law, economics, and medical research—all of which trained them to apply a specific set of methodologies to look at the world. However, they discovered and acknowledged a growing passion for Communication Design. Their decision to return to school—to initiate this compelling shift of their practice—takes courage and dedication. It is a decision that has our utmost respect.

We tell them in their first week that learning the methodologies of a new discipline starts with unlearning. starts with unlearning. Leaving behind what you know in order to see the world anew will lead to questions that trigger rethinking and reshaping of the future. Beyond critical thinking and agency to foster sustainable thinking and social justice, our students develop creative skills that are independent of technology, media, or zeitgeist.

The Class of 2020-21 had to unlearn, learn, and invent faster than we could have anticipated. The COVID-19 pandemic hit right in the middle of their studies. Students actively shaped our altered reality where making—the translation of ideas into form and material—no longer included many of our traditional analog processes. In this context, they have been reflecting critically on their roles as designers in future societies.

In their capstone class, students research a topic or an issue they feel passionate about. Responses of the 2020-21 graduates include investigations into political, social and personal histories; relationships with the material world during isolation; gender roles and social justice; and ways to rethink identity in a post-pandemic world. Besides the shared interest in socio-political themes and form-making, the resilience of the AAS Communication Design community is grounded in the remarkable sense of peer-collaboration that respects and values each individual's unique life experience.

FURNITURE FOR A LOCKDOWN
Jake Berstein

Using only a Japanese handsaw and a power drill, I made what I call "Furniture for a Lockdown." Through many failed attempts, I created a set of three chairs designed to both connect you to your space and to connect the segments of an apartment to itself. With four wheels and a shorter than average seat height, the chairs allow the user to sit, scoot, dance, and move around a space with complete freedom. There are many ways to sit on these chairs, and the very act of using them can elicit things that are rare under lockdown: laughter, play, and freedom. I made the chairs from wood from a local hardware store and scraps leftover from boarded-up businesses during the protests.

Reflect/adoption started off as a personal self-reflection of my adoption experience. After stumbling upon a handwritten note I wrote at age nine to my birth mother, I realized I had never taken the time to sit down and reflect on my adoption story. Over the past 24 years, I have accumulated memories, photos, and thoughts regarding my experience but scattered everywhere—physically and emotionally. I knew as an adoptee, I was not alone. Reflect/adoption is the go-to app for adoptees to reflect on their adoption, communicate with other adoptees, design a memory book with pictures they have preserved, and more.

INTERTIDAL
Dannis Fu

INTERTIDAL is a virtual exhibition that focuses on the natural objects found along the Hudson River during low tide hours. This exhibition is a quiet yet poetic response to this consumerist society. It is crucial to rebuild the ability to identify and appreciate materials and craftsmanship. I want to remind people of the beauty and vitality of tiny things around us.

I collected the most mundane items that were washed up onshore by the tide. These objects are often microscopic, abundant, ignored, underappreciated, and taken for granted. The tradition of appreciating scholar rocks in ancient China inspired my following approach. East Asian countries have a long history of acknowledging natural objects like rocks and trees. Moreover, they have been prominent subjects for their artworks. A wooden cube is used as a physical base to add a sense of significance and elevate

their status. Backgrounds mimic a gallery environment and collages depict the natural environments where I think these objects are originally from or truly belong to. Upon completing the setup of this virtual exhibition, I decided to release these objects back to their natural habitats. I used removable water-based glue throughout this project so that when I placed them back in the Hudson River, they would not harm the environment.

"Recognize them for what they are, and we might just get to the other side." —Glenn Adamson

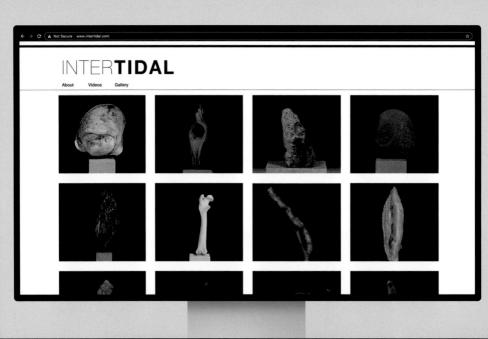

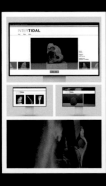

→ dannisfu.com/intertidal2
→ dannisfu.com

Where is the boundary between right and wrong? How do we understand our own and other's morality? How do we reconcile our personal, societal and cultural ethics?

Paradox Magazine explores what morality and ethics mean in the modern context. Curating articles from notable publication sources, the magazine addresses morals, ethics, and decisions at a personal, national, and international level. These articles are paired with dynamic, layered and amorphous imagery mimicking the blurry and incomplete understanding we have of morality in our current day context. The merged and blurry backgrounds are contrasted with rectangular graphical elements, bringing in a sense of contrast true to the topic at hand.

The masthead is set in modified Gopher. The O in Paradox is elongated, emphasizing an open stage for debate and the space between right and wrong. The body copy is set in Temeraire, an academic and serious serif, and the headers are set in Neue Montreal and Gopher, creating a modern feel to the text.

LOSS / FOUND
Nani Harakawa

Loss / Found is a series of experiments on how we might illustrate emotion and attachment through composition. In the form of a catalogue, I conducted a series of interviews and used transcriptions and provided images as material. The front of the book explores the feeling of absence and distance, and the second half of the book revisits the interview in a new light to draw the reader in and illustrate emotional connections.

OBJECT-IVE
Leslie Kay Lim

Object-ive is a series of miniature booklets that explores the creative processes of various artists by examining them through the lens of a tool key to their practice. The project took shape as a manifestation of a semester-long investigation into how concrete objects can ground us and help in processing abstract experiences.

For this iteration, artists of different mediums—including a photographer, musician and illustrator—were interviewed about their creative pursuits and were asked to talk about their "object" within a larger context of making. From why they first picked it up, to the muscle memory it invokes the camera, microphone, and digital pen, respectively, act as approachable entry points for the conversation.

In addition to the conceptual, the tool also serves as a literal introduction. The booklets, featuring a different artist, are designed with cut-outs in the shape of the specific object. It first highlights the object before its technical specifications are presented, but then reappears on various pages to act as a window, enticing readers to turn the page and enter. The cover and back cover also similarly contain perforations that reveal a glimpse of the artist's name and a compelling quote from their interview.

Presented in bright, cheerful hues and handbound with three-hole pamphlet stitching, the booklets' relatively small scale—only measuring 3.5 by 5 inches—also adds to the accessibility and intimacy of the reading experience.

→ lesliekaylim.com/Object-ive
→ lesliekaylim.com

BEYOND BORDERS
      MiJin Kim

Beyond Borders is a publication
that shares experiences and narratives of the Doctors Without
Borders community.

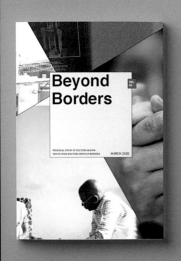

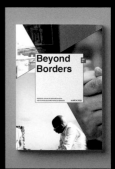

DYSPHAGIA BISTRO: INCREASING PUBLIC AWARENESS ABOUT SWALLOWING DISORDERS

Allison Kobren Allen

Dysphagia—difficulty swallowing—affects up to 15 million adults in the United States each year. Nevertheless, many are unaware of its existence and implications. My professional experience working with the dysphagia population has motivated me to consider ways to raise public awareness about this debilitating condition. Drawing upon my design background, I sought to devise a way to inform the general public about dysphagia in a manner more engaging than say, a stereotypical information pamphlet. I sought to create an experience that would engage people and make them eager to learn more.

Dysphagia Bistro is a pop-up café staffed by speech-language pathologists and speech-language pathology students, who work the most directly with swallowing disorders. The walls of the bistro are adorned by large, radiographic imagery that depict the intricacies of normal and disordered swallowing. Visitors order food and drinks from a menu but instead of selecting specific items, they order food and liquid based upon texture. This exposes individuals to the notion of diet texture modification, a daily reality for many who suffer from dysphagia. After completion of the meal, visitors are encouraged to reflect upon their experience by recording their thoughts on notecards and adhering them to the bistro walls. Their thoughts become a part of the exhibit for future diners. All visitors receive an exhibition booklet which adds informational context to the activities. The booklet seeks to make material more approachable through the use of imagery and typography.

DIET TEXTURE MODIFICATION

Modifying the natural texture of foods and liquids is a commonly employed tactic to improve swallow safety and efficiency. Recommendations consist of a solid and liquid texture. Specific texture recommendations are based upon the aspects of the swallow that are impaired.

SOLIDS:

Food that is softer and easier to chew can help individuals compensate for difficulty chewing and difficulty propelling the food toward the throat for swallowing.

Softer textures may also decrease the amount of food residue remaining in the mouth and throat after the swallow (which can ultimately fall into the airway, a phenomenon known as aspiration).

Most foods can be puréed, chopped, ground, and/or mixed with sauce or gravy to adhere to the recommended texture.

LIQUIDS:

Artificially thickened liquids (liquids with greater viscosity than normal) facilitate slower movement from the mouth to the throat, which can help individuals compensate for impaired timing of the swallow or for difficulty controlling liquids. In some cases, this may prevent aspiration and make swallowing safer.

Images courtesy of Virginia Department of Behavioral Health & Developmental Sciences

TRAVEL MEMORIES
Annachiara Maffezzoli

Travel Memories is a collection of publications that value my experience of family with human connection as the main focus within the travel narratives. Against the backdrop of having the convenience of taking photographs with our phones and amassing huge amounts of images we can access at our fingertips, it is wonderful to recall experiences from the past and memorialize and curate them in the analog medium of a concrete book.

This project intentionally questions the contemporary method of archiving memories, particularly how we consider which are relevant and memorable and what we do to relive them. Through the years, we have shot thousands of photos with several devices and find ourselves with a confusing, chaotic, and mixed number of photos that sit in our devices. Each travel narrative is a selection, categorization and pairing of many photographic memories that honor the warm kindness, stunning views, and unique cultures that can only be seen though the eyes of a conscious traveler. These publications show gratitude toward the open-minded eyes that my family taught me to travel with and at the same time, enhances the light-hearted action of experiencing the world.

MANDALA : THE SACRED CIRCLE
Nittika Mehra

Mandalas are a cornerstone of Hindu and Buddhist culture. There is more to mandalas than what meets the eye. For this project, I decided to reveal its deeper meanings starting with designing a biographical mandala that represents my personality and life philosophy. I then made a 3D model of an informative and interactive Tibetan mandala. One can travel through this mandala while experiencing each of its rings before reaching the center of the mandala that represents completing the symbolic circle of life. Lastly, I created an educational book on mandalas for beginners and anyone interested in knowing more about them.

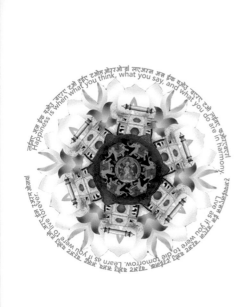

→ nittikamehra.com/portfolio
→ nittikamehra.com

BREEZE ELECTRIC SCOOTERS
Grace Mueller

Breeze Electric Scooters is a fictitious company that is riding the wave of micro-mobility and electric transportation. For this brand experience project, I created the image and wordmarks to define the brand as a fast, fun and portable alternative to current transportation methods. My brand statement is: "Breeze is committed to the manufacture and sale of sustainable electric scooters that will help reduce the need for gas-powered vehicles on our roadways. We believe that every electric scooter we sell will help transform today's gridlock into tomorrow's open road. Go Forward with Breeze."

The typeface chosen for the word mark is Changling Neo Regular. The geometric counters and squared edges provide an industrial quality to the mark. This font is unicase to allow for a variety of combinations. The look is bold and modern to match the Breeze brand. The supporting typefaces complement the wordmark. Basic Gothic Pro Extra Light and Bold are used for the text and Agency Extended and Condensed are used for callouts and headings. The colors and graphics reflect the signs and colors of city roadways, presenting a modern, bold and urban image appealing to a young, urban audience. The imagery for the brand includes photos of cities and suburban streets with cars, pedestrians, and people riding a Breeze showcasing the benefits of Breeze Scooters.

E-SCOOTERS FAST/FUN/PORTABLE

PLACES TO SIT
Denise Mylonakis

Places to Sit is a lovingly curated collection of public city benches. Made for the people by the people, each city bench is a blueprint of those who made it, where it's located, and the people who sit on it. The project was inspired by Montreal's bench variety, extended to New York's historical benches, and finally to Central Park's Adopt-a-bench program. Places to Sit lives on the web and features illustration, photography, motion graphics, augmented reality, and tactile physical elements that have been 3D printed or laser cut into thin pieces of birchwood. By looking at the city's often overlooked public seating and using it as a lens of study, one can better understand the history, people and ultimately, the human experience.

INSECTA REBRANDING
Daniela Pollandt

Sustainability is a concept that focuses on the needs of today without compromising future generations and their needs. Insecta is a rebranding of a Peruvian sustainable vegan fashion brand—inspired by Amazonian insects—that aims to prevent the torture and killing of animals for their fur or skin. Insecta uses materials like pineapple vegetable leather and shiringa vegetable leather to create products ranging from purses to shoes. The visual language is inspired by the colors and patterns of Amazonian insects. After all, as David Attenborough said, "nature is our biggest ally and our greatest inspiration."

MIXED
Rafia Rehman

Identity is not always as concrete as we strive for it to be. Day-to-day we are faced with the notion of defining who we are, but the path is never linear. We try to make sense of life by placing what is around us in categories of things akin. But what happens when we feel like we do not fit into a certain category? Being of multiracial descent can often lead to a blurred sense of identity from a young age. Mixed is a curation of short stories and fearless quotes surrounding the struggle of facing these adversities and finding where we fit. I created Mixed for those out there like me who are trying to find their place to show others and myself that we belong. As human beings we are many things, but the last thing we are is alone.

FALL (OF THE BOURGOISE) 2020
LOOK BOOK
        Caitlin Reilly

This is inspired by Gucci Men's
Cruise 2020 lookbook art directed
by Yorgos Lanthimos and the 90's
teen magazines and catalogues I
grew up with, this is a lookbook for
the New York thrift store,
Beacon's Closet.

→ caitlindesigns.cargo.site/Fall-of-the-Bourgoise-2020-Lookbook
→ caitlindesigns.cargo.site

TALES FROM THE ARCHIPELAGO
Nikki Roxas

Tales from the Archipelago is a print publication that aims to bring together the narratives and experiences of young Filipinos as they try to navigate through a new environment and culture in the United States. One can say that finding a community is not always easy. With the thousands of other Filipinos who move to the US each year for various purposes, how are

they able to foster their own communities?

For this publication, I drew heavily from my lived experiences as a Filipina who moved to a new and foreign city. I gathered narratives from people who have similar experiences and shared in the struggles and triumphs that comes with moving to the US: the homesickness, the feeling of displacement, and the newfound sense of independence. These people include those I am close to, those I have just met here in the

US, and even those who I have never met. All together, these people who come from different backgrounds form this archipelago of stories all housed within this publication.

I hope that with Tales from the Archipelago, readers will be able to identify with the different narratives, know that there will always be a Filipino community out there, and that home is never too far away.

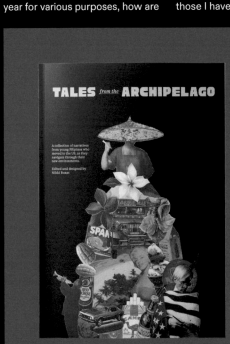

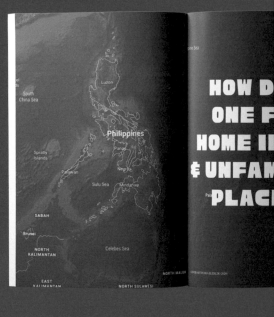

→ issuu.com/nikkiroxas/docs/talesfromthearchipelago_issuu
→ nikkiroxas.com

A. IS THAT YOU? B. CHOOSE
Brooke Shapiro

Pants or shorts? Blue or green? Polyester or wool? Does this match? Or not? White chocolate or dark chocolate? Croissant or granola? Too much or too little? Walk or bus? Soft or firm? Quiet or speak? Simple or complex? Acceptable or unacceptable? Run or bike? Gym or lounge? Book or movie? Keep or purge? Broccoli or bacon? Sedan or sports car? Stay or go? Spend or save? Text or call? Listen or ignore? Music or podcast? Today or tomorrow? Beach or mountains? Rent or buy? 10% vs. 25%? Quantity or quality? Accept or reject? Joint or separate? Proceed or think again? End or continue?

How does the environment around us influence our choices? How do the choices we make influence who we become?

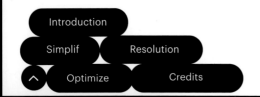

a. Is That You?
b. Choose

Introduction
Simplif
Resolution
Optimize
Credits

Sleep in or Wake up Early?
Coffee or Tea?
Plastic or Biodegradable?
Easy or Challenging?
Less or more?
Just enough or too much?
Light or Dark?
Leather or Vinyl?
Bike or walk?
Larger or smaller?
Now or Later?
Quality or Quantity?
Buy or Sell?
Graduate School or New job?
Downsize or Maintain?
Los Angeles or London?

→ readymag.com/u2600349043/2806043
→ brookearden.design

MANLINESS
Julia Sullivan

Manliness addresses men's mental health and vulnerability. From a young age, boys are taught through societal norms to push away their feelings and neglect their mental health which ultimately leads to negative consequences later in life. I created an exhibit with multiple spaces each focusing on an ideology around masculinity. I used materials, objects, and colors that have been perceived as unmasculine to design my exhibit. For example, visitors would use tissues and pink post-it notes to write their responses to the reflection questions asked in each space. The goal is to break down masculine norms we teach men from a young age and form new ways to approach men's mental health.

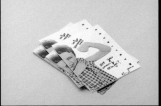

LIMINAL.
Jennifer Wang

Liminal is small-format architecture and design zine publication for art and design enthusiasts. It is a publication that explores the evocative relationship between people and design inspired by the concept of liminality, the transformative potential of the in-between. The inaugural issue is a curated collection of thought-provoking designs that use color, form, and context in ways that expand beyond tradition in these disciplines. Each issue is designed to invite readers into the photography to transport them to places beyond the pages.

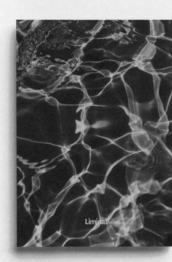

Program Leadership

Director, BFA Communication Design
Caspar Lam

Associate Director, BFA Communication Design
Kelly Walters

Director, MPS Communication Design
Brendan Griffiths

Director, AAS Communication Design
Pascal Glissmann

Program Leadership

Executive Dean, Parsons School of Design
Rachel Schreiber

Dean, School of Art, Media & Technology
Shana Agid

Associate Dean, School of Art, Media & Technology
Nadia Williams

Staff

Program Administrator
Geo Borden

Student Advisors
Aisha Abdelmula, Roy Cohen

Manager of Part-Time Faculty Affairs
Yasi Ghanbari

Design Lab Manager
Joe Hirsch

Student Assistants

Jacob Berstein, Rebecca Greubel, Caleb Hall,
Defne Kaynak, Sophia Kee, Claire Zhang

With Special Thanks to

Mari Al-Midhadi, Katie Brown, Regina La O',
Mohammed Labban, Sofia Moon

Full-time Faculty

Juliette Cezzar
Associate Professor of Communication Design

Brendan Griffiths
Assistant Professor of Interaction Design

E Roon Kang
Assistant Professor of Interaction Design

Lynn Kiang
Assistant Professor of Communication Design

Caspar Lam
Assistant Professor of Communication Design

Pascal Glissmann
Associate Professor of Communication Design

Julia Gorton
Assistant Professor of Communication Design
(Retired in 2020)

YuJune Park
Assistant Professor of Communication Design

Lucille Tenazas
Henry Wolf Professor of Communication Design

Kelly Walters
Assistant Professor of Communication Design

CORE COURSES OFFERED

BFA Communication Design

PUCD 2025 CORE 1: TYPOGRAPHY STUDIO, Fall
Typography is language made visible. This first-semester Sophomore requirement introduces students to the history and current practice of type in all areas of communication design: from the simplest publication to the most advanced screen-based interactive media. Students will learn to see, understand, and manipulate the visual aspect of language as a powerful communicative tool. This class will teach students an understanding of the properties of typefaces, their context and how typography helps readers read and navigate a text. The class will investigate letterform structure and type classification systems, typographic terminology, history of type and printing, principles of spacing, use of typographic contrast in composition, legibility, hierarchy, and typographic form as a tool for expression and communication.

PUCD 2026 CORE 1: TYPOGRAPHY LECTURE, Fall
This lab course works closely with Core 1: Typography Studio to supplement and expand the analytical and critical work in the studio. The lecture focuses on building technical and practical skills towards a fluency in setting and manipulating type within a contemporary digital environment, as well as introducing type history and the foundational typographic concepts shaped by it. Students will understand and use fonts and typesetting software to create and analyze typographic prototypes for both print and screen.

PUCD 2035 CORE 1: INTERACTION, Fall
Core 1: Interaction is designed to introduce students to programming as a creative medium—as a way of making and exploring. The coursework focuses on developing a vocabulary of interaction design principles which can then be applied across a range of platforms. Students are encouraged to experiment with various media, tools, and techniques, ultimately producing a portfolio of interactive and visual projects designed for the screen. An emphasis is placed on typography as it applies to a screen context, research-based problem solving and a learning-through-making approach to technical skill building. Historical and current interaction design precedents will be discussed.

PUCD 2130 CORE 2: TYPOGRAPHY, Spring
This second-semester Sophomore requirement teaches students to be critical users of type. Expanding upon concepts introduced in Core 1: Typography, students will develop more sophisticated techniques for working with texts in multiple formats and contexts. By exploring and discussing historical and contemporary theory related to typography and design, students will also begin to contextualize and apply critical thinking to their own work.

PUCD 2125 CORE 2: INTERACTION STUDIO, Spring
This course exposes students to thorough and elaborate interactive concepts and techniques for applications. It is an extensive investigation in the interface, the mechanism, the controls and the aims of interactive works. Students will learn how to design and develop complex interactive projects and understand how to undertake comprehensive research and direct their thinking process from brainstorming to the final outcome. They will be given the tools to conceive, plan and develop an interactive system and they will become aware of the importance of their role in the development of interactive media.

PUCD 2126 CORE 2: INTERACTION LAB, Spring
This course serves as a complement to Core Studio Interaction. The assignments are built to work in tandem with the projects students are developing in the studio class. The lab is designed around a series of small workshops that teach beginning and intermediate interaction design through a hands-on engagement with HTML and CSS.

PUCD 3095 CORE 3: TOPICS, Fall
This advanced required studio is focused on designing across disciplines within design. Students will apply knowledge of typography and interaction within a specific context in communication design. The first half of the semester will consist of workshops around principles and case studies in multiple interconnected areas, including digital product design, editorial design, design for branding, type design, and motion design, in addition to deeper study of one of these areas within the section. In the second half of the semester, students will develop a larger independent project within a single contextual area, led by their section faculty, demonstrating what they have learned in the first half of the semester across all topics.

PUCD 3060 CURRENTS: CD WORKSHOP, Fall/Spring
This course consists of a series of three workshops, each explore contemporary positions in Communication Design, taught by specialists and working professionals from industry. Each workshop is 5 weeks long and examines a specific topic in detail. Topics of the individual workshops will be posted as they become available. Past workshop topics include a survey of visual culture of 2010s, voice commands and interfaces, generative identity systems, speculative platforms, typography in and out of buildings, and what makes a bad design. Students are expected to engage in all three workshops and must be present for the duration of the semester. Depending on the nature of the collaboration the course might offer a series of smaller assignments or one larger project.

PUCD 3060 CURRENTS: A-GENERATIVE-WEB, Spring
In this course, students will use the generative nature of the web as a medium to shape projects both on and offline. We will practice and analyze using code-frameworks / apis / data to create form, enable performance and encourage social dialogue. Students will adopt a generative mindset: to create rulesets that interact with context(s) to produce an array of outcomes rather than fixed ones. Students will study generative works and theory by evaluating past/present graphic design, modern art movements, experimental writing, procedural architecture, new media art and commercial technology. Projects in this course will start with code, but the final output can live in print, online, in a physical space or as a performance.

PUCD 3060 CURRENTS: BLACK VISUAL CULTURE, Spring
Through a close historical analysis of branding systems, set design, fashion, language and character construction, students will investigate the manner in which Black and African-American identities appear in popular film, television and music. We will compare the visual complexities surrounding cultural representations in shows such as: The Jeffersons, A Different World, The Fresh Prince of Bel Air, Insecure and Lovecraft Country, while also identifying their significance in mainstream culture. We will unpack the ways popular media can guide our visual and material choices and provide a basis for our conceptual thinking and social critique in relation to people, places and objects. In this hands-on-studio course, students will investigate the history of imagery, typography, color and pattern displayed in Black visual culture. Students will be encouraged to develop work across media and explore new tools, methods, and techniques in the creation of digital and print-based responses. As we proceed throughout the semester, we will explore the following questions: What are the photographic and illustrative depictions of Blackness? What is African American vernacular? What are the differences in sitcoms versus serious dramas? How can sound be used to reinforce aspects of representation? What is our understanding of Black identities?

PUCD 3060 CURRENTS: MEMORY AS PRACTICE, Spring
This course looks at the ways that memory and histories are constructed as deliberate experiences through interventions in the archive. We explore how graphic and narrative devices are harnessed to both illuminate and obscure parts of the archive. We look at questions of access and opacity, and press against the notion of the archive as an objective entity. Specifically, this course focuses on two mediums: moving image and interactivity, looking at how the combination of these two subjects can be a potent tool for dynamic storytelling that engages the audience in critical issues such as alternative histories. Primarily, this course will use various video archives, moving from the personal to the collective, as source material for students to explore working in immersive digital storytelling. Students will learn to build their own collections and work with existing archives found in the library or online. At the end of the course, students are exposed to the different processes involved in the creation, reproduction, and distribution of digital content online, responsive design and interactive behaviors. The course encourages students to think about how to combine storytelling, moving image, motion, and interactivity in a design system. Students will learn to identify and integrate interactivity and storytelling to execute immersive design solutions.

PUCD 3060 CURRENTS: DESIGN WITH ARCHIVES, Spring
Archives, collection of documents and records, reveal the history and stories behind certain subjects. In this course students will utilize the archive as inspiration for their design work. Students will work with existing historic and cultural archives (public libraries, museums, publications, social media platforms) as well as create their own archives. The class will explore how the circumstance of time and memory affects the way personal/historical information is perceived today. Class projects will touch on ideas of translation, memory, and open source design. Students are encouraged to experiment as well as work collaboratively with other artists/writers/designers. Through in-class discussions, guest speakers, readings and studio work students will gain an understanding of the importance of the archive while also questioning its role today.

PUCD 3060 CURRENTS: CONTEXT=1/2 THE WORK, Spring
Why does your work look the way that it does? This seemingly basic, yet difficult and often overlooked question will form the base of a collective inquiry which will take multiple forms, principally, a semester-long discussion of how meaning is made through form in graphic design. We will operate from the basic premise that your formal expression as a designer or artist is an outcome of your positionality as a person. This class will seek to function as a parenthesis from your normal modes of production, asking that you pause briefly to step back and reflect critically on the relation of form to content in your own work. The class is intended as thesis preparation for third year students, but will be of value to any student with an interest in history, research, and the making of self-initiated work.

PUCD 3050 COLLAB: DESIGN FOR LITERACY, Spring
This course is intended to integrate the design skills and point of view of students in order to create a product line of re-imagined classic books and market those products on behalf of a social enterprise in their efforts to raise money for a literacy charity. Students will work with the social enterprise, DERT, as contributing designers and will redesign select classic works of literature into marketable on-demand books that are activated as fundraising products. The class will work with DERT to re-design adult and kids classics which will target select audiences who's interested in making meaningful purchases that both enhance their lives while making contributing to a social cause. DERT will donate all profits from its books sales to its literacy partner, The Parent-Child Home Program (PCHP). With over 50 years of proven success, PCHP is dedicated to ensuring that low-income children have access to books, and has the opportunity to enter school ready for success. DERT will work with PCHP and its sponsor, The Reader's Digest Foundation, to market the book products to its various audiences. Team members from PCHP and Reader's Digest will be active in the classes development of their book products, participating in class presentations and critique reviews. Beyond students work in designing book products, the class will focus on research, process, concepting, design execution, teamwork and presentation skills. Although not required, a space for an end of class exhibit would be an added benefit to the class.

PUCD 3050 COLLAB: FUTURE OF PUBLISHING, Spring
This course is specifically designed to bring together two types of students: 1) those who have a background in critical reading and writing but no extensive experience in design and 2) those who have a background in design but no extensive experience in writing and publishing. We will begin with a critical survey of the transmission of written communication from Gutenberg to the present to get up to speed, and in the second half of the semester we will discuss contemporary issues that cross design and publishing through an analysis of contemporary books, magazines, and periodicals across both printed and digital platforms, with a particular focus on the relationship between form and content. The seminar will be the underpinning of a hands-on studio course, where students will get a working introduction to typography, image, layout, sequence, and order, with the aim to design and publish in interdisciplinary teams, both printed and digital, by the end of the semester.

PUCD 4205 CORE 4: SENIOR THESIS 1, Fall
Thesis 1 & Thesis 2 are year-long self-driven investigations into the research, prototyping and design of an identified question, critique, or point of view. It provides an opportunity for design innovation and inquiry through the rigorous research and development of a capstone project, through various pathways across platforms. The goal of the first semester is to research, develop and articulate a thesis concept and create experimental prototypes, including designed presentations of research and process. Thesis 1, in particular, focuses on process, which includes primary and secondary research, ideation, prototyping, documenting and writing about one's own work. Students will be asked to reflect on how their ideas—as expressed through design—sits alongside historical precedent and shapes culture in the present. It provides an opportunity for visual innovation through the development of a rigorous design process. This includes articulation of research, which contextualizes how one's work posits itself within larger historical, cultural, social, and technological frameworks. The semester culminates in two finished projects, a written reflection statement, and presentation of work to guest critics.

PUCD 4210 CORE 5: SENIOR THESIS 2, Spring
Thesis 1 & Thesis 2 are year-long self-driven investigations into the research, prototyping and design of an identified question, critique, or point of view. It provides an opportunity for design innovation and inquiry through the rigorous research and development of a capstone project, through various pathways across platforms. The goal of the first semester is to research, develop and articulate a thesis concept and create experimental prototypes, including designed presentations of research and process. Thesis 1, in particular, focuses on process, which includes primary and secondary research, ideation, prototyping, documenting and writing about one's own work. Students will be asked to reflect on how their ideas—as expressed through design—sits alongside historical precedent and shapes culture in the present. It provides an opportunity for visual innovation through the development of a rigorous design process. This includes articulation of research, which contextualizes how one's work posits itself within larger historical, cultural, social, and technological frameworks. The semester culminates in two finished projects, a written reflection statement, and presentation of work to guest critics.

MPS Communication Design

PMCD 5001 TYPOGRAPHY & INTERACTION 1, Fall
This course teaches students intermediate and advanced methods in typography and interactive design to successfully meet the ever changing challenges of designing and prototyping successful products and services for screens. These comprehensive methods will also support students to complete their projects in other studio classes. Students will learn how to address design problems meaningfully within the context of current design practices, while working towards developing an individualized working methodology. Students will also become familiar with the process of transforming an idea into a functional design by making use of basic web technologies. They will use their newly acquired design vocabulary to critique and critically discuss work produced by themselves and others.

PMCD 5100 MAJOR STUDIO 1, Fall
In this course we will examine the fundamentals of digital product design, including user research techniques, production methods for interactive applications, wireframing, and prototyping. We will investigate the interface, mechanism, controls, and aims of digital platforms. Students will learn how to design and develop complex digital products and mobile applications as they undertake comprehensive research to direct their thinking process from brainstorming to final outcome. Students will utilize tools to conceive, plan, and develop an interactive system, and they will become well versed in their role within the development of interactive media. The course expands on students' existing understanding of programming languages used for digital prototyping.

PMCD 5200 VISUAL CULTURE SEMINAR, Fall
In this seminar we will explore contemporary positions in communication design and discuss its future places in society and industry. The course is an exercise in critical thinking to understand the transformed and expanded nature of globalized visual culture in the 21st century and how design has shifted. Through panel discussions, lectures, and workshops led by industry leaders, researchers, and New School faculty, students will be invited to discuss the cultural landscape of communication design and understand its practices and contemporary working methods. Topics include: counterculture, service design, designer as author, digital craft, social justice and visual narratives, digital storytelling, and digital product design. The diversity of visiting professionals will promote critical interaction with opposing viewpoints as well as provide networking opportunities for students. Students will collaborate in groups to write an essay inflected by one of the lectures or panel discussions that will be published as a microsite.

PMCD 5002 TYPOGRAPHY & INTERACTION 2, Spring
In this course we will build upon knowledge of dynamic content and interactivity by addressing advanced typographic strategies and interactive skills oriented towards publishing and archiving. Sessions will focus on methods relevant to digital production, including content management systems, databases, and responsive workflows. Students will apply their understanding of typography and interaction principles to design screen-based projects from start to finish. This course culminates in a functional portfolio site critically informed by students' design practice and developed in tandem with the Methods & Practices class.

PMCD 5102 MAJOR STUDIO 2, Spring
In this course we will expand on the fundamentals taught in Major Studio 1: Digital Product Design, with an emphasis on integrative user research, advanced prototyping techniques, iterative working methodologies, and development of applications across platforms. Students will learn to identify and solve design problems within digital products, creating systems which engage a variety of outputs, from screens and touch devices to voice control and beyond. The course provides students with an opportunity to acquire the advanced resources, skills, and hands-on experience they need to ideate, design, and evaluate interfaces from a user-centered design perspective. Emphasis is placed on the development of functional interactive prototypes built using contemporary methodologies.

PMCD 5300 METHODS & PRACTICES, Spring
In this course we will explore contemporary working methods and models for communication designers with a focus on digital product design. Students will be exposed to a wide variety of practice models via a series of guest lectures, workshops, and presentations from independent small studios to in-house creative teams and large agencies. As the discipline of design expands, this course attempts to chart novel and alternative working contexts within the industry. Students will discuss professional working processes which include but are not limited to: business communication best practices, business plans, marketing and promotion, bidding, ethics, copyright, editing and packaging work for delivery, and networking.

AAS Communication Design

PACD 1100 CORE 1: TYPOGRAPHY, Fall/Spring
Typography is language made visible. In this course, students will be introduced to the history and current practice of type in various areas of communication design. Students will learn to see, understand, and manipulate the visual aspect of language as a powerful communicative tool. In this course, students will acquire an understanding of the properties of typefaces, their context and how typography helps readers read and navigate a text. Students will investigate letterform structure and type classification systems, typographic terminology, history of type and printing, principles of spacing, use of typographic contrast in composition, legibility, hierarchy, and typographic form as a tool for expression and communication. The course is complemented by Core 1: Interaction. Students will be expected to apply lessons learned from interaction to their type assignments and vice versa in order to form a working method which will be explored further in Core 2 Typography & Interaction.

PACD 1100 CORE 1: INTERACTION, Fall/Spring
This course serves as an introduction to interaction design and prototyping for a web context. Students will undertake projects which cover planning and implementation of web-based projects with a focus on typography, narrative, and experimentation with an interactive screen-based medium. Core 1: Interaction revolves around a series of projects which are conceptualized, wireframed and implemented using both prototyping software and basic HTML, CSS, and Javascript. Students will learn how to design and develop complex interactive projects from initial brainstorming to comprehensive research and final execution. The class will consist of exercises and long-form projects which allow students to develop concepts, ideas, and strategies for web-based projects. The class will be supplemented by lectures, readings, student-led group discussions, and critical writing to reinforce core concepts. The course is complemented by Core 1: Typography. Students will be expected to apply lessons learned from type to their interaction assignments and vice versa in order to form a working method which will be explored further in Core 2: Typography & Interaction.

PACD 1010 DESIGN HISTORY & PRACTICE, Fall/Spring
This class exposes students to significant and great design from the history of visual communications, focusing on the 20th Century. It is not meant to be exhaustive, but provides a foundation of understanding communication design as it exists today. Students will look closely at formal relationships within historical designs and respond in original designs of their own. The class combines lectures, which require additional visual research and reading outside of class, with active making as students will have to design responses to prominent figures and historic moments of the disciplines. Students will also experience basic introductions to color theory and elements and principles of design.

PACD 1200 CORE 2: TYPE & INTERACTION, Fall/Spring
Building upon the Typography and Interaction Core Studios, this course teaches students intermediate and advanced methods in Typography and Interaction Design to successfully meet the challenges of dynamic content in print and on the web. Students will learn how to address design problems meaningfully within the context of current design practice, technology frameworks and how individual processes and methodologies influence a design outcome. In particular, students will explore how an idea can be expressed and modulated across different mediums and how to create flexible design systems that can produce such expression. They will use their newly acquired design vocabulary to critique and critically discuss work produced by themselves and others. Reading and writing will also form an important component of these discussions, as well. The course is the final sequence of the typography/interaction core classes. Methods and concepts taught in these classes will be used as the foundation for all Core 3 courses.

PACD 1500 PROFESSIONAL PRACTICES & PORTFOLIO, Fall/Spring
This course will help students build and refine their portfolios to a professional level and learn the process of preparing for life after school. Students will learn best practices in all aspects of professional work. Students will be challenged to use all their knowledge in the domains of typography and interaction to present work in an articulate manner both in print and online, culminating in the development of a professional portfolio website that builds upon their previous work and interests. The research and investigations undertaken as a part of the portfolio process will help prepare students for Core 3 Capstone.

PACD 2100 CORE 3: CAPSTONE, Fall/Spring
The capstone course is a self-driven investigation into the research, prototyping, and design of an identified question, critique, or point of view. It provides an opportunity for design innovation and inquiry through the rigorous research and development of a thesis project through various pathways across platforms. This class also offers the opportunity to apply previous life experience and academic capacities to the methods and processes of communication design. It will utilize and build upon concepts learned in previous core classes as well as explore individual pathways generated by the Core 3 Professional Practice and Portfolio course. The goal of the first half of the semester is to research, develop and articulate a thesis concept and create prototypes, including designed presentations of research and process. During the second part of this class, emphasis is placed on the students' ability to translate their cumulative knowledge into effective visual communication. Students will develop a competence in cross media design processes and understand the nature of all available communication channels in the creative industries. The senior studies are initiated by topics and not by media or technology.

BFA CD Thesis Faculty

Luke Bulman
Owner, Office of Luke Bulman

Ingrid Chou
Creative Director, The Museum of Modern Art

Dinah Fried
Partner, Small Stuff

Tom Griffiths
Owner, Everything Studio

E Roon Kang
Assistant Professor of Interaction Design,
Parsons School of Design

Caspar Lam
Assistant Professor of Communication Design,
Parsons School of Design

Andrew LeClair
Independent

Prin Limphongpand
Senior Designer, The Museum of Modern Art

Joe Marianek
Partner, Small Stuff

Kelly Walters
Assistant Professor of Communication Design,
Parsons School of Design

AAS CD Capstone Faculty

Christine Moog
Founder, Little Spoons Inc.

Lucille Tenazas
Henry Wolf Professor of Communication Design,
Parsons School of Design

MPS CD Thesis Critics

Atif Akin
Associate Professor, Rutgers University

Jason Alejandro
Assistant Professor of Graphic Design,
The College of New Jersey

Robin Andersen
Product Designer, Dropbox

Sophie Auger
Part-Time Lecturer, Rutgers University

Anne Berry
Assistant Professor, Cleveland State University

Jamar Bromley
Senior Graphic Designer, Samsung

John Caserta
Associate Professor, Rhode Island School of Design

James Chae
Assistant Professor, Hongik University

Flora Chan
Associate Design DIrector, Red Scout

Abby Chen
Designer, The Metropolitan Museum of Art

Hyung Cho
Independent

Glen Cummings
Founding Partner, MTWTF

Meaghan Dee
Associate Professor, Virginia Tech

Tony Dunne
University Professor of Design and Social Inquiry,
The New School

Minsun Eo
Faculty in Graphic Design, Maryland Institute College of Art

Greg Gazdowicz
Typeface Designer, Commercial Type

Barbara Glauber
Creative Director, Heavy Meta

Elizabeth Goodspeed
Independent

Dylan Greif
Head of User Experience, Bloomberg

Peter Hall
Course Leader, BA Graphic Communication Design,
Central Saint Martins

Tori Hinn
Human Interface Designer, Apple

Lucinda Hitchcock
Professor, Rhode Island School of Design

Hanah Ho
Senior Art Director, The New York Times

Eric Hu
Independent

Gaia Hwang
Assistant Professor, Pratt Institute

Moon Jung Jang
Associate Professor, Area Chair for Graphic Design,
University of Georgia

Bo-Won Keum
Associate Designer, Triple Canopy

Meena Khalili
Assistant Professor, University of South Carolina

Anoushka Khandwala
Independent

Minkyung Kim
Assistant Professor, Rhode Island School of Design

David Klein
Senior Graphic Designer, The Museum of Modern Art

Penina Acayo Laker
Assistant Professor, Communication Design,
Washington University in St. Louis

Briar Levit
Associate Professor, Portland State University

Min Lew
Partner, Base Design

Elaine Lopez
Faculty in Graphic Design, Maryland Institute College of Art

Manuel Miranda
Owner, MMP

Elliott Montgomery
Assistant Professor of Strategic Design and Management,
Parsons School of Design

Shem Rajoon
Manager, 15Five

Anna Rieger
Design Manager, The Metropolitan Museum of Art

Juan Carlos Rodriguez Rivera
Assistant Professor, California College of the Arts

Chris Ro
Assistant Professor, Hongik University

Rebecca Ross
Programme Director, Graphic Communication Design,
Central Saint Martins

Louise Sandhaus
Faculty, California Institute of the Arts

Mindy Seu
Assistant Professor, Rutgers University

Andrew Shea
Assistant Professor of Integrated Design,
Parsons School of Design

Emily Smith
Professor, Programme Director Media Spaces MA,
University of Europe for Applied Sciences

Paul Soulellis
Associate Professor, Rhode Island School of Design

Jin Jin Sun
Senior Experience Designer, Adobe

Mariko Takagi
Associate Professor, Typography & Book Design,
Doshisha Women's College of Liberal Arts

Ramon Tejada
Assistant Professor, Rhode Island School of Design

Carolyn Thomas
Independent

Ka-Man Tse
Assistant Professor of Photography,
Parsons School of Design

Rich Tu
Vice President of Digital Design, MTV

Karen Vanderbilt
Senior Visual Designer, Local Projects

Federico Villoro
Independent

Cap Watkins
Chief Experience Officer, Primary

Ida Woldemichael
Associate Creative Director, Wide Eye

Chris Wu
Partner, Wkshps

Xin Xin
Assistant Professor of Interaction and Media Design,
Parsons School of Design

MPS CD Thesis Critics

Sean Adams
Chair, Undergraduate and Graduate Graphic Design,
ArtCenter College of Design

Talia Cotton
Designer, Pentagram

Keetra Dean Dixon
Independent

Tony Dunne
University Professor of Design and Social Inquiry,
The New School

Victoria Duong
Interaction Designer, Frog

Kate Leisy
Art Director, Allbirds

Hoshi Ludwig
Product Design Lead, Instagram

Sigi Moeslinger
Owner, Antenna Design New York

Wael Morcos
Partner, Morcos Key

Igal Nassima
Founder, Superbright

Fiona Raby
University Professor of Design and Social Inquiry,
The New School

Masamichi Udagawa
Owner, Antenna Design New York

Travis Weber
Design Lead, Haus

AAS CD Thesis Critics

Barbara Glauber
Creative Director, Heavy Meta

Allen Hori
Principal, Bates Hori

Lisa Naftolin
Independent

Eric Price
Senior Designer, Wkshps

Anna Rieger
Design Manager, The Metropolitan Museum of Art

Louise Sandhaus
Faculty, California Institute of the Arts

Chris Wu
Partner, Wkshps

Cornell Tech	
2020–21	Rachel Chang, Calen Chung, Trudy Hoang, Charlotte Lomas, Sanjana Navar, Chanjoo Park, Jiayi Xu

Selected Communication Design students have a unique opportunity to participate in a year-long Startup Studio at Cornell Tech. Participants are placed in multidisciplinary teams comprised of the school's engineering and business graduate students to develop and build a vision for a digital product.

CD Tutors	
Spring 2021	Elliot Bohlen, Nico Chilla, Shreya Chittaranjan, Miranda Elder, Trudy Hoang, McKayla K Lankau, Scarlet Li, Ricky Xie, Irene Xu
Fall 2020	Vlora Bajrushi, Nico Chilla, Shreya Chittaranjan, Miranda Elder, Trudy Hoang, Scarlet Li, Haiqingqing Qi, Duncan Williams

Communication Design Tutors are positions awarded to students who demonstrate a commitment to helping their peers build a culture of making and excellence by providing design and code guidance.

Lance Wyman Scholars	
2020–21	Program suspended due to COVID-19
2019–20	Elliot Bohlen, Minxi Chen, Calen Chung, Juriel Furukawa, Peiru Guo, Connie Xu, Wenpei Wang

The Communication Design Faculty honors select junior Communication Design students who have demonstrated an exceptional body of work and a developing sense of creative agency. These students are named Lance Wyman Scholars. Members have the opportunity to engage with faculty and expert designers and interact with like-minded peers in an informal setting to challenge one another to become better makers and community leaders.

Lance Wyman (B.1937, Newark, NJ, USA) is a graphic designer specializing in systems for cities, events, institutions and transit systems. Over the past 5 decades he has helped to define the field of environmental graphics. His graphic design for the 1968 Mexico Olympics identity is widely celebrated as a pinnacle of environmental and branding design. He teaches corporate and wayfinding design at Parsons where he has been a visiting lecturer since 1973.

A PROMISE

Caspar Lam

The impact of Communication Design on contemporary life is so broad and pervasive that its distinctiveness as a discipline has been periodically called into question. The debates over the name of the program at Parsons hints at an anxiety mirrored in the wider profession where faddish terms are unloaded onto an unsuspecting public. With increasingly short expiry dates, today's design thinker or UX/UI designer will and already has joined the webmaster and the type director of yesteryear. But designers are excellent at holding things in tension. What we may call ourselves and what we materially do may all be part of the semantic play of design.

Each successive technological development has resulted in designers adapting to new materials and new methods of production—and hence, new vocabulary—that allow for the dissemination of ideas. The clichéd notion of the democratization of design rendering the designer's role obsolete obscures the reality that designers simply have shifted their operational context. Behind the sophisticated templates and clever filters are the platformed technologies that have been meticulously burnished by designers who now work one step removed from the final artifact while continuing to rely on a deep material knowledge of type and interaction. Interestingly, the precedence for this way of working has been built into the typographic foundations of Communication Design itself. That the very idea of typecasting of visual elements and higher order of practice has now been applied to design as a whole should not be entirely surprising.

While the changes of technology and their cascading effect on design is not a new problem for designers, what is new is the shifting cultural context of making. What has made the Communication Design community at Parsons so unique is the plurality that has organically grown and has been sustained by both the international character of the students that choose to study here as well as the diversity of design practices of the instructors. This plurality is grounded in an idea of friendship and is the key to addressing one of the most pressing questions facing designers today: designing in a fluid, global context.

In looking at the entire ecosystem of design and the many habitats where one could practice, we can generalize two types of designers: those that work in traditional contexts and those that work in the spaces in-between. For designers practicing in traditional contexts, established ways of making give rise to distinct hermeneutics while designers negotiating liminal spaces develop strategies to adapt and translate. Both are vital for the ecosystem of design to thrive.

Because of history and locale, the Communication Design community at Parsons sits firmly in this in-between space where the messy work of translating between materials, contexts, methods of making, and cultures takes place. There is an argument to be made that this is peculiarly American in character, but the mobility of contemporary life means that most designers will study and work in different places throughout their lives. This is certainly true of the typical Parsons student who most likely was born in one country and grew up in another before matriculation. The pandemic may have temporarily stalled such activities, but it has only accentuated how dependent many of us really are on this ability to easily move and work across boundaries.

Over the past decade, the number of incoming Communication Design students has more than doubled. The size and scale of the community has enabled a rich experience for both current and future designers to learn from one another that would not be possible in programs of much smaller scale. In short, it is this variegated experience that allows designers to find their own habitats to thrive. The continued vitality of this community is, thus, contingent on continuing to foster a place where the wonder, theory, and practice of design can flourish.

I have every confidence that it will.

Caspar Lam, Assistant Professor of Communication Design, joined Parsons in 2011 and is the Director of the BFA Communication Design Program.

ABOUT THIS BOOK
E Roon Kang and Andrew LeClair

A book is the product of an intricate patchwork of systems: from a font, with its embedded metrics and variable font axes; to a function, which calculates the arrangement of words in each line of a paragraph; to a template, which defines the repeated placement of text and images. Each of these systems is a product of design. Each was created with specific intentions in a particular historical moment and carries with it inherent cultural associations and biases.

As 908A, we propose that communication designers should focus beyond the surface appearance of things towards these underlying layers of technology. We should investigate our relationship to them and make choices that benefit us, our collaborators', and the world. This practice draws our collective critical attention to the technologies that surround us. It invites us to build new tools and share them, combine existing systems in new ways, and to challenge dominant modes of production.

Our vision for books and other complex documents are workflows that allow editors and designers to write and design in parallel and in conversation, letting the computer handle the necessary logistics. We believe that content should live in simple, interoperable data formats, rather than in complex, proprietary systems, and designers should define dynamic, networked design logics that adapt to changing content without continual manual rework.

This book is built on a lightweight set of interconnected technologies. Content is managed through a flat-file CMS, Kirby. Jarrett Fuller edited the text directly using the human-readable markup language, Markdown. Caspar Lam organized data about the program in tables that were output in a structured text format, TSV. Andrew and E Roon designed layouts using HTML and CSS that gave form to the content as it was written. The book lives as a continually updated preview on a server, which can be used to generate a PDF on-demand using a renderer, Prince.

Each of these tools have their limitations and idiosyncracies. They not only shape the process of making, but they also influence its visual output. Typographic conventions and niceties may not be upheld, even as the tool chain creates new formal possibilities. Many pages in the book are printed with a pattern that reveals the underlying, nested structure of HTML on which the book was built.

This book, at the time of publication, is a collection of 249 Markdown files, 10 templates, and 1,124 lines of CSS. It was generated from the command line in 123.25 seconds on October 21, 2021 at 2:00am.

E Roon Kang, Assistant Professor of Interaction Design, joined Parsons in 2015 and was the Director of the BFA Communication Design Program (2017-2020). Andrew LeClair is a designer in New York and Part-Time Assistant Professor at Parsons.

ACKNOWLEDGMENTS

This project would not exist without the support of the entire Communication Design community. We want to thank the faculty and staff, both past and present, the AAS, BFA, and MPS Class of 2021, and alumni for your belief in this department. In particular, we want to thank Anne Gaines who advocated tirelessly for Communication Design during her tenure as the Dean of the School of Art, Media, and Technology at Parsons.

A book of this scale and scope is a massive undertaking involving many people across design, writing, editing, and production. Thank you to Jake Anderson and ORO Editions for publishing and putting it out in the world and Frits Kouwenhoven of Hemlock Printers for his support, patience, and helping make all of this possible.

Thanks to Johannes Breyer and Fabian Harb of Dinamo, Michelle Morrison of Dropbox, and Håkon Wium Lie of Prince for sponsoring this publication through their respective organizations and for their continued support. Thanks also to our partners at Parsons: Shana Agid, André Allaire, Nadine Bourgeois, Hien Dinh, and Nadia Williams. A massive thanks to Geovanna Borden for her tireless commitment to this department and keeping us all on track.

We owe a huge debt to Anna Robinson-Sweet and Jenny Swadosh at The New School Archives and Special Collections for helping gather resources on the history of the department.

Extra thanks to Claire Zhang for her editorial assistance and attentive eye as well as our other student assistants Jacob Berstein, Rebecca Greubel, Caleb Hall, Defne Kaynak, and Sophia Kee. Additional thanks go to Mari Al-Midhadi, Katie Brown, Regina La O', Mohammed Labban, and Sofia Moon.

We extend a massive thanks to all the designers, lecturers, speakers, critics, and educators who visited our program and shared their wisdom with us over the years. Special thanks to Rachel Berger, Anil Dash, Chris Lee, Renda Morton, Mindy Seu, Andrew Shurtz, and Lynne Yun for graciously allowing us to reproduce their lectures in this publication.

As evident in the pages of this book, the department has continually sustained itself by the community of faculty and students who have remained dedicated to the project of furthering Communication Design during the last century. Our gratitude goes out to every single person who has been a part of this community and to those we have forgotten here. This book is for all of you.

COLOPHON

Published on the occasion of the ten year anniversary of the Communication Design curriculum.

The authors, editors, and Communication Design department have made every effort to secure permission to reproduce the listed materials, texts, illustrations, and photographs. We apologize for any inadvertent errors or omissions.

First published in the United States of America by ORO Editions

PRINTED IN CANADA
ISBN: 978-1-954081-51-2
First Edition

EDITOR
Jarrett Fuller

AUTHORS
Juliette Cezzar
Pascal Glissmann
Brendan Griffiths
E Roon Kang
Lynn Kiang
Caspar Lam
Andrew LeClair
YuJune Park
Lucille Tenazas
Kelly Walters

WITH
AAS, BFA, MPS Class of 2021

DIRECTORS
AAS Communication Design
Director, Pascal Glissmann

BFA Communication Design
Director, Caspar Lam
Associate Director, Kelly Walters

MPS Communication Design
Director, Brendan Griffiths

PROGRAM ADMINISTRATOR
Geo Borden

STUDENT ADVISORS
Aisha Abdelmula
Roy Cohen

EXECUTIVE DEAN
Parsons School of Design
Rachel Schreiber

DEAN
School of Art, Media, and
Technology
Shana Agid

ASSOCIATE DEAN
School of Art, Media, and
Technology
Nadia Williams

MANAGER
School of Art, Media, and
Technology
Hien Dinh

MANAGER OF PART-TIME
FACULTY AFFAIRS
Yasi Ghanbari

DESIGN LAB MANAGER
Joe Hirsch

STUDENT ASSISTANTS
Jacob Berstein
Rebecca Greubel
Caleb Hall
Defne Kaynak
Sophia Kee
Claire Zhang

DESIGN
908A
(E Roon Kang,
Andrew LeClair)

MATERIALS
Paper: Mohawk Options Vellum
Cover 100lb, Cougar Vellum Text
80lb, Pacesetter Gloss Text 80lb
Typeface: Diatype

PRINTING
Hemlock Printers
Printed in Canada

THE NEW SCHOOL
PARSONS

Hemlock

HemlockHarling

Dropbox

Prince

DINAMO

Synoptic Office—

twenty-six.design

908A